Never Come Back

Karen Jensen

DORRANCE
PUBLISHING CO
EST. 1920
PITTSBURGH, PENNSYLVANIA 15238

Dorrance Publishing Co
585 Alpha Drive
Pittsburgh, PA 15238
Visit our website at *www.dorrancebookstore.com*

ISBN: 978-1-4809-8382-3
eISBN: 978-1-4809-8403-5

Contents

front cover, Krause housebarn, #73 Second Street, Gnadenfeld, Molotschna, illustrated by Margie Friesen (Hildebrand)

Dedication

Romans 8:24-25,28,35-36a,38-39

For we are saved by hope: but hope that is seen is not hope: for what a man seeth, why doth he yet hope for?

But if we hope for that we see not, then do we with patience wait for it . . . .

And we know that all things work together for good to them that love God, to them who are the called according to his purpose. . .

Who shall separate us from the love of Christ? Shall tribulation, or distress, or persecution, or famine, or nakedness, or peril, or sword?

As it is written, For thy sake, we are killed all the day long . . . .

For I am persuaded, that neither death, nor life, nor angels, nor principalities, nor powers, nor things present, nor things to come,

Nor height, nor depth, nor any other creature, shall be able to separate us from the love of God, which is in Christ Jesus our Lord.

Deuteronomy 8:2-7

And thou shalt remember all the way which the Lord thy God led thee . . . to humble thee, and to prove thee, to know what was in thine heart, whether thou wouldest keep his commandments, or no.

And he humbled thee, and suffered thee to hunger . . . that He might make thee know that man doth not live by bread only, but by every word that proceedeth out of the mouth of the Lord doth man live . . . .

For the Lord thy God bringeth thee into a good land . . . .

Dedicated to my mother
and her family who lived it.

Foreword

In genealogy we are told to dig far enough. If we haven't found someone in our past who accomplished something truly great and amazing, we haven't dug far or deep enough. But there is the flip side as well. A skeleton will be lurking in the closet. If we haven't found that skeleton, we haven't dug far or deep enough. It was not that I went out looking for a skeleton; it was already there, and came popping up out of my research. Actually, there were two skeletons.

The extraordinary person was my own grandfather. I had repeatedly heard one particular, astonishing story about him, but I didn't know about all the rest of his incredible life. But then, my own grandfather is also one of the skeletons.

Now what do I do with these skeletons? An older cousin remarked that it is the truth, and the truth never hurts. But often, the truth does hurt. The pain this truth could cause is exactly why I have sorely wrestled for some years about including them.

God Himself reveals ugly truth in His Word. For instance, David, a man after God's own heart, was guilty of lust, adultery, then murder to cover up his adultery. David truly repented, so he found forgiveness and mercy but there were still lasting consequences for his sin. Yet David was delivered from his enemies, first Saul, and then his sons, through God's mercy.

A historian said, "I see nothing wrong at all, with the notion of revealing . . . it's better for secrecy to be unmasked." [1]

In spite of my grandfather being one of the skeletons, God delivered him over and over again, through amazing, totally improbable circumstances.

German Mennonites were a fairly godly people as a whole, but not a perfect people, and some were less perfect than others.

The time finally arrived for me to write this story, a story with lessons for us, the living, to learn.

A major lesson seems to be, "Be sure your sins will find you out." They may not have come out then, but they are eventually revealed. Predators need to know the secrecy they think they enjoy now is not forever.

---

[1] Annie's Ghosts, A Journey into a Family Secret, Steve Luxenberg, Hyperion: New York, 2009

The challenge for us as followers of Jesus is to be able to boldly show grace and truth as we address sin and the wounds. Unfortunately, it is normal to cover things up, and doing so in the name of God causes that much more damage. Thankfully God doesn't sweep victims and wounds under the rug. Jesus came as a physician to the sick. He came to bring healing to the brokenhearted, including victims and their families.[2]

The German Mennonites in Russia were blessed by God with great prosperity, for their hard work, thriftiness, and general fairness in dealing with their Russian employees. However, God did not shield them from terrors of war, famine, starvation, deadly disease, rape, and barbaric cruelty. As I uncovered the full story of my mother and her family during extremely tumultuous times, I was drawn into the saga of drama and pathos during the Bolshevik Revolution.

I have been repeatedly overcome by tears; especially when I was working to describe the Great Race to New York. Here I am, a first generation American, living proof by my very existence that they did make it. I know the outcome ahead of time. They made it. They saw the Statue of Liberty. They came through Ellis Island. But I had no idea how close they came even then, on that ship sailing into New York harbor, to being sent back. Why they might not have made it. God had miraculously delivered them yet again, but this deliverance also included great suffering.

Once when I tape recorded interviews with my mother, grandmother, and aunt Marie, I was totally surprised by Marie's husband telling his story for the first time outside his immediate family. He had been deathly afraid for decades that Communists would hear and then hunt him down and kill him because of his and his brother John's exploits leading many German Mennonites to freedom in Siberia across the frozen Amur River into China. But this is another story for another book.

My mother wanted to write this story, but died almost before it was begun. She chose the title <u>Never Come Back</u> based on the story of the cow at Easter.

Since then it has become an obsession to get the audio tapes transcribed, sorted into chapters chronologically, and then do the research to reveal the drama more fully. Others had written memoirs and diaries. I am especially grateful my cousin Will Rempel, as staff writer for the Los Angeles Times, had written several wonderful articles about their life in Russia and escape, but the full story had yet to be told.

For decades I had collected genealogies, manuscripts, copies of memoirs, diaries, and books, and threw them in a drawer. Now that I have the time, it is exciting to pull out a

---

[2] Matthew Staton, e-mail to author, <u>recoveringgrace.org</u>

piece of paper and see what gem will be revealed on its page. I ask relatives a question, and even when they don't know the answer, their replies may contain other hidden gems. It is like putting together a thousand piece puzzle. One book gave clues as to why my Grandfather went bankrupt during WW I. A diary gave me specific dates and the name of the ship my grandfather's sister Susanna Toews and her family sailed on. That was the clue I needed to get the ship manifest, because their last name was totally misspelled. And so it went, gathering clues from this book and that.

When Gnadenfelders have been asked to tell about a certain time in their lives, I found that many who lived through, what seemed to me, the most difficult situations, were not willing or ready to write or talk about it. Some were afraid to cause problems for relatives still in Russia by doing so. Others just wanted to forget it all. Many have not been able to deal with their all too vivid memories and the only respite is to forget or at least try to forget. These people have unbelievable stories of cruelty to tell.

Christians are not protected from pain and sorrow, but in the darkest of times God's love seems to shine the brightest! [3] Walter Loewen

I owe a debt of gratitude:

My husband Peter faithfully drove me on a nineteen day research trip throughout Kansas, Iowa, Nebraska, and on up to Manitoba, Canada to visit German Mennonite heritage sites, museums, libraries, and archives. He took hundreds of pictures documenting artifacts, ran errands, copied thousands of pages at libraries and archives, and carefully proofread and edited this manuscript.

Cousins who supplied answers, pictures, and more documents.

Archivists in a number of Mennonite libraries, archives, historical centers who cheerfully aided my research.

Talented cousin Margie Hildebrand supplied two detailed maps and a number of illustrations including the cover.

Those who read the manuscript and gave helpful suggestions.

Pictures of buildings and or artifacts taken at the various German Mennonite Historical, Heritage, or Museum sites were taken by the author or her husband, Peter.

---

[3] <u>1835-1943 Gnadenfeld, Molotschna</u>, A. Lowen Schmidt, Walter Lowen, pg 77

Quotations from sources appear in italics.
Quotations from Scripture are from the King James Version.

Cast of Characters

Cornelius Krause, born 1818, author's Great Great Grandfather, Susanna's Grandfather, and purchaser of the Rosenhof Estate from Chonuk

Kornelius Krause, born 1856, son of Cornelius Krause, author's Great Grandfather, father of Susanna, first husband of Agatha Dueck

Agatha Dueck Krause Dirks, born 1861, author's Great Grandmother, mother of Susanna

Susanna Matthies Dueck—Agatha Dueck Krause/Dirks' mother

Children of Kornelius and Agatha Dueck Krause:

Cornelius Krause, born 1889, Susanna's older brother

Susanna

Jacob (Jasch) Krause, Susanna's younger brother

Tante Gotcha, Agatha Krause Rempel, born 1899, Susanna's younger sister

Heinrich David K. Dirks, born 8 Sep. 1879, died 6 Feb. 1938 Agatha Dueck Krause's second husband, Susanna's stepfather

Heinrich Davidow Dirks, born 1842, died 1915, first Mennonite missionary sent out by Gnadenfeld—These two Heinrich Dirks are not related

Heinz (Heinrich, Henry) Dirks—Susanna's half brother

Mieche (Maria, Mary) Dirks, Susanna's half sister

Katja (Katherine) Dirks, Susanna's half sister

Aron Johannes Rempel—patriarch of Rempel Clan—author's G G grandfather

Gustav Rempel, born 1835, brother of Aron Johannes, loved Anna Goertz

Anna Goertz Rempel—wife to Aron Johannes Rempel; Anna loved Gustav but was forced to marry Gustav's brother Aron Johannes

Aron A. Rempel Sr.—author's great grandfather, son of Aron Johannes Rempel

Aaron A. Rempel Jr.—author's grandfather, son of Aron A. Rempel Sr.

Maria Schmidt Rempel—wife to Aron A. Rempel Sr.

Maria Rempel Braun—Aaron Rempel Jr.'s oldest sister

Tante Lena, Helena Rempel Toews—Aaron Rempel Jr.'s. sister married Cornelius Toews

Tante Suse, Susanna Rempel Toews—Aaron Rempel Jr.'s sister married Jacob Toews

Johann Toews, Rempels left Gnadenfeld going to USA from Johann's home
Cornelius, Jacob, and Johann Toews are brothers
Rempel siblings married Toews siblings

children of Susanna Krause and Aaron A. Rempel Jr.
   Marie, Ronka (Aron), Gonja (Agatha), Susie, baby Willie

Abraham Rempel (Abram)—Aron A. Rempel Sr.'s, brother, called the Old General
Elizabeth Schmidt Rempel—married Abraham Rempel
Children of Abraham and Elizabeth Rempel:
Tante Greta, (Margareta Rempel Krause)—married Susanna's brother Cornelius
Maria Rempel Krause—married Susanna's brother Jacob, (Jasch)
Carl Rempel —married Susanna's sister Agatha

Siblings Cornelius, Jasch (Jacob), and Agatha Krause
   married
Siblings Margareta (Greta), Maria, and Carl Rempel, respectively

Children of Susanna's brother Cornelius
Liesbet Krause—daughter
Hedwig (Hedy) Krause—daughter
Rudy (Rudolph) Krause—son

Gustav A. Rempel—born 1868, younger brother of Aron A. Rempel Sr., son of
patriarch Aron Johannes Rempel
Elizabeth Electra Dirks Rempel—married to Gustav Rempel
   both Gustav and Elizabeth died leaving their underage children orphaned

Wilhelm Neufeld—husband of Margaretha Rempel, emigrated to America 1911
Margaretha Rempel—sister of Aron A. Rempel Sr.

Dogs Bark

Somewhere in the distance a dog barked. More dogs barked, and Gonja's heart froze in sheer terror. She felt a huge knot in her stomach, and it seemed as if all the air had suddenly been sucked completely out of the room. Dogs barking meant the Makhno bandit robbers were coming. They rode their horses furiously into the yard, burst through the door . . . .

The room was packed, standing room only. Little kids, to see the program, were seated, cross legged, Indian style in front of the first row of seats, almost on top of the feet of people in the first row. The room was hot and stuffy, with so many bodies squished together as tightly as possible, to get everyone inside.

After a hasty supper, their family had rushed in the horse drawn wagon to get to the elementary school in Kalona, Iowa for the school program. Papa had a Model T Ford, but it couldn't be driven when it was rainy, as the tires would get stuck in the muddy, unpaved roads. The children rushed inside the two story brick building with the bell tower on top, next door on the left of the high school building,[4] while Papa found a place to tie up the horses.

For the program, Gonja was dressed as a flower, draped in red crepe paper. But Gonja was hot, and sweaty. The sweat on her face was melting the red crepe paper. Little red streams ran down her face, making her face even redder. Gonja's part in the program was finally over. She had learned a poem about a flower in English, and she had said her poem in English, with a Russian accent to be sure, but she had memorized her poem and said it in English!

Since her part was done, and there was no way for her to join her family sitting somewhere in that crowded room, Gonja found a back door that was open, to let in some cold air, cooling her hot, flushed face.

She stood in the open doorway, enjoying the wind rushing past her face while she gazed in the moonlight at the gently rolling hills of farm fields, dotted with patches of unmelted

---

[4] Today, both the old elementary and high school buildings are gone.

snow. Somewhere in the distance a dog barked. More dogs barked, and Gonja's heart froze in sheer terror. Dogs barking meant Makhno bandits were coming. They would ride furiously into the yard, burst through the door, brandish their sabers, rummage through the pantry, trunks, wardrobes, and search everyone and everything looking for anything of value, turning the whole house into a shambles. People died, even women and children. Oh no! Where could she run and hide? What could she and her family do? The Makhno were coming to take someone away, to kill someone, maybe kill them all. They usually took somebody's father and shot him or chopped someone up with their sabers. Someone would be killed tonight. Maybe a lot of people. Where could they go and hide? They couldn't hide in this school. Surrounding farmlands were virtually bare in winter, so they couldn't hide out there. No, they would be found for sure! Could they get safely back to the farm in time to hide?

2 Kalona Elementary School on left, Courtesy of the Chamber of Commerce, Kalona, Iowa

Rosenhof Estate, Schönfeld, Ekaterinoslav, Russia

It was moving day. Ten year old Susanna was both excited about the new adventure, and sad to leave her beloved Opa (grandfather).[5] Here she lived far away from other families. Only the few families who worked on the estate lived here, and they had to travel several miles to be able to attend church. When she moved to Gnadenfeld, about forty-five miles away, she would be living in a village full of other families, and she would be living almost next door to the church. Then they would walk to church, and she would have lots of other little girls to play with.

Gonja's Mama Susanna Krause had been born in the Rosenhof[6] Estate[7] [8] in the Schön-feld[9] Area of Ukraine, the Ekaterinoslav Volost (province or district). Thirteen Mennonites had bought estates in the Schoenfeld Colony, popularly called Brasol, from the nobleman Lt. Dimitri Nikonow Brasol, who had won his land from Chonuk in a card game. Great Grandfather Cornelius[10] Krause, along with a few other Mennonites, then bought the remaining land for their estates directly from Chonuk in 1869 for just rubles on the acre. The Krause estate Rosenhof was a large sheep and cattle raising ranch of about 800 acres. Some Russian noblemen were willing to sell their large estates because they didn't want to be bothered about maintaining an estate located so far from the Russian capital city—the center of power. Others had a huge gambling debt to be paid. Additionally, in 1861 Czar Alexander II had abolished serfdom. This meant it was no longer profitable for the Russian upper class to continue in the old manner without the sanction of serfdom to keep workers on their land. Indeed, many landowners then found it difficult to sell off their land.[11] The Mennonites initially raised sheep, but then also turned to planting grain, orchards, even some vineyards. Some built dams on the seasonal rivers and

---

[5] Opa Cornelius Krause was 83 when they moved from the Rosenhof Estate.

[6] "Memoirs of Agatha and Carl Rempel," as told to daughter Lonnie R. Lockwood

[7] <u>Constantinoplers, Escape from Bolshevism</u>, Irmgard Epp, pg 22 The Czar gave land grants to noblemen for their service during war. These noblemen only lived on these estates during the summer, and spent their winters in Saint Petersburg. Many noblemen gambled or otherwise lived beyond their means, and had to sell their vast estates at bargain prices to Mennonites. Thus the author's Great Great grandfather bought that sheep and cattle estate Rosenhof, near Schönfeld, in Ekaterinoslav province from the nobleman Chonuk, and Great Grandfather died there before he could move to Gnadenfeld.

[8] <u>Mennonite Estates in Imperial Russia,</u> Helmut T. Huebert, pp 112, 113, 114, 179-182, 363

[9] Schönfeld was also known as Brasol, after the name of the nobleman from whom the settlers bought the land. <u>The Molotschna Colony, A Heritage Remembered,</u> Henry Bernard Tiessen, pg 84. The Schönfeld Colony was started as a daughter colony by the Molotschna Colony to help find farm land for the burgeoning surplus population. Molotschna, Mennonite Settlement (Zaporizhia Oblast, Ukraine), http://www.gameo.org/encyclopedia/contents/M6521.html source <u>Mennonite Encyclopedia</u>, v4, pp. 473-474

[10] Cornelius is the German spelling; Kornelius is the Russian spelling. The author is using Opa, or Cornelius to designate the Great Great Grandfather of the author, and Papa, or Kornelius as Great Grandfather. They would be Opa and Papa, respectively, to Susanna Krause.

[11] Notes on the history of the Schoenfeld Colony, Heritage Cruise 1999, Ron Toews

stocked the resulting reservoirs with fish. Some built brick factories, mills, or small agricultural machinery factories.[12]

After the evening supper, once dinner dishes had been washed and put away, the family gathered in the parlor, while Mama Agatha sat in a rocking chair near the light of the kerosene lantern, quietly knitting new socks, darning old socks, or stitching a new frock. Then Papa Kornelius would read to his family from the big German family Bible. The family spoke Plattdeutch, or Low German, but the Bible was written in that beautiful High German. They prayed in High German as well, believing God could only hear High German prayers. One of the main reasons for the love Papa Kornelius and Mama Agatha had for each other, was the love each had for their Savior, Jesus Christ. Papa Kornelius was careful to lead his family to the feet of the Savior at the close of each day.

Indeed, many of the original German Mennonite villages, that had developed when they first came to Russia, had since grown cold in their love for the Savior, and their lives even reflected a callousness toward the less fortunate. Gnadenfeld was a Mennonite village known for its piety and spirituality. Now they were going to move, not only to a village that held Bible studies and prayer meetings, but they would be living just two doors away from the center of the village, from the grand Mennonite Gnadenfeld church itself. Their new homes were on the side of the street with the large wirtshafts (farms); the opposite side of the street were the Kleinwirtschaften or half farms.[13]

In 1901 Papa Kornelius Krause had bought not one, but two large wirtshafts of about 175 acres each, that actually were next door to each other in Gnadenfeld,[14] Molotschna (of the Taurida province in Ukraine). By mid 1880, a typical Mennonite farmer earned over a thousand rubles profit from grain sales each year, and Kornelius, with his purchase of two large farms, could look forward to a profit of twice that much. A traditional Mennonite farm could have 2 to 4 seasonal workers, each earning between 80 to 100 Rubles. The annual salary for household maids was perhaps half this amount.[15]

---

[12] "Memoirs", Irvin D. Krause, "Descendants of Jacob Krause", self published
[13] 1835-1943, Gnadenfeld, Molotschna, A Lowen Schmidt, pg 6
[14] However, it is noted that when Johann Cornies became the "Mennonite Tsar" in 1817, having been appointed as President of the Landwirtschaftlicher Verein (Agricultural Society) for life, he made a rule that no one was allowed to own more than one farm at a time. From the Steppes to the Prairies, Paul Klassen, pp. 19-20 Perhaps this rule was relaxed before Kornelius Krause bought the two farms. Or perhaps the farms were purchased in the name of his sons. How Kornelius was allowed to purchase two farms located at #72 and #73 on Second Street is uncertain. It appears that Aron A. Rempel Sr. (author's great grandfather) also owned two large wirtshaften #69 and #70 on the same side of Second Street at that time.
[15] Life and Times of a Renaissance Mennonite Teacher: Cornelius A. Klaassen: (1883-1919 and Beyond) Robert L Klaassen, pg 26

Most of the heavy furniture, trunks, wardrobes, beds, tables, and chairs had been carefully loaded the day before into two ladder voge (ladder wagons, used for loading hay in harvest—the sides looked like ladders). Now Papa and the Russian hired hands were loading the feather beds, comforters, and the rest of the smaller parcels. Suddenly, Susanna noticed her papa sweating profusely, taking out his kerchief, and wiping his brow. It was early in the morning, still quite cool, and no one else seemed hot, not that hot. No one else was that sweaty. She watched Papa go into the house and get a big drink of cool water that had recently been pumped from the well. Everyone, including Opa, the hired Russian girls who worked inside the house, and the Russian lads who worked on the ranch, were assembling outside the house by the two loaded wagons.

It was about time to leave, when suddenly Papa fell to the ground. The men carefully lifted Papa, carried him inside, and laid him on the bed in the nearest bedroom. Mama ran to the bedside, and gave orders to unpack the feather mattresses, comforters, and a few small parcels that had just been loaded.

Excitement over the adventure of moving had disappeared. It seemed as if the sun had stopped shining. Would Papa be all right? Tears rolled down Mama's face, as she nursed Papa. Everyone tiptoed around, talking in hushed, low tones, and Susanna, straining to hear what was said, could not understand. A few days later on September 7, 1901 at the early age of 45, Papa died.[16] They buried him in the family graveyard next to Johnny and baby Susanna. Yes, Susanna had an older sister who had died as an infant, and since the first girl needed to be named after the maternal grandmother Susanna Matthies Dueck, Susanna was also given the same name.

Newly widowed Agatha Krause, with a heavy heart, moved away from her friends and family, away from the family cemetery which held her beloved, godly husband and two infants, away from Schönfeld[17] to start a new life. Jakob Schlichting and 3 or 4 Russian men[18] drove the ladder voge and guarded everything. Susanna and Mama, holding baby Agatha, rode in one, while brother Cornelius and Jasch (nickname for Jakob) rode in the other ladder voge.

---

[16] He had a heart condition, so probably suffered a heart attack or stroke.
[17] "History of the Schönfeld Colony, Heritage Cruise 1999", Ron Toews, Today, not much is left of the estates or villages of the prosperous Schönfeld Colony because of its proximity to Guliaipole, the home and base of operations of the anarchist/bandit, head of the Black Army, Nestor Makhno
[18] see APPENDIX B

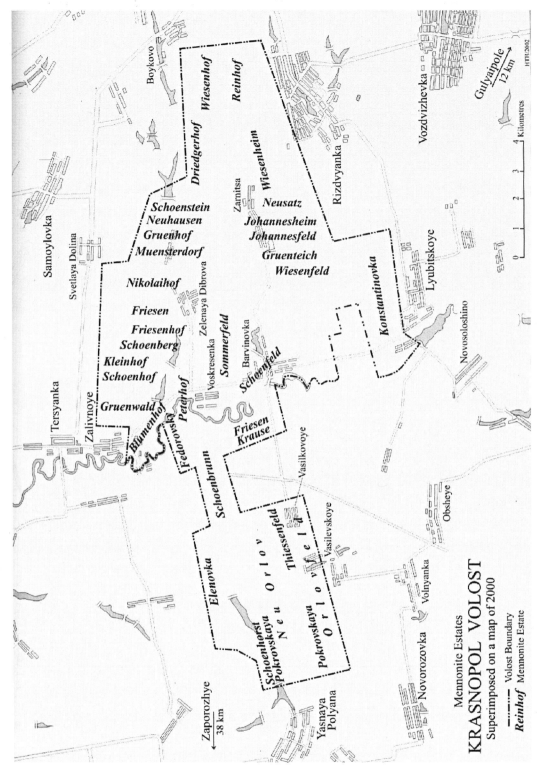

3 map[19] location of Krause' Rosenhof Estate, <u>Mennonite Estates in Imperial Russia,</u>
Helmut T. Huebert, pg 363, used by permission

---

[19] Another map of the location of the Krause estate located in <u>Miracles of Grace and Judgment,</u> by Gerhard P. Schroeder, on pg 261

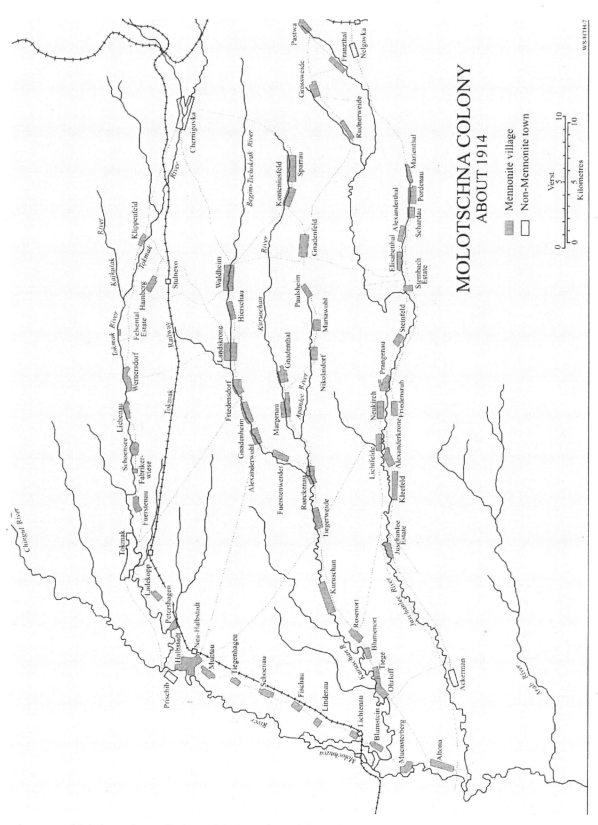

4 map of Molotschna Colony <u>Molotschna Historical Atlas</u>, Helmut T. Huebert, pg 12, used by permission

5 Above, Kornelius Krause Family

From left to right: baby Johnny held by mother Agatha, (who is pregnant in the picture), son Cornelius, son Jacob, father Kornelius, and Susanna (the author's grandmother). Baby Johnny died shortly after this picture was taken. Mother Agatha claimed he died from eating unripened, green fruit the Russian nanny let him eat.

Dad Parents, Cornelios Krausen

6 On the right Agatha and Kornelius Krause

The picture of Agatha and Kornelius Krause, taken circa very early 1899, shows Agatha pregnant with daughter Agatha (born 15 March, 1899).

Gnadenfeld, Molotschna, Ukraine

At their new home in Gnadenfeld, older brother Cornelius wanted to spend the night with the watchman. It sounded like an adventure to this eleven year old lad. Each farmer had his own "barshtan," a big field outside the village where he planted all his cucumbers, cantaloup, watermelon, corn, and pumpkins in one big common area. The farmers pooled together and hired a Russian to guard these patches because in the evening Russian peasants would steal the ripe produce, to try and sell it at a nearby city. The watchman had a simple little upside down "V" shaped hut, with straw spread on the wood floor for a bed. The German farmers took turns supplying the watchman with food and fuel. A Russian maid or one of the children took the evening bowl of borscht[20], and enough bread and salt pork for his other meals the next day until they returned with another bowl of borscht the next evening. Large quantities of ripe watermelon were shipped by train to the cites of Ekaterinoslav, Karkov, Kiev, and others. [21]

Young Cornelius chose a bright moonlit night to spend in the barshtan with the watchman. Cornelius lay down on fresh straw in the watchman's little hut, while the watchman sat outside nearby, smoking his pipe, and recounted tales. "I could hear the creaking wheels of a cart; no, there were several carts. I began to barely make out the outlines of three carts approaching out of the darkness and see them stop."

A gentle breeze wafted in the evening air, and as the moon rose higher into the sky, Cornelius' eyes became heavier and heavier, until at last he fell into a deep sleep. As Cornelius slept, he dreamed.

The watchman continued with his story, "When I saw several men climb down, go into the field, ready to pick the melons, I called out as loudly as I could, 'Rosboyniki, Rosboyniki. Robbers, robbers!' "

As Cornelius dreamed, he walked in his sleep. The watchman saw Cornelius crawl out of the hut, and then walk away in his sleep, and hollered at him, "Stop, Cornelius, stop!" But when the watchman hollered, Cornelius started running. "Stop . . . stop . . . stop, Cornelius, stop!" The louder the watchman hollered, the faster Cornelius ran. It looked like Cornelius was going to run right into that fence between the barshtan and the village. But as Corne-

---

[20] German Mennonite cabbage soup with dill, different from the Russian borscht with beets
[21] The Molotschna Colony: A Heritage Remembered. Henry Bernard Thiessen, pg 20

lius reached the fence, he easily glided right over it in one big bound. Right on the other side of the fence, he plopped down, curled up into a ball, and was sound asleep.

The next morning, when the watchman told the other villagers about it, Cornelius tried again and again to jump the fence, but he couldn't. The fence was just too high. That watchman didn't want anything to do with Cornelius helping him keep watch during the night anymore.

The initial years German Mennonites settled in Ukraine were difficult, but in time the villages with German names spread east along the Molotschna River, *where the soil was deep and rich and black and the eye could see for forty miles in every direction. With German precision, they laid out villages where the main street* (The Mittlestrasse) *ran straight and wide for about* one and one third of a mile, about two versts.[22] *This was bisected by another street in the center. Here they built the church and schools . . . . They had about fifty of these villages with an average population* of around half of Gnadenfeld's 923 in 1908,[23] the largest of any village in the volost (district) with *eighty small farms and forty larger ones.*[24]

In Gnadenfeld, Molotschna, many of the homes of the "small farms" were the original ones, built by the first Mennonite settlers around 1835 when the village was founded. These original homes usually had about three rooms, with thatched roofs, dirt floors, lower ceilings. Even families with many children, always kept these homes clean, neat and tidy.

By the time the Krause family moved to Gnadenfeld in 1901, the villages were prosperous; life was idyllic, a golden time of Mennonite paradise with a nostalgic sense of the halcyon days of forever summer, forever Sunday. A "constable" of sorts resided in the village, but there was no crime, except for attempts by the neighboring Russians to purloin ripening melons.[25] However, as the Mennonites prospered, they became the envy of many of the neighboring Russians. In the beginning, all German Mennonite homes in the Molotschna

---

[22] verst: A Russian measurement of approximately 2/3 of a mile

[23] Molotschna Historical Atlas, Helmut T. Huebert, pg 127

[24] The Batum Story, God's Mercy and Man's Kindness, compiled by Mary Dirks Janzen, Third Edition, Edited by Mary E. Janzen 2011, pg 48, told by Agatha Krause Rempel

[25] Each village was administered by a Schulze (mayor), with the Molotschna Colony divided in two districts. Half the villages were overseen by an Oberschulze located in Halbstadt, and the other half by an Oberschulze located in Gnadenfeld. The Molotschna Colony also had a mutual fire insurance agency and a Waisenamt, which took care of the orphans of the settlement and regulated inheritance . . . . The Molotschna Mennonites were ahead of the other Mennonite settlements in Russia and in America in the realm of hospital and deaconess work. http://www.gameo.org/encyclopedia/contents/M6521.html taken from the Mennonite Encyclopedia Vol 3, pp. 732-737 Krahn, Cornelius. "Molotschna Mennonite Settlement (Zaporizhia Oblast, Ukraine)." *Global Anabaptist Mennonite Encyclopedia Online.* 1957. Web. 4 Jul 2014. http://gameo.org/index.php?title=Molotschna_Mennonite_Settlement_(Zaporizhia_Oblast,_Ukraine)&oldid=120772

Colony of the large farms were exactly the same throughout the village. The newer homes had wooden floors and tile roofs instead of thatch.

They were exactly the same floor plan, situated so precisely the same distance from the road, lined up exactly like German soldiers, with each one perpendicular to the street. They were so precisely aligned, that if you opened the front and back doors of each house on the whole street, you could look straight through from the house on one end of the village clear through all those open doors to the other side of the village. The homes on Second Street, on the Krause-Rempel Street had picket fences. Some of the homes on First Street had brick fences. This was quite unlike the Ukrainian peasant villages, with low-roofed mud huts scattered haphazardly here and there, with sagging doors, bent and broken fences.

7 typical house barn The Mennonite Village Museum, Steinbach, Manitoba, Canada,

The houses were white-washed, with only the color blue used for the trim, since blue was the color of the heavenlies and the only color that was pleasing to God. They were pretty little villages, clean, neat, and orderly, with tree lined streets. *By 1850, the Mennonites had planted over a million trees, transforming the barren south Russian landscape.*[26] Each farm within the village consisted of about three acres. The family was scolded if the garden was not kept nice. There actually was competition to keep it nice. Where piles of straw were to be kept was even mandated as a fire precaution. Each farmer had a place in back of the house where he had a vegetable garden *for potatoes, cabbage, carrots, cucumbers, tomatoes, lentils, beans, onions, garlic, sage, green peppers, red peppers, coriander, peas.*[27]

There was a fruit orchard, and a path with a large variety of tulips on either side, which spoke of their Dutch heritage and former sojourn in Holland. *They lined the streets with elms and surrounded the village with evergreens and hardwoods, such as poplar, oaks, ash, and maples, in a thick windbreak as a shield against the winds and drifting snow, with luscious grass growing on the ground.* [28] [29] Berries grew in these woods that were very good to eat after the first frost. Each farmer had to keep his section of the forest free of weeds.

Farmland to grow grains and pumpkins was outside the village. They mainly grew beautiful, huge pumpkins of all shapes and colors for cow fodder. Streams were dammed to improve pasture land. About one half the farm land was sown with wheat for export, and the other half with barley, rye, and oats for local consumption. Hard winter wheat, now known as Turkey Red, brought better prices. The opening of the seaport at Berdjansk on the Sea of Azov gave the colony access to world grain markets.[30]

Help was plentiful and cheap. The Krauses *had two Russian girls in the house year round with one or two more in the summer. When there was a young child in the house, we always had a young girl as a kind of professional baby sitter. When her services were no longer needed, she sometimes graduated to a cook's position. Most of the Russian peasants were dirty and ignorant, with little schooling, some none at all; they had to sign with an "X" when we paid them.* (There generally were no schools in the Russian villages, and perhaps this was the reason they could not read or write a single Russian word.) However, every Mennonite could read and write well. *They* (the Russians) *were glad to work for the Germans who paid them in money*

---

[26] Life and Times of a Renaissance Mennonite Teacher: Cornelius A. Klaassen: (1883-1919 and Beyond), Robert L. Klaassen, pg 12
[27] The Life Story of Walter Jakob Loewen, Walter Jakob Loewen, pg 5
[28] The Batum Story, God's Mercy and Man's Kindness, compiled by Mary Dirks Janzen, Third Edition, Edited by Mary E. Janzen 2011, pg 48, told by Agatha Krause Rempel
[29] My Memories, Mary Dirks Janzen, page 2
[30] Life and Times of a Renaissance Mennonite Teacher: Cornelius A Klassen: (1883-1919 and Beyond).

and fed them the same good food as they ate. They learned while earning, much as apprentices do today, and carried their knowledge of modern agriculture back to their own farms . . . . They were good-hearted and would give everything they had to someone in need.[31]

When Russian workers first showed up, they were full of lice and had to be deloused with kerosene. They were lazy and had to be watched, supervised each minute. But the laziness wasn't inherent, was not in their genes, but rather resulted from centuries of serfdom, where they never received the fruits of their labors. Even when serfdom was abolished, the former serfs were not allowed to own land, but were relegated to a sort of commune system, where they were moved around every few years, and each family received a number of acres to farm, depending upon the number of adult males in the household. So why would any of them work to improve the house, or barn, or even the land, if someone else would be occupying it in a year or two? They would let the roof leak instead of repairing or replacing it. They would not put in the hard work to spread manure on the fields, just to have the next inhabitants enjoy the fruit of their labors.

Additionally, the Russians were chained to the Russian Orthodox Church, a religious life full of superstition, lifeless religious icons, and dead rituals. The Russian Orthodox priests themselves were illiterate. Catherine the Great's Manifesto had also mandated that Mennonites were forbidden to proselytize Russians, although they were allowed to proselytize Muslims. Only a few Russian hired help came to know Jesus as their personal Savior through their German Mennonite employers.

Susanna and her siblings *worked alongside the Russian young people—hoeing, weeding, and helping in the fields.* They *sang and laughed and talked together as they worked . . . . The boys were good to the horses and spoke to them in Russian.*[32]

The 24 young people were all from Russian Orthodox background and owned icons which they used in their prayers. The girls had a trundle bed in the kitchen, which folded up into a couch. They owned more skirts than blouses, since they wore as many as six or seven at one time to please the boys. The peasant boys just did not appreciate slim girls, so to give themselves the appearance of a chubby girl, a slim girl would wear six or seven petticoats, all gathered and ruffled.[33]

[31] The Batum Story, God's Mercy and Man's Kindness, compiled by Mary Dirks Janzen, Third Edition, Edited by Mary E. Janzen , 2011, pg 49, by Agatha Krause Rempel
[32] Mennonite Foods & Folkways from South Russia, Vol II, Norma Jost Voth, Mary Dirks Janzen, pg 26
[33] My Memories, Mary Dirks Janzen, page 15

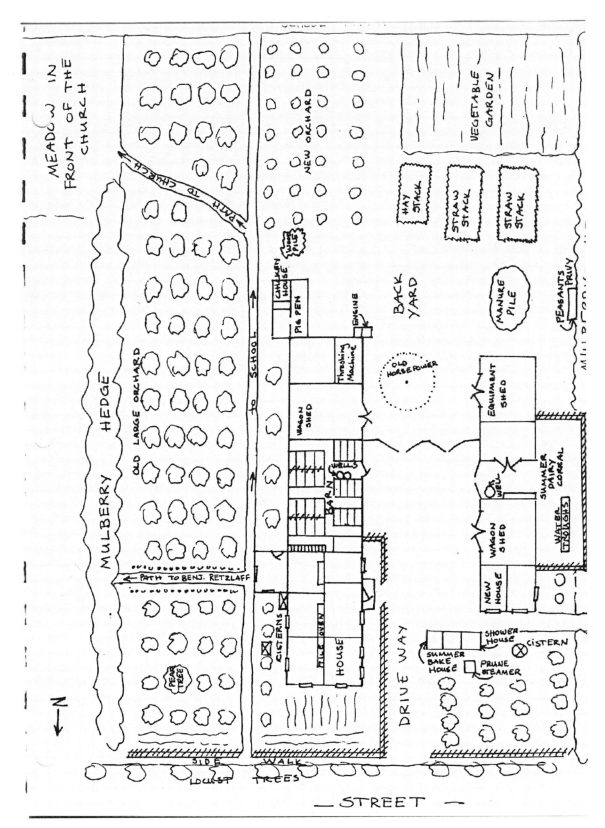

8 map of farm, illustrated by Margie Friesen (Hildebrand)

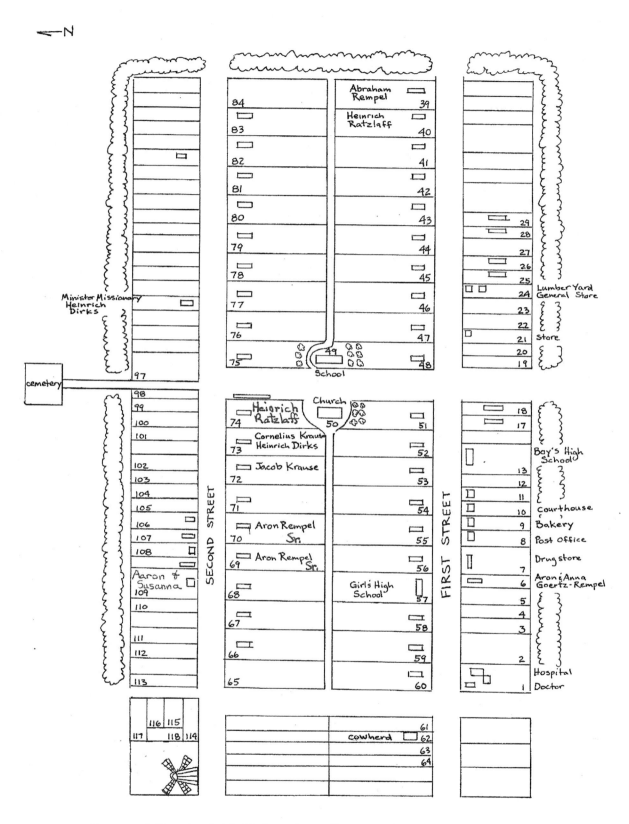

9 map of Gnadenfeld, Molotschna, illustrated by Margie Hildebrand

German Mennonite villages were largely self-sufficient. Although they grew a very fine sugar beet and even some sugar cane, most of their sweetener came from the syrup of boiled down watermelon. They made starch from potatoes, canned all sorts of fruits, which could keep for ten years or more, spun wool from their own sheep, and even cultivated their own silk with their mulberry hedgerows.[34]

In the summer, the family ate outside, placing their table under the two large walnut trees, enjoying meals of Rollkuchen and watermelon, chicken Borscht (a hearty soup of potatoes, meat, cabbage, tomatoes, and fresh dill), or fried potatoes and Kirsches Mooss (fruit sauce/pudding made with cherries).[35] They ate cucumbers with salt, pepper, and vinegar, sliced tomatoes with onions and vinegar. [36] *The hired peasants ate on the other side of the kitchen on the porch, which had a brick floor and steps with Virginia Creeper climbing all around the railing, reaching up to the roof. Here was a table large enough for about five boys and four girls. They ate the same food as we did only they used fewer plates, forks and knives. For example, if there were Borscht or chicken noodle soup, there would be one or two large bowls in the middle of the table, from which the peasants would spoon the soup with Russian wooden spoons. They were good bread eaters and didn't mind if it was sliced thick. They would eat all they wanted, and drink all the milk they wanted. When watermelons were ripe, the whole gang at both tables would eat watermelon for dessert. Milk and watermelon were the only dessert we had in Gnadenfeld.*[37]

The German Mennonite Colonies were an orderly world, where everything was in its place.

On a quiet day, one would hear nothing but the humming of a bee or the occasional chirp of a sparrow. Life in Gnadenfeld was quiet. A person could hear the distant voices of the neighbors singing German lieder *as they were occupied with the same*[38] daily chores, or the Russian lads singing their sad Ukrainian folk songs as *they were working in the barn or hitching a team up to the plow.*[39]

Business people traveled to Germany, England, Japan, and even America, and as a result, brought back new fashions and ideas. People dressed in sturdy, but tasteful and

[34] Constantinoplers, Escape from Bolshevism, Irmgard Epp, "Carl Rempel, White Army Officer", pg 99
[35] Mennonite Foods & Folkways from South Russia, Vol II, Norma Jost Voth, Mary Dirks Janzen, pp.174-175
[36] Mennonite Foods & Folkways from South Russia, Vol I, Norma Jost Voth, Mary Dirks Janzen, pp. 284, 288
[37] Mennonite Foods & Folkways from South Russia, Vol II, Norma Jost Voth, Mary Dirks Janzen, pg 183
[38] My Memories, Mary Dirks Janzen, pg 7
[39] "My Family was Transplanted", audio tape by Mary Dirks Janzen

fashionable clothes. The high buttoned shoes grew higher and higher heels. The young men dressed as fine as anyone in Kiev or Moscow. [40]

Gnadenfeld was one of the more important villages. Most of the villages in the Molotschna Colony had a Hollander type of windmill for grinding their flour. Mama Agatha's father Jacob Martin Dueck had built the Hollander type flour mill that stood in her home town of Brasol, Schoenfeld.

10 Russian workers on Krause/Dirks farm

A similar Hollander type of windmill stood on the eastern edge of Gnadenfeld. On a windy day, the mighty wings with the fluttering canvas would shoot up into the air about ninety feet and then down again. [41]

---

[40] <u>My Memories</u>, Mary Dirks Janzen, pg 33
[41] <u>Mennonite Foods & Folkways from South Russia, Vol II</u>, Norma Jost Voth, pg 60 *All that remains of the era of Dutch windmills is the magnificent reproduction of the Peter Barkman Steinbach mill located at the Mennonite Village Museum in Steinbach, Manitoba, Canada.*

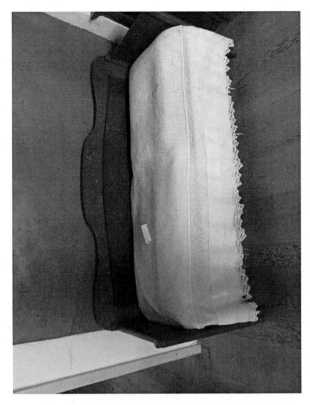

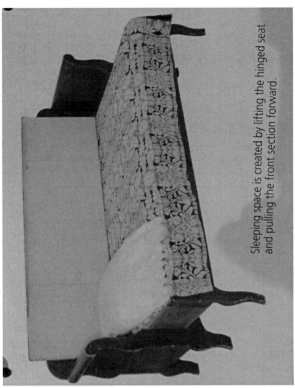

Sleeping space is created by lifting the hinged seat and pulling the front section forward.

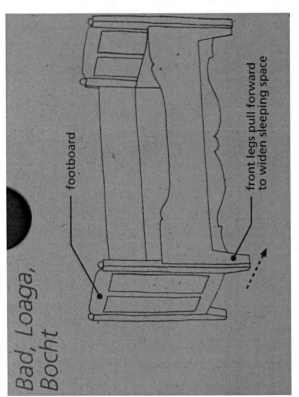

Bad, Loaga, Bocht

footboard

front legs pull forward to widen sleeping space

11, 12, 13, 14 Sleeping Benches, Kauffman Museum, Bethel College, Newton, Kansas Colony.

Agatha had a foreman to run her farms in Gnadenfeld. In the summer, she used to ride out to the grain fields and look over the crops, and often took along gooseberry stems, so daughter Agatha had to ride on the back seat of the wagon. As she looked over the field of ripening grain, Mama Agatha would remark, "Doesn't it look nice?"[42]

15 Hollander type windmill, The Mennonite Village Museum, Steinbach, Manitoba, Canada,

Cornelius was only eleven, and Jacob only seven when their father died. Mennonite boys learned to do hard work as young as age six, working along side their fathers. Mennonites had a Protestant work ethic, believing there was dignity in hard work. Work was a blessing. *God designed man to work. Work is not part of the curse; sweat is part of the curse. It is the intensity of work necessary to earn the bread that implies the curse, but work is a blessing, . . . a sacred duty.*[43]

These German Mennonites in Russia wished to glorify God in all they did. "Whether then you eat, or drink, or whatsoever you do, do all to the glory of God."[44] And so, from a very

---

[42] Memoir of Agatha and Carl Rempel" as told to K. R. Lockwood, pg 4
[43] The Master's Current, Vol. 21, No 2, "Our Sacred Duty," Dr. John Mac Arthur, pp. 3-5
[44] 1 Corinthians 10:3,

early age, the young Krause children learned the value, the dignity of work, whether cleaning out smelly chamber pots in the morning, sweeping the kitchen floor, or mucking out animal refuse from the barn. Cornelius and Jacob were still too young to be in charge of running both large, prominent farms themselves. Still, with a hired foreman and hired Russian laborers, Agatha had been able to manage for two whole years. But Agatha's brother-in-law had other ideas. Gerhard Rempel had married Agatha's sister Maria Dueck, and Gerhard would not rest until Agatha married again. Gerhard pestered Agatha. "Marry your farm foreman," Gerhard nagged. "Marry your farm foreman!" He would not leave her alone.

Either the elders of the church or a guardian, acting as marriage brokers, typically would order second marriages, strongly urging these unions so the village would not be forced to provide welfare assistance. Widows and widowers usually did not remain single for long. It took a husband and wife team to manage all the daily chores. Survival, not love, was often the basis for a second marriage.

Agatha was still a beautiful woman at age 42, but her farm foreman was eighteen years **younger** than Agatha. Two years later, in 1903, Heinrich David K. Dirks and Agatha Dueck Krause did marry. By now son Cornelius was age thirteen, daughter Susanna twelve, Jacob nine, and little daughter Agatha four. Agatha and Heinrich had three more children, Heinz, Marie (Mary or Mieche), and Katherine (Katche).

Was Heinrich, her foreman, marrying Agatha, or was he marrying the two farms? [45]

---

[45] Other such stories of landed, wealthy widows who married their much younger farm foreman also exist in the oral tradition of the German Mennonites from Russia. My Harp is Turned to Mourning. Al Reimer, pg 30

The Large Rempel Clan

It *was a heart-wrenching goodbye between the two lovers in the shadow beneath the old apple trees in the garden in the lowland.* Gustav Rempel of Gnadenfeld and Anna Goertz of the nearby village of Rudnerweide had fallen deeply in love. Then Gustav confided to his older brother Aron Johannes, he was about to ask Anna's father, Franz Goertz for permission to marry her. Immediately, Aron Johannes craftily went to both sets of parents, his own and Anna's, and secured their blessings for him to marry Anna, before Gustav had the opportunity to do so. Aron hadn't courted Anna; he hadn't asked Anna to marry him. Anna wasn't in love with him. She was in love with Gustav, and Gustav with her. That didn't matter in the least. The decision had been made by both sets of parents and that was final. Aron Johannes had stolen his brother's intended bride.

Gustav Rempel grieved over this for a long time and did not marry until later. He was between 30 and 36 years old when he married Miss Sara Görz (Goertz), Anna's much younger sister *and "the fairest of all the girls in the district (Volost)." She bore five sons to him (Gustav) and died during the birth of the sixth child which died as well.*[46]

Aaron A. Rempel came from the large, extended Aron Johannes and Anna Goertz Rempel family. Anna had made the best of her situation, despite being forced into this marriage, and had been a faithful wife to Aron Johannes. More than fifty Rempels were living in and around Gnadenfeld, from the great grandparents, grandparents, parents, children, grandchildren, aunts, uncles, cousins, nieces, and nephews.[47]

There was just the one Krause household in Gnadenfeld. Many Krause relatives had emigrated to Goessel and Hillsborough, Kansas, in America in the late 1880's, while some aunts and uncles still lived back on the Rosenhof Estate. Susanna's grandparents, the Duecks, lived in Brasol. Both Rosenhof and Brasol were located in the Schoenfeld Colony.

The church was the very center of village life. The people of Gnadenfeld, by and large, were known for endeavoring to live by what was right in the eyes of the Lord, according to the Word of God. When the colony was first founded, the preachers had no formal theological training and sermons were generally read. Even spontaneous prayers were forbidden in many of the churches throughout the Mennonite Colonies.

---

[46] Wir Die Braun Kinder, Elizabeth Wiens, pp. 10-11; "Memories", Arthur G. Rempel, pg 19; From the Steppes to the Prairies, Paul Klassen, pg 11; Love and Remembrance, Helene (Rempel) Klassen

[47] Aron Johannes and Anna Goertz Rempel lived in #6 First Street their entire married lives.

16 Rempel Clan 1902
50th Wedding Anniversary, Anna Goertz & Aron Johannes Rempel

17 Rempel Clan with names and numbers (numbers correspond with the numbers on the chart on the following page)

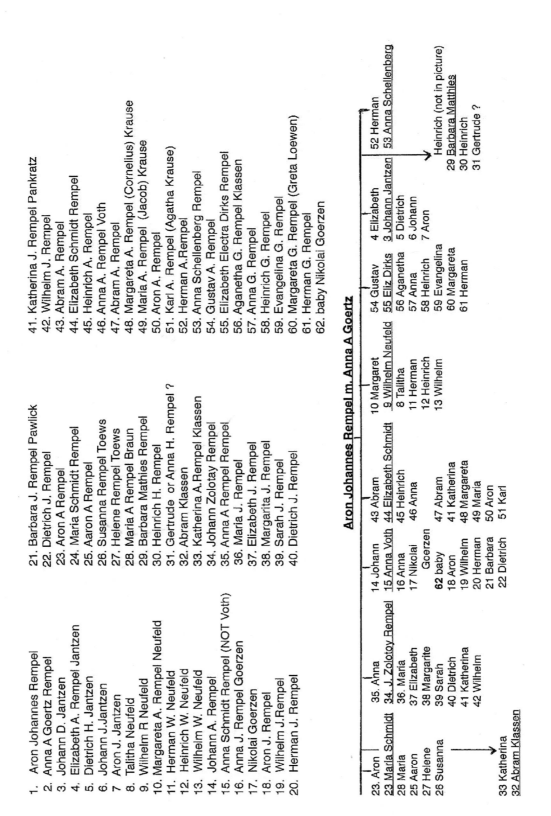

1. Aron Johannes Rempel
2. Anna A Goertz Rempel
3. Johann D. Jantzen
4. Elizabeth A. Rempel Jantzen
5. Dietrich H. Jantzen
6. Johann J.Jantzen
7. Aron J. Jantzen
8. Talitha Neufeld
9. Wilhelm R Neufeld
10. Margareta A. Rempel Neufeld
11. Herman W. Neufeld
12. Heinrich W. Neufeld
13. Wilhelm W. Neufeld
14. Johann A. Rempel
15. Anna Schmidt Rempel (NOT Voth)
16. Anna J. Rempel Goerzen
17. Nikolai Goerzen
18. Aron J. Rempel
19. Wilhelm J.Rempel
20. Herman J. Rempel
21. Barbara J. Rempel Pawlick
22. Dietrich J. Rempel
23. Aron A Rempel
24. Maria Schmidt Rempel
25. Aaron A Rempel
26. Susanna Rempel Toews
27. Helene Rempel Toews
28. Maria A Rempel Braun
29. Barbara Mathies Rempel
30. Heinrich H. Rempel
31. Gertrude or Anna H. Rempel ?
32. Johann Klassen
33. Katherina A.Rempel Klassen
34. Johann Zolotay Rempel
35. Anna A Rempel Rempel
36. Maria J. Rempel
37. Elizabeth J. Rempel
38. Margarita J. Rempel
39. Sarah J. Rempel
40. Dietrich J. Rempel
41. Katherina J. Rempel Pankratz
42. Wilhelm J. Rempel
43. Abram A. Rempel
44. Elizabeth Schmidt Rempel
45. Heinrich A. Rempel
46. Anna A. Rempel Voth
47. Abram A. Rempel
48. Margareta A. Rempel (Cornelius) Krause
49. Maria A. Rempel (Jacob) Krause
50. Aron A. Rempel
51. Karl A. Rempel (Agatha Krause)
52. Herman A.Rempel
53. Anna Schellenberg Rempel
54. Gustav A. Rempel
55. Elizabeth Electra Dirks Rempel
56. Aganetha G. Rempel Klassen
57. Anna G. Rempel
58. Heinrich G. Rempel
59. Evangelina G. Rempel
60. Margareta G. Rempel (Greta Loewen)
61. Herman G. Rempel
62. baby Nikolai Goerzen

Aron Johannes Rempel m. Anna A Goertz

23 Aron | 35. Anna 34. J. Zolotoy Rempel | 43 Abram 44 Elizabeth Schmidt | 14 Johann 15 Anna Voth | 10 Margaret 9 Wilhelm Neufeld | 54 Gustav 55 Eliz Dirks | 4 Elizabeth 3 Johann Jantzen | 52 Herman 53 Anna Schellenberg

23 Maria Schmidt
28 Maria   36 Maria   45 Heinrich   16 Anna   8 Talitha   56 Aganetha   5 Dietrich   Heinrich (not in picture)
25 Aaron   37 Elizabeth   46 Anna   Goerzen   11 Herman   57 Anna   6 Johann   29 Barbara Matthies
27 Helene   38 Margarite   47 Abram   17 Nikolai   12 Heinrich   58 Heinrich   7 Aron   30 Heinrich
26 Susanna   39 Sarah   41 Katherina   62 baby   13 Wilhelm   59 Evangelina   31 Gertrude ?
              40 Dietrich   48 Margareta   18 Aron   60 Margareta
33 Katherina 41 Katherina   49 Maria   19 Wilhelm   61 Herman
32 Abram Klassen 42 Wilhelm   50 Aron   20 Herman
                              51 Karl   21 Barbara
                                             22 Dietrich

18 Rempel clan genealogy chart

19 top left Aron Johannes Rempel
20 top right Anna Goertz Rempel, 1903

Anna (Gortz) & Aron Johannes Rempel
with daughter

1850's in Gnadenfeld, Russia

21 bottom right Anna Goertz, Aron Johannes, and daughter Anna born ca 1854

The Aron Johannes Rempel Family in 1884

Johannes Rempel & Anna

Johannes

Abram

Aron & Marie Schmidt

Heinrich & Barbara Matthies

Anna & Aron J. Rempel

Helena

Gustav

Elizabeth

Katharina

Margaretha

Dietrich Aron

Hermann

Sister Sarah had died at age 17

22 1884 Aron Johannes Rempel family

Anna Goertz brought a strong spiritual influence into her marriage to Aron Johannes by instituting in-home Bible studies and prayer meetings which stressed a personal relationship with Jesus based on forgiveness of sins and acceptance of what Christ had done through His life, death, and resurrection. These Bible studies and prayer meetings were the catalyst for spiritual awakening in Gnadenfeld, and then throughout the Molotschna Colony.

23 Gnadenfeld choir

Standing back row, 2nd from right possibly could be Abram Braun, husband of Maria Rempel, Aaron's oldest sister; 6th from left is Johann Rempel the organist. Author believes the woman sitting in second row from the front, second from the left (labeled Jacob Toews' sister) is really Aaron Rempel's younger sister Helena, who married Cornelius Toews, **not** Cornelius' sister.

Aron Sr. had been elected a reisepraediger, or preacher, for the Gnadenfeld congregation,[48] and was a choir director for the church choir.

---

[48] Aron Rempel Sr. is listed as one of the assistant ministers 1835-1943 Gnadenfeld, Molotschna. A. Lowen Schmidt, pg 22. In another source he is listed as the preacher officiating for the funeral service of Elizabeth Pankratz, born 15 March 1873, died 29 Nov 1878, buried 2 December 1878, daughter of Johannes and Helena (born Ratzlaff) Pankratz.

24 Aron & Maria Rempel family— Left picture
L to R infant son (unknown name); mother Maria (born Schmidt); son Aaron A. Jr. on floor; daughter Maria, standing; father Aron A Rempel, Sr.

25 Aron & Maria Rempel family— Right picture L to R
standing: son Aaron A, Jr; daughter Maria, sitting: daughter Susanna; mother Maria (born Schmidt); daughter Helena; father Aron A Rempel, Sr.

This resulted in a growing interest in missions. The Gnadenfeld Church in 1869 sent a considerable sum of money and the very first Mennonite missionary Heinrich Dirks to mission work in the Dutch Indies of Sumatra, Indonesia. He returned again to Gnadenfeld in 1881. There was no Sunday School, so on Sunday afternoons former missionary Heinrich Dirks, with his long white hair, gathered all the children right below his holy pulpit for their own church time, specifically geared for them. He taught them the *Word of God and told stories of the Bata children from the mission fields. Throughout his life, he kept occupied with the Christian converts in Sumatra. His dearest wish before he died was to once again see his Batas in Sumatra, but those desires were never fulfilled . . . .His last words were, "Now I go home. I am a servant of the Lord."*[49]

---

[49] <u>Gnadenfeld, Molotschna, South Russia 1835-1943,</u> Jacob C. Krause, pp 6-7

#26 Aron and Maria Rempel family

L to R Standing: son Aaron A. Jr., Susanna (married Jacob Toews), Maria with husband
Abram Braun (Author believes Maria & Abram Braun may have lived at #17 First Street)
Sitting: Helena (married Cornelius Toews), mother Maria (born Schmidt), unknown girl,
father Aron A. Rempel Sr. This picture may have been taken at the time of the wedding
of Maria Rempel and Abram Braun.

Gnadenfeld had experienced a pietistic influence, that placed *an emphasis on the Bible
and Bible Study . . . in the life of the believer, . . . and a personal decision of conversion
following repentance for sin.*[50] The sermons focused on salvation and a holy life.[51]

---

[50] Testing Faith and Tradition, A Global Mennonite History, editors John A Lapp, C. Arnold Snyder, pg 44
[51] http://www.gameo.org/encyclopedia/contents/M6521.html   taken from the Mennonite Encyclopedia Vol 3, pp. 732-737
the year of founding, and the number of total church membership, including children

Schönfeld	1868	763
Rosenhof	1870	419
Herzenberg	1881	80
Gnadenfeld	1834	1151

Many conversions had taken place in Gnadenfeld in preceding decades, and new converts had established extra home Bible studies and prayer meetings, not under the auspices of the Gnadenfeld Mennonite Church. These extra Bible studies and prayer meetings earned these earnest Christians the ridicule and derision of the apathetic in the Gnadenfeld Church. This pietistic movement challenged the self-complacency of the Mennonite community. The Mennonite Brethren Church was founded, which only accepted true believers, and administered baptism by immersion. They held that even though a Mennonite attended church regularly, took Communion whenever served, read his Bible, prayed, did "good works," he was NOT guaranteed the kingdom of heaven. Heaven was not earned, but righteousness only came through the death and resurrection of Jesus, who paid for sins on the cross. They did not want to baptize anyone on the basis of a "faith" merely learned by rote.

Unfortunately, with the foundation of this new church, there arose a tendency toward religious legalism with attitudes of pride and self-righteousness, as some considered themselves more spiritual than those in the general Mennonite church.[52]

The early founders of Gnadenfeld, as newly awakened believers, brought lively singing with them as part of their joy in the Lord. Choir practice originated in Gnadenfeld. Singing in four parts was new but quickly embraced. Everybody knew how to sing parts a cappella, and many had well trained voices. Singing Zingen wir aus Herzengrund (Let Us Sing With Heart and Soul); Hallelujah, Schöner Morgen (Hallelujah, Fair Morning);   Grosser Gott; Wir Loben Dich (Great God, We Love You) each Sunday morning produced a most glorious, ethereal sound, filling the hall. Originally, songs were written in numbers, before it was written in the music notation of today. Throughout the village and even in the fields, you could hear singing in German and in Russian; singing in the kitchen, in the barn, weeding the garden, at needlework, at a child's bedside. Instruments such as violin, guitar, and harmonium also were included. The Krause home boasted a pump organ. Since Cornelius and Jacob had taken lessons and could read music, only Cornelius and Jacob could play the organ well. Cornelius also played guitar, Jacob guitar and mandolin, and younger brother Heinz, guitar.[53]

The men and women entered from different doors, at opposite ends of the building, and sat on separate sides, facing each other. This was to help their concentration on the sermon, which could be quite lengthy, delivered by an unpaid, untrained layman, sitting upon an elevated chair, reading the sermon in a sing-song fashion. The simple, almost austere

---

[52] Life and Times of a Renaissance Mennonite Teacher: Cornelius A. Klaassen: (1883-1919 and Beyond), Robert L. Klaassen, pg 14
[53] My Memories, Mary Dirks Janzen, pp. 5, 10

worship service had the pulpit front and center in the church confirming the centrality of preaching. *Sometimes when windows were open in summer, one or two barn swallows joined the service, a most welcome diversion when the sermon was long and . . . eyelids started to droop.*[54]

Often children as young as twelve years old were baptized. The Lord first spoke to Susanna's brother Jakob when he was about 10 years old through the parable of the unmerciful servant. That was when he was saved, converted. In 1912 he was baptized by elder Heinrich Dirks, the former missionary to Sumatra, upon professing his faith in the blood of Jesus Christ to save him from his sin.[55]

Mennonite doctrine mandated adult believer baptism by sprinkling. It was their restriction to only baptize adults, or denial of infant baptism, that had earned Mennonites persecution and martyrdom as anabaptists in the 1500s. Young people around 18 years old or so would take part in Catechism class led by the minister, and then be baptized on Pentecost Day.

Baptismal candidates had spent a long winter of study and prayer, having memorized the catechism answers to the questions. They were now ready to give their testimony of faith in Jesus Christ saving them from their sins, and pledge to live their lives in service to Him. The baptismal sermon commended the candidates for having been born again, for it is impossible to come to God without it. It then challenged them to follow Jesus, wherever He would lead, even through tribulation, suffering, and death.

However, it was easy for prospective members to just memorize the catechism answers, but not really have a personal commitment to live for Jesus. Thus the congregation eventually would be a mixture of those who had really committed their lives to Christ and those who were just going through the motions. After so many daily Bible lessons during all their years of school, plus the catechism lessons for prospective new members, it would be easy for those who were not really broken over their sin, with no longing for righteousness, but a superficial proclamation of faith, to be able to give the right answers, to say all the right words. All who presented themselves would be taken in as members and then were eligible for communion.[56]

---

[54] <u>Mennonite Foods & Folkways from South Russia, Vol II</u>, Norma Jost Voth, Mary Dirks Janzen, pg 57

[55] Obituary of Jakob C. Krause, translated from the German

[56] The author does not have any sermons from Gnadenfeld itself, but does have a book of sermons preached by Johann J. Nickel in Rosenhof, Schoenfeld Colony, the colony where Susanna Krause Rempel was born. The author believes summaries of those sermons are representative of the preaching of that time. Sermons taken from <u>Hope Springs Eternal</u>, John P. Nickel, pg 40

It was the Rempel family that had bought the beautiful chandelier and big pipe organ for the church. Early summer Sunday mornings, the organist would play, and the people could hear the organ all over the village. Only one Rempel knew how and could play it. He had one finger missing but could play beautifully. When organist Johann Rempel was sick, or if someone hurt his feelings, or the people talked instead of listening, he would pout and wouldn't play.

Susanna at age twelve was already blossoming into a beautiful young lady. Susanna, walking along the school path with her girl friends, did not really pay attention to the village lads around her. Aaron A. Rempel, nine years older than she, noticed her and remarked to his friend walking with him, "You see that Susanna Krause? Someday I am going to marry her!"

27 Gnadenfeld Church. Public domain

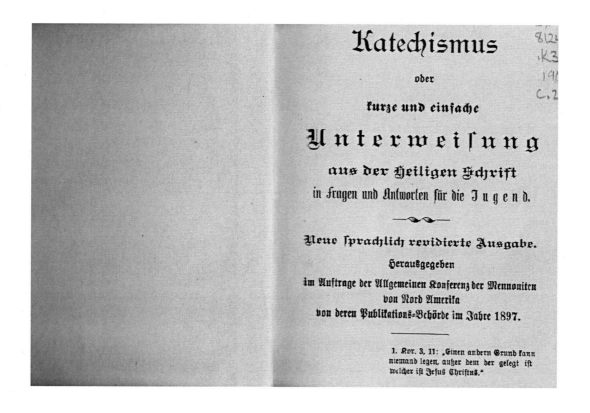

PART THREE
The Redemption of Man

CHAPTER 1
How Redemption was Promised by God

1. Did the Lord God suffer man to perish in sin and misery?

No: He redeemed his people.
Luke 1:68; 1. Peter 1:3,4

2. How did he redeem them?

By giving his only begotten Son.
John 3:16

3. How could God give His Son?

He had to partake of flesh and blood: that through death he might destroy him that had power of death, that is, the devil.
Heb. 2:14,15

4. Was there no other way to redeem us?

No: no one could, by any means, redeem his brother.
Ps. 49:7; Rev. 5:3,4

5. Was only one, our Saviour, to die for all?

Yes: for as by one man's disobedience many were made sinners, so by the obedience of one shall many be made righteous.
Rom. 5:19

29

3. HAUPTSTÜCK.
Die Erlösung des Menschen durch Christum.

1. KAPITEL.
Die Erlösung von Gott zuvor verheissen.

1. Hat Gott, der Herr, den Menschen in solchem elenden Zustand gelassen?

Nein; er hat sein Volk erlöst.
Luk. 1:68; 1. Petri 1:3-4

2. Wodurch hat er es erlöst?

Dadurch, dass er seinen eingebornen Sohn gab.
Joh. 3:16

3. Wie konnte Gott seinen Sohn geben?

Der musste Mensch geboren werden, auf dass er durch den Tod die Macht nehme dem, der des Todes Gewalt hatte, das ist, dem Teufel.
Ebr. 2:14,15

4. War kein anderes Mittel zu unserer Erlösung?

Nein: es konnte auch kein Bruder den andern erlösen.
Ps. 49:8; Offb. 5:3,4

5. Sollte nur einer, nämlich unser Heiland, für alle sterben?

Ja; denn wie durch eines Menschen Ungehorsam viele Sünder worden sind, also werden auch durch Eines Gehorsam viele gerecht.
Röm. 5:19

28

28 Top: catechism, 29 Lower Left: English catechism, 30 Lower Right: German catechism

Romance

Davon spricht mann nicht. About that, we do not talk.
  Old Low German Saying[57]

Onn schämt sikj nijch enmol. And isn't even ashamed of it
  Old Low German Saying [58]

It was the custom for the oldest daughter to take sewing lessons to do all the sewing for the family. Susanna Krause's Mama Agatha did a lot of crocheting and knitting, but she wouldn't let Susanna knit or crochet, wouldn't even let her pick up the crocheting or knitting needles. Susanna was only allowed to sew for the family. Susanna sewed all the clothing for the whole family, even the men's shirts and pants, except for their special Sunday clothes, which would be done by Grunwald, their Jewish village tailor. Susanna could usually be found sewing away on the treadle sewing machine located under the window in the kleinestube (the little room).

31 treadle sewing machine in the kleinestube, the girls' bedroom: Mennonite Settlement Museum, Hillsborough, Kansas

---

[57] In a Rempel-Krause-Janzen Cousin round robin letter, Cousin Connie Easto
[58] Mennonite Foods & Folkways from South Russia, Vol II, Norma Jost Voth, pg 33

Aaron A. Rempel's father Aron Rempel Sr. owned the lumber yard, a store, and the nicest house compared to the other Gnadenfelders.[59] "They had all kind of things." [60]

The son Aaron Jr. had been educated at university, possibly in Kiev. When he was only age sixteen, he traveled to the big cities and bought lumber, iron, and whatever else was needed for his father's stores.

Aaron Jr. was a skilled hunter. Hunting season began in September and the land abounded in fox, rabbit, prairie chickens, deer,[61] and prairie wolves. There was an animal shaped like a kangaroo about the size of a cat, which lived under little mounds of grass. There was also prairie fowl as large as a goose called "Traup." [62]

Aaron and his father were also engaged in repairing and manufacturing plows and other farm equipment for harvesting and cleaning the wheat [63] in a factory in son Aaron's own yard. Eight large Mennonite factories were in Russia by 1911, producing agricultural machines and various farming implements.[64] [65] *Since Russia did not belong to the international Patent Union, Russian entrepreneurs, including Mennonites . . . freely copied and/or adapted European and especially English and American machinery.*[66]

Mennonites were not supposed to act in such a way as to portray themselves as better than others. Equality among them was a virtue. However, they still managed to try and set themselves apart. "My Himmel bed is higher than your Himmel bed." The Himmel bed in the Grottestov (parlor) was used for guests, and you can see the pull-out section to the right. It was called Himmel because it reached toward the heavens (Himmel). However, not all underneath was stacked with feather ticks and comforters, but was often elevated just for show. Usually an extra bed, a Himmel bed, was kept in the living room for company.

---

[59] *The people of the Molotschna were largely self-sufficient. They did have to purchase a number of items: such as sugar, tea, coffee, and spices, as well as dry goods material and some farm machinery. . . A large family would raise from four to six pigs and perhaps a young steer as well. Even the landless, those not engaged in farming, would have a cow or two, some pigs, and a number of chickens. Usually they had a big enough lot where they could grow their own vegetables, a couple of fruit trees, and enough feed for their pigs and chickens.* The Molotschna Colony, A Heritage Remembered, Henry Bernard Tiessen, pg 48

[60] Memories of Susanna Krause But what exactly would make the Aron Rempel Sr. home the nicest of all Gnadenfeld when their floor plans were almost all exactly alike? Was it because the Rempels had a pump organ and a piano, and several other musical instruments? Was it because the beams on the ceilings were decorated with painted flowers? Was it possibly because their floors sported the new linoleum or were painted like linoleum? Perhaps the Rempels had some fine china and sterling silverware? Perhaps the statement "they had all kind of things" refers to their home being the nicest because of special, fancy furnishings, which are not specified. Did they have the highest himmel bed in the Grottestov (Grottestube)?

[61] A Mennonite Family in Tsarist Russia and the Soviet Union 1789-1923, David G. Rempel pg 48

[62] "The Story of Agatha and Carl Rempel", as told to their daughter H. R. Lockwood, pg 7

[63] "Aron Rempel and Johann Ediger sold agricultural equipment." Molotschna Historical Atlas, Helmut T. Huebert, pg 127

[64] 1835-1945 Gnadenfeld, Molotschna, A Lowen Schmidt, pg 9

[65] Mennonites produced a harvester known as the Lobograika, used to cut oats, barley, rye, millet, and hay, and produced a machine called the self-reaper. The Molotschna Colony, A Heritage Remembered, Henry Bernard Tiessen, pg 38

[66] A Mennonite Family in Tsarist Russia and the Soviet Union 1789-1923, David G. Rempel, pg 55

That bed was always made up really fancy with special crocheted lace, or embroidered pillows on it. Everyone showed off their Himmel Bed in the Grottestov.

32 Top: Himmel Bed
33 Bottom: Himmel Bed exposed

Smaller factories employed around 100, with the largest employing about 150 men. The usual workday started at 6:00 a.m., with lunch between 11:30 and 1:00, then work until 6 p.m., when the 10-11 hour workday was done. This was the routine for six days a week. An 8 hour workday was not introduced until the Russian Revolution of 1917. A factory worker earned about 1 ruble a day, with a master mechanic earning around 120 rubles a month. [67]

Once there was a big demonstration of the Rempel farm machinery on the Mordvinovka Estate, owned by Mr. Wiens, Sr. Many people had come from miles around to witness this new fangled threshing machine, but Gerhard Wiens' father was *not impressed with the heavy thing, which took too much fuel to operate and provided no manure for fertilizer.*[68]

Aaron Jr. knew girls. He could have married any girl in Gnadenfeld. He was the catch. The Goosens were some wealthy Mennonites who lived on a large estate away from Gnadenfeld.[69] When Goosens wanted to attend the Gnadenfeld church for any of their three daughters to be baptized, the Christmas holidays, or other special occasions, they always stayed at the Aron Rempel Sr. home. Young people were not baptized until they were young adults and could give a profession of faith in Jesus saving them from their sins, usually around their late teens to early twenties. Father Aron Sr. wanted his son Aaron to marry the wealthy, oldest Goosen girl. Neither Father Aron nor sisters Susanna or Helena wanted him to marry Susanna Krause.[70] The Mennonites who were industrialists, or owned estates, because of their social status, brought a certain air of superiority, a sense of condescension toward those more impoverished. The Mennonite community in Russia, *who prided themselves on their parity or equality of social status, had developed its own class society.*[71]

Wealthy, handsome, debonaire Aaron A. Rempel wasn't the only one who had noticed how lovely the young Susanna Krause was becoming. When she was about sixteen, suddenly two other young lads were always around Susanna. One was Franz Voth, a very good friend of Susanna's older brother Cornelius. He came to her home every day, but never talked directly to Susanna; he was just there. He was aways around, but apparently too shy to say anything directly to Susanna. It seemed he just came to see her brother Cornelius. Finally Mama Agatha noticed Franz was always hanging around.

---

[67] First Mennonite Villages in Russia, 1789-1943, Khortitsa-Rosenthal, N. J. Kroeker, pg 92

[68] Constantinoplers, Escape from Bolshevism, Irmgard Epp, pg,26

[69] Mennonite Estates in Imperial Russia, Helmut T. Huebert,   It is uncertain which Goosen estate it is, possibly the Wintergruen Estate, or Gruenfeld Estate; both were near Alexandrovsk and Schoenfeld, in Ekaterinoslav Volost, pp. 66, 245, 262, 454

[70] The author has no family history to suggest how his older sister Maria, now married to Abram Braun, felt about Aaron marrying Susanna Krause.

[71] Mennonite Foods & Folkways from South Russia, Vol I, Norma Jost Voth, pg 14

34, 35 Two views of Aaron A. Rempel Jr. birthplace, Gnadenfeld

"Why does Franz come each day in the back door?" It was Susanna's younger sister Agatha who knew, "Don't you know? He's in love with Suzy!"

Susanna didn't really notice Franz at first. It was her younger sister who first understood why Franz was always hanging around. Someone else was also noticing Susanna. When Susanna was in the kleinestube (the "little" room where the girls slept) busy sewing, he lurked in the hinterhaus (the dining room, in the center of the house) or in the eckstube (the parents bedroom). If Susanna was helping set the table in the hinterhaus, he was in the vorderhaus (front entryway), where he could slip out the front door. Or he was in the tiny hallway between the hinterhaus and sommastov (called the summer room, where the boys slept) leading to the stahl (barn attached to the house with a fireproof wall of brick, and an iron door). From there he could easily slip back into the barn whenever Mama came back into the kitchen area. When Susanna was outside in the vegetable garden, gathering cucumbers and tomatoes to eat at dinner, he hid behind a tree or behind the summer kitchen, but was always nearby. Her own stepfather was also noticing Susanna. He more than noticed Susanna; he stalked her.

Stepfather was 18 years younger than his wife Agatha, and 12 years older than his young, beautiful stepdaughter. Stepfather was always hanging around, always looking at Susanna. When Susanna went to hang up the clothes on the clothesline, he was there. When Susanna went to fetch butter from the well, he was there. When Susanna went to the vegetable patch to fetch some onions and fresh dill for the borsht, or went to the henhouse to gather eggs, he was there again. He was always there! Mama saw it too. She could plainly see from her kitchen window, that stepfather was stalking Susanna. Poor Mama, but what could she do?

One day Susanna was sitting all by herself on the garden bench, next to the lilac bushes overlooking the orchard. She was enjoying the roses throughout the garden, the one snowball bush, violets and hyssop. Lilac clusters were enormous, their fragrance intoxicating. This time when Franz slipped into the garden, he finally generated enough courage to sit down beside her. He wanted to ask her all sorts of questions: "What is your favorite color? What did you think of the sermon last Sunday? What is your favorite flower? Would you like to go for a walk? What do you like to read? What are your favorite songs? Have you seen the flowers that are now in bloom in the meadow where the cows are pastured each day? Do you enjoy reading? What do you enjoy reading the most? The Bible? The Martyr's Mirror? Something else? "

He came every day, but just never got up enough courage to talk directly to Susanna. Susanna began to look forward to the frequent visits from her shy, silent suitor. She often made sure to sit on the garden bench, shelling peas, or stitching a hem, just to be available. It didn't bother her that he never talked. She had secretly admired Franz, and it spoke well of him that her older brother and Franz were the best of friends. His love and loyalty were almost palpable. And now Franz was frequently coming to the house. But all too often, Franz just ended up finding Cornelius and talking to him. He kept losing all his resolve to finally say something, to blurt out something, anything to the girl of his dreams.

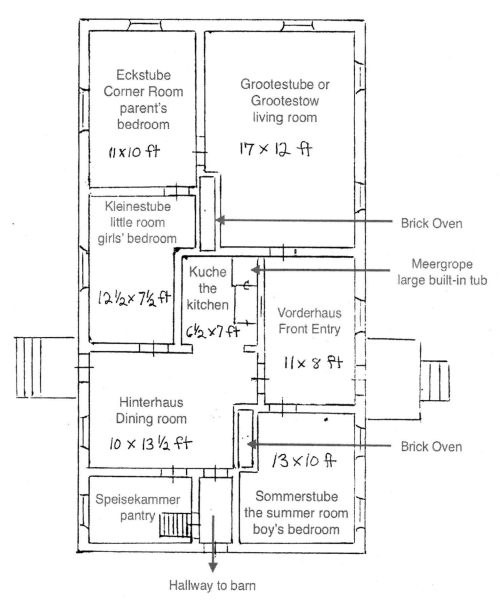

36 typical floorpan of house; The house measured 30.3 Ft by 52.5 Ft

On winter evenings, when the howl of icy wind was heard outside, the hot brick oven made the house cozy and warm inside. While the sun sank into a vast sea of white snow, it was still too early for supper or to light the kerosene lamp. Susanna and her siblings would sit and sing, with Jacob playing the guitar or mandolin. They would later have a simple meal of barley soup cooked with sour milk (buttermilk?), rye bread, liver sausage, onions, and vinegar. Cattle on the other side of the thick pantry wall, comfortable and warm in their sturdy barn, lowed softly. About 9 p.m. the animals would receive their last feeding of the day.[72]

The house was dark, very quiet and still. Brother Heinz was in his bed in the summa-stube. Susanna and her sisters Agatha, Meiche, and Katche were in their pull-out beds in the kleinestube, which was next door to the parents' bedroom in the eckstube. Going to bed was a task. The beds had lids, which were opened and leaned back, then made up with featherbeds, quilts, and pillows. [73]

Susanna was daydreaming of Franz, daydreaming of a wedding and becoming Mrs. Franz Voth.[74] Oh how her heart was fluttering . . . when suddenly Susanna heard faint footsteps coming into her room from the hinterhaus, saw the shadow of someone in the faint moon-light coming in through the door, and then felt someone pulling the covers off her! This happened repeatedly, not every single night, but often enough Susanna could not let her-self fall asleep early. She had to be on guard. Susanna would scream, and stepfather would run out of the room, through the hinterhaus, past the kitchen, into the vorderhaus, through the grottestov, and then tiptoe back into his bed in the eckstube.

Each time Susanna heard someone tiptoeing into the room, coming closer, closer to her bed, and feel the covers slowly being pulled away, she would scream. She never told her Mama. She didn't need to. Mama was in bed in the room next door. The walls between the eckstube and kleinestube were not thick enough to block out the sound of her screams.[75]

Susanna's screams told Mama the complete story. She and her mother never talked about it, never said one word about it, but her mother knew what was happening just the same. How could she not know, with those screams in the middle of the night? Each time when Susanna screamed, Agatha's husband was not in bed beside her. He always came to bed

[72] Mennonite Foods & Folkways from South Russia, Vol II, Norma Jost Voth, Mary Dirks Janzen, pg 161
[73] Ibid. pg 161
[74] Sandi Bergmann remembers Susanna saying while living in Sierra View—she didn't really want to marry Aaron; she was really in love with Franz.
[75] Mennonite Food & Folkways from South Russia, Vol II, Norma Jost Voth, pp. 10—11

a little bit later. Stepfather tried telling Agatha she misunderstood, that he was only covering Susanna up.[76]

37 Top Eckstov, Eckstube — corner room, parents' bed-room;
Mennonite Settlement Museum, Hillsborough, Kansas

38 Bottom Hinterhaus—dining room, pantry beyond—
Mennonite Settlement Museum, Hillsborough, Kansas

---

[76] Susanna said her stepfather ruined her young life. She said her mother Agatha, in marrying a much younger man, ruined her young life, but she still loved and honored her mother.

During the day, Susanna went to the garden to pick some tulips to put on the table for their dinner, and again, stepfather was there. Oh, when would she ever have any peace! She had to be on her guard **all** the time.

The girls in Gnadenfeld and the other German Mennonite villages generally married in their early twenties. Mama began urging 16 year old Susanna to get married young, to get her safely out of the house. That was the only conversation they had about the situation. Otherwise, they never talked about what caused those screams in the night, or the sound of footsteps running away from the girls' bedroom, or why it was so important for Susanna to get married as soon as possible. An unspoken rule of silence reigned, the rule of not airing the family dirty laundry. Silence was caused by the utter shame of what was going on. They were not the cause of the shame, not the perpetrators of the shame; they were the victims of the shame, and yet there still was the unspoken rule of silence: "Davon spricht mann nicht. About that, we do not talk."

Why didn't mother Agatha and Susanna take this matter to the church elders? The congregation was supposed to keep an eye on its members and exercise congregational discipline. Membership in Mennonite congregations was voluntary. An individual became a member of the church through confession of faith followed by baptism.

In the early days in Holland, Mennonite believers were baptized understanding it could very well result in martyrdom.[77] The suffering, persecution, and slaughter in Holland by the Inquisition for the sake of Jesus Christ had purified the church and caused Mennonites to then flee into Prussia. Only true believers were members of the church in those perilous days.

Later, Catherine the Great of Russia invited Mennonites from Prussia to settle the largely uninhabited Ukraine, but mandated that each immigrant village be totally made up of its own church group. Co-mingling of German Catholics with German Lutherans, German Mennonites, or even the Russian people themselves was firmly prohibited.

More than a century after immigrating to Russia from Prussia, the church remained central to all village life. To vote, get married, or own land, a villager had to be a member of the one and only church in the village, but by now the church included the unconverted.

---

[77] Testing Faith and Tradition, A Global Mennonite History, editors John A Lapp, C. Arnold Snyder, pp 19-20

Mennonite congregational discipline ordinarily was strictly applied. Mennonites were not allowed to marry non-Mennonites. They were not allowed to marry Catholics or Lutherans, even German Catholics or Lutherans, and certainly not Russians. Even the Gronigen and Flemish Mennonites were not allowed to marry each other for a time. *There was discipline in cases of adultery, dancing, drunkenness, gambling, indebtedness, tax offenses, extravagant lifestyle by a fine and or exclusion from communion. After a time, with repentance, a person could be readmitted* to the fellowship of the church. A permanently excluded person had no choice but to leave the area.[78]

Why did the church leadership never know about stepfather's actions? Is it because the ones who knew never brought it to the attention of the church leaders for church discipline? Public excommunication in such a small, close-knit village, where everyone knew everybody else, could have been a powerful deterrent to such actions. Actually those kinds of actions are the very things God in His Word directs the church to address.

So the question remains, why didn't Agatha and Susanna go to the church elders for church discipline? Was it because stepfather was charming? Predators often appear good, well mannered, entertaining, likable. They have an outwardly good behavior. But once they have everyone's respect, then the abuse happens. A person cannot judge whether someone is an abuser until a victim comes forth.[79]

Did Susanna and Agatha not bring it to the church elders because the whole Mennonite community would then have looked at Agatha and Susanna as the ones who caused stepfather's heart to lust? Sometimes the culture in close Christian circles not only blames the victim, but requires the victim to first go to the abuser according to Matthew 18 and forgive them. But Matthew 18 was never intended for victims of murder, kidnapping, or sexual abuse. You don't go to the abuser; you go to the police. In Gnadenfeld, that would have meant going to the church elders. They had the authority of police.[80] There were no child protective services. How did families in those days deal with such issues?[81] Was it because of the utter shame of it, that the family just swept it under the rug? Susanna could not

---

[78] Ibid, pg 27

[79] Myron Horst, on ATI Parents Recovery site, 2014 (private access) used by permission

[80] GRACE, Godly Response to Abuse in the Christian Environment   https://www.facebook.com/Godly-Response-to-Abuse-in-the-Christian-Environment-GRACE-102403896480483/

[81] *"Most victims (of sexual abuse) find that their families refuse to admit the abuse actually happened, or else they minimize the damage it caused . . . . They are told to forgive and forget, and when they find this impossible to do, they are seen as stubborn and vindictive. They feel guilty for not being able to 'go on with their lives'; for continuing to feel angry; or for even saying that they have been affected by the abuse at all."* The Right to Innocence, Beverly Engel pg 22

even put it into words? Mother Agatha never even said anything about it either? Each of them just pretended that such things hadn't happened.[82] [83]

Susanna's heart fluttered each time Franz came near, but still Franz never said anything. He just ended up always going to find Cornelius. To Susanna, his love needed no words, and yet it did need expression. Susanna couldn't wait forever. She needed Franz to declare his love, ask her to marry him, and marry her. She needed to get out of the house, and get out of the house soon. No, soon was not good enough. She needed to get out of the house **now**.

As for Aaron, Susanna didn't even notice him. He was so much older, and she was so much younger. Aaron went with the other, older girls all the time. Susanna didn't even care for him.

One day Susanna was invited to the home of Aaron's cousin Susie Voth, to come in and help prepare the lunch. Susie's mother Susanna Schmidt Voth and Aaron's mother Maria were sisters.[84] They made lunch, and Aaron was visiting in the Grottestube at his cousin's home. All of a sudden, Aaron, after coming in the hinterhaus to fetch something, entered the speisekammer where Susanna was working. He stopped short, and told Susanna, "I have to bring them something, but I come back here. Don't you go away." Susanna was scared. "What do you mean?" she thought, "Don't you go away?" She was only sixteen. Aaron was already a grown man. He was older. Much older. Susanna wanted to run home right away. Aaron told her, "You wait a little bit here, and Susie will come." Well, minutes passed, but Susie didn't come, and she didn't come, and she didn't come. Susanna had her own dinner, washed the dishes, and still Susie didn't come back. Susanna dried the dishes, put them away, and was finishing tidying up in the pantry when finally Aaron returned. Then Susanna overheard Susie's mother whisper to the others, "Leave them alone there." Now Susanna Krause felt trapped.[85]

---

[82] In less religious cultures, lust can be fulfilled more easily by adultery or common law marriages free of commitment. But in tight-knit, strict religious communities, uncontrolled lust, must be hidden more carefully. Often in those communities lust is manifest in incest, where the lust can be hidden more easily within the confines of the home. Therefore incest is more prevalent in strict, tight knit, religious communities even today

[83] My Harp is turned to Mourning, Al Reimer, pg 30 This historical novel, set in the same time period, tells of an occurrence known to have happened among the Mennonites, about a much younger man who married a much older widow with property, who had an unmarried daughter, not very much younger than he was, and later the young unmarried girl gave birth . . . I think it was much easier for truth to be told in the setting of a novel, rather than in specific, personal family histories. Such occurrences understandably would usually have been deliberately omitted in memoirs, autobiographies, or biographies.

[84] Susie Voth, daughter of Susanna (born Schmidt) and Herman Voth

[85] Author's Aunt Marie said Susie's mother and Aaron Rempel Jr's mother Maria were sisters. Marie gave Susie's mother's name as Tante Gotche (or Aunt Agatha) but the record does not show an Agatha as a sister for Maria (born Schmidt) Rempel, Aaron Jr's, mother in the family genealogy. If Susie were named after her mother, her mother could be Susanna, (born Schmidt) Voth. However, the author doesn't have a great deal of information on Maria Schmidt Rempel's siblings, and may be missing the pertinent information altogether.

When Susanna went home, Aaron insisted on walking her home. Susanna was so bashful. She felt like she turned beet red, and stayed red the whole way home, she was so bashful. From then on, Aaron was always by her side; he was always around, he wouldn't let Susanna go, but Aaron **talked** to her.

On cold winter nights the young people loved to go for sleigh rides. Each team of horses had three sets of sleigh bells. The lads liked to get the horses to go around a corner too fast in order to tip the sleigh over so they could hear the girls scream. It was all in good fun. Or the young people might gather in a home to sing and play guitar or balalaika. Son Aaron Rempel Jr. was quite musical, playing the piano, flute, pump organ, and guitar. In summer they might enjoy a picnic. Young people had little in the way of outdoor sports. Children used the Mittlestrasse, lined with poplars on either side, to go to school, and on Sunday people strolled along it to go to church. Paths between the gardens were covered with sand and brick so they never became muddy. The garden paths and Mittlestrasse were very romantic settings where young people gathered on Sundays, and often one heard singing, accompanied by a guitar, especially in the spring, with all the world in riotous bloom.

Susanna's family liked to sit outside in the warm evening air, in the moonlight, and listen to nightingales and also Russian workers singing folk songs which ranged from deep and melancholy, to bright and gay.[86]

Cornelius finally did tell Susanna that Franz was madly in love with her, but by then, Susanna already belonged to Aaron.

Choir practice was an acceptable activity for socialization and courting. The choir sounded like everyone had beautifully trained voices. The different sections of the choir learned their parts by singing the numbers, and once they knew their parts, they sang the words of the anthem a cappella, even though they had that wonderful organ.[87]

One day when Susanna and Aaron had gone to choir practice, Susanna's brother Cornelius saw stepfather hide himself behind the mulberry bushes near the Kirchen-steg or Church path, where Susanna and Aaron would return. Previously, Cornelius had noticed stepfather stalking Susanna, which made him very angry. Cornelius ran to get brother Jacob, and together they hid themselves around the corner of the shed housing the

---

[86] Mennonite Foods & Folkways from South Russia, Vol II, Norma Jost Voth, pg 20
[87] "My Family was Transplanted", audio tape by Mary Dirks Janzen

wagons and the pig house. At that corner closest to the school path, they could dimly see stepfather through the trees in the orchard, and would be nearby if needed.

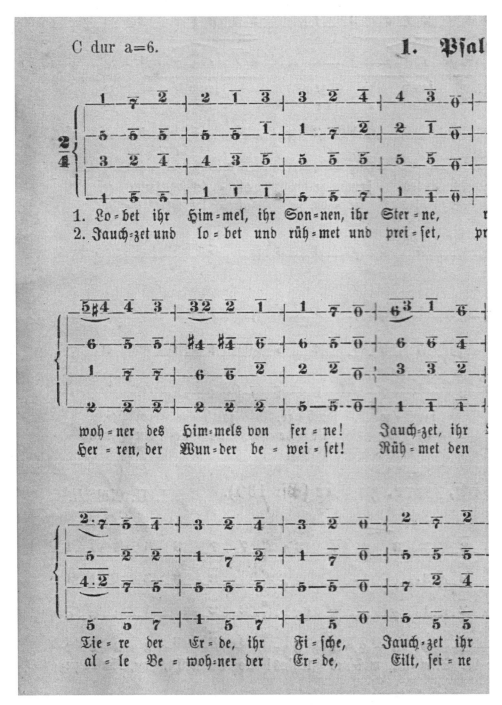

39 old choral music, public domain

Their music was written with numbers (the numbers representing the different notes instead of using notes on the EGBDF staff lines and FACE in the spaces on the music staff).

It was a beautiful early June night. Nightingales sang in the lilac bushes, and organ music floated in the soft evening air throughout the village as organist Johann Rempel practiced. Later Aaron was walking Susanna home along the Kirchensteg when stepfather suddenly rushed out from behind the mulberry bushes, shoved Susanna aside, and hit Aaron in the head with a big rock, causing him to fall to the ground. Susanna cried out just as Cornelius, carrying a big knife, with Jacob in tow, ran up from behind the corner of the building. When Cornelius was mad, he didn't know what he was doing. Was Aaron, lying on the ground with blood gushing from the ugly gash on his head, dead? Cornelius and Jacob caught and beat up stepfather, who then dragged himself off and hid somewhere in the barn. Then the brothers carried Aaron home, where he recovered from a nasty headache. Stepfather, on the other hand, had a hard time explaining all his many scrapes, bruises, and black eye, as he mumbled something about an ornery cow.[88]

Aaron's father still wanted Aaron to marry one of the rich Goosen girls. Stepfather trying to kill Aaron was another reason that Aaron's father didn't want his son to marry Susanna. True, one of the wealthy Goosens was especially pretty, and Aron Sr. was pretty stubborn. He simply didn't approve of his son marrying Susanna. Aaron Jr. never had a doubt. It was aways Susanna, only Susanna. Aaron's mother Maria wanted Aaron to marry Susanna. Perhaps it was Aaron's mother who had helped hatch the plan to get Susanna to visit Susie over at her sister's home to help with lunch that day.

So, when it came time for Aaron to ask permission to marry Susanna, he didn't go to step-father. He went directly to Susanna's mother, Agatha. But would Aron A. Rempel Sr. boy-cott the wedding?

---

[88] Family lore (contributed from Joan Braun, daughter of Jacob Krause) includes one story of Cornelius and Jacob tar and feathering stepfather. Also see Appendix A

Wedding Bells

It was customary to publicly announce an approaching wedding three times, on the three Sundays before the great event.

The evening before the wedding, close relatives, sisters, brothers, cousins and friends would prepare a program where readings were recited and short skits or plays and the wedding gifts were presented.[89] To add a jest of humor, someone would donate a rolling pin, "In case of an emergency," he would explain.[90]

Children would play in a room by themselves. The youth group played Schülleslbund, or Last Couple Out (translated Key on a Ring) which was the most favored of games, since this was one time a young girl could walk arm in arm with a fellow. Bench seats were arranged in a circle, with only enough room for everyone but one. The extra person would have a key ring, which he would jingle, walk around and offer his arm to one young lady. Then the other lads would go find a young lady so they would all be walking around. They provided their own music by singing one of the many folk songs they knew in either German or Russian. The leader, the one with the keys, would drop his keys, and everyone would dash to find a seat. The one left out would be the new leader. [91]

Susanna and Aaron were married when Susanna was just seventeen[92] in the large old church in the center of town, August 9, 1909. Weddings usually took place about two o'clock in the afternoon. Customarily, fathers did not walk the bride down the aisle. Rather the couple entered together, unescorted by the bride's father, and sat on two decorated chairs in the front of the church. There were no bridesmaids, groomsmen, or flower girls.[93] The bridal party and entire congregation were seated for the whole service, except when the couple said their vows, and everyone stood. The sermon stressed that it was God who established marriage and that marriage was a lifetime commitment to each other: *He which made them at the beginning, made them male and female, and said, 'For this cause shall a man leave father and mother, and shall cleave to his wife: and they twain shall be one flesh. Wherefore they are no more twain, but one flesh. What therefore God hath joined together, let not man put asunder.[94]* It was a solemn affair that usually lasted more than an hour.

---

[89] My Memories, Mary Dirks Janzen, pp. 11,12
[90] The Molotschna Colony, A Heritage Remembered, Henry Bernard Tiessen, pg 96
[91] My Memories, Mary Dirks Janzen, pp. 11,12
[92] Age seventeen was young for marriage in Gnadenfeld. Aaron Jr's sisters all married in their early twenties, and the sisters who married Susanna's brothers were also in their early twenties.
[93] Mennonite Food & Folkways from South Russia, Vol II, Norma Jost Voth, pg 145
[94] Genesis chapter 2 as cited by Jesus in Matthew 19:5,6

They had a big reception in Mama's yard. Lots of people were present. Aaron's father was conspicuously absent. Unfortunately, Aaron's mother Maria died of cancer just one month before the wedding. Stepfather was at the wedding, of course, since the reception was held at his home. But he was awfully mad. He sulked in the shadows, and stomped around, but it was too late for him to stop the wedding.

The wedding supper was held in the Schuene (the shed, attached to the other end of the barn, that housed horse drawn vehicles). It had been cleaned out, the walls lined with clean canvasses, long tables set up, with long benches without backs. Garlands of fresh branches, perhaps of wild grape, were hung, to make it look festive and smell aromatic. The wedding supper consisted of plümemooss,[95] home made mustard, cold sliced ham, and two kinds of homemade bread: zwiebach and rye. A long trestle table groaned under loads of plates filled to overflowing with cold ham, zwiebach, and bowls of plumemoos. Teenage girls were thrilled to be asked to serve. Mama had prepared laundry baskets full of zweiback,[96] and friends and neighbors brought even more baskets full. Mountains of zweiback had to be baked for 300 to 500 people, since relatives would come from a distance and the whole village could be present.

At the end of the evening of the wedding day, after games and much singing, the bride and groom stood in the center of a circle, and the bride was blindfolded. The bride gave the myrtle wreath that she wore to the girl that she touched. This lucky girl would presume that she could be the next one to be married, but she did not keep the wreath. The bride would dry, press, and frame it as a family keepsake.[97]

---

[95] Plumemoos, or mooss—a thick fruit soup or thin fruit pudding. It can be something akin to applesauce, as it was when served at the Mennonite Heritage Center, in Steinbach, Manitoba. According to Mary Dirks Janzen, have "cream in Mooss? No! No! No! Gnadenfeld (Molotschna Colony) never had Plümemooss with cream. It isn't right!" Mennonite Foods & Folkways from South Russia, Vol II, Norma Jost Voth, pg 145

[96] Mennonite Foods & Folkways from South Russia, Vol I, Norma Jost Voth, pp. 39 ff many good recipes, tips and advice from a number of Mennonite cooks on making the best Zwiebach —pg 36-37 *the buns were shaped from a rich buttery dough, by pinching off a small ball of dough and placing on top of another larger ball of dough in a pan. Considerable skill is involved in getting them to stay upright together. Tops that slide off or lean over are "lazy zwiebach."*

[97] My Memories, Mary Dirks Janzen, pages 11,12

40 wedding picture of wife Susanna Krause and Aaron Rempel, Jr.

41 backside of wedding portrait

Family Life

Her hellt fäll fonn en kortet Jebäd
onn ne lange Worscht.

He thinks highly of short prayers
and long sausages.

—*Old Low German Saying*[98]

Der Herr hat es uns gegeben,
Ohne Brot is kein Leben.
Solang ein Brot im Kasten

Brauchen wir nicht zu fasten.
Herr segne unser Brot,
Dann haben wir keine Not.
Der Vater, der Sohn und der
Heilige Geist

The Lord has given us bread.
Without it there is no life.
As long as bread is in the
cupboard,
We need not fast.
Lord, bless our bread,
For then we have no need.
The Father, the Son, and Holy
Ghost.

.—*Old German Bread making Blessing*[99]

Susanna and Aaron moved to a beautiful new home. It was not at all like the rest of the farm homes. The floor plan was quite different, with the house facing horizontally toward the street, un-like all the others facing perpendicular to the street like so many German soldiers. *It had more and larger windows. It had hand painted flowers around the ceiling of the living room, beautiful furniture, and potted plants.*[100]

Usually, a young, newly married couple would take turns living in the sommastov of one of their parents, but Aaron already had a new home built on his land across from his father's wirtshaft, where he had been born and had grown up.

So, one of the first things Susanna needed to do as she set up house keeping, was to buy staples for the pantry. She went to the store her father-in-law owned, and bought 5 pounds of flour, 5 pounds of sugar, 5 pounds of salt, 5 pounds of pepper, and 5 pounds of bay leaves.

"What?" exclaimed her mother Agatha! "Five pounds of salt, pepper, and bay leaves? And only 5 pounds of flour? The flour won't even last you a month, and the pepper and bay leaves will last all

---

[98] Mennonite Food & Folkways from South Russia, Vol I, Norma Jost Voth, pg 243
[99] Ibid., pg 75
[100] My Memories, Mary Dirks Janzen, page 28, The author believes this home was located at 109 Second Street. (see map of Gna-denfeld on pg 17)

of Gnadenfeld forever! You probably have way too much sugar, as well. When the butchering is done, then you will need a lot more salt. But now you will need just enough salt for fermenting your sauerkraut. You take the sugar, salt, black pepper, and bay leaves back, and get 25 pounds of flour! "[101]

An exposition was held in Halbstadt, August 14-16, 1909, just a week after Susanna and Aaron's wedding. Those who attended were introduced to a new system of canning fruit, that could maintain the taste, color, and smell of the fruit. A new system of incubating chicks was also introduced, but farmers seemed content with their old technique of "sitting behind the stove." [102]

42 younger siblings at Krause-Dirks home
L to R Maria (Mieche or Mary) Dirks, Agatha Krause, Katherine (Katche) Dirks peeking out, Heinz (Henry) Dirks, cousin Justina Dirks,[103] neighbor and cousin Willie Ratzlaff[104] courtesy of Mary Janzen

[101] story related by Betty Voth, daughter of Jacob and Maria Krause in the Cousin Rundbrief (round robin letter) dated August 2015-2016.
[102] Events and People, Helmut T. Huebert, pp. 111-113
[103] Justina Dirks (born 1904, German Mennonite database: Grandma # 1041876) daughter of Wilhelm Dirks (bother of Heinrich D. Dirks)
[104] Willie Ratzlaff (born 1901 or 1903, Grandma #193849) son of Heinrich Ratzlaff, (brother-in-law of Heinrich D. Dirks)

Susanna and Aaron's first child, Marie, was born 19 May, 1910 in mother Agatha's house.

Now that Susanna was married, Mama Agatha's dressmaker was gone from the home and she needed another. The next oldest daughter Agatha was then sent to sewing school.

It was mother Agatha's first husband Kornelius Krause who had bought, not just one, but two of the big wirtshafts (farms) in Gnadenfeld. Originally, no one was allowed to own more than one farm at a time. If any owner inherited or otherwise acquired another farm, he had to sell one of them.[105] Sometime in the past, this law had been relaxed. Not only had Susanna's father been able to buy two farms, right next door to each other, but Susanna's father-in-law Aron A. Rempel Sr. also owned two adjacent farms just a few farms away on the same street.

Originally, each farm would have been inherited by one of Kornelius and Agatha's two boys, Cornelius and Jacob Krause. Now that Agatha had remarried, Agatha no longer had much to say about what her boys would inherit. In fact Agatha no longer "owned" those two farms. Her new husband "owned" them, so he now controlled the farms. Since she now had three more children with her second husband, two girls and one boy, this youngest boy now stood to inherit both the family farms. Agatha wisely first sent Cornelius and then Jacob to business school to study accounting[106] in Simferopol, Crimea, the capital of their province of Taurida.[107] After graduating, Jacob's first job was as a bookkeeper in Einlage, Chortiza Colony.[108]

— —

"If a person keeps turning like a windmill, he thinks overly much of his fine appearance and displays it." Low German simile[109]

---

[105] From the Steppes to the Prairies, Paul Klassen, pg 20
[106] "Dear Katja, . . . Now I understand why Kornelius and Jasch went off to school to learn accounting and classical music on guitar and mandolin. They must have disliked their young stepfather because of his youth. Now at our old age of 80 plus, we can quite clearly understand that situation caused by a marriage ordered by a guardian, as was customary in those years for widows. Later many tears were shed by husband and wife because of heartache, and hostility from all directions. I blame no one, let God in heaven judge. Only 3 sisters, Susan, you, and I are alive to tell this story. All others are faded into dust, may they rest in peace." Mieche, July 29, 1989 see Appendix A
[107] Information given by Joan Krause Braun, daughter of Jacob Krause
[108] My Memories, Mary Dirks Janzen, pg 33
[109] Mennonite Foods & Folkways from South Russia. Vol II, Norma Jost Voth, pg 61

Opel 14 h.p.

Maintenance Guaranteed.   **14 h.p. 4-Cylinder OPEL Light Touring Car.**   *Trials at any time.*

Price, as Light Touring Car, with Lamps and Horn, £310.

OPEL CARS.

The British Electromobile Co., Ltd., 5-6 Halkin Street, Hyde Park Corner, S.W.

Telephone Nos.: 3238 and 3239 Victoria.   *Telegrams: "Oppidulum, London."*

43 Opel, Public Domain, courtesy of the Nethercutt Museum, Sylmar, California

A half page ad May 30, 1909, in Die Friedensstimme (the German language newspaper of the colonies) pictured an Opel Doppelphaeton (four seater). Aaron had the first and only car in Gnadenfeld, a 1908 Opel.[110] In 1914, there were only two cars in the Gnadenfeld district of the Molotschna Colony,[111] with Aaron owning one of those coveted two. The Ford motor car had an ugly tone to its horn, but the Opel tooted a melodious three notes.[112] Young boys, who could always seem to hear the huffing and puffing from a long distance away, would come running to see it clatter its way down the street. Aaron also had the first and only phone in Gnadenfeld, with the line going between his farm machinery factory and the lumberyard diagonally across town, which belonged to his two brothers-in-law Jacob and Cornelius Toews.[113]

---

[110] Henry Toews, (son of Jacob and Susanna Rempel Toews) told the author Aaron had the only car in Gnadenfeld, an Opel. Author's guess—it probably would have been the same car his Uncle Dietrich Rempel in Caucasus drove, the same car advertised throughout the Molotschna Colony, a 1908 OPEL double phaeton, made in Austria-Hungary, large enough to hold all the people in this story.

[111] Before World War I, there were about 40 automobiles in the Molotschna Colony. The Sudermann brothers . . . became the first distributers in the Molotschna. Henry Bernard Tiessen, A Heritage Remembered pg 32   Hierschau, An Example of Russian Mennonite Life, Helmut T. Huebert, pg 167

[112] First Mennonite Villages in Russia, 1789-1943, N.J. Kroeker, pg 190

[113] Toews, pronounced Taves; Susanna Toews' son Henry remembered seeing that private phone line that went between his home at the lumberyard and the farm machinery factory, which author believes was located at #24 First Street

In the beginning years of the colony, there had been a parity, a social equality of village citizenship. No one member was more important than another. That was the Mennonite way. Mennonite doctrine taught Mennonites to live simply, without ostentation, neither appearing to be more affluent than others, nor exhibiting an extravagant lifestyle.[114]

But with time, the wealthy came to rule over the poor majority. A condescension or disdain for the anwhoner (the landless), considered "lowlifes" or called domkopp (dumbhead) even arose.[115] That was in spite of the fact no land was left for anwhoner to buy, without going far, far away from their home village.

It was not uncommon for some wealthy Mennonite estate owners to purposely dress ostentatiously to show off their affluence. Some of the big houses on the estates sported frescoes, or the work of an Italian painter on the hall ceiling. One featured a bowling alley; another was furnished with ornate black lacquered furniture upholstered in gold velvet. Another included an arboretum with full size lemon trees. Some wealthy Mennonites succumbed to gluttony and became very obese. With servants to do all the menial tasks, a number grew lazy. Some owners even developed sinful appetites and preyed upon their unfortunate female servants. They spied on them in their bathhouse through knot holes that kept opening up, then banished them for what developed "behind their aprons."[116]

Aaron Jr. was disciplined by the church for exhibiting an extravagant lifestyle because of the purchase of his car. He was even removed from church membership for a time. This action was not applied equally and consistently to those who owned vast estates, dwelt in large manor houses filled with fine imported furniture and staffed with many servants. Nor to owners of the fanciest droshky, pulled by the sleekest matched pair of horses. Not even to those whose himmel bed was much higher than others.

The Thursday before Good Friday, Maundy Thursday, the church commemorated the Last Supper of Jesus with His disciples by observing foot washing. Women washed the women's feet, and men washed the men's feet. Aaron and Susanna regularly attended church, and participated in the foot washing ceremony, at least until he was excommunicated for being too worldly by owning a telephone and an automobile. Stepfather was not excommunicated for his misdeeds, but Aaron was. It took many hands to accomplish all the household tasks each day. Russian maids were not a luxury but a necessity. Since there were only a few wells in Gnadenfeld with water free of saltpeter, drinkable water had to be carried from the nearest good well. Cows had to be milked; the house

---

[114] Mennonite Foods and folkways from South Russia, Vol I, Norma Jost Voth, pg 20
[115] The Russländer, Sandra Birdsell, pg 77
[116] Ibid., pp. 56-57, 124

cleaned; eggs pickled; straw or dung fires started; dishes washed after breakfast; noon meals, faspa, and evening meals served. But that wasn't all; the vegetable garden needed to be weeded, root vegetables dug, ripened peaches, apricots, apples, and pears dried and canned, and watermelon syrup boiled down.

The rye bread sponge starter was kept from one bread making to the next. The new batch was started the night before, let rise over night, kneaded and baked the next day. When the dough no longer stuck to the hands and felt good and solid, it was considered ready to mold and let rise the last time before baking.[117]

44 Outdoor Brick Oven, Mennonite Settlement Museum, Hillsborough, Kansas.

---

[117] <u>Mennonite Foods & Folkways from South Russia, Vol II</u>, Norma Jost Voth, Mary Dirks Janzen, pg 57

The large white bread, or Bulkje had a crust that resembled French Bread. Since there is no fat in bulkje, it dried out faster than rye bread or zwiebach. *The brick oven in Russia was heated to a very high temperature and became like a pressure cooker. The bulkje expands; the hot fragrant steam fills the oven and is baked back into the crust, producing bread with a wonderful fragrance. The steam also keeps the crust pliable, allowing the loaf to continue expanding during early baking, which creates legendary bread with a golden brown crust and a superb flavor. It does not burn in spite of the high heat. The moist oven helps caramelize the sugar in the dough which gives the crust a golden yellow color and overall glossy appearance.*[118]

Susanna and her Russian girls knew by feel when the oven was ready. The all pervasive heat, convected by steam coming from the bread, produced the largest loaves of bread, in about half the time of modern electric and gas ovens. *When the fuel had burned down, the glowing embers and ashes were cleared away with a special oven rake and a wet mop which was used to wash the floor. The bread was quickly slipped into the oven with a long wooden paddle so no heat would be lost.* [119]

Every house in Russia had a cast-iron heart-shaped waffle iron, which fit into one of the two big holes in the stove top, in such a way the waffle could be flipped without lifting the waffle iron. The large waffles were served with a sweet white sauce.[120]

Help was especially needed at harvest time, when extra water had to be hauled and heated. Meals included a large meal at noon, a lunch or Faspa at four with zwiebach (a smaller, rich yeast bun nestled on top of a larger bun before being baked)[121] and coffee, then a supper at nine. Chores of milking cows, mending, and ironing didn't stop for the harvest: chores of hoeing the garden, boiling down the watermelon syrup in big meergrope (cauldrons), drying fruit, or canning continued as usual. Russian help was generally treated well by their Mennonite employers, with some becoming good friends.[122]

---

[118] Mennonite Food & Folkways from South Russia, Vol I, Norma Jost Voth, pp. 69-71 American testers finally concluded that American electric and gas ovens do not produce the same results. This cookbook gives instructions for getting steam into a modern oven, and where to write for instructions to make an old-fashioned Russian brick oven.

[119] Mennonite Foods & Folkways from South Russia, Vol II, Norma Jost Voth, pg 58

[120] Mennonite Foods & Folkways from South Russia, Vol I, Norma Jost Voth, pg 121

[121] Ibid. pp. 26, 36-37 *Does the word Zwiebach mean the two buns baked together, or does it mean that the buns were "twice-baked?"—baked and then toasted in the oven . . . . Any zwiebach remaining from Faspa were toasted in the oven. When done properly, the toasted buns lasted indefinitely.*

[122] Paul Klassen related "years later an elderly Russian wistfully shared with a visiting Mennonite that the best years of her life were spent as a servant girl on Grandpa's estate." From the Steppes to the Prairies. Paul Klassen, pg 21

45 Above, kitchen stove
L to R waffle iron, soup pot, meergrope; Mennonite Settlement Museum, Hillsborough, Kansas

A Meergrope, or Copper Cauldron was also built into both the house and summer kitchen. It was used to heat water for baths for the family and for laundry. In late summer watermelon was boiled down for several days into a thick syrup sweetener; tallow and lye was cooked in it to make home-made soap; it was used for rendering lard, cooking cracklings or spareribs; it was used as a large soup kettle to make Salankje (mutton soup), or to cook gallons of Plümemoos for weddings or family reunions.

46 heart-shaped waffle iron; Mennonite Settlement Museum, Hillsborough, Kansas

If a harvest team were to eat the noon meal at the house the next day, the mother of the house knew she had to start preparations the day before. Sometimes women rose as early as 3 a.m., when some of the men had to be in the field by dawn. Neighbors, sisters, aunts, grandmothers would often come to assist peeling potatoes, baking bread, churning butter, butchering chickens, fetching a cured ham, making the mooss or gathering and preparing green beans from the garden. A pail of water, soap, basin, combs, and mirror were placed on a bench outside, and a long roller towel hung on a nail nearby, so hard working field workers could freshen up before the midday meal.[123]

Faspa was initiated to provide nourishment for hard working farmers, as a snack in the afternoon, so they wouldn't have to wait until chores were over and the evening meal served. So around 3:30 or 4:00 in the afternoon, the women served Faspa with zweibach, cheese, sometimes cold meats, sometimes Schnetje (biscuits), Rollkucken cruller or waffles. But always, zweibach, coffee, and jelly were present. Prips, a coffee substitute made from beets, was served to the children.[124]

In getting ready for the Lord's Day, all Sunday meals had to be prepared, as much as possible, the day before. The usual tasks remained: milking, separating the butterfat, churning the butter. Milking was woman's work; Aaron never did the milking. Cleaning the bedrooms, by storing all feather beds and comforters back into the slide out sleeping benches, was routine. Add in wiping pantry shelves and cellar steps, trimming oil lamps and washing their chimneys, butchering and cleaning chickens for Sunday dinner, kneading and baking the Zweibach and bread dough, preparing a big kettle of moos, peeling potatoes, gathering wood for Sunday use, washing the kitchen floor, polishing cutlery with ashes, brushing out the men's Sunday suits, and polishing a row of Sunday shoes. Amidst the many tasks of preparing for Sunday, there was still the Saturday midday meal to prepare. On Sunday, fried potatoes and moos would be served with chicken or cold ham, a simple but quick meal. Only the breakfast dishes were washed on Sunday. Otherwise, the rest was reserved for washing up Monday morning.[125]

With no bathrooms, family members took turns taking a bath once a week in colder months, in a big wooden or galvanized tin tub, set up in the kitchen, with a curtain for privacy. All the water had to be heated in the meergrope, so the tub was never filled. Even so, that water had to be used by several people before it was dipped out and then replaced. Each member of the family dried off with the same linen towel, which became quite wet and cold by the time the last person used it. Otherwise, people usually just washed the face, hands, arms, and feet; that was it.

[123] Mennonite Foods & Folkways from South Russia, Vol II, Norma Jost Voth, pg 198
[124] Mennonite Foods & Folkways from South Russia Vol I,   Norma Jost Voth, Mary Dirks Janzen, pg 405
[125] Mennonite Foods & Folkways from South Russia, Vol II, Norma Jost Voth, pp. 226-229

Each family in the village expected company on Sunday afternoons, and families went visiting without any formal invitation. If your family did not have visitors, your family was one of those going visiting. Sometimes, even three or four families with their children would all be visiting in the same house on Sunday, all staying for afternoon Faspa. Mama would spread her good damask tablecloth over the everyday oilcloth; otherwise that special tablecloth was kept protected in Mama's hope chest.

Adults would eat first, but since as many as thirty or forty children, with four visiting families could be present, including the host family's children, they ate from plates the adults had used. The adults "cleaned" their plates for the children's use, by swabbing them off with a last piece of bread.

Laundry wasn't done in just one day. Clothes were soaked the day before. The wash was put into boiling soapy water, then wrung by hand, and rinsed twice, wringing by hand each time. Laundry water was never wasted, but used to scrub the kitchen floor, even the outhouse. All the rest was carried out to water flower beds or young trees. Everything had to be ironed, and so washday was kjeilkje (noodle) day, the noodle water furnishing a fine starch for ironing on Tuesday. As a young girl, Susanna had learned to iron by first doing pillow cases, handkerchiefs, underwear, and Papa's work clothes.[126]

Just because the harvest was finally in did not mean that the work would lessen. Hog butchering came with the first sharp, cold days, when the meat could then be preserved. Families usually kept several hogs, as pork was more economical than beef. Hogs were easier to raise and grew fat enough to butcher in a much shorter time. Hog butchering, with its promise of fresh seasoned pork, spareribs, cracklings, smoked sausage, and ham, brought neighbors to help. Even minister Ratzlaff, who lived next door, came to help the Krause-Dirks family with their hog butchering.

Women had to fill and boil large caldrons of water, so the pig carcasses could be scalded, shaved, and carved up. Hams had to be trimmed and salted away, meat ground for sausages, and intestines thoroughly cleaned to be filled as sausages. Fat was cut up and boiled in the meergrope, skimmed, and crocks of lard put away. It was said the Germans used every part of the pig but the squeal.

At night the weary people would sit down to a sumptuous meal of fresh pork after the last of the meat and fat had been prepared for winter, and everything had been washed up and put away. All the friends and neighbors who had come to help received gifts of pork, cracklings, and even some

---

[126] Mennonite Foods & Folkways from South Russia, Vol II, Norma Jost Voth, pp. 213-224

bags of cookies at the end of the hard day's work.[127] *A successful butchering was gauged by the number of hams put away and the gallons of lard cooked and poured into big crocks.*[128]

Cooler weather also meant pickling the last of the very small watermelons, canning apple butter and the last grape jelly, filling cellar shelves with rows and rows of summer's bounty. There were red and white potatoes, bushels of dried apples, pickled meat barrels, salted meat barrels, dill pickles, and sauerkraut. A bushel of apples made one and a half gallons of dried apples.

Produce from the garden and orchard was dried, brined, or pickled. Dairy products were turned into clabbered milk, sour cream, and cottage cheese. Separators divided cream from the milk used for drinking and clabbered milk. *The cream was made into butter, for cooking, for sour cream gravy, and for salad dressing in the summer . . . . A milk soup was made with Streusel, flour and milk mixed and rubbed between two hands to form round crumbles the size of rice. These soups were eaten hot, accompanied by bread, butter, and sometimes liver sausage or smoked sausage. There was a lot of clabbered milk standing on the basement floor during the hot season. We (Krause Dirks children) often had clabbered milk on the table. We ate it plain, like a desert. When good and cold, it was delicious. No one ever complained about the food.*[129] [130] Mennonite children basically had two choices regarding food likes and dislikes—take it or leave it. If they complained about the food, like head cheese or liver, they were asked to leave the table. In this way, they learned to like all foods. This little rhyme was quoted to the children when they complained about the food:

Hans Ullarijch	*Hans Ullarijch*
Wrucke wulla nijch.	*doesn't want turnips,*
Kjielkje kräjcha nijch.	*doesn't get noodles.*
Aulsoo bleefa hungrijch.	*So he'll have to go hungry.*[131]

Chairs were reserved for adults, so children sat on a wooden bench along the side. Prayer both began and ended the meal, and no one left the table until father had finished eating and they were excused.[132]

---

[127] Mennonite Foods & Folkways from South Russia, Vol II, Norma Jost Voth, pp. 160-206
[128] Ibid, pg 202
[129] Mennonite Foods and Folkways from South Russia, Vol I, Norma Jost Voth, Mary Dirks Janzen, pg 165
[130] *Clabbered milk as a beverage reminds one of buttermilk. When solid, it is similar to yogurt. The longevity of certain groups of eastern people is often attributed to their diet of sour and fermented milks . . . . Mennonite women today rarely make it, since it requires raw milk.* Mennonite Foods and Folkways from South Russia, Vol I, Norma Jost Voth, pg 167
[131] Mennonite Foods & Folkways from South Russia, Vol I, Norma Jost Voth, pp. 254, 208
[132] Ibid., pg.209

Komm, Herr Jesu, sei du unser Gast, und segne was du uns aus Gnaden bescheret hast. Amen.
Come, Lord Jesus, and be our guest, and let these Thy gifts to us be blest.

Danket den Herrn, denn er isn freundlich und seine Güte währet ewiglich. Amen
Thank the Lord for He is gracious and His goodness is eternal.[133]

Hams were smoked in the chimney of the brick oven. Sixteen to twenty hams, bacon, and countless sausages hung from the rafters.[134] The bacon was left in one slab, and could last almost indefinitely. Fresh, sweet lard made the most beautiful flaky pie crust and the most delicate pfeffernüsse.[135]

47 up the chimney—smoking sausages and ham; Mennonite Settlement Museum, Hillsborough, Kansas

[133] <u>Mennonite Foods & Folkways from South Russia, Vol I,</u> Norma Jost Voth, pg 209,
[134] <u>Mennonite Foods & Folkways from South Russia, Vol II,</u> Norma Jost Voth, pp. 245-247
[135] <u>Mennonite Foods & Folkways from South Russia, Vol I,</u> Norma Jost Voth, pp. 244, 248

Fall was the season for hunting, and Aaron was an excellent hunter. But alas, he often went hunting, leaving Susanna alone much of the time. He brought home so many rabbits, that she grew tired of rabbit stew.

In the years preceding World War I, German Mennonites experienced unprecedented prosperity, with official Russian recognition of Mennonites included in the Duma, the Russian parliament.

It once was against the law to subdivide the farms into smaller farms, to be able to give each son a tract of land. With such large families, it quickly became impossible for grown sons to farm and remain in the family village. Families were large, and soon the land available for farming was gone, not only in the village of Gnadenfeld, but in the whole colony of Molotschna. By the turn of the century about two-thirds of all family fathers in the mother colonies were without land. They were called anwhoner or the landless. Only a few could become teachers, or take up various trades, and those ended up living at the edge of the village in a small house with only a small plot of ground to raise vegetables.[136]

The anwhoner became a problem, especially since only land owners could vote. So the Land Commission was formed by the Mennonites to purchase large tracts of land from Russian estates outside the colonies to form daughter colonies, with new villages. Russian noblemen were eager to sell off these lands to be closer to city life, or to pay off gambling debts. Some of these new colonies were as far away as southern Siberia, where winters were longer and colder, but the land incredibly fertile, due to long summer days. Not many Mennonites were highly educated there in Russia. Because he had gone to university, probably in Kiev, handsome, young Aaron Rempel was elected to the Land Commission in 1911. He represented Gnadenfeld as a member of the local Gnadenfeld Duma,[137], on the land commission,[138] which was founded in 1905. As a member of the Landwirtschaftlicher Verein (Land Commission), Aaron was almost like a territorial governor, traveling about in his 1908 Opel Doppelphaeton granting Molotschna colonists permission to do certain things.

After the evening meal, the family sat at the table, lit by a kerosene lamp hanging from the ceiling, and listened to Papa reading the Bible. When the family had finished reading the entire Bible from Genesis through Revelation, they started all over and read through it again.

---

[136] Testing Faith and Tradition, A Global Mennonite History, John A. Lapp and Snyder C. Arnold, editors, pp. 194-195
[137] Life and Times of a Renaissance Mennonite Teacher; Cornelius A Klassen; (1883-1919 and Beyond)
[138] Hierschau: An Example of Russian Mennonite Life, Helmut T Heubert, pg 220 "Periodically reports of Wolost meetings were published in Friedensstimme. A meeting, presumably chaired by Jacob Duerksen on August 20, 1911, was probably typical of the type of business transacted:
1. Heinrich Unrau and **Aron Rempel** were elected to represent Gnadenfeld at a meeting of the regional Land Commission.

Who shall separate us from the love of Christ? Shall tribulation, or distress, or persecution, or famine, or nakedness, or peril, or sword? . . . For I am persuaded, that neither death, nor life, nor angels, nor principalities, nor powers, nor things present, nor things to come, nor height, nor depth, nor any other creature, shall be able to separate us from the love of God, which is in Christ Jesus our Lord.[139]

Lo, I am with you alway, even until the end of the world.[140]

48 "modern" house; Susanna with Marie 1912

---

[139] Romans 8:35, 38, 39
[140] Matthew 28:20

An Earnest Plea

By 1911 Aaron was making good money, so he and his family were enjoying a very comfortable lifestyle. In late June Aron Sr.'s sister, Margaretha, and her husband Wilhelm Peter Neufeld[141] came back to Gnadenfeld from Halbstadt, where Wilhelm had been teaching religion at the Halbstadt Secondary School and preaching in the Halbstadt congregation. Margaretha and Wilhelm had come to say their final goodbyes to Margaretha's dear, aged mother Anna (born Göerz, Goertz) Rempel, on their way to emigrate to America. The Neufelds had decided that it would be prudent to leave Russia now.[142] Anna would live another 15 years, until 92 years old.[143]

Wilhelm had thought this over long and carefully. A person didn't just uproot himself and his family without taking into consideration all he and his family would be leaving behind. Both Margaretha and Wilhelm would be leaving their extended families. Although the Neufelds had been living in Halbstadt, most of Margaretha's relatives were still in Gnadenfeld. They probably would never again see those left behind. It would be so much better if others would also choose to join them on this adventure to America. After they had visited Margaretha's brother Aron Rempel Sr., they crossed the street to see his son Aaron Jr. and wife Susanna.

Wilhelm found Aaron Jr. next door at the factory. "Consider moving to America with us."[144]

"Oh, but I love it here. This is a great country. We have our beloved church, good schools."

"Good schools!" interrupted Wilhelm. "We German Mennonites are the ones who have the good schools. But the poor Russian peasants are mostly illiterate. Illiterate, hungry, and hurting. There are no schools for them. Such unrest, protests, strikes, riots, utter chaos exist in the cities. After the famine of 1901, the poor peasants deserted the land and flocked to the cities. The peasants see our Czar Nicholas as totally out of touch with reality, and blind to the needs of his hungry,

---

[141] Lehrer Wilhelm Neufeld had been a well-known and much admired choir director in Gnadenfeld from around 1880 through 1900. He also was responsible for Gnadenfeld's church acquisition of its pipe organ. "Gnadenfeld, Molotschna, South Russia_1835-1943," J. C. Krause,_pg 5

[142] California Mennonite Historical Society Bulletin, No 45, Fall 2006, "Russian Mennonite Choral Conductors", by Peter Letkemann, "His colleague in Halbstadt, Benjamin H. Unruh, recalled that W. P. Neufeld suddenly left Russia a few years before the beginning of the War and justified his step in a detailed discussion in his farewell sermon . . . apparently the revolution which shook the Russian Empire in 1905-1907 made him sense further, more powerful crises in the offing."

[143] This was the same Anna Goertz in the picture of Anna Goertz and Aaron Johannes Rempel in the whole Rempel clan in 1902 on their golden Wedding Anniversary, Anna is #2. See pages 24, 25, 27.

[144] From family accounts, we know a conversation took place regarding Wilhelm trying to persuade Aaron Jr. to join him. The conversation here has been created by the author based on historical events with which Wilhelm would have been familiar. In From My Memories written by Wilhelm's son Bill, two reasons for emigration were given: he didn't want his sons in the military, and rumblings of revolt, remembering the revolt of 1905 and the Odessa incident, where massive numbers of Jews were massacred.

desperate people. He has no understanding they are unable to earn enough just to put bread and borscht on their tables.[145] They are suffering terribly, but Czar Nicholas seems totally unconcerned. It seems nothing but his total absolutism holds his empire together.[146] Move to America with us!"

"My farm implement factory is doing extremely well. I have this beautiful modern home. I am one of the wealthiest men in the village. Why leave now?"

"The October Manifesto, the Revolution of 1905 has already occurred, when the Czar's troops fired upon an unarmed crowd, killing over 100, and wounding several hundred others. In former times, the people have viewed and ardently loved the Czar as their "Little Father." He was their supreme ruler but also available to them in such a way they could just walk right up to the palace gates and ask for an audience with him. I have even heard an old couple from Siberia came to see the Czar with a gift of a living, tame sable, but they pled for help, because they had no money for night lodging. Russian peasants formerly believed the Czar could do no wrong; he stood above classes, party politics, and personal rivalries. He desired the good of his people, and had practically unlimited means to assure it. He sought nothing for himself, but profoundly loved all those whom God had entrusted to his supreme care. No reason exists why he should not be the benefactor of each and all. All that's required is that he should know exactly what his people need.[147] However, the people's love has now turned away. Czar Nicholas has shown poor judgement. He ignores the sound advice of Prime Minister Witte and seems to be politically naive. Instead of mourning for the tragic loss of lives on the morning of Bloody Sunday, he callously continued with the coronation festivities planned for that evening. Mobs controlled the streets; red flags flew from the housetops. Russia came to a complete halt. The peasants have never forgotten, nor have they forgiven. What if that Bloody Sunday fiasco has sealed the doom of the monarchy? What if there is **more** revolution? You really should join us," pleaded Wilhelm.

"Na ya. Just a few years ago I was voted onto the Land Commission in our local Duma. I am needed here. Our Mennonite people need me for all the work I am doing in procuring more land for daughter colonies, and developing dams, reservoirs and an irrigation system to ensure enough water during our drought years." [148]

"How can you be so blind to the anarchy growing nearby, with robber gangs raiding and plundering,

---

[145] "The Russian peasant factory worker was sometimes paid only twice a year, and often obliged to sleep beside their machines. Then in 1883 a law was passed that the worker must be paid at least once a month, and the maximum working day would be eleven and a half hours," (instead of the common fifteen hour and former maximum eighteen hour work day). The Twilight of Imperial Russia, Richard Carques, pg 38

[146] At this time the Russian Empire was the largest it would ever be, stretching from the Arctic Circle to the Black Sea, and with more than two-thirds lying east of the Ural Mountains. Ibid pg 11

[147] At the Court of the Last Czar, A. A. Mossolov, head of the Court of Chancellery 1900-1916 memoirs;

[148] From the Steppes to the Prairies, Paul Klassen, pg 19

even raiding Mennonite estates all over the country? We Mennonites have sat in safety and plenty not knowing or caring what is happening to our poor Russian neighbors. We hold ourselves aloof, in arrogance look down on them, and condemn them for their laziness, lice, and itchy fingers. Have we been as guilty of adopting prideful attitudes towards these peasants as the Russian aristocracy? What if this however unintentional slight develops into mistrust and hatred? When we really get to know them, the peasants are a simple, lovable, generous people. Have we separated ourselves from the world ostensibly to live for God, only to enlarge our wirtshaften[149] and form richer, larger estates? We have enjoyed an overprivileged past, which may just catch up with us sooner or later, and it looks to me like it is getting sooner."

"Oba yo. But I am doing real good right now. You see this Opel[150] I am driving?" Aaron's hand caressed a shiny black door and the brass side lights gleaming in the sunlight. "I can put the canvass top down on nice sunny days. What do you think of that maroon upholstery? I am the only one here in Gnadenfeld who has a car," Aaron countered.

"I fear our present prosperity may be a thing of the past. Things will keep getting worse. An anti-German campaign has already started. We have to change the German names of all our villages into Russian names. St. Petersburg has been renamed Petrograd, and our beloved Gnadenfeld has become Bogdanovka. The central Duma wants to revoke our privileged status as pacifists. We'll likely lose our non-combatant exemptions from the military. We hear the Russians crying, 'Russia for the Russians!' as they eye our prosperous villages with envy and jealousy. We have never stopped thinking and feeling like Germans, even though we Germans have been in this land over a hundred years. Can you not see what is happening?"

"I have over 100 Russian workers. They need the work. They depend on me. If I leave, where will they work? I pay fair wages and I pay them on time. Can you say they will be better off if I leave with you?"

Wilhelm scuffed his foot in the dirt and continued, "Maybe **you** are paying them fair wages, and paying them on time, but not everyone is, not even all the Mennonites who hire Russians, I am sad to say. With Russian nobility living such an exorbitantly extravagant lifestyle, and so many Russians suffering so greatly, especially in the cities, I think more and more Russians are embracing the false promise of Communism, 'from each according to his ability to each according to his need.' To these poor souls, it probably looks so good on paper, and sounds so good in speeches.

---

[149] farms
[150] likely painted black because the red or white models would have seemed much too extravagant and ostentatious for a Mennonite

They see we have it good here in our German colonies, but don't understand all the hard work, the scrimping and saving, and even suffering in the early days to get where we are today. All we had we earned by toiling hard to achieve this prosperity. I must admit, Catherine the Great gave us land, lots of land, but nothing to the peasants. That's the thing of it, we didn't rob them of anything, but I am thinking we won't be able to convince poor suffering Russian peasants of that. We don't look or act Russian to them, and it looks like we have the most and the best land. Why wouldn't they be upset?" [151]

"I love this country. We Mennonites are loyal to the Czar. We even have a picture of Czar Nicholas hanging on the wall of the grottestov."

"Are you listening to me? Remember the terrible military disaster with Japan, when General Kuropatkin lost 100,000 men wounded, captured, or killed? Our naval force was almost totally destroyed, and we even lost Port Arthur. What happened to Russia being the greatest empire and one of the most powerful nations on earth? When we read in Revelation about a coming war in which a third of mankind will be slaughtered, I believe we are headed for those dreadfully difficult times. I believe the time is getting short. We Christians need to prepare for the Second Coming of Christ."

Aaron sighed, "Oh no! I love it here, and I am doing really well. My factory is busy. We have orders and more orders. I have seen the improved American farm machinery, and I am adding those improvements.[152] Business is growing. New Mennonite daughter settlements are being colonized, and they all need more farm machinery as well. But you! How can you so easily give up your important, well paying job, going where you have **no** job waiting for you, going with 9 children yet, traveling alone without other Mennonites in a group for protection, and going to a country known for its barbarian way of life?" [153]

At that, the two men turned to go into the house in time for Faspa, the typical late afternoon light lunch of fresh zwiebach, butter, jam, coffee, and cheese. Aaron simply was not persuaded by Wilhelm's argumentation.[154]

To please their Russian workers, Mennonite women had learned to cook borscht and varenekje

---

[151] Jews in Russia then were so restricted in their means of employment and educational opportunities, and facing increasing pogroms, many increasingly favored revolutionary, Marxist ideas.

[152] There was no patent agreement between Russia and USA or Canada, so the farm implement factories freely adopted the new technology and adapted their machinery with the newest inventions from abroad.

[153] The Wilhelm Neufeld family left Gnadenfeld, Molotschna, Ukraine, early June, 1911, traveling by train from Prishib, to Moscow, to Bremerhaven, Germany, then on the ship The Fatherland, stopping at Philadelphia, disembarking in Galveston, Texas, then by train to Kansas, then by train to Los Angeles, California, where the Dick family met them and took them into their home before they resumed their trip to their final destination, Reedley, California. The whole trip took several weeks.

[154] If only Aaron had gone with the Neufelds when they went. It would have saved him and his family a whole lot of suffering, but then there would not have been the rest of this story.

alongside their plümemoos and zwiebach. From their Ukrainian neighbors, Mennonites also learned to spread bread with fresh lard, drink glasses of tea from a samovar, and to sweeten it, Russian style, with cherry preserves, or sip it with a sugar cube between their teeth.[155] Water was poured into the body of the samovar urn, surrounding a wide tube in the center filled with hot coals. When smoke no longer came from the chimney, the samovar was carried to the table. A small china teapot, filled with strong tea, fit into a metal holder on top of the samovar. Each delicate thin glass of tea was made with a few drops of the strong tea from the teapot, and boiling hot water from the samovar's spigot. Tea from the samovar was a special Saturday evening or Faspa treat.[156]

49 samovar; Mennonite Settlement Museum, Hillsborough, Kansas

Harvesting, butchering, canning, scrubbing clothes on the washboard, tending the vegetable garden and cleaning never stopped just because babies came. In August 1911, twin boys were born to Aaron and Susanna, Aron III and Cornelius. One was blond and one dark haired.

Decades later, Susanna complained that nobody had been available to help her with the babies. Her half sisters were only five and six; her younger sister Agatha was ten. August was harvest time. Her mama Agatha and Agatha's Russian household help had to be extremely busy preparing

---

[155] Mennonite Foods & Folkways from South Russia, Vol I, Norma Jost Voth, pg 28
[156] Ibid, pg 406-407

meals for the Dirk farm hands, with no time to spare to help Susanna with the twins.

Sadly, Susanna's and Aaron's twins did not grow big and fat, as normal babies would. Instead, they grew thinner. With the twins, Susanna had a breast abscess that was extremely painful and oozing pus. She almost went crazy with the pain. Little Marie was such a help. Although only a year old, she was potty trained. At night Marie would crawl out of bed, pull the potty jar out from under the bed, put it back again, and go back to bed all on her own. Unfortunately baby Aron died when only 3 months old and baby Cornelius at 9 months.

Susanna was still very young and beautiful. Her husband also was handsome and a gentleman, but their hearts were heavy over the illness and loss of their twin boys.[157] The young couple sat together at the table after each evening meal, while Aaron read Scripture aloud. He read that while David and Bathsheba's child was yet alive, King David fasted and wept, for David said, *"Who can tell whether God will be gracious to me, that the child may live. But now he is dead, wherefore should I fast? Can I bring him back again? No. I shall go to him* (in heaven)*, but he shall not return to me."* [158]

With both of Susanna's arms resting on Aaron's strong right arm, on Sundays the couple trudged slowly up Mittlestrasse, north to the village cemetery to visit the two tiny graves. Tears rolled uncontrollably down Susanna's face, but Aaron remained stoic. German men didn't cry. Men, real men, didn't show emotion, even if they were crying on the inside.

Aaron whispered into Susanna's ear, "Remember how King David mourned and fasted for his dying child, and how he was comforted that his infant son was now with God, and he would see him again?"

Susanna, nodding assent, recalled the words, "*. . . now he is dead, I shall go to him, but he shall not return to me.*"[159] And through her tears she softly whispered, "Yes I am glad that God assures me that he has taken little Aron and Cornelius to be with Him in heaven. Yes, it is comforting that I know I will see our two precious boys again, but why does it have to hurt so much?"

Spring 1912 the little Rempel family was in that grand Opel on their way to visit relatives. It still was frigid as they bumped along on those dirt roads, so Marie was wrapped in a big blue and green plaid shawl. Marie wanted to sit in front with her mother Susanna who was pregnant again.

---

[157] My Memories, Mary Dirks janzen, page 28
[158] 2 Samuel 12:19-23
[159] 2 Samuel 12:23

Susanna was feeling overly big and uncomfortable and didn't want Marie on her lap. What lap? There wasn't a lap any more. Marie didn't like it in back with her aunt and uncle, Susanna's older brother Cornelius and his wife Tante Greta, so she pouted, cried, and fussed the whole way, only she cried and fussed silently or she would get a licking. Aaron liked to drive fast, taking off across the fields, bumping Susanna around. "Slow down, slow down. Why do you drive like the wind?" Susanna blamed her miscarriage on that wild ride across the steppes.

Susanna's brother Cornelius Krause had married Margareta (Tante Greta) Rempel in a big double wedding with Margareta's older sister Katharina (Katja) Rempel who married mother Agatha's brother Peter Dick (Dueck) August 25, 1912.[160]

Newly married couples usually moved into the Sommastov of one of the parents, as Cornelius did with his bride Greta. Susanna's younger brother and sisters were embarrassed by all the hugging and kissing that went on in those days.

Aron III was born 19 July, 1913. It was customary for a baby to be given a diminutive form of his name as a nickname. For instance, Johannes would be called Hans for short, and baby or little Hans would be called Hansel. Baby Abraham would have been called Abramka. Baby or little Aron III would be called Aronka, or Ronka for short.

Besides owning the first car and telephone in Gnadenfeld, Aaron Jr. was also interested in other new technologies, like silent moving pictures. He procured a projector and a film, and showed a moving picture on the side of the barn. Even as an adult, Marie remembered the moving picture about a pretty little land with a river winding through it, but it had no sound.

Aaron Jr. and his father Aron Sr. were probably the two wealthiest men in Gnadenfeld. However, Aaron's income was primarily from his farm machinery factory, manufacturing threshing machines for the farmers, who were most likely buying these machines on credit.[161] What would happen to Aaron's income if these farmers suddenly were unable to meet their financial obligations?

---

[160] My Memories, Mary Dirks Janzen, page 16
[161] RÜCKENAU, The History of a Village in the Molotschna Mennonite Settlement of South Russia, Leona Wiehe Gislason, pg 69

50 shawl, Germans From Russia Heritage Collection, used by permission[162]

---

[162] That plaid shawl that little Marie wore came to America with them. The author received it from her mother, but was never really told the history of the shawl. The author sent that shawl with her younger son on a boy scout camping trip. A California forest fire raged through Mataguay, a camp near San Diego, burning all his belongings. Both sons were safely transported to an emergency shelter at a nearby school. Only while the author was working on this book, did she realize what that little "blanket" had been. She didn't even have a picture of it, but it looked identical to the one pictured at German from Russia Heritage Collection, except it was blue instead of brown, with green as the secondary color, and the same little yellow and red stripes. When she saw this picture of their shawl, she suddenly realized what she had lost in that fire. accessed May 6, 2017, https://www.facebook.com/ndsu.grhc/photos/a.154643828676.147023.127776853676/10155862314243677/?type=3&theater,

51 The young people at the Krause farm in Gnadenfeld.
Jasch Krause and Maria Rempel are on opposite sides of the sleigh

52 Jacob Krause home, with horses

The Beginning of the End

Mennonite identity as a people centered upon their view of nonresistance. It was the Mennonite refusal to fight that had lead to their persecution in Holland and their subsequent relocation to Prussia under the protection of a gracious monarch, until a new monarch arose who demanded military service. When Catherine the Great invited Mennonites to come to Russia, she promised the first Mennonite settlers in Ukraine, exemption from military service in perpetuity. But now that exemption had been taken away.

A majority of Mennonites retained conservative, insular, apolitical views. However, when their own lives were affected, some protested vigorously at every level of government. Otherwise, most held to the slogan, "We are the silent ones in the land."(Wir sind die Stillen im Lande).[163]

A decree by Czar Alexander II demanded military duty from all Russian citizens, including the pacifist Mennonites. A delegation of Mennonites went to St. Petersburg with a petition requesting that Mennonites be allowed to retain their privilege of freedom from military service as promised to them by Catherine the Great. *When they were received by the Minister of War, he discovered that the delegation could not speak Russian. "You have been in Russia for 70 years and still cannot speak Russian!" he exclaimed.*[164] Roughly a third of all German Mennonites in Russia, around 18,000 persons including children, emigrated to the United States or to Canada during 1874-1880 because of this decree.[165] [166]

When Czar Alexander II saw his most productive farmers leaving en masse, a compromise was reached wherein the German Mennonites would be allowed to perform a weapons-free alternative service in the forestry, at their own expense, as non-combatants. Those who did not emigrate, in later years cherished the memory of Czar Alexander II for being so generous as to allow this alternative form of service to their adopted Fatherland. From that time on, Mennonite non-resistance was carried out in forestry service in peace time and noncombatant medical service during wartime.[167] But neither those who emigrated nor those who stayed behind *"understood that there can be no special rights for special groups in a free country."*[168]

---

[163] <u>A Mennonite Family in Tsarist Russia and the Soviet Union, 1789-1923</u>, David G. Rempel, pg 116

[164] <u>Testing Faith and Freedom, A Global Mennonite History</u>, editors John A Lapp, C. Arnold Snyder pp. 198-199

[165] Kornelius Krause (first husband of Agatha Dueck Krause Dirks) had an uncle (his father's brother Jacob Krause, born 1809, died before 1900) who was part of that mass migration, moving to McPherson, Kansas.

[166] A compromise came too late to completely stem the emigration tide. The 18,000 German Mennonites leaving Russia for the USA settled in Kansas and brought with them the hard winter wheat Turkey Red which revolutionized wheat farming in America. <u>The Molotschna Colony, A Heritage Remembered</u>, Henry Bernard Tiessen, pp. 100, 108

[167] <u>Czars, Soviets, & Mennonites</u>, John B. Toews, pp 12, 13, 39

[168] <u>Testing Faith and Freedom, A Global Mennonite History</u>, editors John A Lapp, C. Arnold Snyder, pp. 198-199

In 1861 Czar Alexander II abolished serfdom, but large landowners (both Russian nobility and German Mennonite estate holders) still held 60 percent of the land. Russia did not offer land to her own poor, but offered free land to experienced farmers, German speaking farmers. Their German villages were separated by distance from native Russians, and even separated from each other by religious confession—Catholic, Lutheran, or Mennonite. This social isolation later made Russians suspicious of the "foreign" Germans living among them. Mennonites were largely loyal to the Czar, but remained distinct from the Russian culture. Unfortunately, this separateness lead to a spirit of conceit, a view that Mennonites were superior.[169]

Mennonite farmers, because of their work ethic, innovative farming techniques, and thrift, but also their expansion into raising horses, cattle, sheep, fruits and vegetables, became wealthy, especially in comparison to their Russian neighbors. But it was never easy. The drought of 1833 caused a total loss of harvest. The winters of 1811 and 1824 brought unrelenting snow, and causing severe loss of sheep and cattle. There also were floods, illnesses, and plagues of grasshoppers.

Nevertheless, by the start of the twentieth century, German Mennonite settlements in Russia were prosperous. By late February the ground began to thaw, so in March summer crops of barley, spring wheat, rye or oats were sown. Haying was done from the end of June to the beginning of July. Harvesting grain started in mid-July. Each farmer had a section in each of the four divisions of cropland located outside the village. In this way, no one farmer would have all the best or worst land. The farmers introduced innovative farming techniques including a three crop rotation, with the summer fallow, when the earth rested; then winter wheat, followed by barley, and finally oats. It had become compulsory for each farmer to summer fallow one quarter of his land every year, which did more to preserve moisture on the dry steppe than anything else. The Mennonites also fertilized with manure and ashes, and in the fall planted the hard winter Turkey Red wheat (which German Mennonites also introduced to America's heartland in the 1870s). By December the ground froze. This wheat was favored in markets in London and in regions throughout the Mediterranean for making pasta because of the high quality of flour it produced.[170] Mennonite farmers used sophisticated farming equipment so they could plant and harvest faster than Russian peasant farmers.[171][172] Ukraine, under Mennonite farming techniques, became the breadbasket of Europe, and the Molotschna Colony was considered the best colony in all of Russia, leading Czar Alexander I to visit in 1818.

---

169 The Russländer, Sandra Birdsell, pg 74
170 Mennonite Food & Folkways from South Russia, Vol II, Norma Jost Voth, pg 181
171 Los Angeles Times, Wednesday, August 4, 1982, "A Search for Ancestral Soviet Home", William C. Rempel, page 15
172 1835-1943 Gnadenfeld, Molotschna, A Lowen Schmidt pp 8-10

Russians who worked for German Mennonites were generally treated well and paid fair wages on time. But during the reign of Czar Nicholas II, the plight of Russian peasants who worked for noblemen or who worked in city factories was totally different. In St. Petersburg, the average family of sixteen was crowded into a one room apartment, with no running water. Piles of human waste surrounded the area.

It was said of Czar Nicholas II, he lead a simple life, mostly devoted to his beloved family. However, when the imperial train was detained while the Czar inspected his troops in the region for five days near Roshkovo, that "simplicity" included his daughters going sledding next to the train, using very large solid silver trays as their toboggans. The Czar himself had ordered a spoon for stirring his imperial tea, not from the Fabergé factory, but fashioned by Peter Carl Fabergé himself. It took Peter Carl Fabergé 90 days to handcraft that single spoon Czar Nicholas II would only use once, for he never used any item more than once.

His father had made no attempt to train him as a future emperor, so Nicholas II was totally unfit to rule when he ascended the throne November 1, 1894. He listened to his wife's favorite holy man Rasputin, and appointed ministers who often proved incompetent and corrupt.

The Duma was established to give advice to the monarchy, but it soon became apparent the inept Czar totally ignored the Duma by dissolving it repeatedly. Under previous Czars, the peasants considered their Czar to be the Father of his people, who felt for them as a father should. Czar Nichols II was indifferent to the pitiful conditions of his suffering subjects. He was blind to the actual state of affairs by his belief he owed it to God to continue ruling as an absolute autocrat. He believed his power was divinely ordained by God, inviolable and immutable, so to relinquish any power would be to dishonor and disobey God. He therefore could not, would not, tolerate any argument or debate. In spite of protests and strikes, Nicholas refused to recognize his people were no longer loyally devoted to him. He remained implacable about making changes essential to alleviate their suffering. This caused the eventual demise of the Romanov monarchy and the Russian empire.

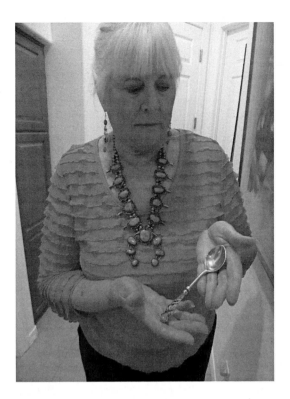

53 A, 53 B

Author holding the Fabergé silver-gilt and enamel tea spoon, (circa 1908-1917) Peter Carl Fabergé, Russian Imperial Cutlery (Court of Czar Nicholas II), courtesy of The Christian Thomas Lee Collection of Fine Art; a private collection

Serbian nationalists assassinated the Archduke of Austria June 28, 1914,[173] which led the Austro-Hungarian Empire to declare war on Serbia's ally, Russia. This in turn led Germany to declare war on France the same year.[174] By August, Germany declared war on Russia. Most Mennonites in Russia failed to recognize this was the beginning of the end of their tidy German world.

Nicholas knew his resources were exhausted from the Japanese-Russo war, in which he had suffered ignominious defeat. But Nicholas believed *there is going to be a war. A short war . . . of course, it is going to be short, all the wars in the past few decades have been short . . . . Durnovo did warn me that the country is not fully prepared for another war, but what does that guy know! He doesn't connect with God, and receive visions from him! . . . improvements in Russia . . . are sufficient to cope with a short war . . . . Before the people even realize the consequences of war and go back to opposing me again, the war will be over . . . when we reach victory, we are likely to receive the Dardanelles. This will give us access to the Mediterranean Sea. What a great deal! . . . such an opportunity! . . . God Bless Mother Russia!* [175]

With the outbreak of World War I, Czar *Nicholas ordered all able bodied men to join the military and fight for their country. Many Mennonites refused . . . . After all, Catherine the Great had given her word: all Mennonites would be exempt from military duties.*[176] Russia was the only European country during the outbreak of the war in which the Mennonites were exempt from all military service. They were under obligation to serve a number of years in forestry on state lands. Since forestry was entirely separate from the military, it was therefore consistent with their profession of faith and the principle of non-resistance.[177] *Nicholas took a slightly different position. Catherine was dead. Russia was being overtaken by German soldiers. That was then. This was now.*"[178] Most refused to fight in the army. With World War I and a national conscription introduced, Mennonites volunteered for alternative service.[179] Susanna's younger brother Jakob Krause, became a Red Cross worker. Opa Heinrich Dirks and Onkel Cornelius Krause served in the forestry service.[180] [181] Tante Suse's husband Jacob Toews served as a medic on a train transporting wounded from the Austrian front to Moscow. Numerous Austrian soldiers were taken as prisoners by the

[173] Hierschau: An Example of Russian Mennonite Life,, Helmut T. Hubert, pg 229
[174] Testing Faith and Tradition, A Global Mennonite History, editors John A Lapp, C. Arnold Snyder, pg 37
[175] https://isedphistory.wordpress.com/russian-revolution/diary-entry-of-tsar-nicholas-ii/
[176] Anabaptist History: "Pilgrims of the Promise", page 182   taken from Mennonite Martyrs, People Who Suffered for Their Faith, 1920-1940, by Aron A. Toews, pp. 31-35
[177] The Principle of Nonresistance, As Held by the Mennonite Church, John Horsch, pg 54
[178] Anabaptist History: "Pilgrims of the Promise", page 182   taken from Mennonite Martyrs, People Who Suffered for Their Faith, 1920-1940, by Aron A. Toews, pp. 31-35
[179] 20% of the male population (over 12,000 Mennonite men) were drafted into the forestry service, and acted as fire fighters, forestry rangers, or guards, serving in isolated areas without communication with the outside world. The Molotschna Colony levied a tax upon themselves to raise almost their entire support, including building barracks, feeding, clothing, and building maintenance. The Molotschna Colony, A Heritage Remembered, Henry Bernard Tiessen, pg 102
[180] My Family was Transplanted, May Dirks Janzen, audio tape
[181] 1835-1943 Gnadenfeld, Molotschna, A Lowen Schmidt; Mary Dirks Janzen "The Good Old Days" pg 55

Russians and sent to camps in Crimea to work in the forests. Because Jacob Toews knew German, he successfully requested he be assigned to supervise these Austrian prisoners, which he did for several years until 1917.[182]

War had been declared in the middle of harvest. To the Mennonite farmers, harvest came first, over anything else, including war. However, the Czar conscripted all their farm laborers. How on earth could they ever bring in the harvest without the manpower to do so? Not only did the Czar conscript the Russian men, but he also conscripted the horses and farm wagons for the military, horses and wagons desperately needed to bring in the harvest.[183] Before the war, on average, each large farm had 8 to 10 work horses, generally needing 5 for pulling a plow, plus two sleek horses to pull the droshky for travel, and two for utility, pulling a hay wagon. Mennonite farmers had to conscript their own sons, older daughters, and even their wives to finish the harvest. When finished with their own fields, Mennonite harvest gangs moved in to do the threshing for the absent Russian farmers. Even though they accepted the help, Russian wives and mothers were not pleased. Their own men were being sent to the slaughter while it seemed to them the Mennonites remained safe as non-combatants. However, most people were confident the war would be over in three, or at the most, six months.

November 5, 1914, Bolshevik members of the Duma were arrested. A few months later they were tried, then exiled to Siberia[184] [185]

Mennonites were able to elect two men, one from the Ekaterinoslav province (location of Chortitza and Schoenfeld Colonies) and one from the Taurida province (location of Molotschna Colony), to the third Duma.[186] *But because of the intransigence of the aristocracy, and a rigged voting system to elect representatives, landowners were heavily represented but peasants were almost eliminated. So the Duma never really had a chance to be an instrument toward representative government. In the end, the emperor instructed his minister Stolypin to dissolve the Duma. "The Duma is dead. Long live the Duma."* [187]

---

[182] The Mennonite Historian, pg 8 East Petersburg, Pennsylvania, Letter to the Editor by Henry Toews,
[183] Henry & John Bergman were conscripted as young German Mennonite boys from Mariawohl (about 4 miles west of Gnadenfeld) to drive teams of horses pulling wagons full of Russian soldiers to the war front. On that trip, the boys saw the White army massacre their own white soldiers and then mutilate the bodies, making it look like the German enemy had done this dreadful deed, in order to rally the country around the war effort. This episode helps to explain the horrible fear Henry and John continued to have of Russian Communists even decades later in the USA. Henry later married Aaron and Susanna's daughter Marie Rempel, September 13, 1931
[184] "Russian Revolution," 1917, Wikipedia http://en.wikipedia.org/wiki/Russian_Revolution
[185] Bolshevik comes from the word bolsbintsvo, meaning majority. Menshevik, mensbintsvo or minority The Twilight of Imperial Russia, Richard Charques, pg 64
[186] A Mennonite Family in Tsarist Russia and the Soviet Union 1789-1923, David G. Rempel, pp. 116-117
[187] The Twilight of Imperial Russia, Richard Charques pp. 32, 120, 157, 158, 173, 192

The familiar pattern of arrests, exile to slave labor camps in Siberia, and executions continued. So many people were hanged that the noose was dubbed "Stolypin's necktie."[188] Stolypin was later assassinated, which meant an end to possible land reforms later, which might have alleviated the volatile situation somewhat.[189]

Mennonites Peter Dück and H. Fröse worked to have the government extend grants to the peasants, limit landholdings of the wealthy, establish an 8 hour work week, but the old aristocracy rejected the recommendations as too socialistic.[190]

A telegram announced a universal draft of all men born in 1896 or earlier, up to age 43, to report to Ekaterinoslav by September 2.[191] Mennonites volunteered for an alternative form of service, either Red Cross or forestry units in the war to avoid killing anyone. About half of the Mennonite men between the ages of 20-50, some 14,000, served in some capacity. 7,000 were orderlies, with 332 of those men from Gnadenfeld.[192] Two military hospitals were formed, with Mennonite women sewing much needed linens. However, just because these Mennonite men volunteered for service in medical units, did not avert suspicion they were German sympathizers.

Mennonites staffed all but two of the fifty hospital trains, trains that would advance as close as possible to the actual fighting, pick up the wounded, and transport them back to available hospitals. Mennonite medics and orderlies realized the closer they went to the war front, the more dangerous it would be, with ambulance trains being most dangerous, and inland hospitals the safest. Should Mennonite non-resistance really mean staying as far away as possible from enemy shells, or should it mean volunteering for the most dangerous assignments to rescue the wounded? Those Mennonite boys who personally knew Jesus as their Lord and Savior were more at peace with going into harm's way, because they knew God is always in control, whatever may happen. And happen it did.

Trains carrying supplies to the war front, and wounded back to hospitals were extremely undependable. A locomotive might stop, detach the train's cars, then leave the train behind. It then became necessary to find another locomotive. An engineer might use the ruse of needing to fill the engine with more water, to abandon the train and take off with the locomotive.[193] Sometimes railroad workers just went on strike for higher pay.[194] Train No 189 was captured, and its Mennonite

[188] Life and Times of a Renaissance Mennonite Teacher: Cornelius A. Klaassen: (1883-1919 and Beyond), Robert L. Klaassen, pg 34
[189] The Russländer, Sandra Birdsall, pg 63
[190] A Mennonite Family in Tsarist Russia and the Soviet Union, David G. Rempel, pg 175
[191] Events and People, Helmut T. Huebert, pp. 148-149
[192] Testing Faith and Tradition, A Global Mennonite History, editors John A Lapp, C. Arnold Snyder, pg 200
[193] Miracles of Grace and Judgment, Gerhard P. Schroeder, pg 9
[194] Hope Springs Eternal, John P. Nickel, pg 234

medics and orderlies became prisoners for the duration of the war.[195] Being captured might not even be their worst fate. With the anti-German campaign underway, any and every German was now suspected to be an alien traitor. Always deadly disease was a threat.[196]

Mennonites serving in the military saw for the first time the enormous gulf between the status of their families and those of the Russian peasants. They saw daily the bestial treatment officers meted out to common solders, the harsh conditions in which the masses eked out an existence, and the hopelessness they felt. Many of the Mennonite young men blamed the old czarist regime for the urban unrest and the soldiers' desertions, and felt relief at the demise of the Romanov dynasty.[197]

The Mennonites had compassion on their neighboring Russians. Churches helped the wives of Russian servicemen harvest their crops. They also gave money to the wives of wounded or sick soldiers totaling more than two million rubles. They collected dried fruit, toasted zweibach, and warm clothing to send to the Russian soldiers themselves. Nevertheless, one thing became clear to the Russian people: Russian solders were being killed by German bullets.[198] [199] These Mennonites were German speaking immigrants from Prussia, which later became Germany, and Russia was at war with Germany. Russians increasingly wondered, "Where did the loyalty of these German speaking people in their midst lay?"

The fact is, German Mennonites volunteered for Russia, not Germany. Austria and Germany had started the war. During previous wars, Mennonites drove the supply wagons for the Crimean War, maintained field hospitals in the Russo-Turkish War, and rendered noncombatant medical service in the Russo-Japanese War. Now they volunteered for medical duty at the front. [200] These German Mennonites were actually loyal to Russia. They were pacifists, but they loved this land. Their refusal to fight was simply because that was what they believed God demanded of them. Sadly, the Russians did not know or understand the religious convictions of their Mennonite neighbors.

The anti-German sentiment grew toward these Mennonites, despite their patriotic love of their adopted Fatherland. November 7, 1914 the German paper Friedensstimme, printed in Halbstadt, Molotschna, was no longer allowed to be published. The German language was prohibited in public

---

[195] Czars, Soviets, & Mennonites, John G. Toews, pp 66, 68, 69
[196] My Harp is Turned to Mourning, Al Reimer, pg 206
[197] A Mennonite Family in Tsarist Russia and the Soviet Union 1789-1923, David G. Rempel, pg 171
[198] Anabaptist History: "Pilgrims of the Promise", taken from Mennonite Martyrs, People Who Suffered for Their Faith, 1920-1940, by Aron A. Toews, page 182
[199] The Molotschna Colony, A Heritage Remembered, Henry Bernard Tiessen, pg 102
[200] Czars, Soviets, & Mennonites, John G. Toews, pp 74-77

meetings, even including the preaching at Sunday services. Mennonites wondered, "How could this be? God only spoke High German, not Low German (Platdeutch), and most certainly not Russian!" They could try to make the case that Platdeutch was really a form of Dutch, and therefore exempt. However, two months later, preaching in German was reinstated.[201]

Carl Rempel (brother to Cornelius Krause's wife Margareta) was reprimanded by both the regional and village police for breaking the decree that no more than three people could gather at once. Since the Russians were afraid the Mennonites would try to aid the German enemy, all pigeons were killed so they couldn't be sent to Germany with messages. In 1915, while working on the family farm, Carl Rempel was drafted into the Russian army and sent to the Caucasian front where he spent two years fighting the Turks. Carl's brother Heinrich was also taken and served in the rear supply. Once when Carl's unit had to retreat for a few days, they found a farm where the family had fled, leaving a pen full of pigs. The men had nothing else to eat, so they shot them. They soon grew tired of just plain pork.

During the two years he was in the White Army, Carl had three horses shot from under him in the cavalry. Once a shot ricocheted and went through his sleeve, just creasing the skin of his arm a little. Another bullet went through his hat, a popach, made of fur, creased in the middle sideways, worn tilted back, and long enough to be used for a pillow. Another time he was leading his mount, advancing slowly, when the Reds let go with a cannon they had captured from the British. It exploded so near Carl that the dirt bruised his whole side. He was buried in dirt except for his boots. He buddies pulled him out but he was unconscious from shock. He woke up in a hospital a couple of weeks later to find he had a concussion.[202]

Even during times of peace, the Czar's ministers were more rivals than colleagues. The secret police, the passport system needed to travel even inside Russia, and universal corruption created stifling bureaucracy with underlying intrigue. This mismanagement carried over into execution of the war.

World War I came on the heels of an inept war with Japan, ending with humiliating defeat, losing Port Arthur (Russia's only ice free Naval base) in the far east to Japan. Casualties had been high, so for the impending World War, available military supplies were negligible. Soldiers were ill equipped, and poorly lead. Only a third had weapons. So the second third of the soldiers was to rush in and grab the weapons of their fallen comrades, and the last third was to grab

---

[201] Hierschau: An Example of Russian Mennonite Life, Helmut T. Huebert, pp. 233-234
[202] "Memoir of Agatha and Carl Rempel" as told to K. R. Lockwood, pp. 9-11

the weapons of their fallen enemy. What armaments were produced were of deadly inferior quality. Acute shortages of not only rifles and ammunition, but food, uniforms, boots, and medical supplies plagued the army. Communication between top generals and various fighting units was intermittent or missing altogether. Transportation was undependable, especially a growing paralysis of railways. Most generals, usually chosen by rank in society and connections at court, were incompetent. It seemed Russia viewed her people as a vast, sustainable resource to prodigally waste. Over four million soldiers were lost within a year. Turmoil at the front lead to insurrection against the officers and even demonstrations against their formerly beloved Czar.[203] A huge rate of desertion should have been no surprise. Gigantic losses gave impetus to revolutionary forces.

Talk of seizing the property of those of "enemy descent," (those who spoke German) increased with continued urban unrest. However, implementation of this rashly conceived property liquidation law was delayed and soon repealed, as the Czar realized he needed the bountiful harvests of his German farmers. Christmas was coming, but there was so much hatred and aversion to anything German, even the "decadent" German custom of decorating Christmas trees was forbidden.[204]

Meanwhile, in this first winter of war, it was going very badly for Russia. Totally ill equipped Russian soldiers desperately looked for weapons and ammo, pawing among mounds of dead bodies after each battle. Left only with empty guns, trembling with fear, and cursing with rage, they sought cover behind walls of their own dead. Now, in their utter extremity, and away from the watchful eyes of their Orthodox priests, many Russian soldiers were becoming open to the Word of God, the wonderful news of the saving grace of Jesus freely offered to them to save them from their sins.[205]

It was easy for the rulers of those belligerent countries to wantonly sacrifice peasants, farmers, the lowest classes, and their sons in war.

Conscription of Russian farm laborers and work horses into the military caused sales for farm machinery produced by Aaron's factory to abruptly plummet to nothing. Why would anyone want to buy a new harvester or thresher, when neither the manpower nor the horses left to operate the farms were available? There were not even enough horses available for the next spring's plowing and planting.

---

[203] Escape to Freedom, Cornelius Funk, pg 33
[204] My Harp is Turned to Mourning, Al Reimer, pg 226
[205] Ibid. pp. 231, 240

Farm laborers were conscripted for military service, but factory workers not. Russian factory workers were exempt from military service for the duration of the war, as the government mandated all factories go into war production. All farm machinery factories, including Mennonite factories, were forced to produce gun carriages, then field kitchens, and finally shells for the artillery, ammunition, and cast casings for land mines and hand grenades. That posed an impossible moral dilemma for Aaron as a German Mennonite pacifist, dedicated to the principle of non-resistance.

But before he had to choose, in December 1914 the government shut off bank credit to German owned business firms.[206] Aaron had sold threshing machines on credit. The farmers were behind in paying him what they owed. He needed a loan to pay his Russian factory workers their current wages. Aaron could no longer get supplies needed to manufacture farm machinery. Those who had bought farm equipment on credit could no longer make payments. When he could not pay his Russian laborers, who really did not understand economics at all, they burned down the factory in retaliation. It was like cutting off one's nose to spite one's face.

Now Aaron had absolutely no hope of ever recouping the money needed to pay them. Aaron went bankrupt. Just plain bankrupt. From being one of the wealthiest men in Gnadenfeld, if not the wealthiest, to bankruptcy, just like that, in one brief moment of time.

The Mennonites had been largely self-sufficient. Stores stocked fabric for their clothing, sugar, pickled herring, and vinegar sold out of wooden barrels, coffee, and school supplies such as slates and pencils. Aaron's father had a thriving lumber yard, and a store,[207] where they also sold sugar, dried plums, coal oil for lamps, coal, nails, bolts of fabric, and other hardware goods, including Alfa Laval cream separators and McCormick Deering binders.[208] Not only villagers from Gnadenfeld but those from surrounding villages, and local Russians shopped there.

---

[206] My Harp is Turned to Mourning, Al Reimer, pg 218, 224, 225
[207] The author believes this store and lumberyard were located at #24 First Street.
[208] The Mennonite Historian, pg 8, Henry Toews, Letter to the Editor,
and Hierschau: An Example of Russian Mennonite Life, Helmut T. Huebert, p 147

54 Ar Ar Rempel ad, public domain 1905 <u>Friedenstimme</u>, Halbstadt

Centrifuges (separators) were used in agriculture to separate cream from the skimmed milk. The ad says in German:

After milk has been separated (skimmed) in this region with centrifuges for a number of years, it has become clear that Alfa-Laval-Centrifuges are the best and most durable.

[The Alfa Laval centrifuge] continues to remove cream from milk after five years of operation as well as it did when new, and is simplicity itself to operate. For instance a machine with a capacity of 10 buckets per hour can be operated by a girl with little physical strength, while setting the machine up and cleaning it is very simple.

Below are the addresses of several owners of Alfa Laval centrifuges, to whom reference may be made regarding the quality of the machine:

. . . .

The Alfa Laval centrifuge was made by a company in Sweden since 1883. Author's Great Grandfather Aron A. Rempel sold these milk separators in his store in Gnadenfeld.

55 Ar Ar Rempel ad, public domain
908 <u>Friedenstimme</u>, Halbstadt

56 Ar Ar Rempel ad, public domain

1907 <u>Friedenstimme</u>, Halbstadt

Highly recommended for spring season.

Hand seeding machines "PLANET" [209]

And also cultivators. These genuine American implements lend themselves as excellent for vegetable gardening (raising).

Also request brochures (leaflets) on concrete brick-making machines

---

[209] William C. Rempel recalls our Grandmother Susanna Rempel said Aaron had a farm implement factory. Susanna was unable to name specific equipment that he manufactured. The author believes it could have included a seed sprayer, cultivator, and/or threshing machine.

The best of the best. Petrol and naphtha (Diesel) motor "Bison"

Winner of 17 awards, Factory established in 1866.

Strong construction. Low number of ?? Ignition most notably simple and reliable. Very quiet and smooth gears. The largest conceivable power deployment. Absolute operational safety. Greatest durability. Quite exceptionally low fuel consumption.

Representative for Russia: Ar. Ar. Rempel, Gnadenfeld, Taurien

The big flywheel enabled greater control in regulating the speed of equipment this machine powered. Oil cups shown on every bearing and two rods along the extent of the machine kept things external so they could be repaired or replaced easily.

The motor was sold by Aron Rempel Sr. The following ad on the next page looks like the same motor was sold by the Toews Brothers. It is possible this motor powered whatever Aaron Jr. manufactured as farm machinery, likely a threshing machine.[210]

Aaron's younger sisters had married two Toews brothers. Susanna Rempel had married Jacob Toews, and Helena married Cornelius, Jacob's brother.[211] Jacob Toews owned a store in Stulnevo, along the railway north of Gnadenfeld,[212] which he sold before the Communists nationalized all property. Maybe it was because Aaron Jr. once had a prosperous farm machine factory, or maybe father Aron Sr. was still angry at him for marrying the wrong girl, but whatever the reason, Aaron Jr. was excluded from the lumberyard and family store. He was Aron Sr.'s only son but was completely shut out of the family businesses. The Toews took over both of them.[213]

But Aaron had a family to support. With his factory now burned to the ground, how was he ever going to be able to do that?

---

[210] Author could find no ads posted in 1913, by Aaron Jr. himself for the machinery he was manufacturing (before he went bankrupt in 1914).

[211] In the Fullness of Time, 150 Years of Mennonite Sojourn in Russia, Dr. Walter Quiring, pg 93, picture #18, the smaller house on the right was built by Aaron'sToews' brothers-in-law. Two Toews brothers and their nephew Peter Toews (son of Cornelius and Jacob Toews' brother Johann), shared the same house. Peter married Aaron Rempel Jr.'s oldest sister Maria Braun's daughter Susanna (Suse). So, Aaron's two sisters had married two Toews brothers, and one of Aaron's nieces had married a Cornelius and Jacob Toews nephew.

[212] 1996 Mennonite Heritage Cruise, Part Four http://home.ica.net/~walterunger/Rudy-4.htm

[213] In later years, Susanna and Marie often complained that Aaron had been shut out of the other Aron Rempel Sr. family enterprises. However the ad for the Naptha Motor by the Toews brothers, posted in 1913, indicates the Toews probably owned the lumberyard in 1913, where they sold that motor, long before Aaron went bankrupt in 1914.

Toews brothers, Cornelius and Jacob, lived together in the house attached to the Lumberyard, where they sold this diesel motor.

The ad says, *Ellenburger, First and cheapest engine for farm and business. Toews Brothers, Gnadenfeld, South Russia, Taurida Province*

Siberia

The Lord's Prayer includes "And Forgive Us Our Debts, As We Forgive Our Debtors."
Matthew 6:12

If we are not prepared to forgive, then God will not forgive us. O how difficult it often is for a child of God to forgive others. Resolve the problem quickly. Do not wait for the other to come to you; take the first step and go to him or her and forgive them.[214]:

Ronka was only about a year old, when Marie ran into the house and yelled for her mother. Ronka had crawled up close to the top of the stairs, outside the barn going up to the barn attic. As Susanna reached the bottom of those stairs, Ronka had just placed his hand on the very top, the platform in front of the door leading to the barn attic door. That platform was extremely high; Ronka still so young. No bannisters or railings existed along the side of the stairs or platform, to keep anyone from falling off. A fall from that height would be bad enough. But at the bottom of the platform was a bisang, or cistern to catch rainwater. Most well water in Gnadenfeld was undrinkable and quite bitter, containing a high level of saltpeter. Only cattle could drink it. Only three wells existed in Gnadenfeld with drinkable water, but this farm did not have one of those wells. So homes and barns had gutters to catch rainwater from tile roofs, and funnel it into cisterns as their drinking water. If baby Ronka should fall into the cistern at the base of the landing on the top . . . .

Susanna yelled, "Just sit there! Just sit there or come back down here. I said, you just sit there or come down here." Slowly, slowly, Ronka sat down. He sat there a little bit and thought about it. Then slowly he started backing down the long staircase until he slipped and tumbled down the rest of the way, falling down at Susanna's feet. When he finally arrived at the bottom, Susanna picked him up, and shoved his head down close to the cistern. "You could have fallen in here where we wouldn't be able to get you out. Marie, you should have been watching him more closely! How could you be so careless?"

Little Marie was thinking, "How can you blame me for that? I am only four years old. Why is it my fault? You are the grown up. Why do you think I am responsible?"

Marie had a beautiful doll with china head, hands and feet, and a muslin cloth body, filled with sawdust.[215] Ronka became sick and wanted to hold that doll. He fussed and fussed for that

---

[214] Hope Springs Eternal, John P. Nickel, pp. 61-62 From a Sermon by Gerhard Nickel.
[215] My Memories, Mary Dirks Janzen, pg 3

doll. Susanna, trying to get Ronka to stop crying, told Marie to let Ronka have the doll. So, Marie reluctantly gave him the doll, and sure enough, he dropped it and broke her beautiful doll, broke fingers off one hand, the nose, and the china head. Her doll was no longer beautiful. It was kaputt. Just plain kaputt. Marie, heart-broken, refused to keep that ugly, broken thing. Crying, she marched straight to the outhouse, and lightly holding the doll by one foot, held it directly over the hole for the toilet seat, and . . . let go.

When Aaron Jr.'s mother Maria died before his wedding, his sisters Tante Maria, Tante Suse, and Tante Lena divided all his mother's special things, the embroidered linens and crocheted table-cloths, all her personal effects. Aaron received absolutely nothing. Well, not absolutely. He did get just one thing. He received the yellow ribbon that said, "MOTHER" which had encircled his mother's casket.

Aaron was a dutiful and obedient son. He didn't want any problems, and so he didn't fight about it. He would never complain. But Aaron's income was now gone, his factory burned to the ground, and he was bankrupt. He needed a way to provide for his family and to pay the back wages of his former employees. Aaron was a man of his word. If he said he would pay them, he would pay them. But how?

Susanna was grieved that Aaron had been shut out of the family businesses. Maybe that is why they had trouble. Aaron would be quiet and Susanna would be the one to bring it up and stir things up. "Your sisters should give you some of those things what belonged to your mother. You go ask them. She was your mother just as much." or "Why aren't you part of the lumberyard business or that store? If you aren't included in those things, what are we going to do? Are you telling me you are going to sell what we have left, and use that money what we now need, and pay those Russians what burned down the factory?"

Lots of times, little Marie would be angry at her Mom for doing that, but she was a child and couldn't say what she was really thinking, "Mom, you need a licking for saying things like that." Then, for days, Aaron and Susanna wouldn't talk to each other. Aaron's feelings were hurt. Neither would ever ask for forgiveness.

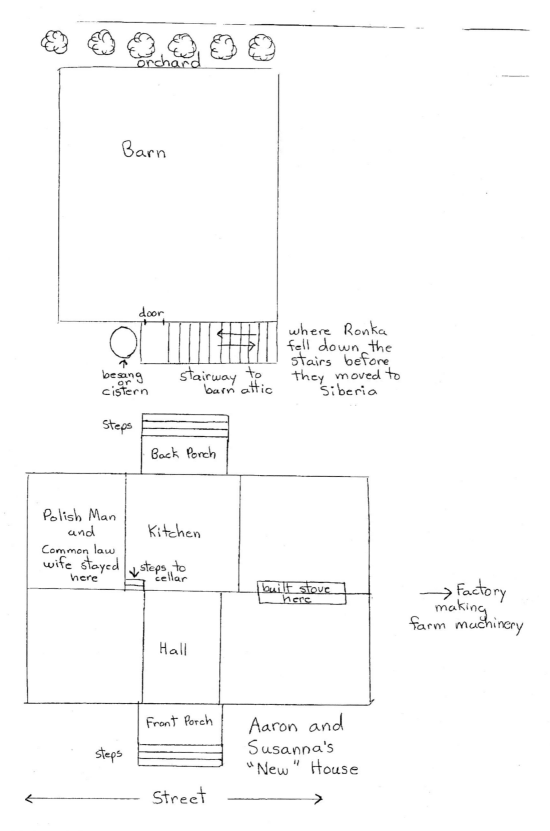

orchard

Barn

door

besang or cistern

stairway to barn attic

where Ronka fell down the stairs before they moved to Siberia

Steps

Back Porch

Polish Man and Common law wife stayed here

Kitchen

steps to cellar

built stove here

→ Factory making farm machinery

Hall

Front Porch

steps

Aaron and Susanna's "New" House

← Street →

59 Aron & Susanna's new modern house, barn, and farm machinery factory next door

103

As was their custom, however, the family finished the day in the flickering light of the kerosene lamp around the Word of God.

Then shall the king say unto them on his right hand, Come, ye blessed of my Father, inherit the kingdom prepared for you from the foundation of the world:

For I was an hungered, and ye gave me meat: I was thirsty, and ye gave me drink: I was a stranger, and ye took me in:

Naked, and ye clothed me: I was sick, and ye visited me: I was in prison, and ye came unto me,

Then shall the righteous answer him, saying, Lord, when saw we thee an hungered, and fed thee or thirsty, and gave thee drink? . . .

And the King shall answer and say unto them, Verily I say unto you, inasmuch as ye have done it unto one of the least of these my brethren, ye have done it unto me.[216]

Not all of Siberia is a formidable, frozen wasteland, with nothing but slave labor camps and mines. Even though winters were long and summers short, southern Siberia, along the Trans-Siberian railway near Petropavlovsk and Omsk, had rich soil, and long summer days, so the land produced bountiful crops of grain. The western area of southern Siberia had vistas as far as the eye could see: miles and miles of flat prairie, or steppes. As a person traveled east, toward Novosibirsk and Irkutsk, mountain ranges with huge forests of birch and larch trees, rose up to majestic heights, which offered great fishing and hunting for Siberian bear, tiger, or coveted sable furs.

To help ease the persistent problem of not enough land for the Russian peasants due to overpopulation, colonization of Siberia had begun when Nicholas II ascended the throne. Mass settlement there began after the disastrous defeat of the Russo-Japanese War of 1905. Each family was allotted 37 acres. The offer of more land for the landless was even more enticing with promises of low railway fares, tax exemptions, a government subsidy of 160 Rubles, and even a 3 year exemption from state service.[217]

A company, actually located in the Molotschna, Ukraine, hired Aaron to work for them selling their farm machinery in Siberia.[218] Newly married young Mennonite couples had difficulty getting farm land in Ukraine. Perhaps they also desired to be farther away from the heavy

---

[216] Matthew 25: 34-40
[217] Life and Times of a Renaissance Mennonite Teacher: Cornelius A. Klaassen: (1883-1919 and Beyond), Robert L. Klaassen, pg 57
[218] Perhaps the person who hired Aaron to sell farming equipment in Siberia was Johann Ediger, the other person in Gnadenfeld who sold farming equipment, Molotschna Historical Atlas, Helmut T. Huebert, pg 127

handed regulation and supervision of the government. Usually, the farther away from the capital, the less government control. So, many anwhoner or "landless" Mennonites also moved to other areas like Siberia. Over 100 villages with some 45,000 Germans had been established by the mother Molotschna colony in Siberia. Around 3,512 Mennonites had settled on over one million acres in and around Omsk, near the Trans-Siberian Railway, to easily transport their produce.[219] The height of their prosperity before the First World War was partly due to the fact that settlers came with money, and settled along railroad lines, so were close to markets. They raised grains, vegetables, and planted orchards.[220] Indeed, some areas were quite pleasant. Petropavlovsk (population about 50,000), had the largest and most beautiful station on the Trans-Siberian railway, and was an important trading center for silk and carpets.[221]

In moving to Siberia, Susanna was now far from her whole support network, her family, friends, and church. She left a close knit community of German Mennonites for the Russian city of Petropavlovsk, with almost no other German Mennonites present for fellowship and support. Nearly everyone there were Russians. Susanna and her mother Agatha were unhappy, and Agatha now wished Susanna had never married.

Marie had enjoyed playing among big, beautiful, pumpkins in the fall. She missed the pumpkin patch and hunting for berries in the woods in Siberia. She really missed their tidy village and playing with all her German Mennonite cousins.[222]

The Tokmak Railway had begun service in the Molotschna December 20, 1913.[223] With railway service now well established the past two years, the family headed north of Gnadenfeld to the train station at Stulnevo, then Ekaterinoslav, Karkov, and Moscow. There they changed to the Great Trans-Siberian Railway headed for Petropavlovsk, Siberia.

The family arrived in Petropavlovsk at dusk in February 1915. The house they rented had been vacant for some time. Even after lighting the big stove in the middle of the house, used to cook, bake and heat the house, it took so long for the stove to heat up, the house remained frigid a long time. They had no beds or furniture when they arrived, only blankets, pillows, and down comforters brought with them on the train. Nothing else had arrived yet, so they spread what they had on the floor.

---

[219] "Molotschna, Mennonite Settlement (Zaporizhia Oblast, Ukraine)", http://www.gameo.org/encyclopedia/contents/M6521.html source Mennonite Encyclopedia, v3, p. 732-737
[220] http://www.gameo.org/encyclopedia/contents/O567.html
[221] the free Dictionary by Farlex http://encyclopedia2.thefreedictionary.com accessed 14 March 2018
[222] Aaron possibly sold his OPEL to pay his debts, or perhaps it had already been conscripted by the Czar's army for use in the war, as were other vehicles in the colony.
[223] Molotschna Historical Atlas, Helmut T Huebert, pg 101

That evening, Aaron went to the store and bought French bread and smoked salmon. Russian French bread was small, only about 8 inches long, 4 inches wide. Usually a person had to buy several. Normally, the father would not be the one who would go out shopping for food, but they had just arrived. It was cold; they were hungry, and it was getting dark much earlier so far north. They had tea with bread and smoked salmon; that was their supper. It tasted pretty good. They couldn't sleep it was so cold. Little Marie crawled into bed with her Mother and Father she was so cold. They were all terribly cold.

While living in that first, rental house, Marie used to visit a Jewish lady with a baby. One day that Jewish lady made some noodles with milk and shared them with Marie, who thought they tasted pretty good.

They had been in that house only a few days, when Susanna, (pregnant with the author's mother) took a nap. When she woke up, she wondered where little Ronka, just a year and a half old, was. A Russian maid was supposed to be looking after him, but Susanna couldn't find Ronka anywhere. Mama asked Marie, but Marie didn't know where he was. Mama called, "Ronka, Ronka! Where are you?" No answer, and no one knew where he was. She looked around, and called and called some more, "Ronka, Ronka, where are you?" She finally found him, just the top of his hair showing. He had fallen into the sewer pit, just outside the front door, where they threw the contents of the night pots. Only his hair was sticking out. Susanna quickly pulled him out, held him upside down, and worked on him to get the filthy waste water out of him. Ronka soon began to sputter as Mama pressed more and more of the water out. It is a wonder Ronka survived!

They did not have running water in this house. They had to buy all of their water and carry it to the house, so Susanna did not have any water to give him a proper bath. "He was stinky," she said. "He was stinky for days!" Susanna was stinky too. Little five year old Marie was scolded for not having watched Ronka more closely. For years Marie would always say, "Be sure to find out that I am to blame, somehow."

The first house in Petropavlovsk had that open sewer pit, with no cover on it, and no wall around it. That house really was uninhabitable. The whole yard was flooded around it for a week, spreading sewer water everywhere when it rained. Aaron went to the police and complained about how unhealthy that place was. The family soon moved to another place.

Aaron's new job was not simply selling company farm machinery. It also was Aaron's duty to get rid of the former salesman for embezzling from the company. This took a long time.

One day Ronka disappeared again, and Susanna couldn't find him. "Ronka, Ronka, where are you?" She looked all over the house. She looked all over the yard. Some Neufelds (no relation), lived with them and helped her look for him. They didn't have a telephone, but Susanna somehow told the police that Ronka was missing. Finally, someone thought of looking under and behind the bed. Behind the bed, beyond the other side of the headboard, was an extra little alcove. Sure enough, he was sitting Indian style, his head leaning against the corner of the alcove, sucking his thumb, fast asleep, holding the little piece of fur he used as his security blanket against his face. When finally finding him, little Marie snapped, "Now be sure to find out somehow that I am to blame again."

About three blocks away to the left of their second house was Ovsiannikova, a sophisticated, modern department store, an imposing three stories high cathedral for shopping within such a small city. The store was built in 1905, and was still the only three-story edifice in the city. An identical store had also been built in Omsk. Ovsiannikova featured a grand carpeted staircase and an elevator. The building was illuminated at night, and had its own power plant to generate electricity needed for the elevator and electric lights.[224]

An enormous stuffed Siberian bear stood guard just inside the store. Poor Ronka was afraid of that huge bear. He wished there would be another way to go in so he didn't have to pass so close to that fierce-some creature. Ronka would keep as far away from it as possible, hiding on the other side of his mother as they entered the store.

It was possible to buy everything: fabrics, footwear, gramophones, fruit, any time of the year. Susanna bought two hats for Marie: a fine straw hat trimmed with cherries for summer, and a red felt hat. They were so pretty; Marie was proud of them. One time a special, beautiful, big doll, two feet tall, was displayed that could be won by someone. Marie desired that doll with all her heart, but she didn't win it.

Another day, Ronka disappeared once again. "Ronka, Ronka where are you?" This time she looked in the alcove behind the bed, but Ronka was not there. She looked here; she looked there. Susanna had stored a rather large box of salt under the kitchen table. Hidden behind the tablecloth she discovered Ronka quietly sitting, dipping his fingers into the salt and licking them off.

The family turned left from their house, walked three blocks to the Ovsiannikova Department Store, then turned left again, and walked several blocks to the Petropavlovsk City Park. It occupied a

---

[224] http://www.petropavl.kz/module/mg106_1.shml

whole block. Marie, Ronka, and Gonja enjoyed a children's playground with sand box and swings. Papa had to put a deposit down for them to use the toys in the sandbox. One could buy ice cream sandwiches that had pink and white ice cream in between thin, dainty wafers. They had to be very careful and eat them before they melted all over their hands. Concerts were held in the bandshell Sunday evenings each summer. People would come, sit, listen to the band, and enjoy visiting with each other. Papa's favorite music was Dvorak's <u>New World Symphony</u>.

The family lived close to the Ishim River. Separate bathhouses had been built right over the river, one for men, the other for women. The floor of each bath house was even with the top of the river. People could sit on a bench in the river that wasn't too deep for the women, but it was too deep for Marie. Mama wanted Marie to take off her slip and go in the water, but Marie didn't want to take off her slip. She wouldn't do it. The women were all naked. They had no bathing suits. Marie just stood on the steps and refused to take off her slip.

Summer in Siberia was really pleasant. It didn't get too hot. The children went barefoot in the summer so they had to wash their feet before getting into bed at night. Fruit wasn't readily available, but Susanna would go to the market and could buy cherries. Mennonites were just getting established in their farms up in Siberia, so fruit orchards weren't plentiful or mature enough to bear bountiful crops yet. Other times she would buy peas. The pea pods were still on the whole vine. The vine was just pulled out of the ground, with the peas still hanging on. When she brought the pea vine home, the children really went after that, pulling off the pods, opening them up, picking out the juicy sweet peas, and popping them in their mouths.

60 above, Ovsyannikova department store; old post card—public domain

61 inside department store; old post card —public domain

62 department store staircase; old post card—public domain

Городской парк

г. Петропавловскъ.   Городской садъ. Дѣтская площадка.

63 City Park, old post card, public domain

One of their rented homes had a long, wide hall, where Ronka would march like a soldier, back and forth, swinging his arms, singing:

Raz va, Raz va.
Tamara ti mi ya.
One, two, One, two
Tamara is mine.

Little Ronka had fallen in love with a little neighbor girl Tamara.

Agatha, nicknamed Gonja, was born 12 October, 1915.
Rasputin, a trusted advisor in government affairs to Czarina Alexandra, wife of Czar Nicholas II, influenced political decisions while her husband Nicholas II was at the war front. He had earned their trust by seeming to help their hemophiliac son Alexi recover from a serious bleed when doctors appeared totally unable to help him.

By the end of 1915, Russia suffered heavy defeats in the war against Germany. The government's appalling disorganization, profligate waste of food and material, coupled with unbridled corruption caused high inflation and rising prices.[225] Severe shortages of food, munitions and other supplies ensued. The confiscation of horses and conscription of man power forced farmers to cultivate less land. Horses that looked like old nags, and wagons that appeared rickety and decrepit were less likely to be taken away from desperate farmers who needed them to produce a harvest.[226]

That first Christmas in Petropavlovsk, Marie received another beautiful doll, to replace the doll Ronka had broken, which she had summarily disposed of in the outhouse. Her second Christmas in Siberia, Marie got a doll bed and new clothes for the doll. Boys would be happy to receive a carved wooden horse or lamb, a metal wind-up train, or a penknife.[227] They always had a large Christmas tree, with candy, paper chains, and beautiful hand blown glass decorations from Germany, that were saved very carefully from year to year. The tree was decorated with delicately and precisely made little animals of all kinds from Germany: cows, chickens, horses, geese. Wax candles in a myriad of colors about 4 inches high were fastened on tree branches with little clips. The children never saw the tree until Christmas morning, when they would get up, and it was as if the tree had appeared like magic overnight. Christmas celebrations included paper poppers from the Orient in all colors, about 5 inches long and twisted on the end. When opened, the

[225] "Russian Revolution, 1917", Wikipedia http://en.wikipedia.org/wiki/Russian_Revolution
[226] A Mennonite Family in Tsarist Russia and the Soviet Union 1789-1923, David G. Rempel, pp. 158-159
[227] My Memories, Mary Dirks Janzen, pg 3

poppers always contained a surprise like a fan made of paper. Each person's gift was at his plate at the table. Christmas was always very special in Russia.

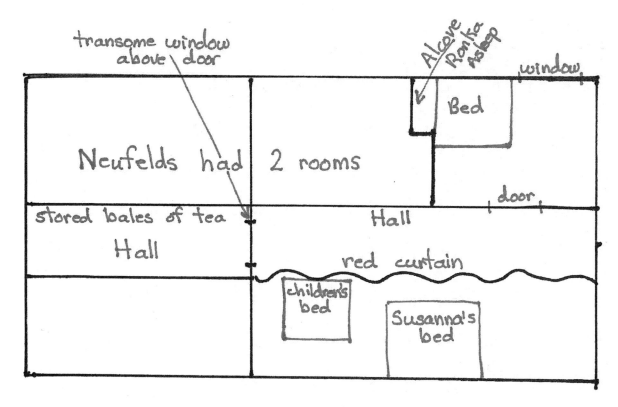

64 home in Siberia with long hall

Aaron was gone from home much of the time. He was away on business trips, visiting the German Mennonite villages around Omsk, to sell farm machinery. When he wasn't away on business, he was away on hunting trips. Hunting was his recreation. Aaron went hunting for wolf in winter and killed 6 or 7 wolves. It was Susanna's role to take care of the household and children. It never occurred to him that it would be good for a father to stay home with his wife and children, to spend time with them. This left Susanna alone much of the time.[228] Susanna, far from family and from her close neighbors and friends, was desperately lonely, unable to share her pain with anyone.

---

[228] <u>California Mennonite Historical Society Bulletin</u>, No, 54, 2011, "The Rempel Family's Escape from Death by Famine", Corinna Siebert Ruth

65 typical Siberian house, illustration by Margie Hildebrand

When Aaron worked in the area, Marie was sent to her father's office about three blocks away to call him for dinner. Without other German children to play with, Russian children made fun of Marie. They called her "German sack of potatoes," and threw dirt clods at her. German Mennonites did not dress like the Russians who wore long skirts to the ankles. The Mennonites dressed fashionably. Whatever was in fashion in Europe was what the Mennonites wore. Once when Marie was skipping to her father's office to call him to dinner, two Russian girls from the country hid in a bush, until Marie got close. They sprang in front of Marie and stuck a stick of tar in her mouth. Marie ran home crying. The Rempel children all were given Russian nicknames: Marie became Mieche, Aron III became Ronka, and when Agatha was born, she was called Gonja.

One day Susanna walked near Aaron's office, and saw something which made her go numb. Aaron had come out of the office with his arm around another woman. Aaron clearly didn't expect Susanna here at this time of the day. He didn't expect her at all. His arm dropped from the woman's shoulders, and she quickly walked away, leaving Aaron and Susanna alone.

Every night thereafter, when Susanna was in bed alone, and Aaron was away on a trip, she cried. Oh, the crying had to be quiet, so the children would not be able to hear her, but she cried all the same. The tears soaked her pillow before she finally fell asleep. She found it was so hard to get up in the morning. It felt like she had no life left in her, but for the sake of the children she did get up. For the sake of the children, she put one foot in front of the other and kept on going. She kept telling herself she had to keep on going, "for the sake of the children."

The Snow Hill

In winter Father built a special snow hill where he piled and stacked snow against the barn almost to the top. He fashioned a long slide and carved a platform on top and steps out of the side. Marie and Ronka could easily mount the top by marching up the steps. If it snowed during the night, the slide was swept off the next morning, so a lot of soft snow accumulated off to the side. Once when Ronka was still quite young, the sled hit a bump, swerved sideways, and dumped him. Ronka fell head first into the soft snow. All you could see was Ronka's little blue coat, lined with fur and gathered at the waist, in a circle, spread like a flower around his little legs sticking up in the air, kicking wildly. Marie, standing on the top of the hill, thought it very funny and laughed, but Ronka did not think it funny at all.

Father poured water on the slide to make it extra slick. Marie would give a little push, then whoosh, down they would go. Whoosh, whoosh, clear through the open gate and out into the street. That sled ride almost took their breath away. But after each ride, Marie and Ronka were right back up the steps for another exciting ride down. Ronka generally was in front, and Marie in back. When she was old enough to join them, Gonja was usually ready to quit before her older brother and sister were. In fact, it was hard for them to stop even when their mother called them to come in for supper.

Later, towards spring, when the snow became softer, they made snow men and had snow ball fights, which generally ended when someone was hit directly in the face and went crying into the house. The children really enjoyed winters in Siberia.

Susanna had a lot of trouble with her teeth. She had a hired man drive their horse to get her to the dentist. Siberian horses were small, with short legs. This horse became so used to going to the dentist that he just naturally followed the route to the dentist. In winter he was hitched to pull a sleigh. One time Susanna just wanted to go for a ride for the fun of it with her friend Mrs. Neufeld. She thought she could drive the horse herself. They took a sharp corner someplace where they missed the road a little bit, went into a ditch, and the sleigh tipped over, dumping Susanna and Mrs. Neufeld into the snow. Siberian sleighs were low to the ground, so they didn't fall very far. The horse was already gone a long way before he looked around to see no one behind him. Right then that horse learned to purposely go around a corner fast enough to tip the sleigh over, dump the people, and take off without them.

There was a rhythm of life for the family in Siberia similar to that in Gnadenfeld, Ukraine regarding daily chores and menus served. Most Mennonites had varenekje (pronounced varenikey), little dumplings of flour, soda, salt, egg, and water made into a soft dough. Mama rolled out noodle dough, cut into small squares, then filled them with a little bit of cottage cheese. The corners of the squares were folded over and sealed with a fork. The ends were pinched together almost forming them into a ball, nearly like a marble, then cooked in boiling water with a little oil and salt added to the water. They were served with a sour cream gravy and fried onions.

Pelmenje were the same little dumplings, similar to Chinese wonton or Italian ravioli, but with ground meat inside instead of cottage cheese. They were kept frozen and warmed by simply boiling them. It was a time consuming task to prepare pelmenje, because each small circle or square of dough had to be filled with hamburger, served without gravy, but with vinegar and black pepper added just before they were eaten. They were small, light, and floated on top of the soup. Good pelmenje should never sink to the bottom.[229] They were Gonja's favorite. "Please, can we have pelmenje tonight?" she often pled. In winter, Susanna made a lot of varenekje and pelmenje, put them in little cloth bags drawn shut with a string tie, and hung them outside in a shed where animals couldn't get them. The air was so cold, it was like keeping them in a freezer. They were then ready to have at any time. Whenever Mama wanted to use them, she merely threw several handfuls into boiling water.

They ate many kinds of soups in Russia: not just Russian borscht, but green borscht or spring soup, meatball, dry bean, green bean, carrot, beef, potato, mutton, or chicken soup.

Mennonite homes customarily had a weekly routine with a rotating menu. For Sunday dinner there could be chicken, goose, ham, a roast, or sausage, and often plümemoos. A simple Sunday evening meal was bread soup, simply crumbling some of their hearty rye bread or even Zwiebach into a bowl of milk and adding a little watermelon syrup. Another simple Sunday evening meal was a rice porridge, with one cup of rice cooked in three cups of milk, served with a little sugar and cinnamon. [230]

In the summer they loved to eat roll kuchen with watermelon. They mixed 3 cups flour, 4 eggs, 1 tsp soda and 1 tsp salt; rolled out the dough, cut it into squares, and fried them in hot oil. They were like flat doughnuts. In the winter, they would have pancakes with watermelon syrup.

---

[229] Mennonite Food & Folkways from South Russia, Vol I, Norma Jost Voth, pg 194
[230] Mennonite Food & Folkways from South Russia, Vol I, Norma Jost Voth, pg 173, 309

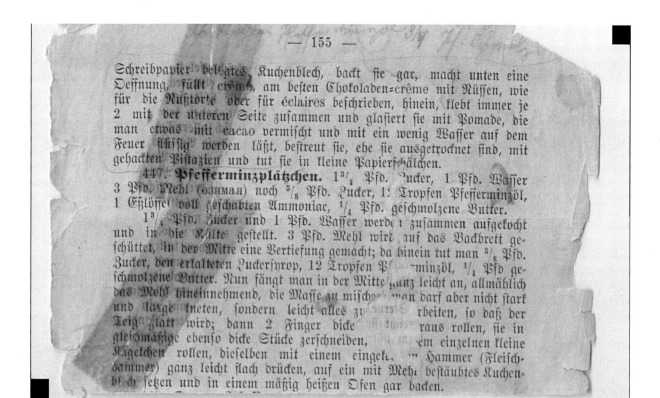

Schreibpapier belegtes Kuchenblech, bäckt sie gar, macht unten eine Oeffnung, füllt crême, am besten Chokoladen-crême mit Nüssen, wie für die Nußtorte oder für éclaires beschrieben, hinein, klebt immer je 2 mit der unteren Seite zusammen und glasiert sie mit Pomade, die man etwas mit Cacao vermischt und mit ein wenig Wasser auf dem Feuer flüssig werden läßt, bestreut sie, ehe sie ausgetrocknet sind, mit gehackten Pistazien und tut sie in kleine Papierschälchen.

447. **Pfefferminzplätzchen.** 1³/₄ Pfd. Zucker, 1 Pfd. Wasser 3 Pfd. Mehl (озимая) noch ⁵/₈ Pfd. Zucker, 15 Tropfen Pfefferminzöl, 1 Eßlöffel voll geschabten Ammoniac, ¹/₄ Pfd. geschmolzene Butter.

1³/₄ Pfd. Zucker und 1 Pfd. Wasser werden zusammen aufgekocht und in die Kälte gestellt. 3 Pfd. Mehl wird auf das Backbrett geschüttet, in der Mitte eine Vertiefung gemacht; da hinein tut man ⁵/₈ Pfd. Zucker, den erkalteten Zuckersyrop, 12 Tropfen Pfefferminzöl, ¹/₄ Pfd. geschmolzene Butter. Nun fängt man in der Mitte ganz leicht an, allmählich das Mehl hineinnehmend, die Masse zu mischen man darf aber nicht stark und lange kneten, sondern leicht alles zu... arbeiten, so daß der Teig glatt wird; dann 2 Finger dicke... raus rollen, sie in gleichmäßige ebenso dicke Stücke zerschneiden, ... em einzelnen kleine Kügelchen rollen, dieselben mit einem eingek... Hammer (Fleisch-hammer) ganz leicht flach drücken, auf ein mit Mehl bestäubtes Kuchenblech setzen und in einem mäßig heißen Ofen gar backen.

66 pfeffuernusse recipe from Susanna's cookbook

Mennonite recipes from old books often omit the amount of flour needed, since the women were all excellent bakers, and cooked by feel, touch and taste. They knew by experience how much flour to use and also often spoke of other "measurements" in terms that are totally unfamiliar to those of us in the 21st century.

1. *1 Glas (Russian glass, slightly less than 1 cup)*
2. *1 spoonful salt*
3. *1 big spoonful flour*
4. *3 kopeks worth of ammonia (bicarbonate of ammonia, or bakers ammonia)[231]*
5. *1 15 cent bottle oil of anise [used to give Mennonite chicken soup its individual character, and considered a necessary ingredient for Christmas Pfeffernüsse Peppernuts) [232]*
6. *a little vinegar[233]*

---

[231] The author's mother Gonja infrequently baked Ammonia cookies. She and her sister would beg and beg Gonja to make ammonia cookies. They were very special. No, no, she did NOT use cleaning ammonia, but a baker's ammonia (ammonia bicarbonate) which is in granular form and difficult to find. Bakeries have baking ammonia. It also has been found at Olsen's Bakery and in Parson's Drug Store in Solvang, California and more recently at the Armenian food store Super King in Los Angeles, or you can now find it on line. Unfortunately, the ammonia evaporates into thin air over time once you have opened the bottle. Never eat raw cookie dough if you have used baking ammonia. Use 1 to 1 ratio to replace baking soda in recipes (1 tsp baking soda = 1 tsp bakers ammonia).

[232] anise—"In Gnadenfeld, mother (Oma Agatha) put anise seed in roast pork. It also adds a good flavor to duck, goose, and chicken. Leg of lamb with anise is very good." Mennonite Food & Folkways from South Russia, Vol I, Norma Jost Voth, Mary Dirks Janzen, pg 253

[233] Mennonite Food & Folkways from South Russia, Vol II, Norma Jost Voth, pp. 273-274

süßen Mandeln und läßt ihn etwa eine Stunde im mittelheißen Ofen backen (siehe allgemeine Regeln). Wenn er aus dem Ofen genommen wird, schiebt man ein breites, dünnes Messer zwischen Pfanne und Kringel durch, um sich zu überzeugen, ob er nirgend festhält und schiebt ihn behutsam aber geschwind auf das dazu bestimmte Brett, welches am besten aus ganz dünnen Holzstäben gitterartig geflochten und mit reinem, weißem Papier bedeckt ist, oder legt wenigstens unter das weiße Papier auf das feste Brett ein mehrfach zusammengelegtes Handtuch oder mehrfach aufgeschichtetes Makulatur- oder Löschpapier, damit der Dampf nach unten irgend wie entweichen kann und der Kringel von unten nicht naß wird. Solange der Kringel noch ganz heiß ist, bestreicht man ihn mit zerlassener Butter und bestreut ihn mit Puderzucker. Leicht bedeckt läßt man ihn erkalten.

378. **Gebrühte Kringel** (баранки, сушки). 3 Löffel Zucker, 1 Löffel Salz, 3 Pfd. Mehl, für 5 Kop. Hefe. ¼ Pfd. Butter, 2 Glas lauwarmes Wasser.

In einem Glase lauwarmem Wasser wird die Hefe aufgelöst, Zucker und Salz hinzugefügt, dann noch 1 Glas warmes Wasser, die ausgeschmolzene Butter und dann 2 Pfd. Mehl hineingeknetet, gut durchgearbeitet und zum Aufgehn an einen warmen Ort gestellt. Ist das geschehn, etwa nach 1—1½ Stunden, schüttet man 1 Pfd. Mehl auf das Backbrett, legt den Teig darauf und arbeitet nun das ganze Mehl in den Teig hinein und walkt ihn, so lange, bis der Teig ganz trocken, fest und sehr glatt ist. Dazwischen schneidet man ihn immer wieder mit dem Messer durch, damit er wirklich durch und durch verarbeitet wird und das Mehl gleichmäßig in sich aufnimmt. Nun werden kleine Teile davon in Rollen ausgerollt und diese dann wieder in kleine gleichmäßige Teile zerschnitten, die man dann zu den größeren Kringeln in etwa 1½ Finger lange, ungefähr 1 kleinen Finger dicke Röllchen ausrollt, indem man das Backbrett und die Finger ganz leicht mit kaltem Wasser anfeuchtet. Dann werden die Röllchen zum Ringe geschlossen, man läßt sie ein wenig aufgehn und wirft sie dann in eine Kasserolle mit stark kochendem Wasser, wartet bis sie an die Oberfläche steigen, hebt sie mit einem Schaumlöffel heraus und auf ein Sieb, wo man sie gleich, so lange sie noch feucht sind, mit Kümmel, Mohnsamen oder grobem Salz bestreut. Sobald sie trocken sind, legt man sie auf ein leicht mit Mehl bestäubtes Backblech und läßt sie in einem ziemlich heißen Ofen schön hellbraun backen.

379. **Napfkuchen mit Hefe.** 2½ Pfd. Mehl, ¾ Pfd. Zucker, ¾ Pfd. Butter, ½ Pfd. Rosinen, 4 Eier, die Schale einer Zitrone, ¼ Pfd. süße Mandeln, 20 bittere Mandeln oder 4—5 Tropfen Bittermandel-Oel, ½ Teelöffel Salz, 1½ Teelöffel Vanillezucker, für 10 Kop. Hefe, 2 Glas Milch.

Die Hefe wird mit einer kleinen Tasse Wasser, 1 Teelöffel Zucker und ¼ Pfd. Mehl angerührt und zum Aufgehn gestellt. Mittlerweile rührt man die Butter zu Schaum, fügt Zucker, Eier, Zitronenschale,

9*

67 — page 131 from Susanna's old recipe book in German

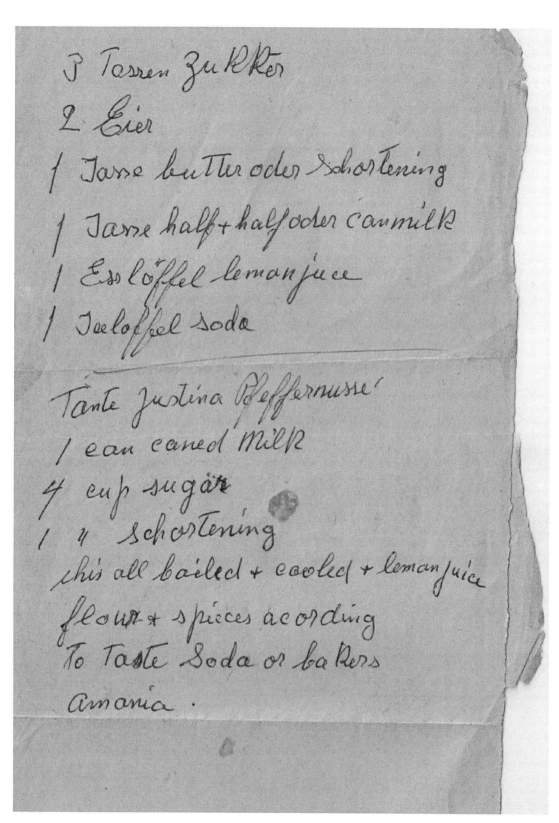

3 Tassen Zukker

2 Eier

1 Tasse butter oder Shortening

1 Tasse half + half oder canmilk

1 Esslöffel lemanjuce

1 Teelöffel Soda

Tante Justina Pfeffernusse

1 can caned Milk

4 cup sugar

1 4 Shortening

this all boiled + cooled + lemanjuce

flour + spices according

To Taste Soda or bakers

amonia.

68 — Susanna's handwritten recipe; note the amount
of flour and spices were not given, —but just "to taste"

Typical weekly Menu

Monday Kjeilkje (dumpling/noodle) day, to make the starch for the ironing to be done the next day, along with onion gravy, smoked sausage, sauerkraut, fried onion.

Tuesday fried or boiled potatoes, with sauerkraut, watermelon, and dill pickles.

Wednesday Rollküake (roll kuchen, or crullers)[234] In winter with jam and watermelon syrup and brined watermelons. In summer with fresh watermelon.

Thursday Borscht, rye or white bread (Bulkje)

Friday Ham, potatoes

Saturday Green Beans, with onion and pork, sausage, or liver sausage, potatoes. The Krause Dirks family had huge pans of Plauts (fruit pastry topped with goose-berries, cherries, currents, apricots, plums, or apples. Sister Katcha became the best baker.

Sunday Lamb or chicken, potatoes, a fruit moos—or watermelon or cantaloupe in summer[235]

Borscht

4	quarts broth, lamb, chicken, beef	Boil the bones, and when tender,
	meat saved from soup bones	remove bones and throw away.
1	bunch fresh dill, chopped fine	Save the meat for later. Chill the
3	large onions, chopped	broth, then remove the fat from
5	potatoes, chopped	the top. Simmer the broth with
1/2	cabbage, chopped	the rest of ingredients. When the
1	quart V8 juice	onions & potatoes are tender, just
3	Tbsp mustard	before serving, add the meat left
1	lemon juiced	over from making the broth.

Add a dollop of sour cream as garnish when the soup is served.[236]

---

[234] The interesting thing to note in Plattdeutch, there is no set spelling. The author has often found numerous alternative ways to spell different words.

[235] Mennonite Foods & Folkways from South Russia, Vol II, Norma Jost Voth, pp. 257-265

[236] Author's Recipe. Borscht is mainly cabbage soup with dill flavoring in a good meat stock, and is better the second or third day after flavors have had a chance to blend. Mennonite Food & Folkways from South Russia, Vol II, Norma Jost Voth, pg 176

Borscht was and still is a staple of both the Russian and the German Mennonite diet. When you have spices and no dill, you don't have Borscht; you have beef soup.

Washing was always done on Monday, ironing on Tuesday. Baking and cleaning would be done Saturday to get ready for rest on Sunday. Plenty of other daily chores kept them busy the other days with sewing, knitting socks, or churning butter. Susanna had learned to knit, so she could provide socks for her own family. Mending and darning holes in the socks always needed to be done. Susanna did have Russian girls to help her, but they tended to sit down and quit working when nobody was watching. As Susanna trained her children, she taught them never to be sitting idle. When they were sitting, they always needed to do something with their hands: darn, mend, crochet rugs out of rags, always accomplish something. Work was a blessing. All work had dignity. Even though mama might not see them, God saw whatever they were doing, or not doing.

In Russia, clothes were not ironed except for dresses. They changed clothes only once a week, and wore Sunday clothes only on Sunday or special occasions. Susanna had a small mangle in Siberia where she pressed sheets and pillow cases.

They didn't go to church in Siberia. Only a few German Mennonites lived nearby, so there wasn't a Mennonite church in Petropavlovsk. The children prayed before meals and before they went to bed.

In the summer, Marie crawled up on the rooftop of the barn, because her girlfriend Lena Sudermann lived across on the other side of the barn. This way they could talk to each other to try and make plans for each day. Lena's father was a merchant with a warehouse to store things like wheat, candy, and salt, to sell to stores. He always had lots of different things in his rooms in the warehouse. One time he stored barrels of candy that was melted together. Lena & Marie helped themselves. They also enjoyed going into the sheds where wheat was stored and stomping on the wheat.

Aaron always had hunting dogs. Drezhnah was a short haired dog, like a German Shepherd. Drezhnah couldn't be used as a hunting dog any more because she was shell shocked, but she was a very good watch dog. The people who had Drezhnah before Rempels, had trained her to sit on a chair next to the table to eat. Susanna didn't allow her dog to eat off the table in their home. Drezhnah had to eat like a regular dog, from a bowl on the floor.

Susanna trusted Drezhnah to take care of her children when she went to market. She would tell him to lie on the front steps and he would stay on guard and wouldn't let anyone through the door. Whenever the Rempel children stopped playing with the neighborhood children and ran to the house to eat dinner, or do chores, often forgetting clothing and toys behind, Drezhnah would pick up all the children had left, and bring it to the house. No matter how many trips it would take, that dog always brought their own things home again.

69 Left— Ronka age 2, Marie age 5,
70 Right —Ronka age 4,[237] Gonja age 2, Marie age 7,

---

[237] Note Ronka with his shaved head. The hair was allowed to grow long for winter, but was shaved for the summer months. A rite of passage for boys to young men was their head was no longer shaved when they advanced to secondary school

A Visit Home

The Rempel family returned to Gnadenfeld for a visit. Susanna enjoyed that trip traveling back and forth from Petropavlovsk, Siberia to Stulnevo, (just a few miles north of Gnadenfeld) Molotschna, Ukraine. Traveling by passenger train, the trip took several days. The family had a compartment all to themselves. No dining cars were on the passenger trains; everyone had to buy food at the train depots. There were always people at the depots selling their produce, bulkje (a big loaf of bread), hot rolls, salami or sausages, and sometimes, in season, fruit like cherries. Samovars with hot water were available on the train to make your own tea. You could even buy some eggs, put them in the hot water, and when you were ready to eat, the eggs were cooked.

About age seven, when Marie visited her Oma Agatha's, she fell in love with a little hand crank sewing machine her Aunt Katche had. Katche (age eleven) promised Marie that when she came back to Gnadenfeld to live, she could have that little sewing machine. Marie never forgot that little sewing machine, and she never forgot Katche's promise.

Susanna missed seeing her brother Jasch (Jacob Krause) because he was away from Gnadenfeld fulfilling his three years alternative military service in the Russian Red Cross.[238] The Rempels, en route to Siberia after their visit in Gnadenfeld, spent the night in a hotel in Moscow, before they would change trains for the Trans-Siberian Railway headed for Petropavlovsk, Siberia the next morning.

Uncle Jasch, on leave from service on a hospital train between the front and the interior, was on his way home to Gnadenfeld for a short visit before going to Crimea, when he met Aaron, on an errand to buy French bread, sausage, and cheese for his hungry family. How happy the family was to see him when Aaron brought Jasch, dressed in his elegant uniform to their Moscow hotel room for a surprise visit! He wore khaki pants, a black leather jacket with a Red Cross emblem, the letters VZS on a white cloth strip on the left sleeve, and a regular military cap with a small Red Cross emblem fastened to its front.[239] The Red Cross collected wounded soldiers from the battlefields, took care of the sick and wounded, and manned long hospital trains. Many such trains were

---

[238] During the war in 1854 when English and French fleets appeared before the gates of the fortress city of Sevastopol, huge contingents of troops moved through the Molotschna. The colonists felt sorry for the soldiers and organized a gigantic assistance plan to provide a lift in thousands of their wagons to the foot-weary soldiers. At the battle site, wounded soldiers were picked up, driven back, and nursed back to health in Mennonite homes. Medicine and doctors were provided by the government, but all the food, assistance, and care were provided by the colonists. Thus was born another form of Mennonite alternative military service. The Molotschna Colony, A Heritage Remembered, Henry Bernard Tiessen, pg 100
[239] Mennonite Medicine in Russia 1800 to 1930, Helmut T. Huebert, pp 146

staffed mostly by Mennonites. By 1917 about 14,000 Mennonites served, half as Red Cross workers and half in the forestry department as noncombatants.[240]

While Aaron, Susanna, and their family lived in Siberia, Susanna's brother Jasch married Maria Rempel, the sister of his brother Cornelius's wife, Margareta. Missionary Gerhard Nickel performed the wedding and the key Bible verse for their ceremony was Matthew 6:35 "But seek first the kingdom of God and His righteousness, and all these things will be added to you." [241]

When they arrived at another train station going north to Petropavlovsk, Aaron left the family on board while he went to buy some food. On his way back with dinner for his waiting family, he passed another train, stopped on a siding at the same station, loaded with Bolshevik prisoners. The prisoners were starving, and begged Aaron for his bread. Aaron was almost back to his famished family, waiting for their dinner, but the prisoners were clearly perishing with hunger. Aaron shoved his bread into their outstretched arms, then saw Susanna watching and waiting on the train platform.[242] "There were starving prisoners in that boxcar! I will just have to go back and buy our dinner all over again."

71 Jasch (Jacob Cornelius Krause), seated far left, in the Russian Red Cross

72 young Jasch (Jacob Krause)

---

[240] 1835-1943 Gnadenfeld, Molotschna, A Lowen Schmidt, pg 17
[241] Obituary of Jakob C. Krause, translated from the German
[242] Susanna's recollection during her 100th birthday celebration, taped at Sierra View, with son Aron Jr. (Ronka) present.

Kirghiz

Give a hungry man bread;
It does you as much good
as if you had eaten it yourself.
—Low German saying[243]

Then shall the king say unto them on his right hand, Come, ye blessed of my Father, inherit the kingdom prepared for you from the foundation of the world:

For I was an hungered, and ye gave me meat: I was thirsty, and ye gave me drink: I was a stranger, and ye took me in:

Naked, and ye clothed me: I was sick, and ye visited me: I was in prison, and ye came unto me.

Then shall the righteous answer him, saying, Lord, when saw we thee an hungered, and fed thee? or thirsty, and gave thee drink? . . .

And the King shall answer and say unto them, Verily I say unto you, inasmuch as ye have done it unto one of the least of these my brethren, ye have done it unto me.

Matthew 25: 34-40

The effects of World War I and civil chaos were also felt in Siberia. All of Aaron's available farm machinery had been sold and all farm machinery production converted into war material. No more shipments of tractors, threshers, or binders would arrive. Aaron was again out of work, and had no income to support his family.

Siberia had wonderful forests full of good hunting. Aaron was an excellent hunter. He killed six or seven wolves, whose furs were used on beds as blankets and on the floors in front of the beds as rugs. Once, sable fur, with its lustrous, sparkling, silky satin sheen, was abundant in Siberia, but sable had been hunted almost to extinction before a ban was placed on sable hunting in 1913. There was still an abundance of fox, rabbit, ermine, and squirrel, with fox and squirrel being the next most valuable after sable. The Chinese preferred squirrel furs for their comparative value, warmth, and durability. Aaron was able to kill enough animals to create a couple of fur coats for Susanna and himself.

Rabbits were plentiful so he provided a lot of rabbit meat for the family, and their skins were used for coats, muffs, and mittens. Siberian rabbits are huge, much bigger than wild rabbits in California.

---

[243] Mennonite Foods & Folkways from South Russia, Vol I, Norma Jost Voth, pg 79

They are white in winter but gray in summer. The family had so much rabbit meat, Susanna finally grew tired of it. She couldn't manage all the rabbits he shot. Father also shot an occasional goose or two, and those made a welcome change from rabbit meat.

Aaron was such a good hunter, he became the game commissar of the hunting league or union, an official position in Siberia paid by the Russians.

The Kirghiz were a nomadic people who lived in Siberia. They drove two-wheeled carts with four foot wooden wheels pulled by two-humped camels. They wore thick fur coats in both winter and summer. They also wore a fur cap with ear flaps, that looked something like a baby bonnet, worn even in the summer, when the Rempel children ran around barefoot, and average temperatures ranged from the high sixties to low seventies Fahrenheit.

They didn't grease those wooden wheels, so when the Kirghiz came to town, you could hear they were coming from a long way off, there was such squeaking and squawking as they drove slowly down the street. The children were told to stay away from those camels; they were mean, and Ronka did stay away, very far away. Long before they even arrived, you could smell them. You could hardly tell which was which, animal or Kirghiz, by the smell. They must have been allergic to soap, water, and bathing.

The nomadic Kirghiz made their living from hunting and selling furs. Siberian furs were known as "soft gold" because their value was comparable to actual gold.[244] Furs were the most profitable exports, although middlemen profited more than the hunters. The Czar counted on the fur trade for positive cash flow in Russia's exports, to fill his treasury with gold and silver. Siberia was where fur-bearing animals grew the thickest, softest pelts in the most desirable winter hues.

The Kirghiz also had horses and sheep. As the Game Commissar, Aaron was in charge of selling guns and ammunition to hunters, so the Kirghiz always came to him to buy ammunition.

They drank camel's milk that had been made into a strong fermented, alcoholic drink, but Susanna wouldn't let the foul smelling drink into the house. It was the job of the Kirghiz children to stir the fermenting mixture in bags made of skins. They also made another fer-mented drink, a kefir called kumis from mare's milk [245] that Aaron and Susanna loved. It was very tasty, so she readily permitted

---

244 Siberian Fur Trade, https://en.wikipedia.org/wiki/Siberian_fur_trade, accessed 10 Feb 2017
245 In the Fullness of Time, 150 Years of Mennonite Sojourn in Russia, Dr. Walter Quiring, pg 158

73 Kirghiz 2 wheeled camel cart, public domain

this one in the house. Kumis was a good probiotic and thought to be beneficial for lung patients. Before fermentation, mare's milk has almost 40% more lactose than cow's milk, and drunk unfermented, is a strong laxative. Fermenting alters the lactose to a source of nutrition for people who are lactose intolerant.[246] But Maria and Gonja were always afraid to even taste it.

Susanna also thoroughly enjoyed kvass, which was another fermented drink made from black bread, sugar, a sprig of mint, and some sultanas, or golden raisins thrown in at the end. The yeast needed for fermentation was supplied by bacteria which always floated around in the air.

The Kirghiz loved Aaron and gave him an official banquet in their tent homes, or yurts. Aaron would be gone a whole weekend with the Kirghiz and he ate with them. They would kill an animal, and eat the whole thing, like a whole sheep, because they didn't have refrigeration to keep any left overs. They would gorge themselves, until they were so stuffed they could eat no more. Whatever else was left over was given to the dogs or thrown away. So they gorged themselves for a day or two, and when it was gone, they would fast, because they had eaten so much they didn't need anything for the next few days. Aaron once entertained the Kirghiz in his own home for a whole day, each Kirghiz drinking at least

---

[246] Wikipedia https://en.wikipedia.org/wiki/Kumis, October 24, 2016

20 cups of tea. The Kirghiz enjoyed tea like all Russians, but the Russian maids told Susanna later, that when they served the Kirghiz, they each put a half inch of butter on the top of their tea. Perhaps that is why their skin always glistened so. They ate everything Susanna cooked, and ate butter all by itself, instead of spreading it on bread.

The Kirghiz often gave Aaron gifts of beautiful furs. One day the Kirghiz, in order to show their appreciation, brought Aaron a gift of a horse and a young wolf they had caught. Of course, not to hurt their feelings, the gifts were accepted. Russian wolves were much larger and more fierce-some than American wolves. When the Mennonites first settled in Ukraine, three men with guns were needed to ride a troika cart or sleigh to protect themselves from the wolves on all sides around them. The Russian wolf indeed was to be feared. Aaron's young wolf was put on a chain, and had a little house to sleep in. But keeping a wolf in the city could prove to be too much of a problem. It was Marie's job to feed the wolf frozen rabbits. Giving the wolf these frozen rabbits was a good way of getting rid of excess rabbit that Susanna didn't want. The wolf was pretty tame with Marie. When she would come, he would act just like a dog, and wag his tail. He would put his feet up on her shoulders, and she could pet him. With Ronka, not so much. If Ronka came near, he would show his teeth and growl. Ronka was aways pretty careful around him. Gonja did not even go near him. With others, he was vicious, and Aaron didn't trust him.

Aaron kept the wolf chained to his house at the bottom of the stairway. One day a lady walked home past the Rempel house carrying a basket of fresh meat she had just bought at the market. That wolf tore loose from the chain, jumped over the fence, ran through the street, and chased that lady. He didn't do anything to her, but he took her meat. That is all he wanted; but that finished the wolf. Aaron said that was it! He knew he needed to get rid of the wolf although they had only kept him about a month.

Hunting and interacting with the Kirghiz was Aaron's recreation. Wildlife included elk, reindeer, wolverine, weasel, bobcat, lynx, fox, beaver, otter, squirrel, wild boar, the gigantic Siberian brown bear[247] and wolf. Aaron was well known throughout the whole region as the best hunter around and was a well-known hunting guide. Thus he became the hunting guide for Czar Nicholas II as well, when the Czar came to Siberia.[248]

---

[247] the wild boar, elk, and Siberian brown bear are considered to be the three main trophy animals of Russia. http://www.rushunting.com/siberian_brown_bear.html

[248] One individual thought Aaron had acted as hunting guide to Czar Nicholas II on Aaron's own estate in Gnadenfeld. Aaron never owned an estate, nor did his father Aron A. Rempel Sr. Czar Alexander I visited the (Mennonite) village of Lindenau April, 1818, and other royals visited the (Mennonite) villages of Steinbach, Juschanlee, and Ohrloff in the Molotschna on their way to their Crimean summer resort. However, after the assassination of Alexander II, the Czars did not travel freely any more. The most prominent person

When his business didn't take him away on long trips, Aaron went hunting practically every weekend which made Susanna very unhappy. She was always home alone, minus the fellowship of friends or family. Her unhappiness probably drove an even bigger wedge between them. Marie and the other children didn't see him much at all. As an adult, Marie remarked that she hardly knew her dad, he was away so much.

The Russian monarchy began to unravel by the summer of 1916. Five strong horses were needed to pull one plow. Government conscription drastically reduced farm production. Fewer consumer goods were available, inflation higher, railways less reliable, so the war became unpopular.[249] Rasputin interfered with the affairs of state, and as the confidant and spiritual advisor of the ailing, neurotic, superstitious empress, he may have had more to do with Nicholas' downfall than the Czar's own ineptitude as ruler.

When a strike occurred in a factory in Petrograd, March 3, 1917, the Czar disbanded the Duma and ordered the strikers back to work. Ultimately, these orders precipitated the revolution. The duma refused to disband and the army openly sided with the workers.[250]
By March 1917 factories had no more coal or wood, and the railway system was totally unpredictable and broken. Cold and hungry peasants were sullen and despaired of this hopeless war, shortages of candles, kerosene, bread, and salt. March 11, Czar Nicholas abdicated and Old Mother Russia was no more. The Czar, thinking he was abdicating in favor of his brother the Grand Duke Michael, actually signed away the Russian monarchy. "Land for the peasant!" and "All power to the people!" were shouted in jubilation.[251]

Once the Czar abdicated, his guards refused to protect him and his family. Without a government keeping law and order, soldiers refused to fight. Riots in the streets brought such chaos, the Red Cross units were disbanded. Mennonite orderlies were sent home. Mennonites found themselves in the unenviable position of being caught between the corrupt government of the Czar and his poor suffering subjects.

Lenin called for his followers to end the imperialist war, give land to the peasants, freedom to the people, and overthrow the provisional government. "All power to the soviets."[252]
With the collapse of the moderate, socialist, Menshevik provisional government, in July 1917, large

to visit the Molotschna Colony after that was the governor of the Taurida Province. The Molotschna Colony, A Heritage Remembered, Henry Bernard Tiessen, pg 92
[249] The Twilight of Imperial Russia, Richard Charques pp. 230-232
[250] Life and Times of a Renaissance Mennonite Teacher: Cornelius A. Klaassen: (1883-1919 and Beyond), Robert L. Klaassen, pg 51
[251] My Harp is Turned to Mourning, Al Reimer, pp. 269-270
[252] The Twilight of Imperial Russia, Richard Charques, pg 244

contingents deserted, taking their arms with them. Often these deserting soldiers plundered on their way home, and many joined anarchist robber bands. Other fresh troops about to be sent to the front, refused to go. Ukrainian peasants, emboldened by the chaos, began raiding their neighbors and seizing land.

A little girl named Susan was born to Susanna and Aaron July 17, 1917. She was named after her mother, and her mother's grandmother Susanna Matthies Dueck. Sadly, the midwife was drunk, baby Susan was sick, and she died soon after birth.

The region came under Bolshevik rule between the fall of 1917 and summer of 1918.

During a riot in 1917, triggered by an increase in the price of flour, a crowd stormed into the beautiful Ovsiannikova Department store, and began throwing all the merchandise into the street. All day long they just threw stuff into the street. They put into effect Karl Marx's slogan, "From each according to his ability, to each according to his needs." Suddenly all of Petropavlovsk seemed to have insatiable needs. All day long little Marie, Ronka, and Gonja, with their noses pressed against the window, watched people running past their home, arms loaded with merchandise from the department store. People ran out from every direction to pillage and loot. "Every man did that which was right in his own eyes." [253]

That evening, they saw a light glowing brighter and brighter in the sky over the city, in the direction of that store, and they heard fire sirens. That store burned all night long. It was thought that someone had carelessly lit a match in the wine cellar. The fire burned two days. Since the store was only three blocks away, both Aaron and Susanna were outside all night long putting out embers that landed on the roof or anywhere else in the yard, so their house would not catch on fire.[254]

From each according to his ability, to each according to his need. But thereafter, there was no more "ability." All the goods were gone, with no more capital to procure more. Each one, from the former wealthiest to the poorest, did without. Communism proved to be the ability of equal sharing of want and misery. They couldn't even get shoes that would fit when their old ones wore out, and people ended up wearing homemade sandals, even in winter.

Since Bolsheviks had the guns, they gained power in all the large cities along the Trans-Siberian

---

[253] Judges 21:25
[254] http://www.petropavl.kz/module/mg106_1.shml The department store's charred walls stood several years, until dismantled in 1926

Railroad, from Petropavlovsk, to Omsk, Novosibirsk, Krasnoyarsk, Irkutsk, and beyond.

Russian peasants and farmers of German descent in the countryside were not sympathetic to Communism. These Siberian peasants were rich and satisfied with life. Previously no gentry resided in Siberia to stifle their economic success. However, the people in Siberia also were not sympathetic to the White Army, who represented arbitrary requisitions of grain and men for the military, high taxation, and extensive corruption.

May 14, 1918, Czech Legion former prisoners of war, caught behind the lines of war in the West, were put in charge of security for the Trans-Siberian Railroad from Samara to Irkutsk. They had interrupted the Bolshevik advance in the summer of 1918. Support in remote Siberia for the White Russian cause was only upheld by the presence of Allied forces and the Czech League. The Russian Aristocracy had been too stubborn and slow to implement social and political reforms.[255] Their reluctance cost them dearly. The Czechs were eager to return home.[256]

Another little girl, also named Susan, was born to Susanna and Aaron December 19, 1918. [257]

74 Ovsiannikova Department Store looted and burned to the ground, public domain

Russians all drank tea. With the railway system in western Russia so snarled, Russia urgently

---

[255] Civil War in Siberia, The Anti-Bolshevik Government of Admiral Kolchak. 1918-1920, Jonathan D. Smele, ed., from a review by Eva M. Stolberg http://www.h-net.org./reviews/showrev.php?id=1925,

[256] Hierschau: An Example of Russian Mennonite Life, Helmut T. Hubert, pg 226

[257] Because the parents still wanted a girl named after her mother and her great grandmother Susanna Matthies Dueck, she was given the same name as her sister who was born earlier but died in infancy. This was a familiar naming pattern among the Mennonites. In fact, Susanna Krause Rempel's own brother Jacob was given his name after an earlier brother named Jacob who had died in infancy.

needed commodities of all sorts. Aaron, once again desperately needing a way to support his growing family, decided to go into the tea business. The Trans-Siberian Railway had been inspired by the beckoning wealth of China. With World War I being fought in the West, and social unrest between Czar and peasants, maybe it would be good to have his money invested in a commodity that everyone used. Tea was hard to get. He thought he could make money on tea. A wealthy man and Aaron formed a business partnership and traveled to the far east, to China. From Petropavlovsk, the Trans-Siberian Railway took them to Omsk, Novosibirsk, Krasnoyarsk, Taishet, Irkutsk, Ulan Ude, Chita, Nerchinsk, Birobidzhan, Khabarovsk, Ussuriysk, to finally arrive at Vladivostok. His partner bought all sorts of commodities, while Aaron bought expensive vanilla and big bales of tea.

Since 1891, an estimated 200,000 Polish rebels, Russian criminals, anarchists, Bolsheviks, and other political prisoners had been exiled to Siberia. Often when train travelers stopped to buy food along the way, they encountered baskarovas (little jails) with such prisoners.

At one of these train stations, when the sun had just dipped beyond the horizon, gas lamps were being lit, and evening stars were just beginning to appear, Aaron disembarked to buy bread and cheese. Returning to the train, he walked past a baskarova with Bolshevik soldiers imprisoned inside. One of the prisoners put his hands through the barred window, and a voice begged him, "Sir, please, please. We are starving in here. Please can you spare us some of your bread? We have had nothing to eat for days." Aaron couldn't see the one calling out to him, and could barely discern men who were imprisoned. Thinking, "I wonder what that poor soul has done?" Aaron shoved his French bread into the faceless, outstretched hands. It wouldn't be much amongst so many, but it would be better than nothing. Aaron then trudged back to buy more bread for his own dinner, and thought no more about the incident.

Today, typical cargo time is 25 days from Moscow to Vladivostok, but during the days of the Russo-Japanese war, the single train track impeded the arrival of war material to the war front, and delayed the removal of wounded to hospitals. Trains remained sidetracked lengthy periods, waiting for oncoming trains to pass. It took Aaron months to procure his bales of tea and then return home. All the while, Susanna was home alone—waiting. . . waiting . . . waiting alone.

Time of Terror

"Property is Theft and Riches a Crime" [258]

John 10:10
The thief cometh not but to steal, to kill, and to destroy.

Psalm 91:1-9
He that dwelleth in the secret place of the most High shall abide under the shadow of the Almighty.
I will say of the LORD, He is my refuge and my fortress: my God; in him will I trust.
Surely he shall deliver thee from the snare of the fowler, and from the noisome pestilence.
He shall cover thee with his feathers, and under his wings shalt thou trust: his truth shall be thy shield and buckler.
Thou shalt not be afraid for the terror by night; or for the arrow that flieth by day; . . .
Because thou hast made the LORD, which is my refuge, even the most High, thy habitation;

The Mensheviks under Admiral Kerensky headed the provisional government for a few months, trying to rally Russia's armies against the Germans. With insubordination and mutiny in the ranks and military forces vanishing, by November 1917, the Provisional Government collapsed.[259] By January 1918, Bolsheviks used the Cheka[260] (secret police) and Red Army to consolidate power. Sudden arrests in the middle of the night and questioning under torture were their tools. Often the poor detainee was never to be seen alive again.[261]

While Aaron was probably on the Trans Siberian Railway, seeking tea, the Cheka was in Gnaden-feld, rounding up Kulak's, or those who were now considered enemies of the workers because they had formerly employed Russians.

Agents from the Gnadenfeld revolutionary committee came to arrest Aaron for the "crime" of once employing 150 men in a farm implement factory he owned next door to his home. By definition of the revolution, that made him an enemy of the working class. *The Bolsheviks in an official bulletin called for a "merciless war" and 'the most pitiless . . . mass terror' against such enemies of the*

---

[258] Mennonites in Ukraine, Amid Civil War and Anarchy (1917-1920) translated and edited by John B. Toews, pp. 44-45
[259] Escape to Freedom, Cornelius Funk, pg 40
[260] Cheka 'the much feared Bolshevik secret police, later renamed OGPU, NKVD, and KGB. The Cheka used arrest, torture, execution, exile to Siberia and other slave labor camps. The purpose always remained the same—to exterminate "the enemies of the working class" which means all those who did not favor the Bolshevik dictatorship. http://alphahistory.com/russianrevolution/cheka/ https://www.systemaspetsnaz.com/history-of-the-cheka-ogpu-nkvd-mgb-kgb-fsb
[261] "A Letter to My Children; The Memoirs of Arthur G. Rempel", pg 29

Socialist revolution as employers. "Capitalists," the Cheka charged, "had for centuries been sucking out . . . all the life juice of the toilers." The Secret Police agents tore up boards from floors and walls [in their former home] *looking for him. By then, however, the factory was bankrupt—an economic casualty of World War I and Aaron was gone, managing a business in Siberia."* [262]

General Wrangel pushed forward from the Crimea, enabling some of the men who had been fighting the bandits in the Crimean mountains to come back home. [263] *Amongst them was Carl Rempel, who had returned to Gnadenfeld in the winter of 1917, his toes frozen from riding on top of freight cars, manning the artillery on those armored trains.*

Carl Rempel had a friend who had served in the Czar's personal guard. Shortly after the Czar's execution, Carl's friend saw Anastasia in a hotel. He saluted her but she immediately turned away not wanting to be recognized. He heard later that she had been saved by a feather pillow and was spirited out of the country. The Royal princesses had previously shown great compassion toward their Russian soldiers by visiting and nursing the seriously wounded on the Red Cross train. *Carl himself was many times assigned to guard a route taken by members of the royal family.* [264]

Carl was surprised to see changes to the village since his absence. People had begun to relax their strict rules. He was shocked to find Susanna's younger sister Agatha had played hooky from school to attend a dancing class. [265]

Late in January 1918, in Tiegenhof, Schoenfeld District, north of the Molotschna Colony, dogs starting barking furiously. Almost immediately, rifle butts banged on the door of a home, demanding admission. When the door was opened, the "guests" lined up the youngest members of the family against a wall, with their arms held up high. One bandit went through all their pockets.

At another home, bandits lined the brothers against the wall and shot them. The young daughter, while holding her little brother only ten months old, ran in front of her father to shield him from the intruders, but she was shot dead. The baby fell to the floor, largely unhurt. The bandits took another adult brother to his home to have him open his safe, but before he could even open it, he was shot in the back of the head. The next day, the remaining family members went to a neighbor's home, and saw the door had been shot full of holes, with three bodies left in the room. The neighbor

[262] <u>Los Angeles Times</u>, Wednesday, August 4, 1982, "A Search for Ancestral Soviet Home", William C. Rempel, page 16
[263] "Gnadenfeld, Molotschna, South Russia 1835-1943", J.C Krause, pg 9
[264] "Memoir of Agatha and Carl Rempel", as told to K. R. Lockwood, pg 10, also see regarding recent DNA studies of murdered family members https://www.livescience.com/7693-case-closed-murders-russian-czars-family.html accessed 13 April, 2018
[265] Ibid, pg 9

who lived in that house came staggering back home. He had been shot in the head, but the bullet missed his brain, coming out of his mouth, shattering his teeth. He had fallen unconscious to the ground, so the bandits had thought he was dead. Later he regained consciousness.[266]

Anarchy was hard at work. The murderers had threatened the Mennonites that they would not be allowed to bury their dead. Many people, including Russians, gathered for the funeral, and the bodies were buried in one mass grave. The pastor spoke on remaining faithful, and being prepared to meet the Lord; their only consolation was in Jesus. "The Lord giveth, and the Lord taketh away. Blessed be the name of the Lord.[267] Above all, love your enemies, no matter what the cost." Many of these violent anarchists and "political activists" were released Russian criminals.[268] The people later discovered that these brigands were from Sofiefka and included three Red Army guards (Bolsheviks).[269]

There was much prayer both in private and in special meetings that implored the Lord to keep the threatening cloud away from us. It came nevertheless. Like a dark storm the waves of anarchism engulfed our entire region and spread misery and fear. [270]

Red army detachments reached Halbstadt, Molotschna February 5, 1918, and suddenly the color red showed up everywhere: red banners, red caps, the red revolutionaries.[271] The "Halbstadt days of Terror," lasting until April 18, began with wide ranging horror of robbery, violence, rape, and murder. Reds requisitioned household goods, cattle, horses, and farm machinery. *The competing White and Red armies, crisscrossing their villages, were constantly demanding food and shelter. The Czar had been their protection. But how could they expect the former Czar or any government to protect them if they were not willing to protect the Czar?[272]*

At first, the Reds only took the best things, but once the more desirable items were gone, they grabbed whatever they found. The poor, plundered victims tried to hide their valuables, but the Reds were quite successful in locating them if they brought along their womenfolk, who did the searching. Torture became a common method for extracting the location of hidden goods.

Everybody thinks only of himself. All property belongs to the state before it is divided up after that . . . . This is the famous doctrine of socialism, cooked up in the Russian witches cauldron! . . . The

---

[266] Consider the Threshing Stone, Jacob J. Rempel pp. 71-74; Hope Springs Eternal, John P. Nickel, pp. 181-185
[267] Job 1:21
[268] Hope Springs Eternal, John P. Nickel, pg 45
[269] Consider the Threshing Stone, Jacob J. Rempel, pp. 72-74, 154
[270] Mennonites in Ukraine Amid Civil War and Anarchy (1917-1920) translated and edited by John B. Toews, pp. 171-175
[271] Escape to Freedom, Cornelius Funk, pg 34
[272] The Russländer, Sandra Birdsell, pg 117

seed grain has all been ground up for food, so how can the land be seeded now? . . . then naturally there can be no harvest. Yet the fruit of all the evil seeds sown in Russia now grows in profusion and ripens quickly.[273]

All ideas of mine and thine . . . mixed. "Your farms, horses, wagons and money, no longer belong to you. They belong to no one and everyone." Much of what had been inherited, worked for, saved for, now ran away like water . . . then God asked the question, "Have you been covetous and avaricious? . . . The idea that they and all their possessions belonged to God was completely incomprehensible to them and never actualized (in practice). There was a second class who said, "My possessions belong to me . . . . I serve God with them" . . . . Some gave a tenth, but added "The rest belongs to me" . . . . There was a third group who said simply, "My possessions belong to the Lord . . . . I give a tenth . . . but it's all the Lord's. These people did not consider it a sin to own a farm. If the Lord provided it, they could possess it and sanctify it with thanksgiving. Yet their hearts did not cling to it . . . . These people had an easier time of it. Their possessions belonged to God and so they calmly allowed God to take them away or continue to keep them if He so desired . . . . Naturally there were not many of these people . . . . God performed a serious operation to free the heart from mammon and to make room for Himself . . . .

A Bible conference in Gnadenfeld especially emphasized that all the suffering did not stem from one human being or another, but came directly from God and should be accepted as such. God did not allow the Bolsheviks to come. He sent them! They were God's messengers sent for our salvation . . . . But the testing was too severe and lasted too long . . . "the Lord has given and the Lord has taken away, blessed be the name of the Lord" came into conflict with the principle . . . that the Bolsheviks deserved punishment. The Bible studies continued . . . . but deep inside people resented what God had sent. [274]

In the vacuum of law and order created by civil war, unparalleled lawlessness of roving soldier bandit bands, especially the robber band of Nestor Makhno, swept in with unprecedented savagery. Barking dogs announced the arrival of pillaging, wanton killing, raping, sheer terror, only to have the bandits vanish in their Russian native villages, where they were often protected by an approving local population. Indeed, even today, Nestor Makhno has become somewhat of a folk idol, sort of a "Robin Hood" to an amazing number of Ukrainians.[275] Rape was so widespread, even as late as 1920, at

---

[273] Hope Springs Eternal, John P. Nickel, pg 198

[274] Mennonites in Ukraine Amid Civil War and Anarchy (1917-1920) translated and edited by John B. Toews, pg 161   Adolf A. Reimer, "How Did It Happen?" Rundschau-Kalendar (1930), 38-54

[275] Mennonite Historian, a publication of the Mennonite Heritage Centre for Mennonite Brethren Studies in Canada, pp. 2, 4-5 There are a number of statues dedicated to Makhno in his hometown of Guliaipole, and a Ukrainian bank commemorative coin featuring him. This article delves into the facts that Nestor Makhno was not always personally responsible for ordering all the brutality that the bandits

least 100 women and girls were still being treated for syphilis in the Colony of Chortitza alone. As pacifists, the Mennonites were powerless to defend themselves and couldn't distinguish the Red Army from the robber bands.

Nestor Makhno, son of a Ukrainian peasant, had been incarcerated in the Lubyanka Prison where he likely was introduced to the philosophy of Anarchism by fellow prisoners, *then released when the Czar abdicated. He was given a hero's welcome in his home town of Guliaipole,*[276] *about 44 miles northeast of the Molotschna Colony, not that far from Rosenhof, Schoenfeld, the estate where Susanna had been born. As a youngster, Nestor had worked for some German Mennonites, where he developed an unbridled fury, an age-old hatred toward all German Mennonites for all their alleged exploitation in the past. "Go and plunder the plunderers!. . .foreign blood suckers ought to be made to pay twice as much . . ."*[277]

Nestor was an anarchist, and a bold, brash strategist. His first order of business was to acquire arms, munitions, and other goods, by "requisitioning" them from neighboring farmers and factory owners, especially the German Mennonites. Nestor Makhno formed his robber band numbering about 3,000 (some estimates run as high as 100,000 at its height)[278] *under a black flag with "Death" inscribed in white letters,*[279] *or a black banner announcing, "Anarchy is the Mother of All Order."*

Day and night Mennonite men were constantly alert, unable to sleep, not daring to even take their clothes off, dead with fatigue. As soon as a dog barked, everyone jumped up and listened for approaching horses and footsteps.[280]

The Russian army experienced massive desertions when peasant soldiers, who heard about the "requisitioning" going on at home, wanted their fair share. The deserters left with whatever guns and ammunition they still had and commandeered trains to get home, resulting in snarling the railway system further, which meant hospital trains were often side tracked or even left without engines, with very severely injured soldiers dying like flies.

---

committed. The Ukrainian peasants, either under other batkas (bandit leaders) or under their own lawless initiatives, did not always strictly follow Makhno's orders, but were certainly stirred on by Makhno's rhetoric. In either case, the amount of barbaric bloodshed remains a historical fact.

[276] My Harp is Turned to Mourning, Al Reimer, pp. 272-273
[277] The Russländer, Sandra Birdsell, pg 12
[278] Mennonites in Ukraine, Amid Civil War and Anarchy (1917-1920) translated and edited by John B. Toews, pg 149
[279] Ibid. pg 141
[280] Master's Thesis, Selbstschutz, Josephine Chipman, pg 157

75 Nestor Makhno, public domain

Unfortunately, the prosperous Schoenfeld Colony (also known as Brasol) was located extremely close to Guliaipole, Makhno's headquarters. Before World War I broke out in 1914, each farmer possessed steam engines, self-tying binders, and even some tractors with ploughs. Many estate owners now also sported new automobiles, like the Opel Doppelphaeton. When these estate owners and farmers had planted their fruit orchards and their "forests of hard woods" in that tree-less steppe, had they shared seedings with their Russian neighbors? What if they had freely given a tenth of their wealth to their Russian neighbors and had invested in their economic development? Had they been good stewards of the wealth which God had entrusted to them? Had they been truly generous in their wages to their Russian farm laborers and domestic help? Had they made their excellent schooling available to their Russian neighbor children? Some Mennonite stories include tales like one wealthy estate owner, who suddenly dismissed his faithful Russian foreman without cause. The *Russian had served for about a dozen years, and then had nowhere else to go, nowhere else to live.*[281]

---

[281] Hope Springs Eternal, John P. Nickel, pg 169

Until the war, these German Mennonites had, or thought they had, good relations with their Russian neighbors. One account is of a Jacob J. Rempel,[282] who visited a former Russian maid and her family during the time of the bandit raids. He was even invited to stay with them overnight and was hosted in a friendly manner. The family made sure to have him sleep in a room with no windows. In the morning, he couldn't open the door to get out. His former Russian maid had slept in front of the door during the night, protecting him, so no one could get to him, showing the extent of the Russian character of hospitality.[283]

In those days, it became commonplace when one heard furiously barking dogs, for Makhnovites to suddenly appear, go storming into homes, swearing and screaming, demanding a large kontributsia, (contribution of money), a favorite form of extortion. They demanded the wedding ring off the finger of a woman, and took her finger with the ring, when the ring wouldn't quickly slip off. They knew German Mennonite women were excellent cooks so demanded a good chicken dinner or borscht with watermelon and rollkucken be prepared. After the meal, they lined the whole family up in the bedroom and made them watch the rape of all the women of the family, from the young teens to elderly matrons. They forced the family to swiftly load their own farm wagons with all the goods taken from the home, and do it with a smile. Often, men were clubbed, hacked, or shot to death. The ongoing horror seemed to be the normal state of affairs.[284] Mutilations were particularly gruesome, violence for the sake of violence.

On one occasion Makhno bandits were in Gnadenfeld, bursting into homes with intimidating force, rummaging through pantries, dressers and trunks searching for weapons and ammunition, demanding entertainment, too. Jacob and Cornelius Krause remembered this incident with "sad" pride how their courageous mother Agatha remained steadfast at her post.[285] In a short period of time, shops, kitchens, cellars, cupboards, and chests were completely emptied.[286] All personal belongings were being systematically liberated. Often, what was not taken was then senselessly destroyed. They might slash feather ticks and the barley straw mattresses, underneath the ticks, and scatter the feathers to the four winds, or slash portraits on the walls. Whatever was left was often burned to the ground.

Changes of clothing were all confiscated, including even a change of underwear. Any piece of clothing that had not been buried in the ground or hidden deep in straw stacks prior to the arrival of the bandits was irretrievably lost. The only manner in which some succeeded in keeping some

[282] no relation of Aaron and Susanna Rempel in this story
[283] Consider the Threshing Stone, Writings of Jacob J. Rempel, pp. 29, 95
[284] Mennonites in Ukraine, Amid Civil War and Anarchy (1917-1920) translated and edited by John B. Toews, pg 7
[285] "Gnadenfeld, Molotschna, South Russia 1835-1943", J.C Krause, pg 9
[286] Mennonites in Ukraine, Amid Civil War and Anarchy (1917-1920) translated and edited by John B. Toews, pg 10

139

of their better clothing was by covering it with patches of odds and ends of old, worn pieces of clothing, and wearing the same things, day in and day out.

As time went on, it became impossible to meet the demands of the almost daily raids. The bandit searches became ever more intensified, more thorough. So no matter how cleverly someone had tried hiding a few precious items, they always seemed to find them, as if the devil himself were directing their searches.

The bandits seemed to believe German Mennonites had inexhaustible resources of every kind to satisfy their lusts. Repeatedly they subjected them to plundering raids during October and November. To the Mennonites, those two months seemed like an eternity. Villages closest to Makhno's headquarters in Guiliapole were the hardest hit. Except for the dreaded Cheka, no other group was feared as much as Makhno and his band of robbers. Nothing could even remotely compare with them in fiendishness.

Sermons in this troubling time of terror included a study of the Lord's Prayer:

"And Lead Us Not into Temptation"
God works with us in such a way that troubles small and large are thrust upon us . . . God is testing our faith in the furnace of adversity making us vigilant so that someday we will stand before Him, more pure than the purest gold.

"But Deliver Us From Evil"
. . . the present time of adversity, tears, and sorrow . . . makes us yearn for that glorious time when sin will be no more, when evil has been overcome, and when God shall wipe away all tears from our eyes.

"For Thine is the Kingdom, and the Power, and the Glory Forever."
. . . the fruits of their disturbances we see around us everywhere: murders, bloodshed, fires, robberies, and destruction. Destruction is what Satan can do very well . . . . Indeed it does seem as if Satan has all the power of the world in his hands now . . . . The waves of anarchy are surging wildly throughout the nation, but when Your Son Jesus Christ, the Redeemer comes, they shall be stilled, for Thine is the power from eternity to eternity! Come Lord Jesus! . . . In the name of the Father all knees shall bow before Him, whether in heaven, on the earth, or under the earth . . . .[287]

---

[287] Hope Springs Eternal, John P. Nickel, pp 62-64

The pacifist Mennonites were urged to never desert their God, even with bloodthirsty bandits pounding on the front door[288] . . . . *heaven and earth shall pass away, but my words shall not pass away* [289] . . . . *And God shall wipe away all tears from our eyes.* [290] They believed they must not resist the bandits in any way to protect their property or even their lives, but they were commanded to love their enemies, to bless them that cursed them. Perhaps their best defense was to hide or run away. *When they persecute you in one city, flee ye into another.* [291]

March 3, 1918, Lenin declared peace at Brest Litovsk. The war had brought nothing but tragedy of countless wasted lives to the Russian people, with no profit, no gain, *but the cost of defeat brought about a still greater and continuing ordeal, the cataclysmic aftermath of revolution.*[292] As part of the peace agreement, Germany was to occupy Ukraine, to help the Bolsheviks quell any Ukrainian nationalism that might arise.

. . . the German Army invaded Russia, which was virtually defenseless since nearly the entire Russian army had deserted.[293] *April 19, 1918, German troops occupied the German Mennonite colonies in the Ukraine. The German army troops were totally surprised to find the people who lived there spoke German. How was it that these people, these Mennonites, who apparently had lived there for generations, still kept their German language and customs?*

Ukraine then experienced alternating brief spells of relative calm, followed by prolonged periods of chaos and cataclysmic lawlessness, of sheer terror. War, revolution, civil war, anarchy, famine and disease utterly destroyed what had been prosperous, peaceful and idyllic. *"Go and plunder the plunderers! . . . foreign blood suckers ought to be made to pay twice as much . . . terror, pillage, and murder was . . . the order of the day . . ."* [294]

---

[288] Ibid, pg 65
[289] Mark 13:31
[290] Revelation 7:17
[291] Matt. 10:23
[292] The Twilight of Imperial Russia, Richard Charques, pg 211
[293] Love and Remembrance, Helene (Rempel) Klassen, editor and translator, pg 23
[294] The Russländer, Sandra Birdsell, pg 12

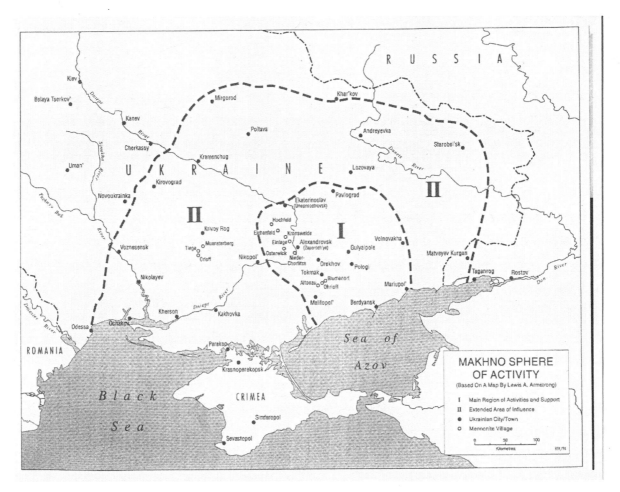

76 map Makhno's Sphere of Activity, <u>Mennonite Historical Atlas</u>, William Schroeder, Helmut T. Huebert, pg 63, used by permission

Few places in Russia experienced such an unbridled era of wanton slaughter, rape and pillage as those areas of Ukraine, under this "Little Father Makhno." [295]

The German army was received as the Mennonite saviors, their deliverers. They talked together, sang "Deutschland, Deutschland über alles,"[296] and even participated in German festivals.[297] However, in their eagerness to welcome the German army, while their Ukrainian neighbors were watching, did the Mennonites ever realize their actions might be considered treason, that they were now traitors, giving aid and comfort to the enemy? How short-sighted was this? Would the German army be there indefinitely to protect them? Could this be just plain folly and stupidity? But their relief from the sheer terror earlier was so great, they did not pause to consider.

---

[295] <u>Miracles of Grace and Judgment</u>, Gerhard P. Schroeder, pp. 43-44
[296] "Germany, Germany, Over All"
[297] <u>Mennonites in Ukraine, Amid Civil War and Anarchy (1917-1920)</u> translated and edited by John B. Toews, pp. 49-50

To Selbstschutz or not to Selbstschutz

The only thing necessary for the triumph of evil is for good men to do nothing. – Edmund Burke

Submit yourselves to every ordinance of man for the Lord's sake; whether it be to the king, as supreme; Or unto governors, as unto them that are sent by Him for the punishment of evildoers, and for the praise of them that do well. For so is the will of God, that with well doing ye may put to silence the ignorance of foolish men. I Peter 2:13-15

Mennonites were Anabaptists who believed only those who confessed their faith in Jesus Christ should be baptized; therefore they believed they should not baptize infants. For this, Anabaptists in Switzerland in previous centuries, had been persecuted, hunted down, imprisoned, and killed by beheading, drowning, being drawn and quartered, or even being buried alive. One Mennonite *had a white-hot bolt pushed through his tongue for having publicly testified to his faith. That bolt had been passed on from one generation to the next.* [298]

In Holland, Mennonites lead a somewhat peaceful life for a time under the pastoral leadership of Menno Simons, a former Catholic priest. These peaceful people believed the Bible to be the Word of God, in spiritual regeneration or a "new birth," and in following the commands of Christ for a life of love, forgiveness, reconciliation, and peace. They believed in a life of non-resistance,[299] otherwise known as pacifism, absolutely refusing military service. With the reintroduction of Spanish rule in Holland with its dreaded Roman Catholic Inquisition, relentless persecution brought about the death of two thousand Mennonites in the Netherlands.[300]

The Mennonites, or followers of Meno Simons, were invited into Prussia and given religious freedom and exemption from military duty. Their progressive farming techniques led to the building of dykes, building Dutch style windmills, and draining large areas of marshland in the largely uninhabited Vistula lowlands of Prussia. They persisted in using their native Dutch language in the pulpit for almost 250 years and thought of themselves as Dutch for a long time. Gradually they accepted Plautdietsch, West Prussian words and phrases mixed with their native Dutch, as their ev-

---

[298] The Russländer, Sandra Birdsell, pg 69

[299] The Principle of Nonresistance, As Held by the Mennonite Church, John Horsch, pp. 22-23 "We confess that civil government is necessary and is a divine appointment. Romans 13, that every man should be subject and obedient to a higher power, not only to a mild and peaceful but also to a tyrannical government, for the reason that there is no power but of God. Therefore all believers, under whatever government they may live, will not complain of heavy burdens, nor will they resist the government or cause trouble or uproar on account of what they may be called upon to bear . . . we are ready to obey the civil government in anything that may be asked of us. And if the government, contrary to justice and right, confiscates our property and reduces us to poverty, we bear and suffer it, since it is impossible for us to escape such oppression without transgression . . . . We obey the government in everything that may be asked of us that is not contrary to the will of God."

[300] Mennonite Foods & Folkways from South Russia, Vol I, Norma Jost Voth, pp. 15-17

eryday language, the language of home.[301] They flourished under Kaiser Frederick the Great. Eventually Kaiser Frederick Wilhelm II, wanting to build up his military might, thought to keep the increasing numbers of Mennonites in check by levying a heavy military tax and forbidding them from buying any land not already belonging to Mennonites.[302] The practice of non-resistance was increasingly difficult to keep during the Napoleonic Wars.[303]

Russia defeated the Turks. She then needed colonists in Ukraine to act as a buffer from the Ottoman Turks to make the land more stable and less vulnerable to invasion. Catherine the Great, herself a German princess, knew these German people were industrious, hardworking, honest, thrifty, generous toward the less fortunate, and could teach the Russian peasants how to work the land. She realized they could accomplish much in a short time to tame the wild treeless steppes, with grass so high even a man on horseback was barely visible. It was a *barren wasteland of a prairie overgrown with useless "bitterkraut" and inhabited only by foxes, field mice,* and nomadic, pillaging bands of barbaric, brown skinned Tartars, called the Nogaies. These were Muslim descendants of the Mongols,[304] *who developed a fondness for horses, which sometimes disappeared from the barns at night, and Ukrainian peasants known as Cossacks (who tilled the soil with wooden plows and harvested the crops with flail and sickle).*[305]

So, in 1763 Empress Catherine the Great issued a Manifesto, inviting German Catholics, Lutherans, and Mennonites to settle the area. She offered Mennonite farmers an exemption from military service in perpetuity, freedom of religion, cheap land, temporary exemption from taxation, and self-government, if they would come and develop this largely uninhabited territory. Thus the influx of German Mennonite families began. Mennonites were allowed to evangelize the Muslim population. However, one main stipulation was Mennonites were to refrain from trying to convert the Russians from the Russian Orthodox faith. In a region only inhabited by the fierce Nogai, nomadic cruel Tartars, or runaway serfs, the colonists initially settled on the banks of the Dnieper River. They brought with them their High German Bibles and song books, some Dutch Bibles, and the Dutch Martyrs Mirror (a book on Mennonite martyrs similar to Foxes Book of Martyrs).[306]

---

[301] Mennonite Foods and Folkways from South Russia, Vol I, Norma Jost Voth, pg 16, 20
[302] From Bolshevik Russia to America, A Mennonite Family Story, Henry D. Rempel, pp. 3-5
[303] Mennonites in Ukraine Amid Civil War and Anarchy (1917-1920), translated and edited by John B. Toews, pg 177
[304] "Gnadenfeld, Molotschna, South Russia, 1835-1943", J.C. Krause, pg 5
[305] Life and Times of a Renaissance Mennonite Teacher: Cornelius A. Klaassen: (1883-1919 and Beyond), Robert L. Klaassen, pp. 6,9
[306] Mennonite Foods & Folkways from South Russia, Vol I, Norma Jost Voth, pg 16, 17 A few Yiddish and some Russian words, including many Ukrainian food words, were added to the dialect while the Mennonites lived in Russia.

As a people, the Mennonites knew little of Germany's history for they had never been part of it.[307] However, Mennonite history was conspicuously absent from their school curriculum. They were not taught the historical or Biblical reasons for their views on pacifism, or non-resistance. They just grew up knowing that they were Mennonite, and Mennonites believed in non-resistance, so they were pacifists.[308]

Following the terrible time of anarchist raids and terror, the German army finally advanced all the way into Ukraine. As their first order of business, they occupied Guliaipole, burned down Mackhno's headquarters, and executed Makhno's brother.[309] The Germans, in their army uniforms, caught three well-known bandits and murderers, and shot them in the sight of everybody. The Ukrainians were watching.

The German army brought peace and order out of totally lawless, anarchy, absolute chaos, massive social upheaval. Finally an end came to the reign of terror.[310] It was little wonder that the Mennonites welcomed the Germans as liberators.[311]

Then too, the German Army's presence brought the German Mennonites a way to recover their lost possessions. The German soldiers ordered that stolen horses, wagons, and other goods be returned. In the meantime, the Ukrainians had learned how nice it was to sleep on feather pillows. The kerosene lamps gave such nice bright light. And what fine field horses! The communist government had told these poor peasants they had a right to take the property of others. During the German occupation, a group of these poor peasants came and begged a wealthy farmer for permission to help harvest his crop in return for a portion. Unfortunately that farmer called them lazy and sicced his dogs on them. If only the Mennonites had at that moment "turned the other cheek" and "after the coat had been taken, given the cloak also." Or, if they had followed Luke 6:30 *Give to every man that asketh of thee; and of him that taketh away thy goods ask them not again*, perhaps they would have been spared such rampant killings later. However, rarely did a Mennonite refuse to accept the return of his goods.

Some of the poorest Mennonites lost the desire to acquire nice things in those days, for they realized that all their earthly treasures could easily be taken away. They might be allowed to keep an ugly old horse, perhaps a small wagon without the coveted springs, a wagon that only bumped along, but would still carry them.

---

[307] Mennonite Foods and Folkways from South Russia, Vol II, Norma Jost Voth, pg 36
[308] Czars, Soviets, & Mennonites, John B. Toews, pp. 41-43
[309] My Harp is Turned to Mourning, Al Reimer, pg 322
[310] Czars, Soviets, & Mennonites, John B. Toews, pg 80-85
[311] My Harp is Turned to Mourning, Al Reimer, pp. 316, 317

With the quartering of German soldiers in the Mennonite villages, now there were guns, loaded and stacked against the walls inside pacifist Mennonite homes.

To selbstschutz or not to selbstschutz, that was the question. Initially, military drills without weapons were held. The more wealth a person had, the more he was in favor of the selbstschutz, or self-defense units, to protect his property. Furthermore, it was considered a most worthy goal to protect the honor of one's mother and sisters. In arguments for and against participating in a selbstschutz, the argument for was rationalized by saying "I only defend myself against the one who is attacking me." [312]

But where was their faith and fear of God in participating in a German armed militia in the midst of their Russian neighbors? What had happened to their history of non-resistance? Had they forgotten the commandment, "Thou shalt not kill?" Had they forgotten that Jesus had commanded them to love their enemies and bless them that persecute you?

Romans 13 categorically decrees that all government is instituted by God, whether good or evil, fair or unfair, with the high calling, the duty of government to punish evil. Therefore all forms of government are from God by divine decree. The Bible doesn't prefer one type of government over another. Therefore, no matter how bad a particular government is, God does not condone any rebellion. And in the Old Testament in the times of the judges, when government ceased to exist, "every man did that which was right in his own eyes." [313]

The Mennonite status of non-resistance was definitely a privilege, a privilege that could not exist without the protection of the state, a privilege defended by those Russians who faithfully served in the military. *What should Christians do in the face of anarchy . . . when murderers and rapists were at your door, did you calmly submit to the lowest form of evil or resist?[314] Had they forgotten their history of martyrdom for the cause of not taking up the sword? Had they forgotten what Menno Simons taught of nonresistance?*

> *"We teach and confess that we know of no other sword, of no insurrection in Christ's Kingdom and church, except the sword of the Spirit, God's Word . . . The aid of the*

---

[312] Author's mother Gonja (Agatha) Rempel often remarked throughout the author's childhood, that if all the Pacifist German Mennonites had fought in the White Army, they could have turned back the tide of the Bolsheviks and saved Russia from Communism. However, it is difficult to determine what would actually have happened. The what if's in history largely remain "what if." But in researching the history of this period, it is highly doubtful that could have been the outcome. A huge disparity between the Romanov Czarist wealth and the poverty of the Russian peasants existed. The Russian peasants just wanted land enough to support themselves, and liberty from taxation and conscription into the military. Even if they were in the Czar's White Army, their hearts were not in his interests. Why should they kill and be killed to preserve his lavish, extravagant lifestyle? Also, because of the prevalent Marxist propaganda, the Russians had begun to develop a spirit of entitlement.

[313] sermon on Judges 21:25 by John MacArthur "How God Restrains Evil in Society," February 22, 2015

[314] Mennonites in Ukraine, Amid Civil War and Anarchy (1917-1920) translated and edited by John B. Toews, pg 5

sword is forbidden to all true Christians . . . Through God's grace which has appeared to us we have transformed our swords to plough shares and our lances to sickles. We will sit under the true vine Christ and under the Lord and Prince of eternal peace, never again will we give ourselves to any struggle or war." [315]

By May 1918, the German army had helped the Mennonites form Selbstschutz units throughout the Molotschna Colony and Ukraine. The young men particularly were drawn into volunteering for the selbstschutz, lured by the dashing uniforms with their shiny buttons and innate duty of protecting one's mother, sisters, and other village females from the depredations of marauding robbers. Those who volunteered rationalized this as strictly an act of self defense, distinct from participation in war. Others viewed it as renouncing Mennonitism itself, as a total compromise of nonresistance.

In the debates that ensued over whether or not to participate in a selbstschutz, some held fast self defense was less sinful than direct military involvement. However, *others considered self defense a worse sin than regular army service, citing Romans 13:4 — that God has ordained the use of the sword by government both for punishment of wrongdoing to protect the innocent, and defense from foreign enemies. Where in the Bible does God say to organize a Selbstschutz?* [316]

One Mennonite Brethren Church in Alexandertal opposed the Selbstschutz with a sermon from Isaiah 59:1,2 *"Behold the Lord's hand is not too short to save, nor His ear too dull to hear, but your sins have separated you and your God."* [317]

Johann J. Nickel, in Rosenhof preached, *"We Mennonites have carried the concept of peace and non-military participation for four hundred years. Now where do we stand? We have mixed up the godly with the ungodly, straying from our God-given path. Many have already taken up the worldly sword in the name of fighting a spiritual battle. They do not trust God any more. What has happened to us, what has become of us? . . . we are not worthy of our name anymore."* [318]

In the heated debate, an officer shouted out :

You farmers destroy the weeds among your grain, without pangs of conscience. Who is Makhno? A weed that is worse than weeds, and he must be destroyed. Furthermore if a rabbit destroys a young tree in your garden, you shoot without further

---

[315] Ibid, pg 176
[316] Ibid, pp. 163-164
[317] Ibid, pg 89
[318] Hope Springs Eternal, John P. Nickel, pg 82

consideration. Who is Makhno? An animal, worse than an animal who must be shot down. If there is someone here who for conscience sake does not wish to take a gun and shoot Makhno, please identify yourself.

Pastor Nickel, *the minister who had spoken the preceding Sunday, replied, "I am the one who on the basis of God's Word will not take a gun." The officer replied, "We will place you before a court of White officers and shoot you down like a dog."*[319]

One man from Halbstadt had seen some of the abused and bleeding from Prishib with their breasts cut off. It became very clear to him what he had to do.[320] *Sadly, such sadistic acts were not limited to just Nestor Makhno and his bandits. There were stories of Red soldiers nailing the epaulets of White officers to their shoulders and that the Whites sometimes buried their enemies alive.*[321]

Henry and John Bergmann, two young lads from Mariawohl, about 7 miles west of Gnadenfeld, had been drafted to drive White Army units to the war front. There they had witnessed the White Army in World War I executing their own men and deliberately disfiguring them by hacking them up, blaming the cruelty and barbarity on the enemy, to spur recruitment and bolster determination to fight the enemy, to reduce the rate of desertion.

Killings, killings, killings!

The necessity of a Selbstschutz did not suddenly emerge overnight, but gradually during months filled with unbearable, catastrophic experiences and unprecedented terror . . . In a gruesome reality we stood helpless before an unbounded, bestial anarchy in which the lowest human traits found expression.[322]

There were more than a dozen changes in regimes between the White, Red, and Black anarchist armies as they swept back and forth over the Ukraine. The Selbstschutz grew out of fear, based on man's instinct for survival. Unfortunately, there was no freedom of conscience to participate or not participate in a selbstschutz. Most pacifists were intimidated, excommunicated from the church, silenced. However, the three villages of Petershagen, Rudnerweide, and Grossweide remained true to their non-resistant convictions, and refused to participate in the Selbstschutz. Very early

---

[319] Master's Thesis, Selbstschutz, Josephine Chipman, pp. 118-119
[320] Mennonites in Ukraine, Amid Civil War and Anarchy (1917-1920) translated and edited by John B. Toews, pg 94
[321] The Russländer, Sandra Birdsell, pp. 304-305
[322] Mennonites in Ukraine, Amid Civil War and Anarchy (1917-1920) translated and edited by John B. Toews, pg 93

on, it was deemed necessary to hire one heavily armed Cossack to keep order. But was not a hired armed Cossack already a form of Selbstschutz? [323]

At a meeting in Mariawohl, it had *been decided that each village will hire four cavalrymen for guard duty. When the bandits come at night, they will shoot in the air, and the bandits will flee.*[324] Unfortunately, in actual practice, the bandits did not flee.[325] It was totally unrealistic, naive, wishful thinking about the extent of sinfulness, cruelty, and brutal savagery of these bandits.

Sentinels were placed at both ends of each village, and at the cemetery in the north. Some Selbstschutz detachments fought in battles near two other villages, where they were joined by Lutheran and Catholic units.[326]

Any attempt to use their hunting guns proved futile, as bandits swept in so swiftly, they bound or killed men before they could even think about defending themselves, then brought out the women who were then "laid on the ground."

Abram Rempel of Gnadenfeld (The Old General, and brother of Aron A. Rempel Sr.) was elected a representative of the Selbstschutz committee, otherwise known as the Wirtschaftskomitee. Their position was clearly spelled out in the minutes: *"we were not a regular military unit and did not wish to engage in any political actions. We only wished to protect ourselves from the bandits until a government in Russia took matters into its own hand."*[327] Carl Rempel joined this home guard or Selbstschutz, headed in Gnadenfeld by his father. Abram was called the Old General because of his long white beard and his reputation as one of the wise old leaders of the village.[328]

The German Mennonites were living in a hell that demanded desperate measures. For centuries they had piously, self-righteously proclaimed the principle of non-resistance. They were supposed to turn the other cheek, to be a suffering church. If someone demanded your coat, to cheerfully give him your cloak also. But was it not evil to be passive in the face of such evil itself?[329]

Having joined the Selbstschutz purely for self-defense, the Mennonite cavalry now rode out on patrols into the Russian villages with the power of the German army backing them, and the desire

---

[323] <u>Mennonites in Ukraine, Amid Civil War and Anarchy (1917-1920)</u> translated and edited by John B. Toews, pg 92
[324] <u>Ibid</u>, pg 87
[325] <u>Ibid</u>, pg 56
[326] <u>1835-1943 Gnadenfeld, Molotschna,</u> A Lowen Schmidt; Jakob P. Dick Remembers: "The Years 1918-1925" pg 56
[327] <u>Mennonites in Ukraine, Amid Civil War and Anarchy (1917-1920)</u> translated and edited by John B. Toews, pg 85
[328] "Memoir of Agatha and Carl Rempel", as told to K. R. Lockwood, pg 10
[329] <u>My Harp is Turned to Mourning,</u> Al Reimer, pg 354

to retrieve all their stolen goods surfaced in full fury, in a raging passionate frenzy. There were excesses, especially in Zagradovka,[330] where Russian peasants, men and women, the guilty and innocent alike, were whipped and even tortured, all while the Mennonites were singing German songs. Sometimes Russian homes caught fire. Eichenfeld villagers were the first to murder Russians.[331]

77 Abram and Elizabeth Rempel
(The Old General) parents of Cornelius, Jacob, and Agatha Krause's spouses

Employers, wealthy landowners, the aristocracy, those who had the most material possessions to lose, formed a White Army under a white flag to oppose the Bolsheviks. However, rival jealousies and factions, old incompetent generals, graft, corruption, no central command, and broken transportation and communication led to its downfall.[332]

The night of July 17, 1918, the Russian White Army drew close to where the Czar and his family were being held captive. The Reds, in panic, and probably at the order of Lenin, secretly executed

[330] Mennonites in Ukraine, Amid Civil War and Anarchy (1917-1920) translated and edited by John B. Toews, pp. 139-140, 153
[331] Ibid, pp. 152,153
[332] She Cried For Mother Russia, Friedl E. Semans Bell, pg 121

all the royal family, along with their servants, where they had been held in house arrest at Ekaterinburg (now Sverdlovsk).

In October, 1918 Gustav (Aron Rempel Sr.'s brother) and family determined to flee the plundering and pillaging of Makhno in their district and left the Marienskaya Estate[333] headed for Gnadenfeld. The family arrived in Gnadenfeld first, because they traveled light, with only the clothes on their backs. Behind them, their oldest son Heinrich lead a caravan of carts pulled by oxen, carrying all they owned. When the caravan didn't arrive on time, Aron Rempel Sr. and his brother Gustav went back looking for him. About midway, they learned of an attack by Nestor Makhno and his bandits. What they didn't steal, they smashed, scattered, or destroyed, and the leiter voge (ladder wagons) returned empty to Marienskaya. Aron and Gustav were then led to a shallow grave where Heinrich's brutally mutilated body was buried beneath the broken doors of one of their wardrobes. They were told, if any consolation, Gustav's son was killed in a hurry. Earlier, two Russian merchants had been slowly put to death with deliberate, for fun torture, including putting burning cigarette stubs into slashes cut in their bodies.[334]

However, when the body was uncovered near an estate belonging to Zerikov, Heinrich's hands were still tied behind his back, his eyes gouged out, and he had suffered repeated stab wounds on his head and neck.[335] Aron Sr. and Gustav returned with the corpse to Gnadenfeld, where a funeral service was held for him in the church. Mother Elisabeth Electra suffered a long period of grief over the brutal murder of her son, and she died of amoebic dysentery in August, 1920.

Kaiser Wilhelm abdicated. When the German troops retreated in November 1918, as agreed upon under the Treaty of Brest-Litovsk, no effective Russian government was left to provide any law and order. The retreat of the German army left a huge vacuum [336] which soon filled with civil war and total anarchy for two more long years.[337]

The Austrians, in a hurry to get home, sold off their wagons, horses, weapons, cannons, machine guns, and ammunition at dirt cheap prices, probably to the Makhnovista, who now had all the money. [338]

November 1918 to March 1919 the Russian White army under General Denikin occupied the area.

---

[333] Mennonite Estates in Imperial Russia, Helmut T. Huebert, pg 291
[334] "A Letter to My Children; The Memoirs of Arthur G. Rempel", pg 25
[335] From the Steppes to the Prairies, Paul Klassen, pp. 72-73
[336] Escape to Freedom, Cornelius Funk, pg 43
[337] 1835-1945 Gnadenfeld, Molotschna, A Lowen Schmidt, pg 25
[338] Hope Springs Eternal, John P. Nickel, pg 249

White officers took over administration of Halbstadt and Gnadenfeld Volosts (county seats).[339]

The Selbstschutz went to the Sebastopol arsenal in Crimea, and were awarded all the *war materials which the Germans had left behind during disarmament, taking five train carloads of arms, munitions, four machine guns, field telephones, hand grenades, steel helmets, spades, picks, etc.*[340]

The German Mennonites had been friends with the enemy. Peasants now joined Makhno's bandits in droves, swearing revenge on Mennonite villages. They talked of killing, and burning homes and barns. Those Russians who had been whipped and stripped of the material goods they had stolen from the Mennonites were now filled with an unholy vengeance and bloodlust. Makhno, who formerly had faced setbacks, now retaliated, laying siege to Blumenfeld and Schoenfeld, two villages located in the midst of bandit territory.

Had Satan himself now entered the former Mennonite Garden of Eden?

In Brasol, two young men . . . were ordered to undress, and then they were hacked to pieces.[341] Their attackers wanted to preserve the clothing so they could wear it. The murderers, in their bloodlust, would grab musical instruments: a violin, guitar, an accordion, and play wild tunes while fellow bandits chopped off a man's fingers, tormenting him further before shooting him. His family might find him later on the manure pile.

Fear gripped hearts when dogs barked, as immediately a black horse, ridden by a black clothed rider armed to the teeth, long hair flying under a large grey fur cap, galloped into the village. Buggies and wagons loaded with Makhnovites suddenly rushed into the yard. Armed men jumped off and burst into the house with shouting and swearing amid the crying of widows and orphans whose husband and father had just been killed.

Prayer services were now more eagerly attended. The message "Today if you hear His voice, do not harden your hearts, give your life to the dear Savior " worked on souls, as this could be the last moment of life.

In another village, a woman persuaded her husband to hide in the garden. With the screams and burning houses, *he crept back towards his house and stumbled over a body. It was his wife. His heart cried out. Suddenly he thought of his children. Horror of horrors! All five mutilated*

[339] Hierschau: An Example of Russian Mennonite Life, Helmut T. Huebert, pg 242
[340] Master's Thesis, Selbstschutz, Josephine Chipman, pg 139
[341] Mennonites in Ukraine, Amid Civil War and Anarchy (1917-1920) translated and edited by John B. Toews, pg 33

bodies were scattered throughout the room . . . . As he ran past his neighbor's house, he barely noticed the decapitated heads of children sitting on the windowsill. His heart cried out in overwhelming agony. [342]

At another home bandits had killed the mother and her seven children, and had placed their heads on chairs around the table.[343]

One of Makhno's men *tore open the mouth of his bound victim, poured lime (used as building mortar) inside, stamped it into his throat and poured water into his mouth.*[344]

The completely helpless cried out ardently for deliverance from the Forces of Darkness.

The emboldened peasants simply marched into the estates and farms throughout the Brasol district, demanding the keys, and that homes be vacated at once. It mattered not that the family had just slaughtered six pigs; they were ordered off with nothing but the clothes on their backs.

*The H. Neufelds left their estate to stay with the Krauses (*probably Susanna Krause Rempel's uncle Johann (her father's brother*) for a while . . . . bandits smashed the furniture in Koop's house to bits . . . . What kind of a civilization is this? WANTON DESTRUCTION! . . . all we possess now is what we saved and brought with us. May we learn the true meaning of the Scripture verse: The Lord giveth, and the Lord taketh away. Blessed be the name of the Lord.* By December 11, 1919, estate owners Jakob Dreidiger and Krause were virtually destitute. And yet the anarchists demanded a payment of 20,000 rubles, or they would be killed.[345] Both anarchists and Bolsheviks demanded huge ransoms be paid to release hostages repeatedly taken from already destitute villagers.[346]

Dreadful destruction was wreaked everywhere. Pigs ran around loose. *The robbers want wealth, but without earning it. They want it instantly, by robbing* and worse . . . . *Let us get out and escape from the "peaceful" country! Jesus is the only One who can make peace.*[347]

---

[342] Ibid, pg 134

[343] Events and People, Helmut T. Huebert, Massacre in Muensterberg, pg 158-160

[344] Mennonites in Ukraine, Amid Civil War and Anarchy (1917-1920) translated and edited by John B. Toews, pp. 115-116

[345] Because of the chaos and utter destruction of this war, family documents for this portion of the family are missing. We can only guess exactly which Krause is referred to, father or son Johann. Susanna's father Cornelius Krause had already died in 1901, hence it certainly was not he. Unfortunately, too many books only list the last name, or the first initial with last name, leaving us to wonder exactly who the person was. Mennonites in Ukraine, Amid Civil War and Anarchy (1917-1920) translated and edited by John B. Toews, pg 11

[346] Hope Springs Eternal, John P. Nickel, pg 187

[347] Ibid, pp. 252-253

A teacher fled, accompanied by his sick wife and ten children, one of whom was an epileptic cripple. One wagon after another passed them on the road, filled with other fleeing Mennonites. None of their fellow refugees offered any help. Finally, one good Samaritan stopped and took the poor crippled child into their wagon, even though their wagon was already full to overflowing with eleven persons, and no room for any more. *The Mennonite Levites and Pharisees who had plenty of room on their own wagons had ignored them as they drove by. They only thought of their own danger.*[348]

Wives were warned not to view the dead. Crows had pecked bodies. A husband's belly had been slashed, and his ears cut off. Another man had his feet burned, his eyes gouged out, his throat slit, and his body cut up. Bandits then tortured his wife by setting her blouse on fire.[349] Corpses were laid in mass graves.

The Bolsheviks started to demand Germans join their collective farms within three days. The Germans refused, realizing their property was going to be confiscated whether they joined or not, and to join the collective would enslave them forever. *One said, "I have inherited one cow and two pigs, and even this is not mine anymore, but belongs to the collective." The workers on one collective farm (formerly an estate) were not allowed to have any money. It was doled out to each one as the manager saw fit. Pure paternalism. It is most astonishing to see what fruit the Revolution is producing. Freedom has now turned into the worst possible slavery of the masses. A few are ruling many in a most capricious manner. This is what happens when man tries to improve the world order without the help of God.*[350]

The Czar's bureaucratic government had been filled with corruption, but was the new Communist order any better? It now took four clerks to register and record the necessary information in order to procure a passport and permission to travel even a short distance from home.[351]

A Russian war refugee bemoaned, *"Who are the Russian soldiers anyway? They're robbers, that's who they are." Many soldiers came to our place in Volhynia and robbed us. They are a lost people. It was the Russians, not the Germans, who finally drove us away, and I fear them more than the Germans.*[352]

The time of terror only lasted three months, from October to December 1919, but it seemed to the people who endured it, terror would never end.

---

[348] Mennonites in Ukraine, Amid Civil War and Anarchy (1917-1920) translated and edited by John B. Toews, pg 131
[349] Hope Springs Eternal, John P. Nickel, pp. 240-241
[350] Ibid, pp. 210-211
[351] Ibid, pg 260
[352] Hope Springs Eternal, John P. Nickel, pg 220

War in Siberia

Admiral Kolchak retreated from the Urals with the Red Army in hot pursuit. The Siberian Cossack Corps and General Sakharov's White Third Army joined with Kolchak's forces near Petropavlovsk, Siberia in August, 1919, where the Whites and Reds met at the Tobol River. *A strong White reserve of about 10,000 men was deployed near Petropavlovsk. The Soviets planned a two pronged attack, one along the Trans-Siberian Railway on Petropavlovsk, and the second attack along the Lalutorovsk-Ishim Railway.*[353]

The Aaron Rempel family could hear fighting in the distance. Three year old Gonja (pronounced Gun-ya) became deathly ill with brain fever (possibly meningitis).[354] Aaron, probably still in the far east, was away from home on his buying trip. Was he alive or dead? Susanna did not know what to do for deathly sick little Gonja. The Red Army was now in the city, and despite fighting going on, she finally decided to run on foot clear across Petropavlovsk, to get a certain German doctor. Mennonite doctors were on salary paid by the German Mennonite community. They only made house calls for patients too sick to go to them. They never accepted money, even if offered, but occasionally would accept a gift of fresh fruit, vegetables, or sausages.[355] Because all doctors had been conscripted into the army, Susanna had to cross the city through gunfire, and travel to where the soldiers were billeted. She knew where the soldiers' barracks were located and this doctor would be working. The neighbor's dog adopted Susanna as his responsibility and accompanied her as she alternately walked and ran across the city to the other side. It took Susanna a whole day to arrive, dodging the fighting and bullets, winding her way here and there, down this street, almost doubling back, and finally finding the soldiers playing cards by candlelight in the barracks. The doctor was totally amazed that she had gone through the fighting in the city to get to him. It was night when the doctor took her with him on horseback to her home, with that faithful, neighbor dog running alongside.

The doctor did not expect little Gonja to live, she was so desperately ill. The German doctor gave Gonja plain medicine. In Siberia it was just plain medicine. He sat with the family for some time and gave Gonja something so she would sleep. Toward morning, little Gonja finally slept. He said that would happen, and if she sneezed, she would quickly recover. Gonja did sneeze, and then

---

[353] the free Dictionary by Farlex http://encyclopedia2.thefreedictionary.com/Petropavlovsk+Operation+of+1919   This source is written from the viewpoint of the Bolsheviks, the Red Army.

[354] http://en.wikipedia.org/wiki/Meningitis   Brain fever describes a medical condition where part of the brain becomes inflamed and causes symptoms that present as fever. The terminology is dated.

[355] Life and Times of a Renaissance Mennonite Teacher: Cornelius A. Klaassen: (1883-1919 and Beyond), Robert L. Klaassen, pg 46

she was better. The doctor did not tell Susanna directly, but told her friend Mrs. Neufeld, that even if Gonja did get well, she wouldn't be right in the head. Her fever had been so high, she would either die or be mentally ill. Gonja recovered, but she was no longer cuddly like she had been. She was extremely tense and easily became restless. Gonja had changed. She never was the same cuddly little girl after her illness.

One day Susanna heard the war was getting very close to their part of the city, and she could hear sporadic shooting. The Rempel family home did not have a basement. Their landlord, who lived next door, told them it would be wise for them to leave their house and go somewhere safer, and he invited them to stay in his basement during the fighting. They spent the whole day down in his basement. The Russian maid who worked for their landlord also was huddled with them in the basement, tightly clutching her religious icon. Bullets went zinging into the house all day long. Susanna cried out the familiar Psalm 121 in prayer, *I will lift up mine eyes unto the hills from whence cometh my help. My help cometh from the Lord who made heaven and earth.*

One cannonball went in a second floor window, through the room, and out a window on the other side, landing in the yard below - - without exploding!

Mama, cuddling her children ever closer to her, repeated Psalm 23, *Der Herr is mein Hirte. The Lord is my shepherd. I shall not want . . . . Yea though I walk through the valley of the shadow of death, I will fear no evil: for thou art with me; thy rod and thy staff, they comfort me.*

Another cannonball came in a second floor window, landed on the floor, and rolled down the stairs to the first floor above their heads, where it stopped - - again, without exploding! The basement was dark with no windows; with no clock, time seemed to stand still. It seemed like an eternity with the zinging of bullets flying past and bombs exploding nearby. Would this never end? How long had they been sitting there? "O Bozhe moy!" the maid cried out in terror, as she crossed herself, rocking back and forth.

Realizing a bomb could set the house on fire, the landlord suggested to Susanna that she should run home and get some of her good things, whatever was important. During a short lull in the firing in their neighborhood, Susanna did run home to get some important papers and a comforter or two. As she was running back, a cannonball shot by her, so close the air moving by knocked her to the ground. Susanna picked herself up, and ran like crazy to the safety of the basement. Hugging and rocking her children, tears streaming down her face, she softly sang, "Nun danket alle

Got," "Now Thank We All Our God" over and over and over again. Fortunately, the armies shot poor shells, many of which didn't explode. Finally the sound of the fighting faded into the distance. All became quiet, and they could come out. They had spent a whole day and night in that basement. Some buildings in the city were on fire making the sky red all around. But when they went to their own home, not one cannon ball or even a bullet had hit their own cozy home. That little house stood completely untouched. Not even one single bullet hole. It seemed miraculous to have escaped undamaged in such fierce fighting.

Marie lay in her bed next to the window, and Susanna had a friend in the house with them to protect them and make them feel more secure. While they talked softly nearby, Marie stared out the window watching clouds scud across the moon. She just couldn't go to sleep. Finally, Marie slipped out of bed, and made her way to her mama. Still shaking, Marie whispered in her mother's ear, "I am afraid."

"Everything will be all right now, you just go to bed now," Mama soothed. The man sitting in a dark corner of the room added, "You do not need to be afraid now; the war is over."

Neighbor friend Lena Sudermann was a year older than Marie, and had already been to school the year before. September, 1919 Marie started school. Papa Aaron Jr. was still away on his long tea buying trip on the Trans-Siberian Railway, and Susanna still had not heard from him for a long, long time. Mama, with tears streaming down her face, worked to sew Marie a brown dress with a black apron, the school uniform in Petropavlovsk, Siberia.

Unfortunately, Marie, who liked school, only attended three days, before the school closed so the Red army could billet soldiers in the school building.

Despite the brevity of her exposure to school, even as an adult, Marie remembered this story from a Russian schoolbook:

A man went fishing. He had a horse and sleigh and went to the river to fish. He caught a lot of fish and had them in the back of his sleigh. He was really happy going home now, and his wife would be really happy for all the fish. On the way home, he saw a fox lying by the side of the road. When the fox saw the man coming, he decided to play dead. So the man picked up the fox and put him in the sleigh, and he thought, "This will be a nice fur for my wife." He kept going, and when he arrived home, shouted to his wife, "Come out here and see what I have! I have so many fish!" When she looked in the sleigh, it was empty. The fox had thrown all the fish out and jumped out himself. Now nothing was in the sleigh. Then the fox had a pile of fish. A wolf came along and saw the fox with a pile of fish. The wolf asked for some fish, but the fox said, "Oh, no. You go and fish yourself. There are women by the river, where they have a hole to wash their clothes. You stick your tail in that hole. When you can't pull your tail out, there will be a lot of fish on the tail. You try all the time. If you can still pull your tail out, just put your tail back in and leave it longer." The wolf went and did as the fox told him to, found the hole, and put his tail in. Finally the wolf decided, "I can't pull it out anymore. Surely a lot of fish are on my tail." Just then a lot of Russian men and women from the village came to the river and saw the wolf. They went after the wolf with their pitchforks, so the wolf had to leave his tail there and just beat it.

The Neufelds lived with Rempels at this time because he was a teacher.[356] He, his wife, and one daughter were allowed to live in the house, and had one room for themselves in exchange for teaching Marie. He also taught two other boys at the same time. The three of them were all German and in first grade.

The Neufeld daughter was about eighteen. She went over to a Jewish neighbor who was sewing a dress for her to ask how the dress was coming along. She wanted Marie to accompany her, because she felt awkward about going alone. When they came in the front door, it was dark with all the chairs and furniture turned upside down. Marie blurted out, "Why is everything upside down?" "Shhhhh," the girl replied, so Marie didn't ask any more questions. The Jewish master of the house had died. There was no casket. They had already carried him on a stretcher down the street to the cemetery, because Jews bury their dead the very same day. They had hired women to wail, "O Bozhe moy! O Bozhe moy! O My God! O My God!"

Many Czech soldiers were in Siberia. During World War I, Czechoslovakia had been a part of Austria-Hungary, and Czech soldiers had to fight on the Eastern front for Austria. Many of them didn't like the Austrian Emperor and did not want to fight against Russia so they preferred to be captured by the Russian troops. The Russian Military began to form a Czechoslovakian Legion with these captured troops. Czech soldiers were caught in Russia after the October Revolution. They couldn't get home by going west, but were promised safe passage home going east to Vladivostok. Trotsky later broke this promise and ordered their arrest.[357]

---

[356] The first names of these Neufelds is unknown. Not related to Wilhelm and Margareta Neufeld.
[357] http://en.wikipedia.org/wiki/Revolt_of_Czechoslovak_Legion

Admiral Kolchak had handed security of the railroads over to the Czechs, who wanted to look like they were doing a good job of railway security. They thought perhaps they should shoot a German instead of a Russian. So, when Aaron arrived back in Petropavlovsk with his bales of tea, he was promptly arrested and falsely accused of committing sabotage. His situation looked extremely serious until his Kirghiz friends in the hunting union intervened, guaranteed Mr. Rempel's political dependability, and the Czechs released him.

Finally back home again, Aaron was able to line up his tea bales along the side of the long, wide hallway where Ronka had marched proclaiming his love for Tamara, with plenty of room left for the family to walk.

August 20 to October 31, 1919, Soviet troops were in Petropavlovsk, between the Ishim and Tobol Rivers. They were pursuing Kolchak's armies, trying to "liberate" all of Western Siberia. A strong White reserve of about 10,000 men was deployed near Petropavlovsk.[358]

One Monday morning, a neighbor called Aaron to come and help him defend his property. Communists were robbing his place. Papa took his gun and went to the neighbors.

During good times, Susanna had three Russian maids. She had to have three because the Russian girls were lazy and would sit down and not do any work as soon as she walked out of the room and wasn't watching them. It took three Russian maids to get the work of one good German. They were filthy dirty and would steal things. And the lice! All the Russians had lice. During these troubled times, Susanna only had one Russian maid. While Papa was gone helping their neighbor, Susanna's Russian maid suddenly quit. She didn't tell Susanna when she quit, but when she did, she stole Susanna's brand new galoshes, and an expensive, very fine wool shawl, so fine a person could pull it through a wedding ring. Susanna had had it in her chest, but in the morning it was gone. Susanna had a number of things soaking Sunday evening, getting ready to wash them the next day, but the maid had wrung them out and stolen them, too. The maid knew exactly what she had soaked and what she wanted to take. A cooler had been made in the yard by digging a hole, lining it with straw, and keeping milk, cream, and butter fresh in it with ice. Those things were gone as well. Somehow that maid seemed to know when the Reds were coming so she could safely steal a number of things.

Rempels lived in a neighborhood with a lot of wealthy Jews. One Jewish girl had two thick braids that reached way below her waist. Marie had marveled at her long hair. But the same morning

---

[358] the free Dictionary by Farlex http://encyclopedia2.thefreedictionary.com/Petropavlovsk+Operation+of+1919, accessed December 21, 2017

they discovered the Russian maid had stolen so many of their belongings, they also discovered all those neighborhood Jews had disappeared. They had completely vanished overnight. How had they known to disappear?

When Bolsheviks occupied the city of Petropavlovsk, one of their first acts was to redistribute goods "from each according to his ability to each according to his needs." Bolsheviks ransacked the whole city. Suddenly, Communists burst into the Rempel home, loaded up all the tea bales, and took them away. Now all their money was gone. The Rempel needs were becoming greater and greater, but their ability was reduced to about zero.

Admiral Kolchak needed more manpower. His back was against the wall; the Red army increased daily. Kolchak found supporters among foreigners, among the allies, but not among his own Russian people. About this time, the Czechs were eager to return to their own newly established homeland, and the Western Allies viewed Kolchak as "A Lost Cause."[359]

Because the Kirghiz had interceded for Aaron, to deliver him from death, the Czechoslovakian Legion and Admiral Kolchak now knew about the men in the hunting union. Aaron and the Kirghiz all realized that they would be conscripted into the White army. After talking it over, the members of the hunting union all decided it would be better to volunteer, since then they could choose the military branch where they would serve. So they all volunteered to serve in the Air Force, including Aaron Rempel. He chose to serve as a noncombatant mechanic in charge of airplanes and machinery[360] because he was a notable mechanical expert, especially on fuel-powered machinery. This expertise made him especially valuable when drafted into service, as he kept their trucks rolling and even worked on airplane engines. Aaron ended up supervising a supply train providing maintenance support for the troops under Admiral Alexander Kolchak and again was gone from home for months.[361] That is how a pacifist German Mennonite became a high ranking officer in Russia's White Army Air Force in the autumn of 1919.

While Aaron was away for this extended period, Susanna never heard from him. There were no letters. Not even one.

---

[359] Civil War in Siberia, The Anti-Bolshevik Government of Admiral Kolchak. 1918-1920, Jonathan D. Smele, ed., from a review by Eva M. Stolberg http://www.h-net.org./reviews/showrev.php?id=1925,

[360] California Mennonite Historical Society Bulletin, No, 54, Fall 2011, "The Rempel Family's Escape from Death by Famine", Corinna Siebert Ruth http://www.calmenno.org/bulletin/fall11.pdf

[361] Los Angeles Times, Wednesday, August 4, 1982, "A Search for Ancestral Soviet Home", William C. Rempel, page 17

An offensive on Ishim mounted by the main forces of the Soviet Third Army on October 18 forced Kolchak's troops to begin a retreat all along the front. Petropavlovsk was "liberated" on October 31 after three days of stubborn fighting. Having lost up to 50 percent of their men from the attacks of the Soviet armies and Siberian partisans, Kolchak's demoralized troops withdrew to Omsk.[362]

Once a Russian officer and his wife were billeted at the Rempel home. They fell in love with Drezhnah, but the Rempels wouldn't sell them their beloved dog. She was a favorite of the children. The wife, however, just had to have that dog. When Marie, Ronka, Gonja and little Susie woke up, they missed Drezhnah. "Drezhnah, Drezhnah," they called and called. But Drezhnah never came. They went outside and continued calling, "Drezhnah, Drezhnah."

Finally a neighbor strolled over, "That Russian Officer and his wife put the dog they bought from you up on one of their horses, and left very, very early this morning, while you were still sleeping."

"But we didn't sell them our beloved Drezhnah!" wailed the children.

"They must have lured Drezhnah with a lump of sugar, or she would never have gone to them," mused Susanna, but it was too late. Drezhnah was gone for good.

After the fighting in their neighborhood, Ronka and two of his friends had fun looking around for unspent shells that still had powder in them. The idea was to get the powder out. Suddenly a spark burned some skin off Ronka's hand. Ronka went running in the house and cried that somebody shot him. Mama didn't believe him.

One day Susanna was making Gonja's favorite meal, pelmenje. She had prepared the hamburger for the pelmenje, and left it standing in a bowl on the table. The Rempel's last dog with short fur and white and brown spots, gobbled all the hamburger up when nobody was looking.

Meanwhile, the Bolsheviks quartered a Red Communist soldier in their last home that now had only three rooms. He was a real Communist, and told the children that there was no god. Marie gasped aloud, "No God? How can this be?"

---

[362] the free Dictionary by Farlex   http://encyclopedia2.thefreedictionary.com/Petropavlovsk+Operation+of+1919

Mama quickly hushed her, and hurried Marie off to another room. "Shhh. you will just make things worse. Just remember what God has said in His Word, 'The fool hath said in his heart, 'There is no God.' [363] When that soldier says, 'There is no god,' what kind of a person is that man?"

Marie didn't have to think very long, "He is a fool. God calls him a fool."

"Yes, but we must not say that out loud while he is living here with us, or bad things could happen to us."

Susanna's Bible was well read and worn so she had bought a new Bible at the Ovsiannikova Department Store before it had burned to the ground. This Communist soldier living with them found Susanna's new Bible. He took it and wouldn't give it back to Susanna, even after much pleading. "Religion is the opiate of the masses," he stated triumphantly. "You won't need this anymore. No one needs this anymore!"

Susanna still had her old Bible. When the soldier wasn't looking, Susanna put it in the kitchen, made it look like a cookbook, and kept it near the medicines.

"Mama, why is your Bible near the medicines here in the kitchen?"

"Shhhh. That Bolshevik soldier who doesn't believe in God, took my new Bible and he won't give it back to me. We will lose this one too if he finds out it is also a Bible. Pretend it is a cookbook. Actually it is a cookbook, of sorts, with the recipe for life. We need these 'recipes' for living."

> *The law of the Lord is perfect, converting the soul: the testimony of the Lord is sure, making wise the simple;*
> *The statutes of the Lord are right, rejoicing the heart: the commandment of the Lord is pure, enlightening the eyes.*
> *The fear of the Lord is clean, enduring forever: the judgments of the Lord are true and righteous altogether.*
> *More to be desired are they than gold, yea, than much fine gold: sweeter also than honey and the honeycomb.* Psalm 19:7-10

Mama and Marie chuckled quietly about their little secret, then finished making the beds, and sweeping up. Since the Bible was in German, and the Russian soldier couldn't read German, he

---

[363] Psalm 14:1a

was convinced it was only a cookbook, so she was allowed to keep her "cookbook." Susanna didn't like that Communist soldier living in her house at all. He was a foul-mouthed, ill-tempered, impatient, dirty soul, so finally she went to the office in charge of quartering the soldiers, complained about him, and asked if she could get a better man put into their house. So, surprisingly, they replaced him with a German prisoner of war named Ferdinand.

Susanna hung a red curtain to fence off his bed so Ferdinand had a little privacy for himself in their tiny three-room house. Because he played with the children, the children didn't feel like it was too bad if they played tricks on him. They felt free to do it. They put a bowl of water in his bed and covered the bowl by pulling a sheet over it. He caught on. He didn't lie down in it, but he chased after them and laughed about it. It was all in good fun.

Now soldiers were billeted in houses all across the city. Ferdinand grew to love Susanna and wanted to marry her. What was Susanna to do? She didn't know if Aaron were dead or alive. She hadn't heard from him for months. Was she already a widow, and didn't know it? And if he had died in battle, would she ever even be notified?

Surrender

Admiral Kolchak's greatest supporters were the Allies, not the Russians themselves. When the Allies realized that Kolchak did not have the support of his own people, they also withdrew their support for his war effort.

Aaron Rempel's Air Force unit was located in Novosibirsk. The war effort was going badly. They were surrounded and outnumbered. There was such a rout, such panic, each man decided to save himself as best he could. Aaron's whole unit deserted and ran away, except Aaron Rempel, who found himself alone with all the equipment and airplanes. Desertion of soldiers was the White Army's worst problem. Men didn't want to fight a hopeless war.

In utter despair, Aaron trudged toward the city, then sat on a grassy knoll, meditating about what to do now. He cried out to God, "*Lord, how are they increased that trouble me! Many are they that rise up against me. Many there be which say of my soul, 'There is no help for him in God.' But thou, O Lord, art a shield for me, my glory, and the lifter up of mine head. I cried unto the Lord with my voice. He heard me out of his holy hill. Some trust in chariots, and some in horses: but we will remember the name of the Lord our God.*" [364]

"Oh God, I am utterly at your mercy. You know I can't trust in chariots, horses, or even all these guns, ammunition, and airplanes that have been left behind. Everyone else has deserted. They have all fled. I am the only one left. I am as good as a dead man. What shall I do? Please save me and save my wife and children! If I don't get back home, what will happen to them?"

When Aron looked up from prayer, he noticed a poster fastened to a wooden fence. It was a proclamation from the war department by Comrade Leon Trotsky, that anyone who had served in the Kolchak army who would turn over all the weapons that they had and join the Red forces would be forgiven and treated as equals with the Red Soldiers. Aaron would have to trust that the Reds would honor this promise. Anyway, it sounded like a possible way to save his neck and save his family.

So Aaron went to the government office indicated on the poster to turn himself in as a prisoner of war and join the Red army. The man at the information center told him to go down the hall to a

---

[364] Psalm 3:1-4, and Psalm 20:7

certain office, and tell those people what his intentions were. When he came to the door he was looking for, a soldier standing guard outside wouldn't let him in. So an argument ensued. Aaron kept insisting, "I need to see the officer in charge," each time louder than before. The soldier standing guard outside refused to let him in.

The office door had been left partway open. Pretty soon a voice from inside shouted, "Let that man in!"

So the soldier standing guard outside the office said, "Well, OK, Comrade, you can go in."

Aaron entered the room, looked around, and saw another, smaller office off the large main room. A man sat behind a desk in that smaller, adjoining office. The man behind the desk said, "Come in, Comrade."

Aaron went in with his hat in his hand, and stood quite a while. The Red officer sat, and just stared at him. Finally the Red officer told him to sit down, and continued to stare at him for ever so long. The drawn out silence was so awkward, Aaron could hear the clock quietly ticking in the background. Aaron thought, "This is very unusual, a Red officer asking a White officer to sit down." After scrutinizing him even longer, finally the Red officer asked, "Do you remember me?"

"No, I don't know you. Why should I remember you?"

He then asked Aaron if he had been in the far east, to Krasnoyarsk, Irkutsk, Chita, Khabarovsk, Vachkotov, Vladivostok?

Aaron said, "Yes, . . . yes, I have."

Do you recall giving a prisoner at a train station at Chita[365] [366] a loaf of bread?

Now Aaron remembered, "Yes . . . yes I do. Yes, I remember. I was on my way to buy bales of tea to sell in Petropavlovsk to support my family."

---

[365] A katorga is a Tsarist slave labor camp for political prisoners. The notorious Nerchinsk Katorga was in the Chita Oblast, near the border to Mongolia. https://en.wikipedia.org/wiki/Katorga accessed 11 Feb 2017
[366] Years later, Aaron learned this was the same Baskarova (little prison at the train station) in which his son-in-law's brother John Bergmann had once been imprisoned as well.

The Red Officer clearly was excited now. "I was that man in that train station jail. I was that prisoner. You saved my life. We were so very hungry. We were starving, and you gave us your bread. You saved my life, and now I can save yours. What do you want?"

"Well," said Aaron. "I want to turn over the White Air Force to the Red Army and join myself."

The Red officer asked him, "How many of you are there?"

Aaron replied, "The others all disappeared. I am the only one left."

"Well, that is very unusual to turn over the whole unit and you are just one man. How can you do that?"

"Because I know where the airplanes and all the equipment are."

The Red officer, who was a Jew, laughed and said, "I know you are a good man because you proved yourself, and I will accept it because you gave me your French bread when I was really hungry."

He commissioned Aaron as a Red officer, and gave him papers authorizing Aaron to immediately take his family from Siberia back to their families and ancestral home in Ukraine, before returning to serve in the Red Army as an expert mechanic.[367]

That is how a German Mennonite pacifist with the stroke of a pen became a lieutenant in the Red Army.[368] With those papers, Aaron could travel anywhere because he was now a high-ranking Red Officer. They allowed him to take himself and his family out of Siberia to Gnadenfeld, now renamed Bogdanovka.

Back in Petropavlovsk, one day Susanna was going to market, when she again saw something that made her go numb. She saw Aaron, her own husband Aaron, with his arms entwined around some other woman. He had been gone from home for six months, and now here he was, but with another woman. She felt so betrayed. They were in a carriage, so Aaron didn't see Susanna standing in the street. The way they were cuddling together in that carriage, Susanna thought Aaron was already married to this other woman. She feared she and the children had been abandoned.

---

[367] from a cassette tape by John Bergmann, relating the story Aaron must have told him innumerable times; This is the story the author heard as a little girl which led her to research the rest of this incredible story
[368] Los Angeles Times, Wednesday, August 4, 1982, "A Search for Ancestral Soviet Home", William C. Rempel, pg 17

When Susanna came home, she took Marie aside, who was her oldest, and told her they no longer had a father. Their father was gone. He was married to someone else now, and he was never coming back. Susanna really believed that. Susanna also wanted the children to believe that. She didn't want them to want Daddy back, because she had seen Aron with that other woman, sitting together like man and wife in that carriage. She felt so bereft, so betrayed, so abandoned. Susanna asked young Marie "How would you like a new father?"

Marie and the other children loved having the German prisoner Ferdinand around. He played with them in a way their father did not, because father was hardly ever home. They loved to play tricks on Ferdinand, but Marie most definitely and vehemently said, "NO!" As much as Marie liked the German prisoner, she did not want him as her own father. Marie let it be known in no uncertain terms, "If you marry him, I will not cooperate. I want my very own father, and that is that!"

For this cause shall a man leave father and mother, and shall cleave to his wife; and they twain shall be one flesh. Wherefore they are no more twain, but one flesh. What therefore God hath joined together, let not man put asunder."[369] Susanna remembered their wedding sermon, but it gave her no comfort.

When Aaron finally came home very shortly thereafter on Palm Sunday, the German soldier Ferdinand was still quartered in his home. Now Aaron was lying beside Susanna again at night. When confronted, Aaron had told Susanna that the woman she had seen with him in the carriage simply had a bad toothache, and he was just taking her to the dentist. Susanna didn't believe him. After Aaron rolled over and went to sleep, Susanna was still awake for a long time, awake and crying silently inside. No sound, but tears streamed down her face soaking her pillow. She was sobbing inside.

---

[369] Genesis chapter 2 is cited by Jesus in Matthew 19:5,6

Traveling by Train

Susanna had always enjoyed traveling by passenger train back and forth from Siberia to Gnaden-feld for visits in peacetime. The trip each way would take about a week. With papers in hand, the family prepared to leave Siberia immediately, by the end of March 1920, hoping to reach Gnaden-feld in a week or two at the most.

The Petropavlovsk Train Station, built in 1904, was the largest station on the Trans-Siberian Rail-way and was considered the most beautiful.[370] The Trans-Siberian railway had only been built with one track line, which worked sufficiently well in peacetime. Few places existed for trains to pass each other going in opposite directions. Consequently the White Army could not move men and armament efficiently or fast enough to supply the army when needed. This contributed to the fall of the White Army just as it had to Russia's defeat in the Russo-Japanese War in 1905.

With his Red Army identification papers, Aaron was able to move his family, unchallenged, back to Gnadenfeld for the last time.[371] They had tickets, like in the good days before the war, but the train was full already; the doors were already locked, so windows were opened and people pushed their way inside through them. Susanna was the last one in the family to get on. She pushed in when the train already had started to move, and she just barely made it.

Each family member had to carry certain things. Aaron carried the heaviest suitcases. Marie had to carry the next heaviest, because Mama usually carried Susie in her arms. Then Ronka had to carry things. Gonja always had to carry the night pot, wrapped discretely in a cloth.

Now all of Russia was in upheaval, and passenger trains no longer ran. They often had to wait at a train depot for a week or two for the next train of any kind. To get back to Gnadenfeld, the family had to travel by freight train. Now everyone traveled by freight train in box cars.

Two windows were located at each end of the boxcar, with a deck built about five feet above the floor under these windows. Aaron aways tried to get his family situated on the top of one of the decks, so the children would be able to look out the window, and the family could be slightly distant from the Rus-sian passengers who were aways so full of lice. There could be enough room for them to lie down and sleep at night. Sometimes boxcars would be stuffed with people, jammed inside like animals.

---

[370] the free Dictionary by Farlex   http://encyclopedia2.thefreedictionary.com/Petropavlovsk+Operation+of+1919
[371] Los Angeles Times, Wednesday, August 4, 1982, "A Search for Ancestral Soviet Home", William C. Rempel, page 17

The Russians always had lice, lots of lice. Rempels were not used to having lice. Whenever they were packed so closely together, they were sure to get lice from the Russians. The lice would bite, and their victim would itch terribly. Susanna killed adult lice by rubbing a mixture of kerosene and lard on heads, but this did not get rid of the eggs. The eggs were laid along strands of hair and stuck. Nothing would kill the eggs. Marie felt she was especially blessed with lice. They liked her overly much. It seemed she was always smelling of kerosene, because her mother was always putting kerosene on her head to kill lice. It was difficult to get hot water and be able to clean themselves, so they just couldn't get rid of them.

Once when they were finally on a train, and it was already moving, one Russian was wearing a black coat thick with lice. They had bites of fire, and carried the dreaded typhus fever.[372] Marie could see the lice crawling all over that man from where she was standing on the platform near the window. All the rest of the Russians saw his lice, too. The man was so full of lice, it was even too much for the other Russians, so they threw him off the moving train. People sort of felt sorry for him, but they just could not tolerate all those lice.

Everything was out of order. Toilets didn't function, and water was scarce. Sometimes when the train arrived at a station, a person had to walk a long way to get water. When Aaron bought food for the family at train stations, he would buy a pot of hot water, so they could make their own tea. They put eggs in the hot water, which were boiled by the time they wanted to eat them. People living near the railroad brought produce to sell at the depots, like cherries in the spring.

Once while stopped at a depot, Susanna wanted to wash Marie's hair. The only container for washing her hair was the night pot. So Susanna and Marie walked to find water to wash her hair, and Marie carried the night pot and pouted. She didn't want her hair washed in a night pot. It would be thoroughly clean, but still, in a night pot? They walked by some soldiers who laughed at Marie's pouting face.

Freight trains were slow and undependable. One would go a couple of days but then stop and stand still the next couple of days. The single track from Siberia back to Moscow and Ukraine meant trains had to wait for each other to pass. Too often the train waited fully a week at a depot before moving on. This was typical of train travel throughout war torn Russia. It now took months, instead of days to travel from Siberia to South Russia.

---

[372] Los Angeles Times, Wednesday, August 4, 1982, "A Search for Ancestral Soviet Home", William C. Rempel, page 14

They could try and find a room to rent somewhere, or just try to get along as best they could at depots. Usually they just stayed at the depot. For amusement while waiting for the next train, often Marie and Ronka would sit next to the train tracks, pick up small stones, and line them up on the top of the rail. Their parents did not watch them closely, so never told them not to do so. They didn't have much money to rent rooms because the communists had taken all their tea which they could have sold.

One time the family was in a rented room, and Aaron heard that the train was going to go again. He hurried back to his family. "Hurry, hurry, we must pack and leave immediately. The train is leaving now!" The family packed as quickly as possible, and hurried as fast as Gonja's little legs could go, hurrying to the train station. He wanted them to run, but they couldn't while all carried as much as possible, and the loads were heavy. Just as they arrived, the train was already pulling out. Aaron was really upset that they had missed that train! Now they would have to wait at least another whole week before the next one, and Aaron was never late for anything. Never! His supply of money was extremely limited and dwindling quickly, with not enough to rent another room. It was the next day before the family heard the news. The very train they had just missed had derailed and fallen into a deep ravine! No one survived. Years later, Marie recalled, "It was an act of God that we missed that train." [373]

The next week, when another train arrived which could take them further, they were ready. The trestle and the tracks had been fixed. They didn't miss this train. The train passed slowly over the ravine where the other train lay in ruins. People near the windows could see the locomotive and boxcars lying crumpled down below, and were quietly somber as the train chugged slowly past. Crowded in together, everyone remained silent for a long time, while the train slowly picked up speed and went on, winding its way through the Siberian steppe.

The fighting was in their path. At the depot in Kharkov only about 200 miles short of their destination, the family was forced to camp out at the depot with hundreds of other stranded passengers. It had already taken them two months to travel the 1,800 miles from Petropavlovsk, east of the Ural Mountains. Along the route, food was scarce and lawlessness rampant. [374]

Lots of thieves usually roamed around the train stations. Aaron stacked up their suitcases next to a wall and had the family all lying on top of the suitcases to protect them. Susanna had one case with all new material for sewing new clothes, including some wine colored material for making a

[373] A Rempel Story, video of Susanna Krause Rempel and Marie Rempel Bergmann by William C. Rempel
[374] Los Angeles Times, Wednesday, August 4, 1982, "A Search for Ancestral Soviet Home", William C. Rempel, page 1

dress. She intentionally placed this particular suitcase under her feet. Susanna was the first in her family to awaken. Susanna was confused, and couldn't make sense of why a dirty sock was sticking out of her suitcase. That looked strange. It was hard for her to wake up and make sense of it all. As she picked up the dirty sock, she noticed a big slit in the suitcase. Her head seemed foggy. and she felt nauseous. She reached for a familiar object on the ground in front of her and broke into tears. It was her dental bridge, now missing its gold teeth. Someone had reached inside her mouth, removed her bridge and stolen her gold teeth! She felt so violated. "*They reached even into my mouth.*" [375] They must have been chloroformed, so they would not wake up. The robbers had slit the suitcase open and stolen all Susanna's new material. They also had taken Aaron's vest with important papers.

Finally, they were back on a train headed toward Gnadenfeld. The train hadn't left yet, when Marie heard a ruckus outside. Three young boys had been captured for stealing food. The soldiers beat them with metal rods on their heads and back. Marie felt sick, and left the window. Shortly she heard three shots. The boys had been taken out back and shot to death.

---

[375] _Los Angeles Times_, Wednesday, August 4, 1982, "A Search for Ancestral Soviet Home", William C. Rempel, page 14

War in Ukraine

December 6, 1918, the German Army and the Selbstschutz met Makhno, the Black Army anarchist, at Chernogovka, on the eastern edge of Ukraine. Makhno actually outnumbered their forces, and fighting was fierce, but they were able to repulse Makhno, who aimed to utterly destroy the Molotschna Colony.[376]

In January, Makhno joined forces with the Bolsheviks, and a week later the Selbstschutz was defeated when faced with Mackhno and machine-gun fire.[377]

Villagers were awake at night, watching . . . . waiting. They would put children to bed fully clothed. A barking dog jolted them upright, in fear and panic, awaiting the arrival of a rushing horde.

In the village of Schoenfeld, where Susanna worshipped as a little girl before moving to Gnadenfeld, and her mother Agatha had married Kornelius Krause, the people were in such a panic one night, they fled leaving uneaten suppers on their tables. Some poor souls had no horses or wagon, so were left behind where they could only stay, pray and await the unknown, bravely singing "What a Friend we Have in Jesus."

When a certain Makhnovet bandit was presented with the Christian offer of forgiveness and everlasting life through the atoning work of Jesus on the cross for his sins, he contemptuously replied,

> Do not try to change me with advice to read the Bible and believe in God.
> We Makhnovtsy, as partisans and anarchists have only one program,
> only one desire and aim, —to enjoy living off somebody else's property,
> to rob and kill as we please. We will not change and we will be a menace
> to others as long as we live. Nothing will change us, not the Bible, nor
> God, neither Hell nor Heaven. We will live this way as long as possible.
> And when that is no longer possible, we will commit suicide, and only when
> Mother Earth has covered us will we be harmless.[378]

---

[376] My Harp is Turned to Mourning, Al Reimer, pg 355
[377]. Master's Thesis, Selbstschutz, Josephine Chipman, pg 143
[378] Miracles of Grace and Judgment, Gerhard P. Schroeder, pg 77

By February 28, 1919, Reds arrived in Gnadenfeld. Halbstadt was occupied by the more disciplined Bolsheviks. The much more feared Makhnovites entered Gnadenfeld. To where could they have fled? The road to the Crimea was already blocked before the Reds reached the villages of the Gnadenfeld district. We had gladly given them all our possessions—land, grain, horses, whatever they wanted. We were now free of our possessions as never before.[379]

While the Mennonites generally were not extravagant in their lifestyles, still they were the privileged ones. Differences in language, religion, culture, with their distinct architecture and village layouts in their prosperous, neat, and tidy little isolated villages, made them cultural islands separated from their poor struggling Russian neighbors. Those differences were enough to arouse jealousy and would make them easy targets. While the Mennonites had been blind to the plight of their Russian neighbors, they also had been blind to the coming upheaval and time of terror.

In hindsight, we wonder why the Mennonites did not evangelize their Russian neighbors and reach out to them more. In Catherine the Great's Manifesto, Mennonites were prohibited from proselytizing the Russian Orthodox. Russians, by Russian law, had no freedom of religion but were bound to remain in the state Orthodox church with its many shrines and painted icons, incense and flickering candles, and dead orthodoxy filled with lifeless patriarchs and saints. Mennonites were only allowed to evangelize the Muslims living amongst them. It was even permissible to openly evangelize the riffraff, low lifes, thieves, whores, and ruffians. Mennonite Brethren Church members actually did some limited evangelizing of their own Russian farm workers.

Generally, the Mennonites, bound in their rigid forms of worship, held contempt for their untidy, lazy, superstitious Russian neighbors. They could have learned much from them regarding the joy and spontaneity of their Russian culture. Though some had been converted and baptized (but in secret, since it was against the law), there was no lasting success amongst the Russians. Eventually the Edict of Tolerance of 1905-1906 gave more wide spread freedom to Russian people from the Orthodox Church, such as the Old Believers[380] who had always been persecuted, banned, and destroyed. The 1906 Constitution also legalized Mennonites associating with Russian Baptists and evangel-izing Orthodox Russians.[381] Beginning in 1917, for the first time, Mennonite missionaries were allowed to move freely among Russians and Ukrainians. This missionary outreach began in New Samara.[382] [383]

---

[379] <u>Mennonites in Ukraine, amid Civil War and Anarchy (1917-1920)</u>, Translated and Edited by John B. Toews, pg 169

[380] believed in the Gospel of Jesus Christ, so were outside the Russian Orthodox Church and persecuted for their faith

[381] <u>RÜCKENAU, The History of a Village in the Molotschna Mennonite Settlement of South Russia</u>, Leona Wiehe Gislason, pg 84

[382] <u>Testing Faith and Tradition, A Global Mennonite History</u>, John A. Lapp, Arnold Snyder, pg 198

[383] Some of the most cruel, brutal robbers and murderers, while imprisoned with a Russian Orthodox priest, testified they learned of the forgiveness of sin through another prisoner, a Mennonite believer. These robbers then accused that priest of causing them and

The war front kept moving back and forth through Gnadenfeld.[384] Villagers repeatedly heard thunderous explosions of artillery shells, bursting shrapnel in the sky, the continuous tat-tat-tat-tat of machine gun and rifle fire, cavalry galloping down the street, occasional war planes, and bombs dropping, forming craters here and there. Aaron's cousins were among those sent out to collect the dead from the fields of battle.[385] Once an American biplane passed over Gnadenfeld. Amazingly, only a couple of villagers were killed by the fighting all around them.

Prisoners were stripped of their uniforms and allowed to walk in their unbleached underwear begging for food. Agatha cooked a whole pail of meat soup for them and set out a bunch of wooden soup spoons on the *bench in the back yard. Heinz, Mieche, and Katja watched through the window the way they enjoyed the soup and bread. No chairs. No plates.[386]*

Then General Deniken of the White Army was able to involve the Selbstschutz in 2 military operations. The first operation overran two Russian villages south of Gnadenfeld and 5 captured bandits were taken to the Gnadenfeld cemetery and executed. In the second operation, White forces took up guarding positions, while the Selbstschutz attacked the Russian village directly, and the Makhno bandits fled. The Selbstschutz then realizing somewhat their blunder and their vulnerability, but still unaware that they were fighting the very army that would soon reign over them permanently, persuaded White commander Colonel Malakhov to sign a memorandum stating the Selbstschutz was just for self-defense, and would be disbanded once civil order was reestablished. Whatever army was occupying, whether White, Red or marauding bandits, they requisitioned whatever they wanted. Only the White Army occasionally offered to pay, but in worthless Czarist paper money.[387]

Unfortunately, although the Selbstschutz men were brave and courageous, they were poorly trained and organized, with no decisive leadership. After their defeat their operational maps revealed a complete lack of strategy, focusing on military objectives with no tactical value.[388] It seems those Mennonite villages which had provided the most Selbstschutz resistance, suffered the most, both from the Makhnovites and the Bolsheviks.

By early 1919 the combined forces of Makhno and the Red Army defeated the Selbstschutz, with the Red Army occupying Gnadenfeld on March 11. Then followed days of anarchy and terror, with

---

their families to only know lives of desperate crime, because the priests had never given them the Gospel with its freeing power from sin. Beneath the Cross, Cornelius Martens, pp 146-155

[384] 1835-1943 Gnadenfeld, Molotschna, A Lowen Schmidt, Jakob P. Dick Remembers: "The Years 1918-1925", pg 57

[385] "A Letter to My Children; The Memoirs of Arthur G. Rempel", pg 27

[386] "My Family was Transplanted", audio tape by Mary Dirks Janzen

[387] Czars, Soviets, & Mennonites, John B. Toews, pg 87

[388] Master's Thesis, Selbstschutz, Josephine Chipman, pg 150

intermittent occupation by the White armies, first under General Deniken, then General Wrangel, but also the Bolsheviks and Makhnovze.[389]

The Reds came to the village to punish the villagers for their participation in the *Selbstschutz*.[390] In their anger the Russians had sworn to kill all the inhabitants and burn the villages to the ground. In total desperation, the Mennonites humbled themselves before God, confessed their sins and prayed to God for mercy . . . . *"Brethren, we have sinned, have neglected the help of God, and have relied on the arm of the flesh as our source of strength. There is only one way for us; repentance and confession of sin and back to our God." Repentance and prayer occurred in the very room where formally the Selbstschutz was foolishly, inexpediently, injudiciously, unwisely, organized. A committee was elected to negotiate with the Reds . . . a terrifying assignment . . . .*[391]

Carl Rempel hid out in Crimea for about eight months, having been an officer in the defeated army and a member of the Selbstschutz. The Reds would have shot him on sight.[392] Not only were those in the Selbstschutz afraid of reprisals, but the whole German community was afraid because they had given aid and comfort to the German army.

On March 19, 1919, the village elders Benjamin Unruh and teacher Cornelius Wiens (men who had refused to participate in the Selbstschutz) humbly appeared before victorious Colonel Dobenko, to plead for Mennonite lives, "Mr Dobenko, please forgive us!"

Then the general let them have it. "You damned renegades from the faith of your fathers! For 400 years you could not take arms, but now for your damned Kaiser Wilhelm." Three times they had to hear, "You damned renegades from the faith of your fathers!"

Three times they cried out, "Comrade Dobenko, forgive us!"[393]

They presented copies of the minutes forming the Selbstschutz Wirtschaftskomitee, clearly stating, *we were not a regular military unit and did not wish to engage in any political actions. We only wished to protect ourselves from the bandits until a government in Russia took matters into its own hand."* A memorandum from Colonel Malakhov stated *"the Selbstschutz was just for self-defense, and would be disbanded once civil order was reestablished."* The Mennonites bargained with the Bolsheviks that the Mennonites would turn in all their weapons within three days and

---

[389] Molotschna Historical Atlas, Helmut T. Huebert, pg 95
[390] "Memoir of Agatha and Carl Rempel" as told to K. R. Lockwood, pg 12
[391] Mennonites in Ukraine, Amid Civil War and Anarchy (1917-1920), Translated and Edited by John B. Toews, pg 86
[392] "Memoir of Agatha and Carl Rempel", as told to K. R. Lockwood, pp. 9-11
[393] Events and People, In Russian Mennonite History, Helmut T. Huebert, pg 154

would allow the Bolsheviks to plunder for three days. In return, the Bolsheviks would spare their lives. They pled for mercy, but any members of the Selbstschutz that were found would be executed.

A mass killing did not happen. People saw the wondrous hand of God in this. [394]

It was July 1919 when Mennonites in Ukraine were freed from Bolshevik terror as General Deniken of the White Army occupied Gnadenfeld and was lodged in the town hall. Some Mennonites joined Deniken's White Army when it arrived. Deniken's forces caught 4 members of the Red Army, and released them. When the Reds began to run, they were shot in the back. *The villagers buried them in wooden caskets at the new cemetery. After six months some of our men were ordered to dig them up. With pomp and sarcastic speeches against us Germans, they were taken to their Russian village to be buried again.*[395]

---

[394] Mennonites in Ukraine, amid Civil War and Anarchy (1917-1920), Translated and Edited by John B. Toews, pg 182
[395] 1835-1943 Gnadenfeld, Molotschna, A Lowen Schmidt, pg 57

Beyond Hope

"We see before us a starving and freezing Russia, a land torn apart by class hate . . . ."[396]

"Woe to the rich. But who is still rich?"[397]

We have created the Russia of today. We, the atheists, are to blame for all the misery. We killed the conscience of men and women, and they have turned Russia upside down.[398]

God has extraordinary means to bear us up when ordinary ones fail. He can turn poisons into antidotes, hindrances into furtherances, and destructions into deliverances. The ravens give Elijah food. A whale becomes Jonah's ship, and pilot too. An almighty God can work without means. God often brings His people into such a condition that they do not know what to do. God is with His people at all times, but He is most sweetly with them in the worst of times. ~ Thomas Lye

Houses in the German villages aways had a barn attached to them. Attached to the far end of the barn was a shed to store farm equipment. The wall between the house and barn was built of brick with a heavy iron door, making a fire-proof separation between house and barn. Farmers didn't have to brave fierce winter storms to do their chores. The barns generally contained stalls for twelve horses, six cows, a bull (when it was their turn for use of the village bull), and a separate stall for calves. A typical farm might also have enough pigs to slaughter, chickens for eggs and meat, perhaps a dozen geese, several dogs, and enough cats to keep the mouse population under control.

During winters, for about five months, all livestock was kept inside the stable or barn. The fodder, (hay, oats, beets, and pumpkins—animal feed) was stored in the barn attic above the animals. The roof was high and steep pitched. On occasional, sunny days in winter, the cattle and horses were let into the yard for exercise and relaxation, but those days were few and far between.[399]

Wheat, oats, barley and beans were stored in the Dachstube, or house attic, along with smoked hams and sausages in barrels of ashes, and sacks of dried apples and cherries. Marie had always enjoyed playing in the beans because they were all kinds of colors.

---

[396] <u>Mennonites in Ukraine Amid Civil War and Anarchy,1917-1920</u>, Translated and Edited by John B. Toews, pg 39, Abraham Kroeker, "The Year-end (1917/18)," <u>Volksfreund II (XI), no. 20 (January, 1918), 2.</u>
[397] <u>Mennonites in Ukraine Amid Civil War and Anarchy,1917-1920</u>, Translated and Edited by John B. Toews, pp. 44-45
[398] <u>Beneath the Cross</u>, Cornelius Martens, pg 92
[399] <u>The Molotschna Colony, A Heritage Remembered</u>, Henry Bernard Tiessen, pg 34

By August and September 1919, the competing armies each requisitioned wagons to transport food, munitions, the wounded, and troops. Horses needed for farm work were depleted by about half, and time to do the yard and field work was greatly diminished. In spite of an abundant crop in 1919, food supplies rapidly dwindled. Food supplies which had previously generously supplied a very large family for a full year and a half or more, now were depleted by the ravenous Bolsheviks in a mere six weeks, as if there would be no end to the bounty they were wasting.[400]

Bolsheviks tore open walls, roofs, and floors. They seized whatever they could transport and ruined whatever was left behind. Books were torn and trampled upon, bedding cut open and feathers scattered in kitchen, cellar, and attic. Furniture was smashed or soiled. What was still useful was distributed to poor people or stored in factory warehouses.[401] Factories were now the property of the workers, yet people stole as much as possible and produced little. The cows lowed in the barns with hunger; hens, ducks, geese, dogs, cats, everything ran around hungry. Calves, sheep, and swine grunted and bleated. Glass jars of canned fruit were smashed; flour poured out; books and photographs thrown in the garden.[402] It was senseless, total wanton wastefulness and destruction.

Now also came the time of confiscatory and impossible government demand for grain and other foods, including poultry and live stock. A wry political joke was told in Gnadenfeld. A rooster had hanged himself and had left a note explaining, that since the government had counted the whole flock, and had demanded one egg from every member of the flock every day, he had to kill himself since in no way would he ever be able to comply with that demand, and he feared the punishment more than death itself.[403] There were several cases of animals committing suicide. A cow's head had been stuck on a fence post, with a sign saying before Communism, there had been lots of hay and grain to eat, and now the cow was only given straw and had to deliver so much milk as a tax to the government that life was not worth living.[404]

While the White and Red armies fought in and around Gnadenfeld, Communists had plundered the village before the Rempels returned. Even when they were not fighting in the neighborhood, Bolsheviks often raided, then demanded entertainment as well. Barns and storehouses were empty—no horses, no seeds, and hardly a glimmer of hope for the future . . . . In many homes bread was no longer baked, replaced instead by a steady diet of soup made of turnips and milled

---

[400] <u>Mennonites in Ukraine, Amid Civil War and Anarchy (1917-1920)</u> Translated and edited by John B. Toews, pg 81
[401] <u>Ibid,</u> pg 60
[402] <u>They Came From Wiesenfeld,Ukraine to Canada,</u> Translated and edited by Katherine Martens, pg 59
[403] "A Letter to My Children; The Memoirs of Arthur G. Rempel", pg 29
[404] <u>The Russländer,</u> Sandra Birdsell, pg 332

Makucha—these were the ingredients on so many recipe cards from those times.[405]
The farmers swept their attics to collect the last grain to comply with the requisition orders. [406]

When Communists took the grain, they not only took food, but also insulation for cold weather, and seed to plant next year's crops. The Communists just threw sacks of grain out of attics onto the muddy ground. Many sacks split open, spilling precious seed all over the mud. Then the Communist soldiers' horses trampled much seed into the ground, wasting it, and leaving almost nothing for the people to eat, let alone plant the next spring.

Communist ideas predominate . . . . Even the gods would despair of the stupidity of their ideas . . . . Everybody wants to live in affluence and avoid work, thus forgetting that prosperity can only be achieved through honest labor. Work must come before play is what we taught our children and it applies to adults as well.[407]

The Cheka registered everything. No one was allowed more than one change of underwear or more than one pillow for each person in the household.[408]

Grandmother Agatha hid her family jewels in the bake house, but one day a Russian came and went directly to the hiding place. No one could be trusted, and even some of the Mennonites were Red.[409] As traitors, some treated their fellow Mennonites more harshly and cruelly than the Makhnovites. The traitor Letkemann from Halbstadt encouraged his fellow Bolsheviks to each kill as many as forty Mennonites by January 1, 1920.

Bolsheviks imprisoned one group of men in a cellar. Some were taken out individually and shot, the rest fired upon through barred windows. Finally, a hand grenade was thrown in the cellar. Nothing was left but bloody, mangled corpses. [410]

Mennonite Peter von Kampen lead a strong Selbstschutz which never took prisoners. The one rational for forming a Selbstschutz, "I only defend myself against the one who is attacking me," had been replaced by a spirit of vengeance.

---

[405] "Gnadenfeld, Molotschna, South Russia 1835-1943," Jacob C. Krause, pg 9
[406] 1835-1943 Gnadenfeld, Molotschna, A Lowen Schmidt; Jakob P. Dick Remembers: "The Years 1918-1925," pg 57
[407] Hope Springs Eternal, John P. Nickel, pp 175-176
[408] Mennonites in Ukraine, Amid Civil War and Anarchy (1917-1920), Translated and Edited by John B. Toews, pg 60
[409] "Memoir of Agatha and Carl Rempel" as told to K. R. Lockwood, pg 12
[410] Mennonites in Ukraine, Amid Civil War and Anarchy (1917-1920), Translated and edited by John B. Toews, pg 120

The first and one of the most gruesome massacres occurred in Eichenfeld, October 26, 1919[411] where Makhnovists systematically killed all male inhabitants, shooting them at one end of town, and hacking them with sabers at the other end. From nine o'clock in the morning till four in the afternoon, thousands of anarchists moved through Eichenfeld.[412] Each surviving wife would stumble into her neighbor's house only to discover the same tragedy had befallen their neighbors. Eighty-two people were left dead.

Muensterberg was burned to the ground. Only one home remained, which was immediately dismantled, carried off to Russian villages, and used as building materials. Ninety-eight people, including eighteen women and thirty-six children, including babies in the cradle, lost their lives.[413] Often after one of these raids, small children were seen wandering about sobbing, lost and dazed.

Earlier, villagers from the Zagradovka Colony had sent a punitive detachment to Russian villages where they beat and tortured innocent and guilty alike. On November 29, 1919, the Zagradovka and Blumenort massacres occurred. A number of men were herded into a cellar, which then was doused with gasoline and set on fire.[414] One man wrote he escaped dressed as an old woman, and fled along with his wife, hearing behind him the cries of burning animals and people who had been covered in gasoline and ignited.[415]

In Zagradovka, women were raped and farms burned to the ground. Some two hundred two people died in Zagradovka; twenty-one more in Blumenort were buried in a mass grave.[416] When it was all over, the villages of Gerhardstal, Eichenfeld, Neuhorst, and Neuendorf had vanished; Reinfeld, Petersdorf and Paulheim had only a few walls left standing. A resident who had managed to escape recalls the sight which greeted him when he returned, "There was no one to be seen in our village. The next day, with the help of survivors from a neighboring village, the dead were buried in a mass grave."[417]

---

[411] http://www.mhsbc.com/news/pdf/RB07-3_2001_Summer.pdf, Mennonite Historical Society of British Columbia, pg 5, accessed 14 March, 1018. pp. 27 May, 2001, A reunion was held at the Makhno Eichenfeld massacre site by ancestors of those who were able to flee. What the author found extremely interesting was the testimony of the Russians who were just small children and lived nearby when these atrocities occurred. They did not share the extreme hatred of the Makhno for the Germans. The following is what the local Russians recalled, or what they remembered their parents telling them about the Germans who had lived in these villages, which are now completely gone. *They were very punctual people, cultured, clean—not 'our people.' There was no hostility toward the Germans in the local area. I remember that their villages were very beautiful. There were pear and apricot trees everywhere—all planted by the Germans. With us everything was run down, disheveled, dirty. With them, everything was cultured. Our people worked for the Germans as cooks, cleaners, and gardeners.* pg 83 *My parents told me that the Germans were hardworking and orderly; even their six-year old boys worked side-by-side with their fathers. They paid decent wages, and they were honest about paying them."* pg 86 Nestor Makhno and the Eichenfeld Massacre, by Dyck, Staples, & Toews Wikipedia

[412] Eichenfeld, Dubowka, Heinrich Toews, translated from the German by Arthur Toews, pg 78

[413] Often, if it were just a small group of Mackhno bandits that had come upon a small group of Germans, Russian peasants would try to intervene, usually to no avail. Events and People, Helmut T. Huebert, "Massacre in Muensterberg", November 29-December 1, 1919," pages 158-160

[414] Escape to Freedom, Cornelius C. Funk, pg 50

[415] Master's Thesis, Selbstschutz, Josephine Chipman, pg 160

[416] Mennonites in Ukraine, Amid Civil War and Anarchy (1917-1920), Translated and edited by John B. Toews, pp. 139-140, 184-185

[417] Master's Thesis, Selbstschutz, Josephine Chipman, pg 159

December 11,1919 estate owners Dreidiger & Krause[418] were executed in Schoenfeld.

By December 23, 1919, not only did the bandits rob and loot, but they also tortured to find hidden treasure. The question was, should people just abandon what they owned and flee to some safer place? But was a safer place to be found anywhere at all in Russia?

By winter 1920, the last Mennonites had left Schoenfeld and returned to the mother colonies of Chortiza and Molotschna. Some seventy farms had been totally devastated. Only bare walls, dried up gardens, chopped down orchards and forests, and unseeded grain fields populated by every kind of weed were left. Schoenfeld Colony had become a desolate wilderness.[419]

Death came to Schoenfeld. Not just the death of many of her people, but death to the village itself. Nestor Makhno made the district his head-quarters.[420] As the people fled, and left the village totally deserted, it's fate was sealed. Neighboring Russians came and demolished the buildings: church, school, store, and homes. They tore down each and every brick, door, and window, then used them as building materials in their own villages.[421] After all, that meant German Mennonites would never be able to come back and claim those buildings as theirs, ever again.[422]

In retaliation for Mennonites forming a Selbstschutz or joining the Volunteer White Army, Makhno ordered the entire Mennonite population be slaughtered. The order was promptly carried out in two villages—no one was spared—men, women, children. Prayer meetings were held. *"Dear God, we have been put to shame with our selbstschutz. Forgive us and be merciful to us." "God forgive us our sins. We trusted the flesh for our strength!"* Nothing more could be done. A few days later the Makhnoviks stormed in, shouting and discharging their weapons, filling everyone with fear and anxiety.

Inexplicably, the Makhnovites changed their mind. They took pity in their murderous killing spree. An order came the remaining villages be spared after all. *But when we (*Makhnovites*) entered the villages, we relented. We did not know why, but we felt sorry for them and could not do it.*

---

[418] Either Susanna Krause Rempel's grandfather Cornelius or uncle Johann (Kornelius Krause's brother), Probably Cornelius had already died ca 1910, so Johann was the one executed.

[419] Mennonites in Ukraine, Amid Civil War and Anarchy (1917-1920), Translated and edited by John B. Toews, pg 10

[420] Hope Springs Eternal, John P. Nickel, pg 246

[421] Miracles of Grace and Judgment, Gerhard P. Schroeder, pg 90

[422] A 1999 tour to Schoenfeld found "only three old farm machinery buildings and just one structure from Schoenfeld village itself still standing, from its German Mennonite past. Everything else is gone; nothing else is there". Notes on the history of the Schoenfeld Colony, Heritage Cruise 1999, Ron Toews

You (God) wonderfully protected us (Mennonites) in one respect. What we feared most did not happen—we did not lose our lives. We knew God in His great mercy had heard our cries.[423] Even though the mass slaughter of the whole Mennonite population had been averted, looting continued. The Makhnovites searched attic, cellar, barn, straw stacks, and even found clothes hidden, buried in the manure pile. Boots and shoes were long gone, and everyone wore wooden sandals and torn clothes. The populace walked about as specters with blank expressions, fallen cheeks, dressed in rags, covered in old blankets or remnants of old coats.* [424]

In Gnadenfeld, when Makhno himself was stationed at Johann Rempel's house, an agent of the Red army was discovered in Benjamin Unruh's garden behind the mulberry hedge. He was dragged into the street in front of the Hollander windmill and killed with their sabers. Then the Makhnovze tried to trample him into the ground by riding their horses over the corpse. But the horses could not be made to step on the corpse.[425]

Makhno's motto was, "Anarchy is the mother of all order!"[426] Whatever they could not take they destroyed, burning homes and barns. Makhno and his men killed 240 persons in Zagradowka, 63 in Ebenfeld, 58 in Steinbach, 81 in Nikolaipol, and 12 in Gnadenfeld. There was hardly a village that did not mourn at least several who had been murdered.

The villages of Petershagen, Rudnerweide, Grossweide, which had refused to participate in the selbstschutz experienced **no** *deaths following the collapse of the Selbstschutz and the carnage that followed. The others experienced an average of eleven dead per village as a result of the Selbstschutz.* Those three villages were repeatedly respected and commended by the Red authorities.[427]

A minister in Wiesenfeld and Zagradovka dared preach against the Selbstschutz and was excommunicated. The Lord spared him and protected him while some of those who had excommunicated him were murdered. The Old General Abram Rempel sought refuge in Crimea.[428]

It was at this point, too, that people began turning to God in desperation. Many came to know the Lord, experiencing for the first time the meaning of "Rufe mich an in der Not, so will ich dich erretten" — "And call upon me in the day of trouble: I will deliver thee, and thou shalt glorify me." [429]

---

[423] Mennonites in Ukraine, Amid Civil War and Anarchy (1917-1920), Translated and edited by John B. Toews, pp. 63, 91-92, 170-171
[424] Mennonites in Ukraine, Amid Civil War and Anarchy (1917-1920), Translated and edited by John B. Toews, pp. 64, 66
[425] 1835-1943 Gnadenfeld, Molotschna, A. Lowen Schmidt, pp. 56-57
[426] 1835-1943 Gnadenfeld, Molotschna, A. Lowen Schmidt, pg 24
[427] Mennonites in Ukraine, amid Civil War and Anarchy (1917-1920), Translated and Edited by John B. Toews, pp. 89-90, 181
[428] Ibid, pg 90
[429] Psalm 50:15 The Batum Story, God's Mercy and Man's Kindness, compiled by Mary Dirks Janzen, Third Edition, Edited by Mary E. Janzen 2011 pg 74

Since Makhno's activities somewhat helped the Bolshevik cause, they had allowed him the freedom to do as he pleased for a time. Makhno even joined the Red army for a while. Later, however, Makhno fell out of favor, and was himself on the run. Once, while escaping from the Bolsheviks going toward Romania, Makhno stayed overnight at the home of Suse and Jacob Toews and Helena and Cornelius Toews in Gnadenfeld.[430]

January 1, 1920, the Reds, no longer needing extra harassment by the bandits to further their cause, began rounding them up and executing them. They caught Trifon Pravda, one of the most gruesome leaders under Makhno, but by the grace of God, Trifon escaped, later confessed his sins, and became a true follower of his Master and Savior Jesus Christ. There were also other Makhnovtsy who turned to Christ, who were eventually exiled to Siberia for their faith. Trifon's brother Senjka Pravda, Koljka Ermolovsky, and Yerik Grosa, three of the most depraved Makhnovtsy, were being chased by the Reds . . . . When the wheels of their cart hauling their machine guns broke to pieces, Koljka and Yerik abandoned Senjka. A previous injury had left Senjka with two amputated legs, so he couldn't run away on his stumps. Senjka, who had previously boasted about killing his brother (Mitjka) and 56 or more other men, pulled out his gun and sent a bullet through his own head. Now Mother Earth covered him and rendered him harmless.[431]

January 16, 1920, a funeral was held for thirteen men who had been locked up as prisoners by the Bolsheviks in a shed that was then set on fire. [432]

The bandits, who had absolutely no concept of personal cleanliness or hygiene, were so full of lice, people could see them crawling on the collar, sleeves, and pocket flaps of their dark clothing. Rats carried the Rickettsia organism, causing typhus, which was then transferred to humans by lice. The incubation period could take up to two weeks, but onset was usually abrupt with extremely high fever, a constant headache, and rash. It could lead to stupor, vascular collapse and kidney failure.[433] Not only had the Makhnovites slaughtered people, but Mennonites and Makhnovites both succumbed to typhus in droves.

Most people had no change of clothes, including no change of underwear. To kill lice, members of a family took turns undressing, trying to keep warm under such covers as the family still possessed, while the other family members wrapped the underwear and outer clothing in paper or cloth, and

[430] Suse and Helena Toews were sisters of Aaron A Rempel, 1996 Mennonite Heritage Cruise, Part Four, http://home.ica.net/~walterunger/Rudy-4.htm
[431] Miracles of Grace and Judgment, Gerhard P. Schroeder, pp. 177-178
[432] Mennonites in Ukraine, Amid Civil War and Anarchy (1917-1920), Translated and edited by John B. Toews, pp. 18, 19
[433] Mennonite Medicine in Russia, 1800 to 1930, Helmut T. Huebert, pp 172-173

placed them into the oven, to kill the lice in the heat. Or they would crush the blood sucking varmints between their thumb and finger nails, or by whacking the seams of the garments with a hammer. In some Mennonite villages, almost everyone contracted typhus, with as many as 30% to 40% dying. The bandits died like flies.[434]

Hospitalization was generally of no help, since medicine, beds, and blankets had all been previously purloined. Schools were turned into makeshift hospitals, with male students drafted into serving as orderlies, and fresh straw strewn on the floor as makeshift beds. The men were made to strip down to the waist, where one could then see lice crawling over the entire body. However, usually only a few days later, these student orderlies also succumbed to disease. Many Makhnovtsy arrived at the hospitals, and so many died, the wagons bringing bandits were no sooner empty of the sick, when they were immediately filled again with the dead. Toward the end, bandits didn't even bother to pick up their comrades, who were left lying in their quarters, stables, or even in the streets.[435]

Many villagers were much too weak from disease to dig graves for their loved ones. When they did so with much difficulty, then moved the corpse to the cemetery, they often found another corpse had already been placed into the open grave.[436]

Help came from the Molotschna colony to the south: food, clothing, medical supplies, and help to bury the dead. This was complicated because various body parts often had to be gathered from dismembered corpses. Recovery parties would enter a house and find two decaying Makhnovite bodies. In an adjoining room four persons occupied one bed: a father with his sick children. The mother had died earlier. As it turned out the father was already dead. The children said he had not moved for three days. Bodies of Makhnovites lay in all the houses and barns, while horse cadavers littered the barns.[437]

Women took to wearing light, home sewn caps, to cover their bald heads, shorn to get rid of lice. The villagers didn't have shoes any more, only home made sandals.[438]

Disease followed the armies, with 160 dead of typhus in Osterwick, Einlage 100, and Kronsthal 66.[439] In many homes there was no one well enough to care for the sick. In 12 households everyone had died, and in Eichenfeld, 22 widows of the men slain by the Makhnovites suffered from typhus.

---

[434] Miracles of Grace and Judgment, Gerhard P. Schroeder, pp. 123, 130
[435] Miracles of Grace and Judgment, Gerhard P. Schroeder, pp. 137, 139
[436] Ibid, pg 124
[437] Mennonites in Ukraine, Amid Civil War and Anarchy (1917-1920), Translated and edited by John B. Toews, pg 69
[438] Miracles of Grace and Judgment, Gerhard P. Schroeder, pg 166
[439] Mennonite Historical Atlas, William Schoeder, Helmut T. Huebert, pg 138

Herzenberg

It was June, 1920 when at long last Aaron, Susanna and family approached Ukraine by train. Instead of taking only a week or so, this trip had already taken more than two months, and they still had not arrived in Gnadenfeld.

Because of fighting between the Whites and Reds right in Gnadenfeld itself, the train had to stop again near the German village Herzenberg, or Heart Village.[440] Aaron and Susanna again were stranded without money at Herzenberg. What were they going to do now?

Susanna sat down with the children. Aaron paced back and forth with his hands behind his back, back and forth, back and forth. He always paced when he was thinking really hard. What could they do? Aaron paced some more. Back and forth. Back and forth. Farther they couldn't go. They couldn't even go back to Siberia. Back and forth. Back and forth.

Ronka noticed green peppers for sale, beginning to turn red. Susanna noticed a group of men standing nearby talking, and she realized they were speaking Plattdeutsch, or Low German. The men had brought watermelons to the depot to ship. Two kinds of watermelon were grown, those that ripened early, and dark green ones that ripened later. For longer storage and shipping long distance, the darker green ones were better.

Susanna urged Aaron to go talk to them, but Aaron balked. He didn't want to, but Susanna kept urging him, "You go talk to them. They are our people. They talk Plattdeutsch. What else can we do? We can't do anything else. You go **talk** to them."

Back and forth. Back and forth. Aaron kept pacing back and forth. Stuck now in Herzenberg, what could Aaron possibly do? They were so close to Gnadenfeld, but the war was in the way, totally blocking their path. Back and forth. Hands clasped behind his back, Aaron kept pacing. Susanna finally went over to the men talking Platdeutch and very reluctantly, Aaron, too, strolled over, only to discover that not only were they German Mennonites, but one of the men was also named Rempel. He was not a blood relative of Aaron's, but he was related to Susanna by marriage. Susanna's mother Agatha's sister, Maria Dueck, had married Gerhard Rempel. Peter Johann Rempel, standing right in front of them in Herzenberg was one of Gerhard's brothers who actually had lived in

---

[440] http://www.mhsbc.com/famhistories.html Herzenberg, in the district of Pavlograd, province of Ekaterinoslav, Ukraine, Russia. This village prospered particularly by raising. sheep. During 1919-1920, 18 adults died of typhoid fever.

Gnadenfeld when young. He even looked like Uncle Gerhard. Peter looked at Aaron and said, "Why don't you come and stay with us?" What a small world! And what a provision of God! This Rempel relation by marriage took the Aaron Rempel family into his own home. They didn't even really know each other. He had no idea how long this family would live with them or how long he would have to support them.

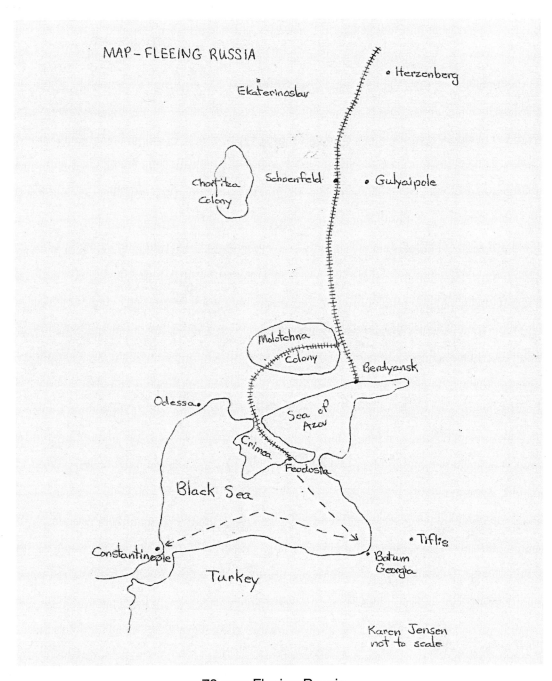

78 map Fleeing Russia

family into his own home. They didn't even really know each other. He had no idea how long this family would live with them or how long he would have to support them.

Only a year and a half earlier, on 29 September, 1918, three families were murdered in Herzenberg by the Makhno bandits.[441] *In one instance, villagers were looking for a missing boy, and later found him under his bed, with his nose and ears cut off, and palms sliced up. He had wound himself up in the sheets to try and stop the bleeding and pain . . . . In another home they raped the women while the rest of the family was lined up against the wall and forced to watch. Suddenly one soldier stuck his sword though the stomach of the baby in the cradle. He held it up on his sword. The baby could not cry but only gasped for breath. As he held it up, another soldier proceeded to cut off its little feet and hands.*[442] Often Makhno bandits then burned houses and/or barns to the ground, with only a few able to escape their village.

Now Jakob Rempel, Peter Johann's only surviving son, was gone. By the time Aaron Rempel's family arrived in Herzenberg, only Peter Johann and his two daughters remained. Barking dogs had announced the arrival of marauding bandits, who then immediately burst into the Peter Rempel home. True to form, they had the women cook them a meal, then raped them.[443] Makhno had taken their son Jakob and hacked him to pieces in front of the family as recently as February 13, 1920. It was so hard on the mother Katharina Klassen Rempel, she died only two days later. The two daughters Katharina and Anna Rempel Martens never smiled after that. No joy in life was left in them anymore. Katharina's husband Abram Martens had died a year earlier.[444] Despite all this, Peter Rempel seemed to be a happy man. He was very funny sometimes; he had a great sense of humor, and was "so down to earth talking."

In spite of their great sorrow, this Peter Johann Rempel family took the Aaron Rempel family in, and gave them their summer room. Marie, Ronka, Gonja, and little Susie really enjoyed staying with the Herzenberg Rempels, who had all kinds of apple, cherry and other fruit trees. They joined the host Rempels for meals, just like they were their own family, and with hearts overflowing with thanksgiving they sang, "Nun danket alle Got (Now Thank We All Our God)" for abundantly supplying all their needs.

---

[441] Master's Thesis, Selbstschutz, Josephine Chipman, pg 116
[442] Constantinoplers, Escape From Bolshshevism, Irmgard Epp, pp. 169, 181
[443] Author assumes this rape occurred, since rape fits the known modus operandi of the Makhno bandits, these girls never smiled again, and both died early,
[444] Neither sister lived very long. Katharina Rempel Martens died Aug. 1922, and Anna Rempel followed October, 1,1924, both dying in Herzenberg—Genealogy information taken from GRANDMA genealogy database

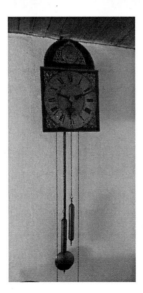

79, 80, 81, 82, 83

Kroeger clocks; Top to bottom: Mennonite Heritage Village, Steinbach, Manitoba, Canada; Kauff-man Museum, Bethel College, Newton, Kansas; Mennonite Settlement Museum, Hillsborough, Kansas

German Mennonite village homes in Herzenberg all had the same floor plan as those in Gnaden-feld and other Mennonite villages in Russia. Each house had a summer room, middle room, corner room, living room, and hallway. Usually the boys in the family slept in the summer room, so called, because heat from the brick stove in the kitchen did not reach it, so that room remained cooler in summer. Summer temperatures could reach as high as 102 degrees, but that was rare.

The Peter Rempels had a gaggle of geese, which chased Gonja, nipping at her legs, and she was afraid of them. Ronka had nightmares about them chasing him when he couldn't run.

Marie did go to school a little in Herzenberg for a couple of months, She was put in 3rd grade, be-cause she was 8 years old, almost nine and big for first grade. She had no idea what was going on in the classroom because she hadn't had first or second grade. So Marie was made to stay after school and work, but didn't tell at home because she was afraid she would get a licking. Ronka was still too young for school.

Aaron let the people of Herzenberg know he could repair all kinds of things. Stores had all been ran-sacked, the merchandise stolen by Bolsheviks or Makhnovite bandits. People were unable to buy new commodities any more, so they needed to mend whatever they had. People brought clocks to him. Kroeger clocks[445] were distinctively Mennonite, made right there in Rosenthal, Chortitza Old Colony, Uk-raine. They were found in almost every Mennonite home. The ring of the clock echoing through the entire house would tell mother and father when it was time to start a new day, make breakfast, feed the horses and cattle and send children off to school.[446] The hands, pendulum, and weights were all made of heavy brass, so required frequent polishing. The faces were hand painted by the clockmakers' two daughters, with numerous subjects: flowers, birds, mountain scenes. The clocks were so well made, they lasted a long time, and would be handed down from generation to generation. During the time of terror, with the marauding Makhnovites destroying much of what they didn't steal, almost everything needed repairs. Clocks hung all over the walls in the summer room where the family lived. At night the Rempel family could hear the tick tock, chimes, all kinds of clock noises as they slept in the summer room.

People brought Aaron sewing machines, watches, and even pots and pans with a little hole that needed mending. He was handy at fixing almost anything. One lady came to him with something wrapped up in a cloth, and she was rather shy about it. It was her night pot that had a hole. Mul-tiple farmers brought their wagons of grain into the neighbor's farm yard to be threshed, but his threshing machine broke down. Aaron also repaired the threshing machine. He had lots of work.

---

[445] Picture #32 shows another Kroeger clock in the Grottestube, located to the right of the himmelbed. Also see picture #92.
[446] First Mennonite Villages in Russia, 1789-1943, Khortitsa-Rosenthal, N. J. Kroeker, pg 86

Gnadenfeld—Home Again

If we lose the German language (Platdeutch Low German), then we lose much more than a language. ~ A Mennonite Prophet's Warning[447]

General Wrangel sent directives to his White Army generals ordering an offensive to begin against the enemy before dawn June 20, 1920 in the direction of Gnadenfeld. At 5:00 a.m. the attack began . . . . Pressed on all sides, pounded by artillery, strafed by machine guns of White aircraft, the Red Army started to panic. Many Red cavalrymen abandoned their exhausted horses and fled on foot, hiding where they could. In all, the Whites captured 40 canons, 200 machine guns, almost 3,000 horses, and took about 2,000 prisoners. The following day, June 21, a church service was held thanking God for the victory. [448]

Both Red and White armies had armored trains during the civil war, which included cannons mounted on the railway cars. The summer of 1920, when the Red Army occupied part of the Molotschna Colony, armored trains also patrolled the tracks of the Tokmak Railroad, running east and west to the north of Gnadenfeld.[449]

Soldiers from the White and Red armies were quartered in homes, depending upon who was occupying the village at the moment. Sometimes the village changed hands as much as several times a day.

When Red soldiers were quartered in homes, all the bedding was infested with lice. As children came home from school each day, they undressed to put their clothes into the oven to cook them hot enough to kill vermin. A typhus epidemic struck, and villagers died from typhus, cholera, amoebic dysentery, malnutrition, and other disease.[450] Deaths from disease often significantly exceeded deaths from the savagery of war. Around 300 soldiers a day died of typhus at Melitopol.[451]

Some soldiers boasted to their unwilling hosts, with little children listening, once the Bolsheviks were in total control, they would take all children away from their parents and train them to be good Communists. Even babies would be put into the Communist nurseries, while older boys would be made to fight in the Communist army.

---

[447] Mennonite Foods and Folkways from South Russia, Vol II, Norma Jost Voth, pp. 59-60
[448] Molotschna Historical Atlas, Wiliam Schroeder, Helmut T Huebert, pg 138-139
[449] Hierschau: An Example of Russian Mennonite Life, Helmut T. Huebert, pp. 170-173
[450] "A Letter to My Children; The Memoirs of Arthur G. Rempel," pg 29
[451] Mennonites in Ukraine Amid Civil War and Anarchy (1917-1920), Translated and Edited by John B Toews, pg 68

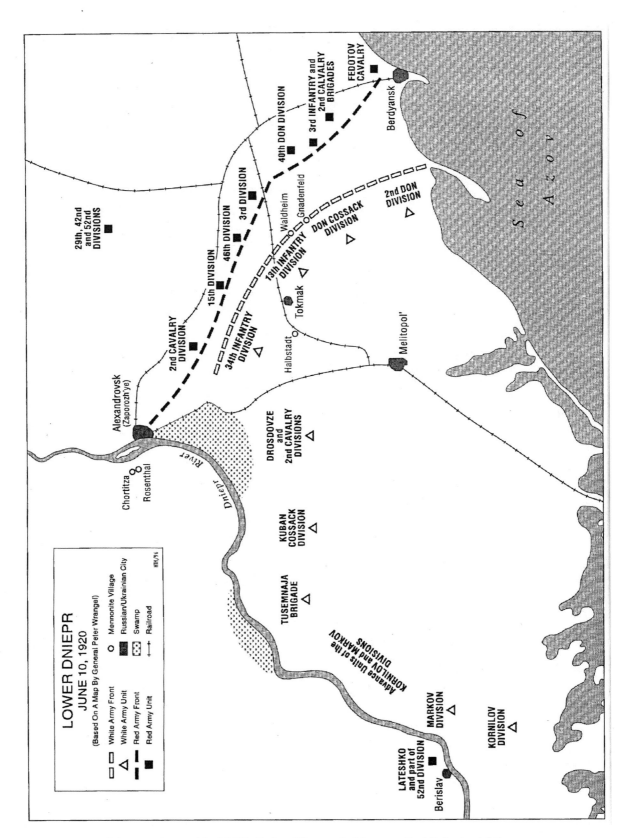

84 map **June 10, 1920**, Peter Wrangel, <u>Mennonite Historical Atlas</u>,
William Schroeder and Helmut T. Huebert, pp. 64, 138-139, used by permission

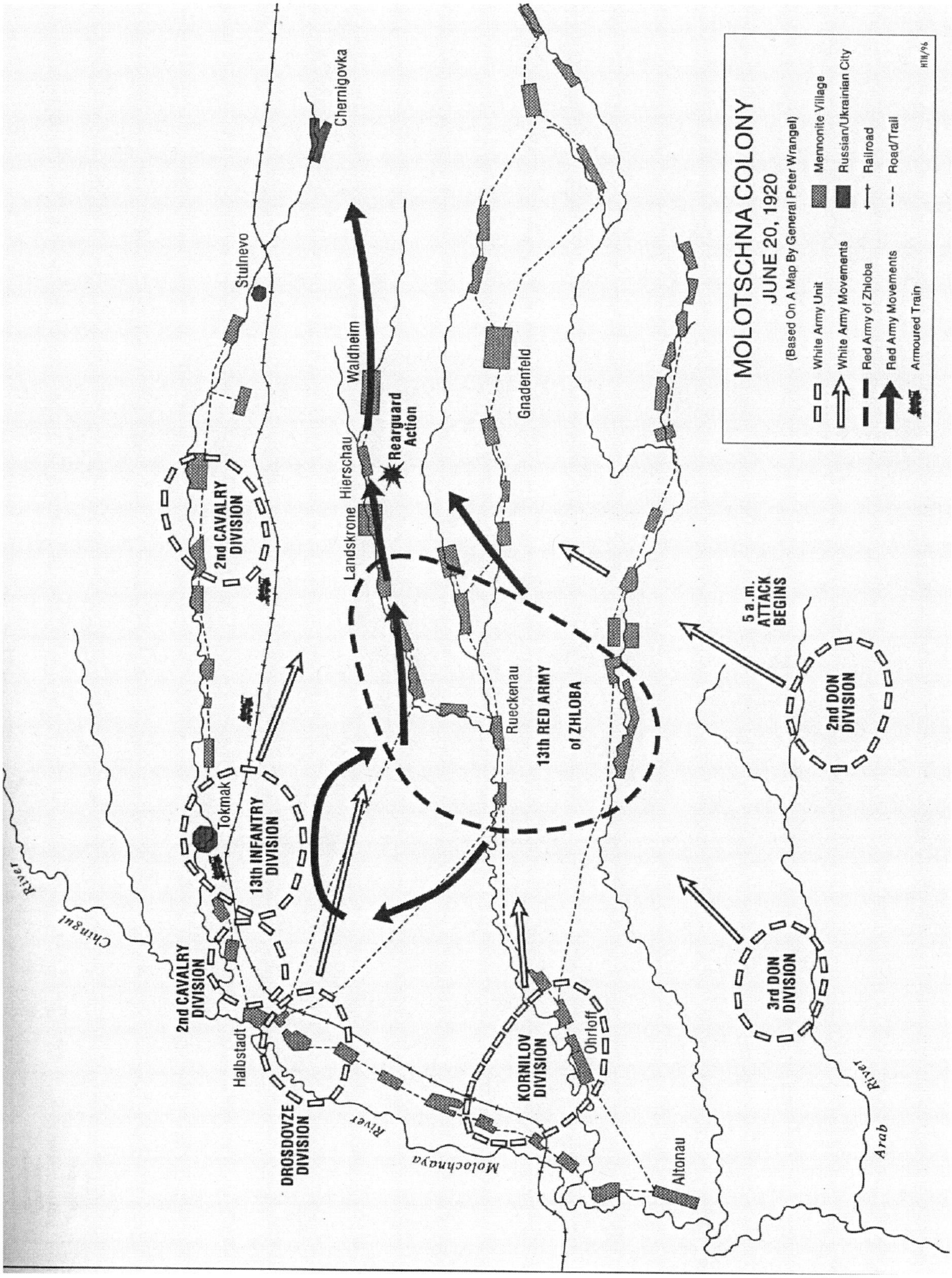
MOLOTSCHNA COLONY
JUNE 20, 1920
(Based On A Map By General Peter Wrangel)
White Army Unit
White Army Movements
Red Army of Zhloba
Red Army Movements
Armoured Train
Mennonite Village
Russian/Ukrainian City
Railroad
Road/Trail
Chernigovka
Stulnevo
Waldheim
Rearguard Action
Hierschau
Landskrone
Gnadenfeld
2nd CAVALRY DIVISION
5 a.m. ATTACK BEGINS
Rueckenau
13th RED ARMY of ZHLOBA
2nd DON DIVISION
Tokmak
13th INFANTRY DIVISION
Chingul River
2nd CAVALRY DIVISION
Halbstadt
DROSDOVZE DIVISION
Molochnaya River
KORNILOV DIVISION
Ohrloff
3rd DON DIVISION
Altonau
Arab River

85 Map Molotschna Battle **June 20, 1920,** pp. 13, 102-104 Molotschna Historical Atlas, Helmut T. Huebert, used by permission

The poor children would go to bed but be unable to sleep that night or for many nights to come, frightened that their whole, dear family would be separated forever.[452] [453]

The White soldiers attempted to pay their unwilling hosts with inflated, worthless rubles for food and other provisions they requisitioned. The Reds just took and plundered what they wanted. Oma Agatha hid some thread and needles, but the Bolsheviks found her buttons and plundered those as well. So the villagers covered seeds with cloth to create buttons. Cherry pits made the best buttons, but they also used beans, which unfortunately tended to sprout in damp weather.

Agatha's mother Susanna Matthies Dueck had moved from Schoenfeld to live with her daughter. When Gnadenfelders still had plenty to eat, even though Susanna Matthies Dueck was nearly blind, she would peel and cut apples by the hour to dry. [454] Great Grandmother Susanna Dueck owned a treasured "Grandmother's cap" (haub) that she kept in her trunk, to wear on special occasions to church, weddings, or funerals. It was a great privilege to be able to wear such a cap as soon as a woman was married, decorated with black lace and ribbons. Later, new styles came in, and the young married women started wearing a bow instead of the cap.[455]

A Bolshevik soldier throwing grain sacks out of the attic noticed Great Grandmother's precious cap hanging on a peg. He plunked it on his own head, and rode off on his horse. The family cried and laughed at the same time because not only had the Bolsheviks taken and spoiled all the grain and taken Great Grandmother's beloved haub, but because that soldier looked so funny riding off with the cap on his head.

Wrangel's White Army fled to Crimea, October, 1920. Gnadenfeld was suddenly filled with fleeing soldiers causing confusion and panic because no one knew who and where the enemy was.[456] Waiting Allied ships in Crimea took on as many fleeing men as possible, almost swamping them.[457] Still, because of a shortage of ships and too little room on the ships, many were left on land to face a cruel end by the Red Army. Many Mennonite lads managed to escape, but once they arrived in Constantinople, the French tried to press them into the French Foreign Legion. With the help of the Mennonite Refuge Home, they were rescued once again.[458]

---

[452] From Bolshevik Russia to America, A Mennonite Family Story, Henry D. Rempel, pp. 15-16
[453] They Came From Wiesenfeld, Ukraine to Canada, translated and edited by Katherine Martens, pg 38
[454] My Memories, Mary Dirk Janzen page 32
[455] Also see picture #87, Anna Goertz is wearing a Haub, a Grandmother's Cap
[456] Mennonites in Ukraine Amid Civil War and Anarchy (1917-1920), Translated and Edited by John B Toews pg 86
[457] Molotschna Historical Atlas, Helmut T. Huebert, pg 95
[458] Constantinoplers, Escape From Bolshshevism, Irmgard Epp, pg 260

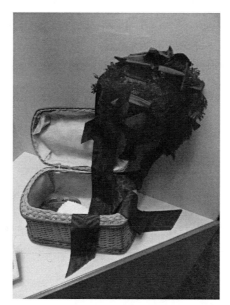

86 Upper Left   Jakob Martin Dueck

87 Upper Right Susanna Mathies Dueck. Oma Agatha Dueck Krause Dirks'
parents Jacob Martin H Dueck and Susanna Mathies A.B. Dueck.
Susanna is wearing her treasured grandmother's cap in this photo.

88 Bottom—Haub, or Grandmother's cap, Kaufmann Museum, Newton, Kansas

*Mennonites from the Mennonite Central Committee, a relief arm of the Mennonites in the United
States, arrived in Constantinople on their way to help provide relief to their suffering, starving fellow
Mennonites still in Russia. They listened to the stories of the refugees, of the Communist takeover,
of their losing their homes and families, of the atrocities, the barbaric cruelties, and simply could*

not believe that these stories were true. "There are no people like that. It's devilish! Kill and murder in front of on looking families!" They just could not believe that such things could happen.[459]

Once war in Gnadenfeld was over, Rempels were finally able to leave for Gnadenfeld. The family traveled one hundred miles from Herzenberg to Gnadenfeld in a horse drawn ladde voge, or Leiterwagn with straw in the middle, and suitcases piled on top. They didn't have any roof, canvas cover, or top. These huge wagons were used to carry a lot of grain at harvest time. Usually farmers had two to four such wagons, depending on the size of the farm.[460]

The family stayed one night in a Russian[461] village. Russian homes were small, usually only one or two rooms. A person entered through the yard covered with curlicue droppings of chicken manure, which would stick to one's shoes, and be dragged inside. Sometimes the Russians even kept a goat and/or a pig in the house, especially in wintertime. It was sort of half house, half barn, with animals and people together in one room. They had a big brick oven, which took up half the room. They baked in that oven, cooked on it, and in the winter would sleep on it, often with a baby's cradle suspended from the ceiling above it. The Rempel family slept in a loft. The odor of tobacco drying in the rafters, kerosene, and dankness of the stamped earthen floor permeated their clothing. The Russians had been oppressed by their rulers so long, they seemed satisfied as long as they had some bread, vodka, and bacon. Or were they? [462]

A man trying to escape from the Red Army was hired as a chauffeur to drive the ladde voge. Red soldiers at check points didn't question the family about him because he was just the chauffeur and Papa had those special papers given to him when he surrendered to the Reds, so they drove right through the line. When they arrived in Gnadenfeld, the chauffeur went on his own way. [463]

The Indian summer of 1920 lasted well into November. The weather was still fairly warm. Wispy clouds stretched across the sky; red, golden, and brown leaves floated earthward. Storks, nightingales, swallows, wild geese, cranes, and herons had flown to their winter quarters. Then came a day when the sun could not pierce the dense fog until late morning.

---

[459] Constantinoplers, Escape From Bolshshevism, Irmgard Epp, pg 227
[460] The Molotschna Colony, A Heritage Remembered, Henry Bernard Tiessen, pg 32
[461] In taping family memories of life in Russia, family members always referred to their Russian neighbors as Russians, even though there were Ukrainians in the Molotschna.
[462] The Batum Story, God's Mercy and Man's Kindness, compiled by Mary Dirks Janzen, Third Edition, Edited by Mary E. Janzen 2011, pg 49, told by Agatha Krause Rempel; The Ruslӓnder, Sandra Birdsell, pp. 52-53
[463] It is unclear how Aaron would have the necessary papers at this check point when his papers had been stolen from the vest he was wearing as they slept at the train station in Karkov.

89 Russian (Ukrainian) peasant home, illustration by Margie Hildebrand

The steppes were so flat, plodding along on a ladde voge, the Rempels could finally see Gnaden-feld some distance away. It was a welcome sight. As the sun set and dusk enveloped them, they saw flickering lights from lamps being lit in many homes. They went straight to Susanna's mother Agatha's home. Agatha's family had just finished eating supper, so Oma Agatha went back into her kitchen to prepare the weary travelers fried potatoes and eggs.

Marie was so happy to see her Oma Agatha and her aunts, uncles, and cousins, but she quickly re-alized they were not as happy to see them.[464] Now there were six more mouths to feed, and Susanna was expecting another baby. The fighting armies, the Reds, and Makhnovista bandits had pretty much taken everything away from the people, so it had been difficult just feeding themselves day by day. The Aaron and Susanna Rempel family moved into Oma Agatha's summer room.

For the school Christmas program, everyone sat in rows facing the Christmas tree at church. Stu-dents recited their short pieces and sang with the entire student body. They watched in wonder as

---

[464] A Rempel Story, video of Susanna Krause Rempel and Marie Rempel Bergmann by William C. Rempel, grandson and nephew

the huge tree was lit, the light going from candle to candle on a single white string, from the bottom to the very top. Surely this was the loveliest tree ever. The tallest men stood by with little wet mops, checking on the candles to make sure the tree did not catch on fire. The lamps were turned down low for the singing of "Stille Nacht, Heilige Nacht." In former days, days of plenty and prosperity before the villagers had been so completely plundered, when they were children, Cornelius, Susanna, and Jakob would have written out their Christmas wish poem precisely in their best penmanship. Also for weeks before Christmas, they would have practiced the verses to be recited at church. Then the teacher brought out rewards—"large baskets of small paper bags filled with nuts, an orange, some hard candy, (no chocolate), an apple, and a German storybook." [465]

Christmas morning, Susanna and her brothers would wait impatiently for Papa to finish his chores and wash up. Then they would present their beautiful Weinachswunsch (Christmas wish) folders, with wishes written in their best penmanship to Mama and Papa Christmas morning, and recite memorized verses before they could enter the Grotestow (living room) and see the Christmas tree for the first time. Under no circumstances, would children help decorate the tree. In good times the tree was decorated with beautiful hand blown glass ornaments from Germany, along with cookies, gilded nuts, apples, and colored paper chains. Only after the children had recited their verses, Mama would go into the Grotestow alone, light the candles, come back, and open the door. Candles, held by gilded or silver holders that clipped on to the branches of the tree, sometimes slipped a little, starting a little fire here or there, which was immediately extinguished with a little wet mop. The smell of scorched fir needles added to the festive spirit, but the rule was never leave a lit Christmas tree unattended. [466] [467]

Plates were laden with nuts, an apple, perhaps an orange, pfeffuernusse and ammonia cookies.[468] Gifts lay unwrapped, on each person's plate.

Little girls received beautiful dolls with china heads, and for succeeding Christmases, a wardrobe for the doll. Sometimes a new dress or an apron was among the gifts. *There might be hand-knit mittens, a shawl or gloves, aprons, or petticoats, and German story books. For the boys there might be a carved wooden horse, or lamb, a penknife, a small wind up metal train that ran along the floor, or hand-sewn shirts . . . .*[469]

---

[465] Mennonite Foods & Folkways from South Russia, Vol II, Norma Jost Voth, Mary Dirks Janzen, pp. 79-80

[466] From My Memories, Bill Neufeld, pp. 45-46

[467] Author's mother Gonja often reminisced years later about the magical quality of the Christmas tree lit with real candles.

[468] Ammonia cookies are NOT made with cleaning ammonia, but with a granular baker's ammonia. *Many of the old recipes call for ammonia or ammonium carbonate. It was once made from the antlers of deer and called salt of hartshorn. The ammonia must be finely ground and combined with dry ingredients or dissolved in warm liquid. Mennonite Foods & Folkways from South Russia Vol I, Norma Jost Voth, pg 327*

[469] Mennonite Foods & Folkways from South Russia, Vol II, Norma Jost Voth, Mary Dirks Janzen, pp. 79-80

90 Weinachswunsch folder, public domain

German Mennonites celebrated three days of Christmas, honoring the three persons of the Trinity. Day one was celebrated at home with the parents, day two with one set of grandparents, and day three with the other set of grandparents. The children lined up with other children to recite their wishes before not only the grandparents, but also aunts and uncles, expecting some sort of a treat, such as a little candy, a kopek, or a bright blue flowered kerchief filled with pfeffernüsse (button sized cookies).[470] [471]

---

[470] Mennonite peppernuts (pfeffernüsse) more closely resemble Dutch than German cookies in texture and flavor, seasoned with a blend of anise, coriander, cardamom, cinnamon, nutmeg, and pepper. They were flavored *with orange and lemon rind and brushed with rosewater. The leavening was, and still is, bakers' ammonia . . . . Testers said the best peppernuts are crisp and very spicy. Anise is the most popular flavor. Pepper enhances the other spice flavors . . . . Grind star anise with a mortar and pestle or use anise oil. Do **not use anise extract** although it is cheaper, as it is of poor quality, adulterated with alcohol . . . . Store peppernuts in an airtight container for at least a week before serving as they definitely improve with age. Mennonite Foods & Folkways from South Russia Vol I,* Norma Jost Voth, pg 340, 366, 368, 396

[471] There are definitely differing opinions about how peppernuts should taste: T*he ammonia peppernuts were bigger than a walnut, had **no** peppermint flavor,* Mary Dirks Janzen, or P*eppernuts were the size of half dollars and **had** the flavor of peppermint.* Mennonite Foods & Folkways from South Russia Vol II, Norma Jost Voth, pp. 371, 373

Almost nothing was available for mothers to use for the great Christmas celebration of 1920. Perhaps Oma was able to save a little bit of flour for making a few pfeffernüsse. No oranges, no story books. Perhaps they had been able to scrounge a few apples or nuts from the orchard, and save them for this most special time of year.

Shortly after Christmas, Aaron left his family and went back to Siberia to fulfill his obligation and serve as an officer in the Red Army. It was truly merciful that the Red Officer he had surrendered to permitted Aaron to travel all the way from Siberia to get his family back to Gnadenfeld before fulfilling his new duties in the Red Army. The family had no idea when Aaron would return again, or if he would ever return again.

Marie had never forgotten that little hand crank sewing machine Katche had promised to her. Now that the family did return to Gnadenfeld, Marie remembered, but Katche told her she had never made any such promise.

Since Susanna had done all the sewing for the family before she married, her younger sister Agatha took sewing lessons to take her place. But after the Bolsheviks were in power, money was inflated and worthless, so Oma Agatha had to barter for high school tuition, and piano and sewing lessons for her daughter Agatha with beans and bean soup.[472] By now, sister Agatha had become an expert seamstress, and could even make slippers.

One day Ronka passed his uncle Cornelius and Jasch Krause' house looking for his cousins. He suddenly was attacked by the neighbor's big dog, which bit him three times, finally grabbing him above the knees, giving him blood poisoning. A woman finally arrived with some alcohol to sterilize the infected bites, and Ronka recovered.

Sometimes Gnadenfeld had terrible windstorms. Windstorms were much worse now that much of the "forest" of hardwoods which once encircled the village had been cut down for firewood for military trains by marauding armies. The once lush windbreak was nearly gone. Gonja had gone out of the kitchen, down the steps, off the porch, around the barn to the outhouse. She made it to the outhouse all right, but she couldn't get back from the outhouse to the kitchen door. Gonja tried to run even faster and harder, but try as she might, the wind wouldn't let her get back to the kitchen door. She ran for all she was worth, wailing loudly, arms flailing about like a windmill, but getting nowhere fast, until Marie ran out and pulled her back in.

---

[472] "Memoirs of Agatha and Carl Rempel" as told to K. R. Lockwood, pg 12

91 hand crank sewing machine; Kaufman Museum, Newton, Kansas

92, 93 The Grottestov, the Mennonite Settlement Museum, Hillsborough, Kansas

The life of the house centered around the central brick stove. *The German brick stove was incredibly versatile and economical, as it used wood twigs (picked up from the floor of the fruit orchard), dried manure, and even dried grasses for fuel. The steppes of the Ukraine had no trees when the Mennonites first arrived, and so not only was the steppe grass fed to the horses and cattle, it was used as fuel. Later, wheat straw, along with corn and sunflower stalks were also used. The top layer of the manure pile was spread on the fields as fertilizer. The bottom of the manure pile was used for heating. In the summer, the children were required to take the composted cow manure, moisten it with water, add rotten straw, and mash it all together with their bare feet. It was then molded into forms, and manure bricks were turned out of the forms to dry in the sun. As the sun rose higher in the sky and the day warmed, steam rose and their smell permeated the whole neighborhood. Once dried, the bricks were then stacked in a shed for winter. The manure bricks would glow and glimmer slowly and retain heat for a whole day. There was no smell or odor to it and it proved to be an excellent fuel supply for the long winter nights.[473] Dried dung cakes held the heat much better than straw.[474]*

The kitchen stove also had iron plates on top, surrounded by tiles with recessed openings for kettles and pans. There were two long ovens at the bottom where huge loaves of bread were baked daily in prosperous times. Twigs and branches from pruning the orchards were kept for holidays. Straw was burned the rest of the time. The straw typically was kept in the hallway between the kitchen and the barn.[475]

Oma Agatha didn't like it that her grandchildren from Siberia could only speak Russian, but not Plattdeutsch, so she wouldn't talk to them. She let it be known that she wouldn't speak to them until they spoke Low German. Little Gonja felt very rejected.

After the evening meal, the whole family was in the Grottestov near the warmth of the large German brick stove. Oma Agatha and the children sat around a table in the light of a kerosene lantern, hanging from the ceiling on a chain. Oma Agatha taught them to sing songs in Plattdeutsch, which helped the children learn Low German faster.

While they sang, their little dachshund began barking in the Vorderhaus (front entryway). When Oma Agatha checked, she discovered the straw kept for heating the brick oven had caught fire in the kitchen. While everyone else just stood around in bewilderment about what should be done,

---

[473] The Molotschna Colony, A Heritage Remembered, Henry Bernard Tiessen, pg 74
[474] Mennonite Foods & Folkways from South Russia, Vol II, Norma Jost Voth, pg 24
[475] "Memoirs of Agatha and Carl Rempel", as told to K. R. Lockwood, pg 3

someone ran to Cornelius and Jake Krause's house next door. Cornelius ran over, threw water on the fire, and put it out. It had never occurred to anyone there to throw water on the fire themselves. Oma Agatha took everyone to the Achstov (or Die Eckstube, corner bedroom/parents' bedroom), and had people sit on the bed. It was so smoky, Marie was choking on the smoke, but it was too cold to go outside to get fresh air.

Right after New Year's, Marie came down with malaria. Gonja also got malaria about the same time, but she didn't get very sick. Gonja was sick with malaria again when the family reached Batum on their way to America. Marie never became sick with malaria in Batum like the others did. She was the only one in the family who was so very sick with malaria at this time, but it apparently gave her some immunity later on.

About then Susanna's younger sister Mieche came down with smallpox, so Oma Agatha had the nebengebiet or nebenhaus made up for the family to stay in so they wouldn't get the pox too. The nebengebiet was a room in a nearby shed for men to sleep in during harvest when the weather was warm. They nearly froze to death in that little house, until brothers Cornelius and Jasch took Susanna and all her children in with them and their two families in the other Krause farm house right next door.

Both Cornelius and Jasch were married. Cornelius had three children, and Jasch had one, so with the addition of Susanna and her four children, they ended up with eight children in that house. Cornelius' three were Liesbet 6, Hedwig 5, and Rudy almost 1. *When Rudy was born, Hedy was asked what she thought of her new baby brother, to which Hedy replied, "I would rather have a pet sheep or goat!"* Rudy's mama Tante Greta had to carefully position Rudy's cradle under the window during the war to protect baby Rudy from flying bullets.[476]

Marie started attending school again. The Dorfschule, the village grade school, was located in the center of the village on the Schulensteg (school path), opposite Gnadenfeld's grand Mennonite Church. The school had two large classrooms. Grammar school had first through third grades meet in one room and fourth through seventh in the other. As students entered the room, they passed the teacher's desk and chair, and came to long desks for each grade, which reached from one side of the classroom to the other, with an aisle at each side of the room.[477] Boys and girls sat separately on long benches. It was easy to see who the best pupils were, because they were seated by rank. They learned the Bible in school each day. They had a Bibliche Geshicte, a Bible

---

[476] handwritten memoir by Rudy (Rudolph) Krause
[477] My Memories, Mary Dirks Janzen pp. 1-2

with pictures. The very strict teachers even had to look after the children on Sundays and often took them for long walks in the afternoons.[478]

They studied geography, pronunciation, penmanship in Russian, and Bible and the German language in High German. They spoke the every-day low German or Platdeutch, at home, on the farm, in the kitchen, and around the village. Platdeutch was not a dialect of High German, but of Low German, which is a separate language. The original Low German of the Netherland Mennonites of Gronigen and East Friesland was carried to Prussia when they emigrated to the Grosses Werder of Prussia. This was a swampy delta at the mouth of the Vistula River, where they drained the swamps to create rich farm land.[479] As an everyday language, Mennonite Platdeutch was without formal grammar, syntax or spelling. [480]

94 typical sommastov, or summer room,
the Mennonite Settlement Museum, Hillsborough, Kansas

---

[478] The Batum Story, God's Mercy and Man's Kindness, compiled by Mary Dirks Janzen, Third Edition, Edited by Mary E Janzen 2011, pg 47 told by Agatha Krause Rempel
[479] Mennonite Foods and Folkways from South Russia, Vol II, Norma Jost Voth, pp. 34 36, and From My Memories, Bill Neufeld, pg 8
[480] Mennonite Foods and Folkways from South Russia, Vol II, Norma Jost Voth, pg 37

Platdeutch was left behind Sunday mornings in church. On Sunday they read Luther's Bible in High German, sang High German hymns, heard High German sermons, and uttered High German prayers. *Low German is at the heart of our (German Mennonite) experience and culture in a way High German never was and English never can be . . . . Arnold Dyck referred to Low German as the soul and sinew of our way of life, as the very essence of Mennonite identity.* [481]

If a child misbehaved or didn't know his lessons well, Lehrer (Respected Teacher) Lenzmann at the Central School would assign Psalms to be learned after school time. Some students developed quite an extensive knowledge of those Psalms.

Children took sack lunches or went home for lunch if the home was close by. A child could put his lunch in a special door in the oven, that heated the whole schoolhouse, and have hot soup at lunch. There was no physical education. The children went outside for recess and played games: Drop the Handkerchief, Hide and Seek, Last Couple Out, and Jacob, wo bist du? (Jacob, where are you?). Jacob would be blind-folded, and the children would call out, "Jacob, wo bist du?" then run away so as not to be caught.[482] They played ball games and had recess every hour. School was from 8 am till 11am, dinnertime, then from 12 noon till 4 pm.

Good penmanship was stressed even for drills and homework. At Christmas, students wrote several pages of wishes and blessings in their best penmanship. They studied religion in the morning. It was a Mennonite School, not Russian.[483]

In High School boys and girls went to separate schools. There were no Mennonite universities. The very few who could afford it, went on to study engineering, law, or medicine, usually at a university in Germany. Many of the Mennonites learned to speak, read, and write Russian, and to appreciate great Russian literature and writers like Dostoevsky, Tolstoy, and Pushkin.

Catherine the Great had promised the Mennonites they would have complete control over the education of their children, but Catherine the Great was no longer alive. By the late 1800s, new czars began their Russification programs. They renamed German villages with Russian names. They also insisted Mennonites serve in the military, and even demanded German Mennonite schools have a native Russian teacher. A German Mennonite teacher could still teach the classes in Ger-

---

[481] Mennonite Foods and Folkways from South Russia, Vol II, Norma Jost Voth, pg 36
[482] My Memories, Mary Dirks Janzen, pg 9
[483] In addition to the elementary school, Gnadenfeld was one of the few villages that had the secondary educational system with its Zentralschule (Central School) and also a Mädchenschule. (Girls' School). Boys and girls from surrounding villages would room and board with Gnadenfelders to attend high school. The Molotschna Colony also furnished teacher training and business schools. http://www.gameo.org/encyclopedia/contents/M6521.html   Mennonite Encyclopedia Vol 3, pp. 732-737

man and Bible. The children had to learn arithmetic in Russian, but they learned Bible stories in German, not the Plattdeutsch spoken at home, but High German, as found in books. With grammar it was different; they learned grammar and songs in both Russian and German.[484]

Most German Mennonites still had a German accent even though they spoke Russian each day. But Marie, Ronka, and Gonja spoke the beautiful Russian one finds in books and learns in school since Russian was all they had spoken in Siberia. It differed from the Russian spoken by the peasants of Molotschna.[485]

Because of the war and their flight from Siberia, Marie hadn't attended first or second grade. The family had arrived in Gnadenfeld in November, and Marie had only attended school a short time in Herzenberg. She was nine, almost ten, too big for first grade, so they placed her in third grade. Again she didn't understand what was going on in the classroom. The teacher in the Gnadenfeld Dorfschule simply ignored her in the classroom, as though she was stupid.

Other Gnadenfeld children wore clogs to school, but Marie, Ronka, Gonja, and little Susie wore felt boots, which were common in Siberia. They looked cozy and warm and reached to their knees.[486]

Susanna and her children stayed in the sommastov (summer room) and ate with her brothers' families. While Susanna and her four children stayed with her brothers, all the children had plenty of fresh milk to drink because Oma had given Sasha, a wonderful milk cow, to Susanna. Somehow, the Cornelius and Jacob Krauses always seemed to be able to have enough bread for everyone.[487]

95 felt boots; AHSGR (American Historical Society of Germans from Russia), Fresno, CA

---

[484] My Memories, Mary Dirks Janzen pp. 2, 8
[485] Ibid, pg 28   It is also probable that the local "Russians" spoke Ukrainian, which would be different from the Russian required in their schools.
[486] Ibid, pg 28
[487] Many accountants found employment with steam mills in various Mennonite villages. Maybe that is why Josh and Cornelius always had bread—they may have been paid with flour, which was otherwise unavailable to almost everyone else.

Maybe man does not live by bread alone, but that bread sure could fill aching stomachs. Susanna's brothers were so very good to her and her children. At this time Jacob was working in accounting [488] for the Gnadenfeld [489] volost (county seat).[490]

Marie was quite sick with malaria every other day. A little girl who lived across the street died, but Marie couldn't go to the funeral because she had malaria. The rest of the family was at the funeral for the little girl. Tante Suse saw Marie had been left alone, "Did they all leave you? What do you especially want to eat?"

Marie answered, "Cherries. I especially want cherries."

The next day Tante Suse brought Marie a jar of her canned cherries, a jar that had somehow escaped the pillaging Bolsheviks and bandits.

Susanna was not well either, and the baby was coming. Oma Agatha wanted her daughter near by when the baby was due. Mieche had recovered from the pox, so Oma asked Susanna and the children to return to her house.

After moving back in Oma's house, little Susie cried because she was so hungry. They always seemed to have bread to eat living with her Krause brothers, but living with Oma again, Susanna had nothing to give her. Susie wanted bread, and there was no bread. Mama asked Marie, Ronka, and Gonja to take little Susie to Aaron's married sisters, Tante Lena Toews and Tante Suse Toews and ask for a piece of bread for Susie. They not only gave Susie a piece, they gave each of the children a big, thick piece of bread and put cottage cheese on it. They each nibbled slowly, savoring every bite, making the wonderful treat last as long as possible. The children hadn't had anything so wonderful for a long time. The Toews aunts were good cooks and Tante Suse knew how to do fancy cooking. The children liked the bread and cookies they baked when enough ingredients were available to make them.

The spring of 1920, farmers had little to no seed and few horses to plow and plant what little seed was to be found. Considerable land remained fallow. Communist rules now dictated that each

---

[488] formerly had been an accountant in Berdjansk and Kitchkas for several years, Obituary of Jakob C. Krause, translated from the German
[489] information given by Joan Braun, daughter of Jacob Krause
[490] Like a county seat—Gnadenfeld was the 'county seat' for half of the Molotschna Colony, and Halbstadt was the 'county seat' for the other half of the colony. *The whole Molotschna Colony was divided into two districts, volosts: Halbstadt consisting of 32 communities and Gnadenfeld district which consisted of 29 communities. The offices of administration were in Halbstadt and Gnadenfeld respectively.* The Molotschna Colony, A Heritage Remembered, Henry Bernard Tiessen, pg 90

farmer plant some corn, potatoes, and melons for nearby Russian villagers, using his own seed, paid for by his own money.[491]

Most of the sheep had been taken by the Communists, so little to no wool was available to knit socks. During spring and summer months, the villagers again raised silkworms. Gnadenfeld once had enjoyed a thriving silk industry, but it had come to an end with competition from Italy.[492] Yellow silkworms were again ordered and established in trays on tables in the attic. It was the children's job to gather fresh mulberry leaves from mullberry hedgerows separating the farms to feed the worms each morning. Their crunching, like the sound of rain beating on the roof, could be heard all over the house.[493] In autumn when big and mature, the silkworms spun their cocoons on branches. The cocoons were thrown into boiling water so the threads would loosen and unravel. It was tricky to find where to pick at the end of the string to unravel it, leaving the brown debris of shriveled pupae in the water. It took 200 silk strands to spin a thread strong enough to sew on a button, or mend a garment.[494] In good times, the cocoons had been sent away to be spun into thread. Now one of Susanna's younger sisters had learned how to spin the thread, which could be knit into socks that were so strong they could hardly be worn out.

Marie was only ten when she learned to darn socks. If Susanna saw anyone sitting idle, she always gave them some work to do. When Marie was first married, she always felt guilty if she didn't have something to do.

After the revolution, times were hard, and all sorts of commodities, including necessities were scarce. Commercial egg coloring for Easter could no longer be bought. So the resourceful Mennonite women used what they had on hand:

> red beet soup for red coloring
> dried onion skins for a golden brown
> wild lilac with purple berries, which had been pressed the previous fall and kept in a little
> > bottle with some alcohol
> green from tender young leaves or green wheat sprouts
> carrot soup for orange[495]

---

[491] Mennonites in Ukraine, Amid Civil War and Anarchy (1917-1920), Translated and edited by John B. Toews, pg 61
[492] 1835-1943 Gnadenfeld, Molotschna, A Lowen Schmidt, pg 8
[493] "Memoirs of Agatha and Carl Rempel", as told to K. R. Lockwood, pg 5
[494] Miracles of Grace and Judgment, Gerhard P. Schroeder, pg 169
[495] Mennonite Foods and Folkways from South Russia, Vol II, Norma Jost Voth, pg 119

Easter

Throw the cow over the fence some hay. ~ Old Low German saying[496]

Easter Celebration began with a foot washing ceremony by baptized members of the church on Maundy Thursday. Ronka, Gonja, and the other children generally dreaded Stelle Friedach, or Quiet Friday, as they had to sit still and be quiet all day long, because it was such a dark day remembering Christ's crucifixion. No visiting, laughing, or playing was allowed that day. All baptized members wore black, and their fathers wore their long-tailed coats when they went to church. Festive occasions such as weddings were not permitted during Easter week. It was a time for serious reflection on the death, burial, and resurrection of their Savior.

Saturday was a day of preparation for Easter Sunday. In prosperous times, before the civil war, Russian hired help was allowed to return home at noon. The Paska (Russian Easter bread) and zwiebach had to be baked, lamb had to be prepared to roast the next day, and wood piled, ready to be put into the oven Sunday morning. Mama started the sponge (yeast dough) for the Paska Friday night, adding flour and kneading the dough in the morning, until the high mushroom shaped Paskas came from the oven in mid-afternoon, and were lined up on the kitchen table waiting to be frosted. Paska would then be eaten for Easter Sunday breakfast and with Faspa.[497] Besides the Easter baking, it was mandatory the whole farmyard be raked and swept clean.

Mama started growing wheat or oat grass in some bowls about two weeks before Easter to create grassy "nests," in which to "hide" colored Easter eggs. Mennonites only colored their eggs, but did not decorate them delicately as the Russians did. Their work ethic kept them from wasting time on something that would be destroyed as soon as you ate the eggs. Spending time embroidering was acceptable on long lasting items as pillow slips, tablecloths and dresser scarves, or crocheting doilies or lace for dress collars, but not on elaborately decorating eggs, when chores needed to be done.

Mama put the number of eggs in a bowl for each child that matched each child's age, so Marie had 10 eggs in her bowl. The bowl was hidden somewhere in the house for Susie, and in the farmyard for the older children. Easter Sunday morning, Marie knew she had found **her** bowl when she found the bowl with just 10 colored eggs. No more, no less. Ronka would look for 7, Gonja for 5, little Susie for just 3 eggs.

---

[496] This was often repeated by the author's mother Gonja Rempel.
[497] Mennonite Foods and Folkways from South Russia, Vol II, Norma Jost Voth, pg 126

A typical Easter dinner would be boiled ham or roast lamb, fried potatoes, bread and butter, home-made mustard, plümemooss, and colored, hard boiled eggs. The afternoon Faspa would typically have paska and cheese paska (like a mild flavored cream cheese with raisins), canned fruit, coffee with sugar cubes (otherwise reserved only for Sunday Faspa), and colored, hard boiled eggs.

A new breed of cattle from Germany was introduced and crossbred with the Ukrainian grey cattle, resulting in a cow known as the Molotschna German Red Cow. The average annual milk production was 580 gallons[498] with a very high butterfat content. Butter was produced in great quantities and shipped to the surrounding towns and cities.[499] This new breed produced less milk than their former Frisian cow, but was much hardier.[500]

Gnadenfeld's Russian herdsman announced the moment the sun arose in the sky when villagers should rise and chores should begin by blowing his horn. Susanna and Oma could be heard rustling in the kitchen in the lamplight, stuffing straw into the big central brick oven. The sun would be a round, warm ball by the time breakfast was eaten. After cows were milked early in the morning by peasant girls,[501] they listened for the horn and the crackle of a long whip signaling the time for the cows to be turned out to pasture. The children enjoyed going to the street to watch the cows depart. It was a great embarrassment not to have the cows ready when the herdsmen came by.[502] They were collected by a Russian herdsman and his family, and driven to a common pasture.

While the cows were away during the day, manure was hauled away and barns thoroughly cleaned. In good times, chickens, ducks, geese, pigs, and crickets lived in Oma Agatha's barn. Porcupine lived in the area too. Each village in the Molotschna had at least one stork family, some villages had two. It was considered good luck to have the stork nest on your roof. Swallows nested in the barns, so barn doors were kept open during the day. Marie loved to watch the swallows dart in and out of the barn, make their nests of mud, and later see the little, open, yellow beaks stick out when the mama bird came back to feed them. Horses and colts were also turned out to pasture, where they remained the whole summer. Gnadenfeld was two versts[503] long and the pasture was one mile further away from town. There was a good well at the pasture, but it required a great deal of manpower to pump enough water to water all the livestock, about 400 cows and calves and over 300 horses. [504] [505] [506]

---

[498] 1835-1943 Gnadenfeld, Molotschna, A. Lowen Schmidt, p 8
[499] The Molotschna Colony, A Heritage Remembered, Henry Bernard Tiessen, pg 34
[500] Hierschau, An Example of Russian Mennonite Life, Helmut T. Huebert, pp. 140-142
[501] Milking, feeding the calves, and making butter and cheese was traditionally the work of women in Russian Mennonite villages. Mennonite Foods and Folkways from South Russia, Vol I, Norma Jost Voth, pg165   Milking the cows continued to be Susanna's responsibility even in old age, while she lived in Alaska in the 1940s.
[502] My Memories, Mary Dirks Janzen, pg 29
[503] a verst is about 2/3 of a mile, so two versts would be about one and a third mile, "Gnadenfeld, Molotschna, South Russia, Memories of Good Times and of Hard Times", Jacob C. Krause, pg 1
[504] My Memories, Mary Dirks Janzen, pg 29

In the fall when all the crops were in, the cattle were driven onto the stubble fields. Due to fall rains, plenty of wild oats, barley, and grasses had grown so the herd could eat to their heart's content.[507]

If young Marie and her siblings had time, they would walk to the picket fence along the street and watch the cows come home. Only in the evening once the cows had returned and were milked, with separators humming, and chickens roosting, the barn doors finally would be latched for the night. Then was heard a chorus throughout the village of supper bells ringing.

It was a Saturday evening, the Saturday right before Easter, March 26, 1921. As always, the Mennonites had made Easter bread or Paska, baked in coffee cans and decorated with frosting on top. Cornelius' wife Margareta and daughter Liesbet had finished the beautiful paska. Round loaves all sat with their frosted domed tops, ready for breakfast Easter morning. They had just finished cleaning up the kitchen by washing the kitchen floor when the bearded village herdsman, in baggy pants and high leather boots, with a blast on his horn, had announced the return of all the cows from their daytime pasture. He watched as each beast plodded down the wide treelined street, faithfully turning into its own gateway. All the cows, but one.

Sasha, Susanna's cow, had become confused. She forgot where she was. She forgot where she really should be going. Perhaps she simply wasn't paying attention and was daydreaming wonderful cow daydreams so just walked on like she had done so many times before, without thinking, when suddenly she wasn't quite so sure about where she belonged. Oh dear, now what to do? All the fences, houses, and yards pretty much looked alike. Sasha had been Oma Agatha's cow, but now she belonged to Susanna Rempel's family. Susanna had lived with Oma, then with her Krause brothers, but now she lived with Oma again. In her confusion, Sasha had absent-mindedly walked to the open front door in Lisbet Krause's house and walked right in. Sasha saw the other door in the kitchen was open, leading directly to the barn. That looked like a good idea, so she walked on through the house, right through the kitchen. But before she got all the way through the kitchen, Sasha left a present, a generous pile of manure on the freshly scrubbed brick, kitchen floor!

Liesbet's sister Hedwig lead Sasha back to her own home, to Tante Susanna's next door, at Oma's house. In the meantime, Liesbet and her mother had to clean that kitchen floor all over again. Liesbet was not happy, not happy one little bit!

[505] The Batum Story, God's Mercy and Man's Kindness, compiled by Mary Dirks Janzen, Third Edition, Edited by Mary E. Janzen, 2010, pg 49, told by Agatha Krause Rempel
[506] Mennonite Foods and Folkways from South Russia, Vol I, Norma Jost Voth, Mary Dirks Janzen, pp. 163-164
[507] The Molotschna Colony, A Heritage Remembered, Henry Bernard Tiessen, pg 34

Easter morning could not have been more beautiful. Susanna had hidden the Easter nests with eggs. Each child looked for his own Easter egg nest. Gonja found hers inside the outdoor bake oven, just beyond the summer kitchen. Then, in the best clothes they had during those hard times, with their shoes all shined, everyone headed for the church in the center of town. Another family shouted, "Christos Voskres!" (Christ is Risen!), and the Rempels replied, "Voistynu Voskres!" (He is risen indeed!) No longer did the children have to be quiet. It was a day of triumphant joy. All over the village, people could hear the majestic church organ playing, the music wafting in the soft morning breeze a half hour before the service would start.

96 Paska, Russian Easter Bread displayed on the table under the plant

It was a sunny day in March, and if Gonja could have ordered it, it could not have been more beautiful. The sky was a deep, deep blue; meadowlarks twittered in the bushes; bees busily hummed in lilac bushes in full bloom with majestic, deep purple spires. Fragrances of many lilacs and fruit trees along the path blended together to make the loveliest smell in the world. Nothing could mar this day!

People came from all directions with more hellos and greetings, and smiles on all the faces. Ronka and Marie were ahead of Gonja, with little Susie holding Mama's hand. As the family passed Oma's lilac bushes, Gonja couldn't resist picking a small bouquet. Gonja wanted to run and skip and hop and sing all at once, and that was just about what she was doing. But all of a sudden, everything changed. There was a hush, and the family came to an abrupt and complete stop.

Liesbet blocked the path. She stood with her face beet red and hands on her hips. The way she stood plainly said, "Don't take another step!" After taking a deep breath, Liesbet screamed out, "I hope you go back to Siberia and you **never** come back!" Liesbet let them know she was not pleased with having to wash the kitchen floor a second time after their cow had left a present on it! Liesbet's father Onkel Cornelius moaned, "Oh, Liesbet, don't say that! You don't really mean that!"

When Liesbet's angry tirade ended, they walked to the grand old Gnadenfeld church, but Gonja was no longer running, skipping, hopping, or singing. In fact, Gonja's feet dragged as she slowly followed behind her family, and Mama had to urge, "Hurry up, Gonja, church is about to begin already." Her beautiful day didn't seem so bright and cheerful any more. Her hand holding the lilac bouquet slowly opened, as she dropped the lilacs by the side of the path.

Magdalena

Papa Aaron returned to Siberia to fulfill his duty as a Red Russian officer right after Christmas, and the family had not gotten any letters or news from him. Susanna and the children returned to Oma's sommastov before Easter, and Magdalena was born June 1, 1921.

Then Marie, Ronka, Gonja, and little Susie all came down with whooping cough. Whooping cough is especially dangerous for a little baby, let alone a newborn, so the children all had to sleep with their bedding on the kitchen floor to try and keep away from little Magdalena to keep her from also getting whooping cough. Little Susie went blind from whooping cough. Papa's sisters Tante Lena (Aunt Helena) and Tante Suse (Aunt Susanna) lived together and these two aunts took Susie to live with them for the month while the whole family had whooping cough. Susanna just had too much to do with a newborn and three sick children, to also take care of Susie who was now blind.

It was no use. At six weeks old, Magdalena also contracted whooping cough. Susanna came out of the summer room to let Marie see her baby sister one more time before she died. Just then Marie looked out the window to see a red sky. There was a fire in the village. The next day they learned the Schmidt children (relatives of Papa Aaron's mother Maria Schmidt Rempel) had their house burn down. Their mother and father had already died, leaving ten orphaned children. The youngest child had gone to the attic to feed some kittens. He had taken a saucer with grease in it, and a rag for a wick for light when he went upstairs. He had tripped, dropped the burning wick into the straw on the attic floor, and set the whole house on fire. Nobody got hurt, however, now ten orphans were homeless.

Susanna told Marie, "Magdalena is extremely sick and she won't live long. Do you want to come in and see her?" The other children did not get to see her again after they had been banished from the summer room with whooping cough. Magdalena died that very night. Marie was the only sibling who ever saw her again before she died in July, when only six weeks old.

Someone in the village made a tiny casket. It was a simple wooden box with a lid, in the shape of a casket. Susanna made the lining, mattress, a special puff quilt pillow, decorations, and netting for it. A special room like a cellar, for viewings, had been dug into the ground near the church, to keep bodies cool. Marie went with her mother to get her baby sister, dress her, and decorate the casket for the funeral. Magdalena was a pretty little baby with very light blond hair. No screens were on the windows, which were open, so already flies had laid eggs on her. Susanna and Marie cried as they brushed the eggs off before dressing her.[508]

The funeral was held in Grandma Agatha's yard, under a big walnut tree, between the summer kitchen and the porch off the kitchen. Abram Rempel, Aaron's uncle,[509] gave the funeral sermon. He said, "Things will change from now on. Sometimes when things look the darkest, then all of a sudden, it gets lighter." The two big lilac bushes beside the porch were in bloom. It was a beautiful day, but it was so sad. Magdalena had been born, sickened, died, and buried, all without Papa even seeing her. Aaron still wasn't home.

Ronka did what most boys do. He roamed through the forests and orchard with other boys his age, climbed trees, checked birds' nests, and slid off the straw heap. Then they found some un-spent bullets from the war and other war explosives and made a pile of them. Out in the fruit or-chard the boys first made a pile of paper, twigs, and the explosives, then poured sand on top. The trees were in bloom. It was a beautiful time of year. Gonja was standing right over the pile when the boys lit it on fire.

Meanwhile, right after Magdalena's funeral, Susanna and Marie had gone to the Toews sisters' home at the opposite end of town to get little Susie and bring her home. On their way back home, suddenly they noticed Susie had opened her eyes and could see again! Oh, were they happy! Just then Liesbet Krause, Cornelius' daughter, came running, "Tante Susanna, Aunt Susanna, Gonja is burned! Gonja is burned!" Ronka's fire had exploded right in her face and burned Gonja's forehead and her hair!

"Ach du lieber!" cried Susanna, as she ran to find out what was left of her little Gonja. It was a wonder that it didn't blind or kill her, and Gonja was fortunate enough to grow up into a beautiful young woman despite this accident.

The day after the funeral, Marie sat on the steps, and looked down the road toward Uncle Corne-lius' place. She was still sick and weak from malaria. She saw a thin, sickly stranger come trudging slowly up the path. As he approached, Marie had no idea who he was, until finally she realized it

---

[508] This funeral parlor was located in a cellar about 30 feet away on the north side of the church. My Memories, Mary Dirks Janzen, pg 12 *Next we went to the church, beside which stood a small funeral parlour. It had been built when Aaron Rempel (Sr.) was mayor. There is a cellar underneath, with places for the storage of two bodies up until funeral time. Upstairs there is a hearse and related equipment.* Hope Springs Eternal, Translated from the German and Edited by John P. Nickel, pg 12

[509] Abraham A (or Abram) Rempel was a teacher and minister, the father of Cornelius' and Jacob's wives, and father of Carl Rempel who later married Susanna's younger sister Agatha Krause. Susanna's siblings married Abram Rempel siblings. The Abram Rempel home was located at #39 First Street.

was her own Papa come home again! She could hardly recognize him, he looked so much older, so thin and emaciated.

Marie ran screaming into the house, "Mom, Dad has come home!" Susanna had been taking a nap, and she woke up with a jerk. Had she just been dreaming that he was coming home? No, it was really true. He had come home. He was standing right before her, but oh, she could hardly recognize him. What had happened to him in these six plus months? Even though Aaron was now home, and would be taking care of them again, Susanna still remembered seeing him with those two other women. How could she forget?

Aaron had served in the Red Army and caught typhus.[510] He was then left in a Red Army field hospital where day and night bodies of the dead were carried from a room he shared with the dying. He fled from the hospital, and was taken in by his good friends Peter and Sarah Petrofsky.[511] Peter and his common law wife Sarah only lived in a one room shack, but they divided it in half with a curtain, put their bed in one half for Aaron, and had nursed him back to life from the brink of death. They literally had saved his life.

Now Aaron had brought Peter and Sarah back with him to Gnadenfeld. She was Russian, he Polish. Neither were Christian, and both smoked. Aaron then moved them into his own vacant house at the other end of the village near the windmill, to make themselves as comfortable as they could despite having no furnishings to speak of.

Petrofskys moved into the Eckstov/Eckstube, the same room that had been Aaron's and Susanna's bedroom before they had moved to Siberia. Not only was Susanna unhappy about them not being married and living together in sin, but they were living in sin in her very own bedroom! They were desecrating **her** bedroom by their fornication. She was also deeply distressed about them living off Oma Agatha. This was not right! Agatha refused to give them extra food for the Petrofskys. What a dilemma! Susanna didn't like them. Peter was the kind of man who would just live with other women, but never marry them. And yet, they had done so much; they had given Aaron their one and only bed and nursed him back to health. He surely would have died from typhus if he had stayed in that filthy army hospital.

---

[510]   http://en.wikipedia.org/wiki/Typhus Fatalities were generally between 10 to 40 percent of those infected, and the disease was a major cause of death for those nursing the sick. Between 1918 and 1922 in Russia after World War I, during the civil war between the White and Red armies, typhus killed three million, mostly civilians.
[511]   It is unclear in listening to audio tapes of memoirs, whether the name was Petrofksy, Petrotsky, Gerofsky, Gerotsky, or something similar

Shortly after Aaron came home, the family finally moved into their own home, while Petrofskys still occupied die Eckstov. They had no furniture, including beds, since they had to quickly leave Siberia without them. The two families slept together in the same house, but Susanna couldn't give them any food. They had no food of their own to give. Oma Agatha still provided food but only for their own family. To keep from starving, Peter shot and cooked crows for Sarah and him to eat. Susanna made them feel uncomfortable, so they eventually moved across the street and stayed awhile with Opa Aron Rempel Sr. before they left Gnadenfeld.

Since the Rempel home was vacant while Rempels lived in Siberia, rats had eaten through the floor from the cellar. Also the Cheka had earlier torn apart portions of the house looking for Aaron. Initially, it was a nice, more modern house, but now it suffered serious damage.

Houses made of bricks had walls about a yard thick, which provided good insulation. The resulting window ledges held flowerpots of geraniums and parsley. Shutters outside all windows were closed in summer to keep it cool. With no screens on the windows, flies buzzed in whenever windows and doors were open. They landed where sunlight shined on the wall. Sticky rolls of fly tape, unrolled and hung from the ceiling, did a good job of catching flies. But they were not as good at catching flies as the Gonja flycatcher. Gonja stood where sun shone on a wall thickly covered with flies. She would swipe her hand and catch a fist full of flies. Even as an adult, Gonja was able to catch a fast flying fly with her bare hand.

Before the family had moved to Siberia, Aaron had planted an orchard of apple, pear, plum, apricot, cherry, and walnut trees. Each farmer had an orchard. Peach trees were unusual. Toews had a peach tree, but others in the village did not. There was a kind of little pear called Kruchev. It didn't ripen until it was nipped by the frost; then it would get mushy. Only then could it be eaten. Otherwise it would pucker a person's mouth. Those pear trees were huge, and usually they were planted next to the street where they would shade the yard or the house. All the time they lived in Siberia, Marie remembered that orchard in Gnadenfeld, and thought about all that fruit. Now that they had moved back, the first thing Marie did was to run to that orchard to see if she could find any fruit. She did, and she ate as much as she could.

The former stove had burned coal, but because of the war, coal was unavailable. Aaron took out the wall between two rooms and built a brick stove in the opening so the rooms on each side would be heated. Mama would cook on it and bake in it. The new stove could burn straw or dried manure bricks, if any were available with far fewer farm animals. Formerly, children also had the chore of gathering twigs from their forest wind break and pruned branches from the fruit orchard, both now very scarce.

Little Susan became unhappy when she knew her mother and father were upset with each other. "I don't like anybody here," she announced loudly to no one in particular.

Susanna tried to sooth little Susan, "You are just too troubled."

Susan replied, "Yes, I am very troubled. I just don't know what is going on."

Susanna quieted the children. She always did, "It is not as bad as you think."

"How do you know I think it is bad?"

"It just is not as bad as you think. Just leave it at that." And for then, little Susan just left it at that.

Drought and Famine

"Where there is no bread, there is no life." Old German saying[512]

"Socialism is a philosophy of failure, the creed of ignorance, and the gospel of envy. Its inherent virtue is the equal sharing of misery." Winston Churchill

Ever since German Mennonites had immigrated into Ukraine at the invitation of Catherine the Great, they had a crop year after year. About every 13th year was not so good, but they still had a crop without any irrigation. It was all dependent upon the rain, but they always had a crop. Always. When it did not rain, the Mennonites prayed for rain. It wouldn't take long, and then it would rain.[513]

The Mennonites practiced good farming methods like fertilizing the ground with animal manure and ash from the stoves that heated their homes. Farmers had a special shed called the ash house where they stored ashes from their ovens for spring planting. Farmers mulched the ground, so wheat came up abundantly. They let the land rest every 3rd year and rotated the portion of the land they let rest. In the Bible, God instructed His Israelite people to let land rest every 7th year, but the Mennonites let a portion of it rest every 3rd. Mennonite farmers could harvest from 35 to 45 bushels of wheat per acre, and sometimes even more annually.[514]

Under the Czar, Russia shipped grain to Europe: to Germany, France, and Turkey. Most Molotschna wheat went to the seaport of Berdjansk, on the Sea of Azov. English, Italian, and Greek ships would dock constantly at Berdjansk and fill their holds with the fine winter wheat. Russia was so rich, they could raise enough for themselves and others. Ukraine became known as the breadbasket of Europe. [515]

Harvests of the Russian peasants were not so abundant. When Tsar Alexander II abolished serfdom in 1861, some lands formerly belonging to nobles were given to peasant village communes, but not to individual peasants themselves. Every few years, the village redistributed the land among the peasants according to how many men were in the family to work the land. So when redistribution time came around, the size and location of the land apportioned to a Russian peasant family changed. Every few years the people were required to move. Since they would never profit from improvements like putting a new roof on a house or a barn, digging ditches, or fertilizing

---

[512] Mennonite Foods & Folkways from South Russia, Vol II, Norma Jost Voth, pg 58
[513] Henry Bergmann, audio tape
[514] The Molotschna Colony, A Heritage Remembered, Henry Bernard Tiessen, pg 42
[515] Ibid, pp. 42-44

the land, they had no incentive to perform or invest in that work. Sometimes the plot of land was many kilometers away from his house in the village, and it would take a half-day's driving. Russian villages were mostly primitive and unkempt. Their cattle were skinny. Therefore Russian agriculture was stagnant.

No wonder the Russian peasants were receptive to the empty promises of Bolshevik propaganda of another, final redistribution of land. The Bolsheviks never did give any land to the people; they only collected the people on communes to work for the benefit of the bureaucratic state. In Communist Russia, only the state owned any land.

Peasant huts commonly had no beds or ventilation but plenty of vermin, with three generations living together. No wonder they suffered a high infant mortality, and recurring epidemics of diphtheria, typhus, malaria, and *syphilis possibly more widespread than anywhere else in the world.*[516]

After the unrest and riots of 1905-1906, Petr Stolypin allotted some government land to a limited number of qualified peasants, based on the number of males sixteen to sixty years old. So, between 1906 and 1909 some peace was restored, as many small Ukrainian villages were formed under this program, mostly arranged on the Mennonite model. Even though these peasant villages were a startling success, it didn't entirely quell the popular unrest.

Some Russian peasants noticed the success of the German Mennonites and imitated them as well as they could. They saved money and bought land from the gentry who were eager to sell the land to work within the Czarist government and live in the city. The peasants who did imitate the Germans rapidly became prosperous and extremely anti-Bolshevik. Sadly, however, their prosperity then made them targets of both Makhno and the Cheka, and they also were later rounded up as hated Kulaks and sent off to imprisonment, death, or a slave labor camp.[517]

Under the Czar, Russia had enough grain to feed her own people and to export all over Europe, but the Russian harvest in 1917 was below normal. Bread riots broke out in the spring of 1918. The harvest of 1919 was super bountiful. Cherry, apricot, apple, pear, and plum trees were all so laden with fruit, boughs hung low to the ground, like the villagers had never seen before. Villagers cut the fruit, baked it in the oven, and spread it out on a screen to dry. The fruit was dried out in the sunlight during the day, and brought in at night. After three or four days, the dried fruit was bagged and stored in a dry place.

---

[516] The Twilight of Imperial Russia, Richard Charques, pg 24
[517] http://www.krausehouse,ca/krause/EasternFront.htm   accessed Feb 8, 2013

Pillaging by the armies caused all the bounty of that super harvest of the summer of 1919 to be smashed, looted, and totally depleted, so famine set in. Now the formerly neat and tidy, orderly German villages were unkempt, full of ruts, with broken fence posts and smashed hedges.

Since the Makhnovesze had stolen even extra changes of clothing, now Mennonites' everyday clothing was worn to pieces, almost gone. A once formerly wealthy widow was left with only the bed she slept on and the clothes she was wearing.[518] Even the linoleum was stripped off their floors.[519] Many children could not even go to school, particularly in winter, because they did not have enough clothing to stay warm. In Gnadenfeld, the situation was also critical, although probably not quite as desperate.

The summer and fall of 1920 brought a drought like they had never before experienced. Normally they had a number of different kinds of melons and cantaloupe. That summer, the largest watermelon were only the size of grapefruit. They were just as sweet, but a lot smaller. Usually they grew to be about twelve pounds.

A natural tax, payable in kind (that is, a grain tax was to be paid with grain, or a milk and butter tax on the milk cow was to be paid with milk and butter) was instituted. Farmers were assessed before harvest, well before a farmer knew what amount he would harvest or even if he would have any harvest at all. So this tax bore little relationship to what was actually harvested. The amount of tax was arbitrarily assigned based on what the Bolshevik commissars believed Mennonites had formerly raised, but totally ignored the reality of the drought. The Commissars apparently believed if the Mennonites did not meet their tax quotas, it was because they were not working hard enough or they were hiding produce. The winter of 1920-21 was cold and dry. Little rain fell and little seed was sown, as almost no seed was available. Grasshopper plagues and hailstorms created even more devastation.[520]

Communists had confiscated nearly all their food supply, and completely destroyed their ability to raise more. Marauding soldiers had trampled the gardens. Beets, cucumbers, and potatoes disappeared. There was no ripening fruit left on the fruit trees in the orchards. The people started eating pumpkins and mamalega (cornmeal made into a porridge)[521] both of which formerly had been raised only as cattle feed. The Gnadenfelders now made Aupelmooss (a thin pudding or thick soup) from pumpkins. They ate dried beets, chaff, dried weeds, ground up corn cobs, dogs,

---

[518] Hope Springs Eternal, John P. Nickel, pp. 190-191
[519] Ibid pg 224
[520] Lost Fatherland, John B. Toews, pg 47
[521] Mennonite Food & Folkways from South Russia, Vol I, Norma Jost Voth, pg 280

227

cats, gophers, crows, field mice, horse meat, cattle which had died whether from disease or starvation, the remains of processed linseed,[522] and even resorted to eating leather. Villagers even mixed ground bark or clay into their bread. They didn't know how to smile anymore.[523] Some 326 individuals died of starvation in the neighboring Halbstadt Volost, and 62 more died in the village of Gnadenfeld itself.[524]

Not only was seed gone for planting next year's crops, their draft horses for farming had also been taken by raiding Communists. The horses needed for plowing were few and far between. The village of Sparrau had only 53 horses for 49 Wirtshaften, while the 19 landless households had a total of five. In earlier years, each Wirtshaft would have had a complement of 12 horses, with five horses needed to pull each plow. The number of cows was also depleted, with only about 1.2 per household. The weakened horses and cows often shared plow pulling duties. Many of the men needed for the hard farm labour were killed, or had fled. Farmers carefully swept their attics to find each and every grain, separating out mouse droppings from their meagre returns.[525] Some farmers had tried hiding seed grain, but when they were discovered, they were usually killed on the spot, and the grain taken. Only a lucky few had any grain left for seed.

The Bolsheviks and marauding robber bands had already stolen their livestock, food, and all the means of growing more food. Additionally, this was the most severe drought and famine that land had ever known. *Now we have only one class in our society, the poor. The beggar's staff for all!* It became a land full of beggars and the suffering. *And where shall one go and beg? Nowhere is there a fruitful field or a full pocket.*[526]

A very tall man about six foot eight, the specter of death, came knocking daily. Different people in the village would invite him to come in to have lunch with them. He made the rounds among the villages. During the summer, when they had some watermelon, they usually served rollkuchen (a rectangular, twisted donut) with the watermelon. Susanna had made a big batch of rollkuchen, and had invited him to help himself. Before she knew it, **all** her rollkuchen was gone. To feed her own family, Susanna had to prepare it all over again. Later, this poor starving man found a dead dog, which he ate and then died.

A decrepit figure known to all as the "one-armed Jew" walked from village to village peddling needles, thread, shoelaces, and whatever else he could carry in his pockets to sell. Villagers always

---

[522] Mennonite Food & Folkways from South Russia, Vol II, Norma Jost Voth, pg 269
[523] A Rempel Story, video of Susanna Krause Rempel and Marie Rempel Bergmann by William C. Rempel, grandson and nephew
[524] Hierschau: An Example of Russian Mennonite Life, Helmut T. Huebert, pg 271
[525] Ibid, pp. 267-270
[526] Czars, Soviets, & Mennonites, John B. Toews, pg 114

knew the names of everyone else; even the common village idiot was addressed by name, but no one ever had the inclination to inquire where the one-armed Jew lived, how he lost his arm, or even his name.[527]

Grandma Agatha's family had a little black dog, part dachshund. One day he did not come home, and a few days later they found his little feet under the mulberry hedge near their neighbor's home. Someone had eaten him.[528]

Two boys had gone out on their farm to uncover some food they had hidden from Makhno and the Communists. But after they had uncovered it, some Makhno came riding up on horses out of no-where. They saw that this family had hidden food from them, so they killed one boy in front of his brother, and then killed the other boy, too. A Russian caretaker who witnessed it, pretended that he was a Makhno bandit also, so they let him live, and he later told the family what had happened.

Now when Susanna had anything to cook, she had to fill all the cracks around the windows or doors with rags so starving people outside would not smell the food and come look in the windows at them eating and pound on the door for food. Swelling numbers of unforgettably creepy and insidious characters went begging from house to house, pleading for anything to eat.[529] As it was, the children were always awfully hungry, and the family never had enough to eat.

Because of the acute shortage of farm animals for farming, many fields had been abandoned. Even straw and dung were scarce to use as fuel. Families had to cut and dry weeds, then haul them home in a cart, one man pulling, another pushing.

Matilda Regier's sister[530] was odd, truly strange. She seldom left the house or was seen by other people. She made all sorts of things with paper (perhaps scherenscnitte or origami?). She had a cat, but during the famine, since she couldn't feed the cat anymore, she wanted Papa Aaron to shoot her cat while she cradled it in her arms.

One mother had a pot of millet porridge on the stove, heating up for dinner, but while the family was outside in the garden weeding, a beggar boldly came into the house, and stole their dinner

---

[527] "Memories" by Rudy Krause, dated 13 July 1990

[528] The Batum Story, God's Mercy and Man's Kindness, compiled by Mary Dirks Janzen, Third Edition, Edited by Mary E. Janzen, 2010

[529] "Gnadenfeld, Molotschna, South Russia 1835-1943", Jacob C.Krause, pg 9

[530] Matilda Regier or Regehr (daughter of Lehrer Sudermann, teacher at the Central Schule) lived next to the Toews lumberyard, per Rudy Krause Memoirs and Marie Rempel Bergmann. Perhaps the mental retardation and/or mental illness present in the colonies was the result of much intermarriage throughout the decades, what genealogists call endogamy.

for that night. A neighbor later found the empty pot in his outhouse.[531] "We were terribly hungry," Susanna explained decades later. "At first you cannot even sleep at night. It makes you very tired, but you cannot sleep. After a while it doesn't hurt; you get used to it. You have to work; you have to wash; you have to keep going . . . but I don't remember how we did." Food became more valuable than gold. [532]

As the situation deteriorated, the Molotschna villages appointed delegates to go abroad and ask for assistance both for relief efforts and to emigrate from Russia. Mennonites in Canada and the United States began developing plans to rescue friends and family from the clutches of death in Russia.

The famine continued from 1921 until 1924 in some parts. Between 5 to 6 million people died. Efforts by the American and Dutch Mennonite Relief Agencies saved many Mennonites still trapped in Russia.

Much later the Mennonites learned that more people from Guiliapol and the surrounding district (which had been Nestor Makhno's center of operations) had died of starvation during the famine than anywhere else in Russia.[533] Makhno himself fled to Paris in 1921, where he died as an alcoholic in 1934.[534]

---

[531] "A Letter to My Children; The Memoirs of Arthur G. Rempel", pg 29
[532] Los Angeles Times, Wednesday, August 4, 1982, "A Search for Ancestral Soviet Home", William C. Rempel, page 16
[533] The Eichenfeld Collection, Compiled by Arthur Toews, pg 44
[534] Master's Thesis, Selbstschutz, Josephine Chipman, pg 162

Last Christmas in Russia

Rules haft en Enj   ,   Everything has an end
Bloss ne Worscht nijch.   except a sausage.
Dee haft twee Enja.   It has two ends.

~ Low German Saying[535]

The whole village was in church for the Christmas program on Christmas Eve 1921. It was truly a big, exciting occasion! The big moment came when the huge tree was lit. With no electricity, a couple of men, with candles attached to long sticks, lit candles that were four inches high. Those candles were just like the ones on their own tree at home. Hot candle wax dripped on Ronka, sitting Indian style under the tree, but he was afraid to move. Christmas was special, with the fragrance of the tree needles in their nice, big, old church all decked out in Christmas greenery.

There were poems, skits, little plays, and each school age child had a part. The schoolmaster had drilled the Christmas story . . . beginning with John the Baptist, then the birth and life of their dear Lord Jesus. But the story of the birth of the Christ Child meant so much more on Christmas Eve. After each child had said his piece, he received the gift of a small paper bag filled with nuts, candy, an apple.[536] In better years, they would even have received a German story book and perhaps some halva (Turkish candy, a coveted delicacy), but now all the cookies and candy, what little of it there was, was home made.[537]

The organ music from that big organ, played by relative Johann Rempel and the singing of Christmas carols, especially "Stille Nacht" was glorious! Sometimes the choir was divided into two halves, each half standing on an opposite balcony. The ethereal antiphonal singing brought tears to many eyes. Songs were memorized so they could be sung any time, any place, and for any occasion. The same chorales which were sung in church were sung at home, on festive days, in the evening, when mending or spinning, in the field, when hoeing weeds in the potato patch, or gathering in grain to thresh. A person could hear the men singing while performing their chores in the barn among the cows and horses, and while driving a team through town. Everybody learned to sing from early childhood on, and they did a lot of it in Gnadenfeld. Young people had books containing German and Russian folk songs telling of young lovers, loneliness, or sadness. One time, choir director Opa Aron Sr. rehearsed "When the Rooster Crows," a song some people thought didn't

[535] <u>Mennonite Foods and Folkways from South Russia, Vol II</u>, Norma Jost Voth, pg 201
[536] <u>My Memories</u>, Mary Dirks Janzen, page 4,
[537] "Gnadenfeld, Molotschna, South Russia 1835-1943" Jacob C. Krause, some of the story books were by Christina Schmidt

belong in church. They knew more than a hundred songs, which they sang often, to lighten their hearts or express a great disappointment: [538] Hab oft im Kreise der Lieben (What Joy it is to be Among my Loved Ones), Im Schensten Wiesengrunde (The Beauties of the Meadows), Nun Ade du Mein Lieb' Heimatland (Good-bye My Home and Country), Nachtigal, o Wie Singst du so Schoen (Nightingale, how Singest Thou so Beautifully?).[539]

All the German Mennonites knew how to sing parts, and the singing was heavenly, especially at Christmas. Little Susie loved to sit next to her Papa just to hear his deep, baritone voice. What a wonderful sound came out of his mouth. She snuggled up to him just to be closer to that sonorous voice.

The family spent the first day of Christmas together in their own home. When Aaron came back from Siberia, he brought a model Zeppelin, tied on a string, with a motor. Ronka held it up on a pole, and round, round, and round it would go.

That night, to keep warmth in the house, Susanna closed the damper, but she closed it too early, and the house filled with smoke while they were asleep. Marie became ill from the smoke. She seemed to be the most affected. The next day was the second day of Christmas, so they went to Tante Lena and Tante Suse's home. The men made their own cigarettes and all smoked. They hand rolled their cigarettes using tobacco that was little better than the peasant's vile makhorka.[540] Marie was still sick from the smoky house the night before and their smoking was making her worse. Tante Lena noticed that Marie was sick, so she took her away from the smoking men, to a couch in a cool room, and told her to lie down. She covered her up with a down comforter, and Marie went to sleep. When Marie woke up, she felt much better, feeling Tante Lena had saved her life.

---

[538] My Memories, Mary Dirks Janzen page 5
[539] The Molotschna Colony, A Heritage Remembered, Henry Bernard Tiessen pg 18
[540] A Mennonite Family in Tsarist Russia and the Soviet Union, 1789-1923, David G. Rempel, pg 109

Arrested

The children should have been asleep when Neufelds, their neighbors from across the street, visited with Susanna and Aaron late one evening. Whispering and hushed voices told the children this was "grown-up talk" they didn't want children to hear. Marie could tell Mrs. Neufeld was crying softly. Susanna had made a little candle by putting some grease in a dish and lighting a small piece of cloth as a wick. There was no kerosene anymore. The two doors were wide open between the rooms where the girls were supposed to be asleep and the Grottestov where the grownups were visiting. Marie heard Mr. Neufeld say he feared the dreaded Cheka was coming for him that night.

The Cheka always arrived in the middle of the night to arrest someone. When people heard a car coming, it usually was a harbinger of bad news.[541] Somebody would be taken away for questioning, perhaps torture, imprisonment, exile, or even death. The cars that once had been owned by prosperous Mennonites were now used by the feared secret police.

Marie heard Mama and Papa imploring, "Dear Father in Heaven. I beg you to help us. We are helpless, and You are mighty. Help us in this dark hour. I pray for Mr. Neufeld, for the Neufeld family, for myself and my family, and for all the men and their families in our village. Be merciful and gracious, Dear Sweet Savior."

No dogs barked that night. All the dogs had been eaten. Marie feared what the news would be the next morning. Sure enough, Mr. Neufeld was gone. The Cheka had taken him.

While Carl Rempel hid in Crimea, his brother had been arrested in Carl's place. When he was released, he was never the same afterwards. He seemed to walk about in a kind of daze. Once, when his two sisters held an engagement party, he was missed. His brothers found him in his room. In answer to their queries, he asked, "You think I've never seen one?" and he went on rocking and reading.

Meanwhile Carl Rempel was still hiding out in Crimea. While at choir rehearsal with other refugee soldiers in a Russian church, Carl, his cousin Wilhelm (Willie) Rempel,[542] and two others were

---

[541] Hierschau: An Example of Russian Mennonite Life, Helmut T. Hubert, pg 168
[542] Wilhelm Rempel was the son of Johannes Aron Rempel: another brother of Aron Sr., Abram, and Gustav Rempel.   Wilhelm Rempel was engaged to a cousin of Henry Bergmann. Henry Bergmann later married Aaron & Susanna's daughter Marie.

suddenly arrested. They were imprisoned in a cellar for about two weeks, then moved to another cellar in another village.[543] Carl had been tortured and sentenced to be shot.

Communists came to Aaron Rempel Jr. and asked him to repair a motor in a piece of agricultural equipment, and crate it to be shipped. Aaron agreed to mend it if they would free his cousin Carl Rempel. Henry Bergman's cousin Willie Rempel also had been arrested and sentenced to be shot. Willie's fiancee came to Aaron and begged and begged him to intercede on Willie's behalf. The Communists agreed to free both Carl and Willie. Aaron had temporarily forgotten about another imprisoned cousin, and later terribly regretted he had not been included in the bargain.

Before Aaron had actually completed the task of repairing the machinery and crating it, suddenly Carl and Willie both were released. Carl began the long hike home from Crimea, four or five hundred miles, after he managed to obtain false identification papers.[544] He made it back home to Gnadenfeld in November. Afterwards he was quiet all the time. He seldom would laugh at anything. Life had become very serious. Carl had left prison desperately lonely, unable to share his great inner pain. He needed to quickly leave Russia forever; otherwise the Bolsheviks could and probably would change their minds and continue to hunt him down to kill him.

All the Abram Rempel boys eventually returned home, except for Carl's handsome brother Abraham, who was with the Red Cross Medical Unit. Always something of a dandy, and no doubt wearing a good uniform, the Reds suspected he was an army officer, which he was not. Anyway, they fatally shot him without warning. The Russian nurse he was engaged to marry found him lying in the sand and had him buried in a Russian cemetery. [545]

After Carl returned home, he immediately talked Susanna's younger sister Agatha into marrying him, saying among other things that he had sort of had his eyes on her since she was in first grade.[546] Carl Rempel and Agatha were engaged and Carl's father (the Old General) gave them their wedding rings. [547]

Four men from Gnadenfeld, including Abraham Rempel (The Old General)[548] along with Abraham's son Heinz (Heinrich) Rempel, Heinrich Epp, and Heinrich Dirks were all suddenly arrested by the

---

[543] Memoir of Agatha and Carl Rempel as told to K. R. Lockwood, pg 11
[544] Ibid, pg 11
[545] Ibid, pp 11-12
[546] Ibid. pp. 11-12
[547] Constantinoplers, Escape from Bolshevism, Irmgard Epp, "Carl Rempel, White Army Officer, pg 100
[548] Abraham Rempel, The Old General, was the **brother** of Aron Rempel Sr, **uncle** of Aaron Rempel Jr, and the **father-in-law** of Cornelius and Jacob Krause and Susanna's younger sister Agatha Krause

8th Red army division, falsely accused of hiding some grain from the authorities, imprisoned, and sent by box car to Tokmak, shuttled from city to city on the railways, and finally to a prison in Tarachtacha, a suburb of Kiev.[549] Traitor Mennonites sometimes acted as informers, directing either robber brigands or Bolsheviks to places still not looted.[550] Abraham also had been a part of the Selbstschutz and both a teacher and a minister in the church. Atheistic Communists eventually executed or exiled most of the teachers and ministers they could find. Little children in the family wondered, "Why doesn't daddy come home? Why couldn't he even say, 'Good-bye?' Why is daddy arrested and punished? What has daddy done wrong?" They would even go outside each evening and wait for him to return. That empty ache would follow them the rest of their lives.

There were no telephones, newspapers, radios, or bus service for communication with neighboring villages. News from 200 miles away reached Gnadenfeld at best in two weeks to a month. But news did travel with visitors passing through, and the villagers weren't particular about whether the messenger was Mennonite, Catholic, Jew, Lutheran, or Russian.

Only the men attended meetings where they discussed the news bought by these messengers, conditions in other villages, and how well the new provincial government was functioning or not. Suffering and hunger was intense and growing, with little hope for improvement. Staying here meant starvation and death. Hope meant setting their eyes on the other side of the Russian border, any country, only away from this destruction. Mennonites no longer had a Fatherland in Russia.

Sixty-two men who had participated in the failed selbstschutz escaped with the White Army through Crimea to Constantinople.

Letters reached the colony from Abraham Kroeker, (former editor of the Mennonite German language newspaper Friedenstimme), fleeing from the Cheka. He had successfully procured exit documents in Batum, Georgia by the Black Sea, sailed to Constantinople, and on to America. News of his successful escape spread like wildfire.[551] His journey to Constantinople had taken just six weeks.[552] Also, Selbstschutz participants had successfully fled through Batum. News came from Crimea where a prosperous colony of Mennonites lived and some wealthy estates were situated. A group of families in Crimea had organized to leave Russia and immigrate to America. They aimed to sail from Feodosia, Crimea to Batum, Georgia, where they would get exit visas,

---

[549] 1835-1943 Gnadenfeld, Molotschna, A Lowen Schmidt, Jakob P. Dick Remembers: "The Years 1918-1925", pp. 56-57
[550] Hope Springs Eternal, Jon P. Nickel, pg. 191
[551] http://www.krausehouse.ca/krause/EasternFront.htm California Mennonite, Historical Society Bulletin, No. 54, 2011 - http://www.cal-menno.org/bulletin/fall11.pdf
[552] Mennonites in Ukraine Amid Civil War and Anarchy (1917-1920), Translated and Edited by John B. Toews, pp. 185-186

then sail to the promised land.[553] At that time, Bolshevik rule was not yet firmly established in Crimea, so perhaps exit documents would be easier to obtain there.

As the likelihood of starving to death grew steadily worse, many logically concluded that if no help or relief were available in Russia, surely the unknown dangers of emigration could be no worse. Would it not be wiser to at least attempt to go where help might reach them sooner?

During the winter of 1921-1922, quiet meetings were called to lay plans for departure. Five families and three bachelors decided to venture out together by faith: Oma Agatha Dirks' family of five, Tante Suse and Jakob Toews' family of four, newly married Carl and Agatha Rempel, Aaron and Susanna Rempel's family of six, Kornelius Heide family of four, and several single young men: Jacob Loewen, Johann Pankratz, and Solomon Schmidt.[554] Plans progressed meeting by meeting, step by step, prayer by prayer.

The men negotiated to rent one boxcar for this whole group to travel to Feodosia. Passport photographs, signatures, immunizations, permits from local and provincial authorities to leave, and a legal stamp of approval by the county secretary were needed.[555]

Word came by the end of January, Aaron's uncle Abram, cousin Heinz, father-in-law Heinrich David K. Dirks, and Heinrich Epp had been pardoned. However, they were not actually released until February 14, when they set out on foot for home. Unfortunately, Heinrich Epp had already died on Christmas Eve, and Abraham was so weak from typhus, he and his son Heinz had to return.

Meanwhile Abram's brother Gustav Rempel and son-in-law Cornelius Krause needed money for travel to rescue their relatives. Someone remembered that Abram Rempel had buried some gold coins near the gooseberry bushes. After frantic digging in numerous places, the coins were found so Gustav and Cornelius set off. Gustav and Cornelius found Abraham and Heinz in a hospital so filthy and full of lice the seams of their bed clothing were lined with them. Abram had suffered typhus since New Years, had a gaping wound on his leg, then a large carbuncle (boil) developed on his back. Abraham was far too sick to take back to Gnadenfeld with them, so they dressed Heinrich in clean clothes, hoping to come back for Abram later when he had recovered. Cornelius Krause hurt his leg and was pretty lame. Gustav then contracted typhus and died. Cornelius returned with Heinz, and reported Abraham died February 9 [556] and Gustav died March 5.[557] They were buried

[553] "My Family was Transplanted", audio tape by Mary Dirks Janzen
[554] The Batum Story. God's Mercy and Man's Kindness, compiled by Mary Dirks Janzen, Third Edition, Edited by Mary E. Janzen 2011, pg 3
[555] "My Family was Transplanted", audio tape by Mary Dirks Janzen
[556] The author has found conflicting dates from family memoirs- -the men were released February 14; Abram set out then turned back,

in Tarachtacha without caskets, a sermon, or a song. Memorial services were held for Abraham and Gustav in Gnadenfeld without any caskets.

As for Gustav's death, since his wife Elisabeth Electra had died August, 1920 before he made this trip, their remaining underage children were now orphans. Little Rudy, their youngest, had died at the age of nine, probably of pneumonia, weakened by the famine. Dietrich had a gun and shot sparrows and crows for food. Later the gun was taken away from him, but the children did not have to resort to eating cats and dogs. They were taken in by Gustav's oldest brother Aron A. Rempel Sr, who then moved them to a little house next to his implement store in Gnadenfeld.

Beggars and marauding military had brought lice, and with lice, the inevitable typhus into the village. Susanna's younger sister Mieche Dirks contracted typhus in January 1922.[558] Mieche was situated in the Grottestov for easier nursing by her mother, who soaked her bed sheets in cold water from the horse drinking trough, wrung them out, and wrapped them around Mieche to bring down the high fever and delirium. Mieche's beautiful braids were cut off, then her head was shaved to help bring down the fever.[559]

While Mieche was still bedridden with typhus, Great Grandmother Susanna Dueck Matthies[560] suffered a stroke and died at the age of 78 on February 17, 1922. Her funeral was held in the same place as the wedding reception for Susanna thirteen years before. Normally, in good times, the family would provide a Faspa (a light lunch of coffee and zwiebach) after the burial service at the cemetery God's Acre, about a half mile outside the village. Now they had not even enough food to feed their own family.

Susanna's younger sister Agatha prepared to marry Carl, son of Abraham and Elizabeth Rempel. Her brothers Cornelius and Jasch had married Margareta and Maria, daughters of Abraham and Elizabeth Rempel. Siblings married siblings.[561] Susanna had also married a Rempel (Aaron), a cousin of these other Rempels. Oma Agatha once remarked, "Don't you know anything else but marrying Rempels?"

---

and then died February 9. It appears that Heinrich Dirks was the first to return to Gnadenfeld, alone. Then Susanna's brother Cornelius returned with Heinz, sometime after burying Gustav in Tarachtacha, and sometime before Susanna and Aaron left for America.

[557] There is some confusion about whether it was Jacob Krause, his brother Cornelius, or both, who went on this rescue mission. In From the Steppes to the Prairie, Paul Klassen, pp. 76-78 names Jacob Krause as the one who went. Another memoir by J. P. Dick (son in law of Abraham) names Cornelius, whom he says also contracted typhus, but recovered by the grace of God.

[558] The Batum Story, God's Mercy and Man's Kindness, compiled by Mary Dirks Janzen, Third Edition, Edited by Mary E. Janzen 2011, pg 3, told by Mary Dirks Janzen

[559] "My Family was Transplanted", audio tape by Mary Dirks Janzen

[560] Susanna Dueck (born Matthies), mother of Agatha Krause,

[561] Oma Agatha"s brother Peter Jakob Dueck had married another Abram Rempel daughter Katherine.

When Sister Agatha was still young, her school teacher had noticed a young Rempel lad (Carl) smiling at her, and somewhat admonishingly remarked about it to her. Agatha replied that he was only the brother of her two sisters-in-law, who had married her two Krause brothers.[562] Someone else had remarked the Krauses and the Rempels should all just move in together, but Agatha had just tossed her braids and said, "There are too many Rempels in our family now. Not for me!"

Carl played a tuba which had been made in Germany, a mandolin from Italy, a German 12 stringed guitar, and the Russian balalaika. He had a beautiful tenor voice.[563] Carl had enjoyed a wonderful home, always filled with music and laughter. It was a large household, but a happy one. His mother Elizabeth Schmidt, a small person, was good to all and never known to quarrel with anyone. She was a good cook and housekeeper but tolerated all sorts of pets in the house, all kinds of birds, dogs, and cats. They had a Russian wolfhound who stood as high as the table top, yet was very pretty, mostly white with black. He could catch jackrabbits weighing 8-10 pounds. They also had a Dachshund, a German Spits, and a Russian mongrel.

Carl's childhood home also had a pet magpie named Max who was housebroken and used to scream to have the door opened so he could go in or out. He used to play with marbles, string, shiny things, and hid those that appealed to him. His favorite food was, of all things, cottage cheese! He would carry a gob of it in his beak out of the bake house where he would smear it between the bricks in the joints. He then would fight any other bird who tried to come near it.

In the barnyard were Banty roosters, hens, pigeons, and four peacocks. When the men found mice in the grain fields, they killed them and lay them out on the tailgate of the grain wagons. Storks and cranes used to fly out to meet the wagons, then stalk along behind, eating the dead mice. They looked rather comical.[564]

Carl and Agatha married just before they fled Russia. Even though Sister Agatha Krause was an excellent seamstress, the dressmaker in town came to the home and made her wedding gown out of a finely woven bedspread, with tiny stitches and fine tucks. She was paid in milk and came to the barn every night to collect. Their own silk thread was used to stitch the gown and they rented a silk veil for two loads of hay. The groom was dressed in homespun sports coat and "Frenchie" pants he bought by chopping and delivering a load of firewood.

---

[562] "Memoir of Agatha and Carl Rempel" as told to K. R. Lockwood, pg 1
[563] Ibid, pp. 5, 8
[564] Ibid, pp. 5, 8

The wedding day March 15 was dreary with rain mixed with snow. In church the bride and groom sat on one side of a plain table and the minister on the other. The choir sang, and the minister preached an hour long sermon.

For the wedding feast, Carl's family supplied one loaf of white bread which was rationed among the guests.[565] Agatha's family did not have a goose, but Cornelius and Jakob must have had one, and so they also served a delicious goose soup[566] and plumi moose made with the very last jar of canned plums.[567]

Once upon a time Gnadenfeld families enjoyed the companionship of all sorts of animals, but now the village had become strangely quiet without dogs or cats. Sometimes, villagers were desperate enough to slaughter farm work animals, which were also skin and bones. But then, how would they ever be able to plow and plant without the work animals? Ground up corn cobs were added to their bread. It didn't add nutrition but it helped fill the belly. It was as if the land itself was spewing them out.

---

[565] The severe famine meant many families had nothing to share with wedding guests, so many weddings were simply quiet, limited family affairs.
[566] "My Family was Transplanted", audio tape by Mary Dirks Janzen
[567] "Memoir of Agatha and Carl Rempel" as told to K. R. Lockwood, pg 12

Farewell

The wicked borroweth, and payeth not again: but the righteous sheweth mercy and giveth. Psalm 37:21

Life had become intolerable under the new Bolshevik government. All property had been nationalized; all grain needed for seed had been confiscated. People already were starving as it was, but the future looked even worse. Always before, these hardworking Germans had hope of a better future by the sweat of their brow, frugality, and saving for the future; but now all the fruit of their labors was no longer theirs.

Since Wilhelm and Margareta Neufeld had emigrated to America in 1911, their letters back to Gnadenfeld gave a good sense of abundant work opportunities and typical wages. These letters described the admission process at Ellis Island, but noted that not all were admitted. Ellis Island really was an "Island of Tears." Towns in southern and eastern Europe had a surprisingly rich source of information about life in America. Letters from émigres arrived regularly, often containing money, and these letters had a powerful effect in encouraging more immigration. *The cottage of the recipient becomes at once a place to which the entire male population proceeds, and the letters are read and re-read until the contents can be repeated word for word . . . .* Immigrants stood a better chance at admission if they had money, a skill, a place to go, and no obvious physical or mental problems.[568]

Preparations had to be made as quietly as possible so as not to alert Communist authorities. Jacob and Suse Toews hid coins on their clothing by making them into buttons.[569] Brothers Cornelius and Jasch would not risk their own necks but would rather stay home. They feared the difficulties of emigrating were too great, and believed that the drought and famine could not possibly last any longer; conditions just had to improve soon. They also believed that with their frugality and strong work ethic, Mennonites could regain economic prosperity under the relative order brought by the new Bolshevik government.

Cornelius and Jakob Krause also had good advice regarding what was needed for this courageous undertaking. Since, they said, this journey would take as long as three weeks, they would need plenty of food. Each one scraped together whatever grain they could find anywhere: wheat, barley,

---

[568] Annie's Ghosts, A Journey into a Family Secret, Steve Luxembourg, pp. 200-201
[569] The 1996 Mennonite Heritage Cruise, Part Four, pg 1, http://home.ica.net/~walterunger/Rudy-4.htm accessed Feb 10, 2013

oats, and even the mash in the horse feeding bin, ground it into flour, baked bread, sliced and toasted bread to fill two burlap bags with toasted zwiebach. They butchered the last heifer. Their dapple grey horse broke a leg and needed to be shot, which provided horse meat. It took four men to butcher the horse, cut up steaks, grind hamburger, and mix horse meat and heifer into sausages. All this seemed to be ample provision for a three week journey.

Villagers in Gnadenfeld had heard about other German Mennonite families living in Crimea who planned to emigrate to America. They intended to avoid alerting Bolshevik authorities by traveling to Batum to get the necessary legal documents to travel on to Constantinople, Turkey. Batum, or Tiflis, both located in the Caucasus, was an ideal place to contact the Turkish consul.[570]

To flee from Russia, instead of saying they were going west to freedom, they would say they were going to Crimea to visit a relative. The Communists would never give permission to young men of military age to leave the country. Aaron's papers from his Red Army superior gave his family and the group traveling with him authority to travel to Crimea.

The Communists had already nationalized all the land, so former landowners could no longer sell land. Aaron and Susanna, having recently arrived from Siberia with very little other than the clothes on their backs, had little to sell. They did sell all their household belongings for a box full of money. Each family needed as much money as possible to get them all the way to America. They expected to be in the United States in just a few months.

Agatha's family auctioned off what belongings they could, including the steam engine which powered their threshing machine. They had more than one burlap sack filled with inflated paper currency. Brother Jasch came to check on their progress, and assured them that with luck they could get to New York in three weeks time, so the two burlap bags of toasted bread and one of beef and horse sausages, and one more of inflated paper money looked like fantastic provisions.

The Mennonite Central Committee[571] had just recently set up a kitchen in Oma Agatha's old house. The day before they left, they had a real meal of rice and some kind of meat at noon. The next morning, the day of their departure, they had hot soup, and for the first time in their lives, they had hot cocoa, which was something out of this world! Susanna was not hungry on that drizzly morning

---

[570] The Batum Story, God's Mercy and Man's Kindness, compiled by Mary Dirks Janzen, Third Edition, Edited by Mary E. Janzen 2011, pg 1, told by Mary Dirks Janzen
[571] From a population of 20,706 in the Molotschna in 1922, 11,134 received relief food thanks to the MCC http://www.gameo.org/encyclopedia/contents/M6521.html taken from the Mennonite Encyclopedia Vol 3, pp. 732-737

Saturday, March 22, 1922.[572] Her lack of hunger may have been due to morning sickness. She walked out of Gnadenfeld for the final time that day, unaware she was pregnant again.[573]

The emigrants all gathered at John (Johann) Toews' place at the other end of the village from his brothers Jakob and Cornelius.[574] Cornelius and Tante Lena (Helena) Toews stayed in Gnadenfeld with Aaron's father, Aron Sr. Susanna's married brothers Cornelius and Jacob Krause and their families were present to say good-by. Gonja marched right up to Liesbet, with hands on both of her hips, looked Liesbet straight in the eyes, and blurted out, "You know we are leaving, but we are not going back to Siberia. We are going to America, and we will **never** come back."

"No, no, I don't want you to leave," wailed poor Liesbet. As it turned out, Gonja and Liesbet never saw each other again.

Someone special was there to say good-by to Susanna. When Franz Voth was young and in love with Susanna, he was unable to talk to her. Now Franz especially sought out Susanna, took her hand and said with tears streaming down his eyes, "We may not see each other again this side of heaven."[575]

Before leaving on this trip, Aaron had accumulated lots of inflated money. Seventeen million rubles normally would seem to be more than sufficient, but now was almost totally worthless. Some rich people who had silverware but no money came to the gathering, but not to say good-by and give well-wishes. This particular family had needed money a few months earlier, so Aaron had loaned these rich people some money in exchange for their "pawned" silverware. Now they wanted their silverware back but didn't have money to repay the loan and redeem the silverware. Still, they demanded that Aaron give it back anyway. Papa didn't want to give the silverware back until he was paid. A big argument ensued. Papa needed that silver to pay for the trip. Grandfather Aron Sr. talked Papa into giving the silverware back, but Papa was awfully angry. That family took their silverware back, but didn't pay Aaron anything they owed him. So Aaron and Susanna had to leave without the money they so desperately needed.

Susanna recalled, "That family was Mennonite, but they were not Christian." Aaron again was reduced to trusting the Grace and Mercy of God. As an adult, Ronka reflected on this terrible hardship,

---

[572] Easter Sunday was a week later on March 30, 1922

[573] Los Angeles Times, Wednesday, August 4, 1982, "A Search for Ancestral Soviet Home", William C. Rempel, page 17

[574] The author believes Johann Toews home was located at #60 First Street.

[575] Susanna said of Franz Voth, "That was a good man. I could have married him. Pop was very jealous if I talked about him." From genealogy records, we know Franz married Katharina Wiens, born 22 April, 1892 in Mariawohl. They had two sons, Harry born 15 Feb 1926 and Walter Voth, born 26 May, 1921. The author's assumption from these birth dates, is that Franz probably did not marry until around 1920, just before Susanna and Aaron Rempel returned to Gnadenfeld. It is unknown when Franz died, possibly in exile at the hands of Stalin. (http://www.blackseagr.org)

"Sometimes during the process, you say, 'Lord, do you think I can handle this?' " It was such a sad gathering with these families leaving Gnadenfeld forever, when this terrible argument arose on the verge of their separation. They might never see each other again. That stingy family stayed in Gnadenfeld, and the Rempel family ended up in America. Of those that stayed in Russia, all men and boys over 16 were later deported to work in slave labor camps in the frozen wasteland of Siberia, and most were never heard from again.

Some people warned, "You go to your death, all of you,"[576] or "in a month you will return, starved and in rags."[577] Some said they were crazy to leave home, downright foolish, because conditions had to get better. Others wistfully said they wished they could join the group, but simply didn't have enough money.[578]

Finally the time came to say, "Auf Wiedersehn." To tearful friends, Susanna said, "We will see you in heaven." And when she turned down the road with her family, she never glanced back again.[579] "We were like the Israelites leaving for the Land of Canaan. We didn't know how we would come to America, but we trusted God."

Finally the group set off. It was kind of rainy, drizzling the whole way, not really hard, but enough to make it miserable. Everything became wet and soggy.

Three ladde voge drawn by horses had been procured to take the families on the three day trip to the train station. All their possessions, food, supplies, blankets, cooking utensils, family Bible, photographs, only the essentials, were in those wagons, along with those who needed to ride. All who could, had to walk. Oma Agatha Dirks' family and Toews each had one. Susanna was pregnant, but she had to walk. There was no room for her, and the Aaron Rempels did not have a wagon. The Toews let Aaron and Susanna's small children ride in their wagon. Mieche who was recovering from typhus and her aged mother Agatha rode.

The Dirks family had hired an uncle by marriage to drive them. When the wagon sank in the muddy spring mire, he threatened to abandon them unless they paid him more. Oma Agatha, riding on

---

[576] Los Angeles Times, Wednesday, August 4, 1982, "A Search for Ancestral Soviet Home", William C. Rempel, pg 1

[577] From Bolshevik Russia to America, A Mennonite Family Story, Henry D. Rempel, pg 29

[578] A woman in the nearby village of Alexanderkrone, Molotschna, made journal notes on the backside of sweetened condensed milk can labels, since no other paper was to be had. Her entry for March 22, 1922, the same date the Rempels started their long journey out of Russia, *The body just doesn't have the necessary strength and I always feel tired . . . . The relief kitchen now has supplies for only two weeks because the Americans have withdrawn their help here in order to help in other places. The only hope now is Mr. Willing . . . and when he also declines, then humanly speaking, there is no hope for us—we will all die of starvation.* Mennonite Foods & Folkways from South Russia, Vol II, pg 120

[579] Los Angeles Times, Wednesday, August 4, 1982, "A Search for Ancestral Soviet Home" , William C. Rempel, pg 1

top of the load, gave him all of the family silver to get them and their belongings to their waiting railway car at the train station.[580]

Once upon a time this land had been good to them, very good indeed! They all loved this great land of Russia, and it tore their hearts apart to think of leaving; leaving it forever. Not looking back, they trudged on in light rain.

Walking two days in the rain, they began the journey by singing "Jesu, geh voran, auf der Lebensbahn" (Jesus, Lead the Way Through Our Life's Long Journey). But soon they were wet, cold, miserable, and the singing died out. It was enough effort to just keep going, putting one muddy foot after another, passing through the German Mennonite village of Paulsheim.

In Mariawohl, just 7 miles west from Gnadenfeld, Heinrich Bergmann, a young man of 22, peered out the window of his home, and wondered about this group of loaded wagons, with only a few people riding, but most walking, plodding steadily on in the falling mist. They were moving, headed west, but where in the west?[581]

For their first overnight stay, they reached the Mennonite village of Rueckenau, about 21 miles from Gnadenfeld. Carl, with his wounded leg, walked along carrying personal belongings and travel money in two suitcases.[582]

The next two days they continued walking, passing through other villages: Tiegerweide, Kuruschan, Rosenort, Blumenort, Tiege, Ohrloff, Muensterberg, Blumstein, until they arrived at Feodrovka, where they caught the train. A boxcar was waiting for their group. After loading the baggage, there was no floor space left, so they had to settle themselves on top of all the baggage. They had to pay bribes all along the way to get the train to move.[583]

When the train finally arrived in the city of Feodosia, Crimea, the place had the smell and pallor of death, death everywhere. People, dead and dying of starvation, were lying around all over. People

---

[580] "Memoir of Agatha and Carl Rempel" as told to K. R. Lockwood, pg 13
[581] Remarks made by Walter Bergmann at the Fiftieth Wedding Anniversary of his parents Marie Rempel and Henry (Heinrich) P. Bergmann, Sunday, September 13, 1981
[582] Dueck Family Genealogy, Jacob P. Dick, pg 45
[583] This report, written by Mary Dirks, was found in mother's (Agatha Krause Dirks) cookbook, by my sister Katja, Mrs. Herman Niebuhr. *We began our journey toward America March 17, 1922, . . . leaving our beloved homeland forever. Our caravan of walking people and laden wagons first reached Rueckenau. We overnighted there and after walking another full day, we reached Lichtenau. Next day we arrived at Feodrovka, where a boxcar was waiting for us. Personal belongings in the boxcar made it a crowded place, especially at night, when people stretched out on the floor. We were 27 [persons]. A week later reached the seaport of Feodosia. We stayed 16 days. Sea travel to reach Batum took 5 1/2 days. We left Gnadenfeld in the rain and arrived in Batum in the rain.* The Batum Story, God's Mercy and Man's Kindness, compiled by Mary Dirks Janzen, third Edition, Edited by Mary E. Janzen 2011, pg 46

with wheelbarrows or small hand carts picked up the dead and nearly dead alike, and carted them off for burial. [584]

The group found a place to stay next to the ocean in a two-story hotel, near the bottom of some hills. The children had never seen the ocean before. It was such a new experience, they could not quite get enough of the sight of that vast expanse of water. Once inside their quarters, dried zwiebach was passed around. It was not so crisp now, after two days in the rain. In fact, it had started to grow some green mold, but they had no other food. Food was too scarce to waste, even if money to buy any were available, which it was not. They heard a knock at the door where they were staying for the night. Marie opened the door and saw a little girl begging for food. She was just skin and bones, but had a big stomach. Marie just stood looking at that poor starving little girl, and as hungry as she herself was, just handed her that limp, green piece of zwiebach. To her dying day, Marie wept each time she recalled that starving little girl.

Others in their group witnessed a starving boy, who appeared to be about ten or eleven, dressed in a sack, with holes cut out for his head and arms, who snatched a loaf of bread from under the arm of someone attempting to hold it while paying for it. The man yelled to stop that thief. The poor boy fell in the mud, and a crowd quickly gathered around him and kicked him while he stuffed the bread in his mouth as fast as he could.[585]

While they lived near the ocean, they saw all kinds of things wash up on shore like onions and oranges. Shell fish (perhaps mussels, oysters, or clams) were available, but at that time the group did not realize that they were edible, so they ignored them.

Grass grew in a lot across the street from the hotel, so they took some knives to dig up the grass and plants to eat.[586] Each morning as they went out to dig up grass, or fetch water, they saw dead and dying people lying in the street. They had seen many starving people before at home in Gnadenfeld, but this was much, much worse.

They spent about two weeks in Feodosia before a ship arrived to transport them to Batum.[587] Marie had never seen a ship before they arrived in Feodosia. She had no idea how they would ever get

---

[584] From Bolshevik Russia to America, A Mennonite Family Story, Henry D. Rempel, pg 36
[585] The Batum Story, God's Mercy and Man's Kindness, compiled by Mary Dirks Janzen, Third Edition, Edited by Mary E. Janzen 2011 pg. 67
[586] Marie still cried even decades later, as the author, recorded her on tape as she related this tale.
[587] From Bolshevik Russia to America, A Mennonite Family Story, Henry D. Rempel, pg 37 It only took the Aaron Rempel group about two weeks after arriving in Feodosia to be able to leave for Batum. This was probably due to those papers given Aaron by the Communist Officer for saving his life with a loaf of bread. It seemed as long as Aaron had those papers, he could travel everywhere. For other Mennonites trying to go to Batum, it seemed nearly impossible to get the necessary passport and visa.

onto that ship, and it scared her silly. She shook all over from fright. But after they walked up the gangplank together as a family, it wasn't as bad as she had feared after all. It actually wasn't a big ship. It was always drizzling, and they had booked the cheapest passage, which meant being out on the open deck for the whole trip.

Papa always seemed to find a little bit of overhang, that provided slight protection from drizzle. This time it was right next to the gangplank and the door going down inside. So the family watched all the other people come on board and go down into the ship. Behind them were windows which looked down into the deck below. To their amazement, three couples of midgets came on board and then went down into the ship. They were perfectly formed people, but extremely short, and old. A person could easily see they were old because their hair was grey and they had wrinkles. The midgets had been hired by the ship to provide entertainment for the trip. While underway, the children looked in the windows, and saw people dancing inside.

Mama had given her family some zweibach to nibble on, but it didn't take long, before people came running up from downstairs, and ran out of the door, to the railing. When the people inside started getting seasick, they had to run right past the family to get to the railing. That finished the children as well; they became seasick and ran to the railing too.

Batum

In 1922 Batum was far from the governmental bureaucracy of Moscow, the center of Bolshevik rule. At the same time, it was closest to Turkey, where the necessary passports could be obtained to leave Russia forever. Since 1921, Batum no longer was an international seaport, with ships going directly to America, which necessitated traveling to Constantinople to get a ship to America from there. [588]

Rain 300 days a year created continual dampness, and dawn typically emerged under a mantle of thick fog, which gradually dissipated with the rising sun. The hills were lush with verdant undergrowth, rising to majestic snow-capped mountain peaks. Palms lined the main street. Lemon and orange trees, ferns, and magnolias flourished in the park. It was incredibly beautiful. It was also surrounded by swamps, however, that never dried up, infested with malaria carrying mosquitoes.[589]

The city was overcrowded with refugees: Greek, Armenian, Jewish, and now German Mennonites from Russia. Therefore it was almost impossible to find anything for shelter, as everything was occupied! [590] *Newlyweds Carl and Agatha Rempel stayed in an old chicken coop. One night a blacksmith offered lodging for Aaron's family, where they slept on the floor of his waterfront blacksmith's shop.* They entered through a narrow gate, where old scrap iron, broken wagons, and tree trunks were lying all around. During the night *Susanna was abruptly awakened by noises and persistent nudging. They didn't know the room came with pigs. "I thought we were as low as we could get," Susanna recalled. "How much lower can you be than to be sleeping with the pigs!" [591] They later realized that they were sharing their lodging not only with pigs, but also cows and rabbits that were allowed to roam freely in the yard and into the shop.[592]*

The first group of Mennonites from Crimea who had arrived in Batum three months earlier had rented two large sheds, for about 100 people, with rows of families lying next to each other like sardines on each side, with an aisle down the middle. It took great care not to step on someone when going out or coming in. The front of the shed was open, and some roof tiles were missing, so rain poured in through holes in the roof. The climate was so wet, the walls were completely

---

[588] see map, picture #78

[589] Mennonites in Ukraine Amid Civil War and Anarchy (1917-1920) Translated and Edited by John B. Toews, pp. 185-187,

[590] Ibid, pg 187

[591] A Rempel Story, video of Susanna Krause Rempel and Marie Rempel Bergmann by William C. Rempel, grandson and nephew and William C. Rempel, Los Angeles Times, Wednesday, August 4, 1982, "A Search for Ancestral Soviet Home" page 17

[592] California Mennonite Historical Society Bulletin, No, 54, 2011, http://www.calmenno.org/bulletin/fall11.pdf and Mennonites in Ukraine Amid Civil War and Anarchy (1917-1920) Translated and Edited by John B. Toews, pp. 187-188

grey, covered with fungi because the mold penetrated right through the cracks in the walls. The cement floor, where they made their beds, was completely broken and dirty, covered with straw, infested with bedbugs and other parasites.[593] *Lice—oh man! Lice and mosquitos! Often, the refugees had only a coat for bedding, and a worn out jacket for a pillow. Partitions of some sort were made between families using boxes, trunks, suitcases. These sheds had a door at each end, with no partitions, no furniture, and no windows for ventilation. Everyone had to use an outdoor privy, very primitive sanitary and cooking conditions. New arrivals had to squeeze in somehow. The place came to be called Octentactensich, or Eighty-eight, after the address 88 Petrogradskaya Street.*[594] [595]

At one point the group of refugees heading for America swelled to over 300. By the end of May 1922, few, only about ten percent, had any hope of contacting friends or relatives to sponsor them to enter the United States. It also became apparent the meager refugees' food supply would run out soon.

People died daily. Fortunately, a Lutheran church permitted the Mennonites to bury their dead in their cemetery. Those having to do the burying were themselves weak from hunger and disease. *As soon as a person died, worms emerged through the nose and mouth. It was terribly gruesome. There were no coffins. Generally bodies were just wrapped in a sheet, and the dirt thrown directly on top with just a short Bible passage read and a couple of prayers uttered.*[596]

When the infant son of the Henry D. Rempel family (no relation to the Aaron Rempels) died, they cut the rockers off his cradle, and buried him in what remained. When their daughter Katya died, the family came to the hospital and noticed the left side of her face was covered. Removing the cover, they saw that part of her face had fallen in. They were told by an attendant that her face had been gnawed by rats. But another Mennonite refugee informed them when he had worked as an orderly in the Russian army, some orderlies poisoned those soldiers so seriously injured that they could not recover. On the second or third day after receiving the poison, their cheeks had

---

[593] Mennonites in Ukraine Amid Civil War and Anarchy (1917-1920) Translated and Edited by John B. Toews, pp. 187-188

[594] The Batum Story, God's Mercy and Man's Kindness, compiled by Mary Dirks Janzen, Third Edition, Edited by Mary E. Janzen 2011 pp. 8, 29

[595] *This report was found in mother's (Agatha Krause Dirks) cookbook, by my sister Katja, Mrs. Herman Niebuhr, (written by Mary Dirks) . . . . All 27 of us spent the night at an open grain warehouse near the railroad. Then we were allowed to stay three nights at a crowded place where the Crimean group lived (88 Petrogradskaya). Our men walked to the Turkish village and rented a room for each family. But 15 lira per month was too costly. We had to move. A unique attic room in the home of a retired Russian general was our next abode. His family lived downstairs; his chickens occupied one room upstairs. We rented the other room, 8 X 8 feet, which had held pigeons, for our family of five. It had to be scrubbed and disinfected from top to bottom. Papa made three cots and we moved in. Here we spent some of the happiest days as a family. We could live by ourselves, such a contrast to life in the boxcar or even with the Crimean group in town. We enjoyed the most beautiful view of the sea on one side and snowy mountains on the other. The local people said that beyond these high, snow-covered mountains lay Mt. Ararat.* The Batum Story, God's Mercy and Man's Kindness, compiled by Mary Dirks Janzen, third Edition, Edited by Mary E. Janzen 2011, pg 46

[596] The Batum Story, God's Mercy and Man's Kindness, compiled by Mary Dirks Janzen, Third Edition, Edited by Mary E. Janzen 2011 pp. 78-79

fallen in. That is what had been done to their daughter. She had been poisoned![597] Next their son Mitya became sick with malaria. He was taken to the hospital where he contracted typhus and also died.

When Abraham Reimer's father died, they dug a hole vertically straight down, wrapped him in a sheet, put a pillow on top of his head, and shoveled the dirt on top.

Sometimes so many died at the same time, and family members back at #88 were so weak from starvation and malaria, often by the time they came to the hospital to check on beloved relatives, they discovered they already had died and were buried in a mass grave.

The Kornelius Heide Family who had traveled with the Rempels, became so disheartened, they left Batum and returned to Gnadenfeld. So did two of the single young men. Jakob Loewen had to go to the hospital sick with typhus. Before he left for the hospital, he loaned some money to his friends so they could get their passports, and left the rest of his money with them for safekeeping. When Jakob recovered and left the hospital, his friends had already left for America with all his money. Now totally broke, he had to return to Gnadenfeld, still suffering from malaria.[598]

The Rempels heard later Kornelius Heide died in Gnadenfeld. The new Communist government demanded a certain quota be met in crop production. If that quota were not met, the father was sent to Siberia. If the father was absent, they took the son. These men were sent to Siberia, never to be seen again.[599] All men who returned to Gnadenfeld later perished from starvation, disease, or in a slave labor camp in Siberia.

Many of their group contracted malaria and typhus. Paradoxically it seemed like the healthiest, strongest young men died first. It took bribes to get good quinine to recover from malaria. It was so bad, of the whole number of German Mennonites, only Marie Rempel and two men never came down with malaria in Batum. Some whole families died. Both parents in some families died, leaving their children orphans. In one family of six, only the mother survived. In another, the mother and five children died. Only a fourteen year old daughter remained of one family of eight. [600]

When people came down with malaria, they just lay on their bed, shook and shivered, they felt soooo cold. Others would just step over them. After an hour, they would sweat like the dickens,

[597] From Bolshevik Russia to America, A Mennonite Story, Henry D. Rempel, pg 48
[598] The Life Story of Walter Jakob Loewen, autobiography, pg 2
[599] The Batum Story, God's Mercy and Man's Kindness, compiled by Mary Dirks Janzen, Third Edition, Edited by Mary E. Janzen 2011 pg 71
[600] Czars, Soviets, & Mennonites, John B. Toews, pp 125-128

then get so weak, they couldn't get up, even to go to the bathroom. Some didn't really feel sick, but just had that terrible fever; otherwise they felt healthy."[601]

In Batum, all the other families lost someone, except the group that traveled with Aaron and Susanna. An estimated 150 people died there.[602] Miraculously, no one died in Agatha Krause Dirks family, Jacob and Susanna Toews' family, the newlyweds Uncle Carl and Aunt Agatha, or Aaron and Susanna Rempel's family. At Susanna's 100th birthday celebration, Ronka recalled those terrible times, "We couldn't afford to die."

Aaron's box of money ran out in Batum. They all thought it would only take a few months to get to the United States. It took gold to purchase fake identity papers, so newlyweds Agatha and Carl Rempel sold their wedding rings and Carl's beautiful, German seven string guitar for their papers and to buy food.[603]

While still in Batum, the Rempels moved closer to the ocean, the Black Sea, into a big two-story unfinished house built on stilts. These homes were built five to six feet off the ground because the tide often came far inland. The stilts were simple, just trees with the bark removed. The climate was so temperate, no walls were needed. Home-made rugs carpeted the floor where people slept without beds. The people lived simple lives.

The Rempel family lived in one room twelve by twelve feet. All they had were a few blankets, pillows, and their own clothes. A Turk lived in another room, and the Jacob and Susanna Toews family lived in a room at the other end of the house. They stayed in this place a long time. Everyone did all their cooking outdoors even though It drizzled almost daily.

One time the Turk gave them a taste of what he had cooked. It had smelled very tantalizing with all his spices. Another time he shared some corn on the cob, which was different and very tasty. It grew in rows all around there. Daily rain irrigated the corn crop, and coyotes came right up to the house.

It was just a gorgeous country, with narrow streets and steep hills, where bushes and blooming flowers grew profusely. One day during a walk on a big mesa that overlooked the ocean, they passed a pool of water. An uncle, not realizing how deep the water was, went in to wade. He didn't know how to swim and nearly drowned. Fortunately, someone in their group knew how to swim and saved his life.

---

[601] "Never Come Back"-Lancaster Mennonite Reunion audio tape, transcription pages 2-3
[602] Los Angeles Times, Wednesday, August 4, 1982, "A Search for Ancestral Soviet Home", William C. Rempel, page 17
[603] Constantinoplers, Escape from Bolshevism Irmgard Epp, "Carl Rempel, White Army Officer", pp.100, 101

Both Aaron and pregnant Susanna came down with malaria. All their children except Marie got malaria. Malaria makes a person sick one day, but not so sick the next. All they wanted to do was sleep on the floor all day long on their sick days. Marie had malaria in Gnadenfeld, so being well now, she had to gather wood by the stream for cooking. Especially after a hard rain, brush was caught on bushes and trees so was easy to gather. She stored the brush and corncobs under the house so they would dry out and burn easier. Ronka could help her on his better days. A place dug out of the hill was used as a stove to cook their meals.

Having heard about a group of Mennonites stranded in Batum, Wilhelm P. Neufeld (Aaron's uncle) from Reedley, California arrived in Batum, October, 1922,[604] and gave each family $40.00.[605] He also was instrumental in getting food for the starving Mennonites through the Near East Relief Agency[606] to provide a monthly ration for each person over the age of 17, which lasted until aid was cut off December 31, 1922:

22 and a half pounds of flour
12 pounds of rice
12 pounds of oatmeal
6 pounds of beans
2 pounds of sugar
4 cartons of condensed milk

The Mennonites, considered sugar and rice as luxuries, so sold them to buy rye flour and potatoes. But the beans were not edible. No matter how long they presoaked them, no matter how long they cooked them, or even cooked them in baking soda, those beans remained like hard little rocks.

Absolutely astounded at the misery and suffering he encountered, in letters back home, Wilhelm P. Neufeld pled with the Mennonites for all sorts of help: "Many have had malaria for three or four months and cannot get better. They are getting weaker and weaker and will eventually die. Even if they are recovering, they need only get their feet wet once and they relapse . . . . They walk about peering through sunken eyes, bent and exhausted with pale faces and fallen cheeks.

---

[604] Mennonites in Ukraine Amid Civil War and Anarchy (1917-1920) Translated and Edited by John B. Toews, pg 186
[605] "Memoir of Agatha and Carl Rempel" as told to K. R. Lockwood, daughter, pg 13
[606] The reason for the presence of the Near East Relief Agency was the genocide of the Armenians by the Turks. Since the Ottoman Empire had been defeated, the Allies were talking about declaring the land inhabited by Ethnic minorities as separate countries. The Turks, realizing that if there were no Armenians, then the Allies could not demand a "liberated" Armenia, began a whole-sale genocide of the Armenians. The Near East Relief Agency had been set up to supply relief to those fleeing Armenian refugees that had flooded Batum at that same time.

The most essential items include:

1. *Better accommodations.*
2. *Free medicine and medical help*
3. *Clothing, shoes, and stockings*
4. *Better and more nutritious food. The Near East Relief provides us with monthly provisions, but they are insufficient especially the flour. They also supply no fat, which is badly needed . . . the unpalatable beans are also to be replaced by something else."*

Signatories, W. P. Neufeld from Reedley, California, and J. B. Jansen from Sebastopol

Oct 20, 1922, Wilhelm Neufeld gave a sermon on Psalms 42 and 43
Why art thou cast down, O my soul? . . . hope thou in God with the voice of joy and praise . . . .
Why art thou cast down, O my soul? . . . hope thou in God: for I shall yet praise Him . . . . Yet the Lord will command His loving-kindness in the daytime, and in the night his song shall be with me, and my prayer unto the God of my life . . . . Why art thou cast down, O my soul? Hope in God: for I shall yet praise Him . . . .[607]

A few families who had earlier made it to Constantinople (now Istanbul), sent word back to Batum that agents from the Mennonite Central Committee Relief Agency were now in Turkey to help them immigrate.[608]

The Rempel family moved higher up on the mountain. The higher altitude made a big difference in cooler, dryer conditions, and was farther away from the mosquito filled swamps. Aaron had to go to town to work on getting their papers to leave for Turkey. Aaron had the strength to walk down the hill and make it to the train. Some time in the afternoon, Marie had to go down the hill to meet her father with a little stool. All of them had made little stools from reeds. He would walk uphill only so many steps and then he would have to sit down. He simply did not have the strength to make it all the way without resting.

The refugees, all from different villages, each had their own fire, but they all ate together. Some refugees who had butchered and roasted animals had so much food, they gave the Rempel children some of their meat. Many of these wealthy people died because once they

---

[607] Mennonites in Ukraine Amid Civil War and Anarchy (1917-1920) Translated and Edited by John B. Toews, pg 194; Also, "The Mennonite Refugees in Batum." Deutsche Mennonitenm Hilfe Files, Mennonitische Forschungsstelle, W.P. Neufeld and J.D. Janzen, Weierhof/Pfalz, Germany

[608] The Batum Story, God's Mercy and Man's Kindness, compiled by Mary Dirks Janzen, Third Edition, Edited by Mary E. Janzen 2011 pg 28

were able to secure plenty of food, they gorged themselves. The Rempels were too poor to die. They never had enough to eat, but they didn't die from overeating. They were again reduced to the grace of God.

The UnIted States had a very strict immigration quota. Paraguay seemed to be the only country willing to take these German Mennonite refugees, but they would need to pay their own travel costs.[609] When finally granted, exit papers were only good for about 30 days. If a member of the family became too sick to travel, the papers would expire, and new papers had to be procured.[610] Once they were well enough to travel and had papers, then they needed a ship to take them to Turkey; but often, no ship was in Batum for many days. Time itself seemed to conspire against them ever leaving Batum alive.

Because hordes of refugees were in the city, Georgian officials would gladly have given them their exit visas. However, now Soviet bureaucrats presided who were reluctant to grant them. The Allies in power in Constantinople designated the Italians to grant visas to the city of Constantinople. Since one Italian official had insulted the Communists, the Italians were banned from Batum. Therefore the refugees also needed to travel to Tiflis to the Italian Consulate, a sixteen hour trip by train from Batum.[611]

Finally, in desperation, Aaron Rempel and the other men in their group, including his brother-in-law Jacob Toews, took the train to Tiflis, the capital of Georgia, to try to purchase fake papers with gold coins or jewelry to become Polish or Bulgarian citizens. They sought forged fictitious papers as citizens of some other country to obtain their exit visas to go to Turkey, but they were promptly arrested and thrown in jail. They had passports from Russia, but now they were in Georgia, and Georgia did not recognize Russian passports. Their families back in Batum had not the slightest idea what had happened to them. Eventually they were hauled off like criminals to the consul's office, who didn't want to be bothered, and so they were released.

In peace time, they would have bought passage straight to New York City from Batum, transferring to whatever ships necessary, without traveling to Constantinople. But the United States government did not recognize the Russian Communist government, so they had to get passports from the nearest country which would permit them to pass through it, and that was Turkey. They returned to Batum without any exit visas. Only after the Italians and Bolsheviks had mended relations were refugees able to obtain exit papers and visas in Batum again.[612]

---

[609] Mennonites in Ukraine Amid Civil War and Anarchy (1917-1920) Translated and Edited by John B. Toews, pg 189
[610] Ibid. pp. 185-186
[611] Czars, Soviets, & Mennonites, John B. Toews, pg 128
[612] The Batum Story, God's Mercy and Man's Kindness, compiled by Mary Dirks Janzen, Third Edition, Edited by Mary E. Janzen 2011 pg 30, told by Peter Martin Janzen

It was so discouraging going down time after time, yet not to be able to get the needed money and papers. One time Aaron went down the hill, still sick with malaria. He and his family were stuck. It looked hopeless. He just sat, and didn't care any more. His body had just given out, and he had just given up. When Peter Janzen came by, he remonstrated, "*Mensch du hast familia du mast. Man, you have a family to take care of.*" Then Aaron recalled the words of Psalm 37:23,24 *The steps of a good man are ordered by the LORD, And He delights in his way. Though he fall, he shall not be utterly cast down, For the LORD upholds him with His hand.*

Aaron cried out, "Oh God of my righteousness. You promise me that You hear me when I call, not after I call. You are the true and living God who hears and answers prayer. You have proven that by delivering me with a loaf of bread. You are the living God, sovereign, able to deliver, wise, and righteous. You know these passport officials are so unrighteous. I am stuck here. I can't go forward. I can't go back. I'm trapped here. Have you delivered me with that loaf of bread just to abandon me and my family here? I am so sick, am totally lacking energy, without hope of ever making it to America."

Placing his palms down on the ground, and pushing up with his arms, Aaron slowly straightened up, rose to his feet, and started putting one foot after the other, plodding on. That got him going again.

Grandson William C. Rempel in the video A Rempel Story asked Susanna, "Did you ever lose hope?" "No, I never did. I trusted in God." By remembering past mercies, she had confidence to trust Him again and again.[613]

The young bachelor Peter Janzen had been elected one of the leaders of these desperate refugees. He wrote letters to every relief agency he could think of, (such as the Red Cross, the Near East Relief Agency, and the Mennonite Central Committee) pleading for their merciful help: " You already know . . . of the overthrow of the Czar and the liquidation laws which were carried out so violently during the civil war and which gave way to ever increasing terrible forms such as starvation and bands which destroyed homes, farms, and country . . . . Witness to this described terror are the empty barns and cellars, the untended fields, the many fresh graves, and the camps of emigrants in the harbors."[614]

Aaron and Susanna finally obtained their exit visas to leave Russia for good and boarded a steamer, an absolutely filthy ship, for the 700 mile voyage over the Black Sea to British occupied Constantinople, where they arrived 8 months after leaving Gnadenfeld.[615]

---

[613] A Rempel Story, video of Susanna Krause Rempel and Marie Rempel Bergmann by William C. Rempel, grandson and nephew
[614] The Batum Story, God's Mercy and Man's Kindness, compiled by Mary Dirks Janzen, Third Edition, Edited by Mary E. Janzen 2011 pg 44, letter by Peter Martin Janzen
[615] California Mennonite Historical Society Bulletin, No, 54, 2011, http://www.calmenno.org/bulletin/fall11.pdf

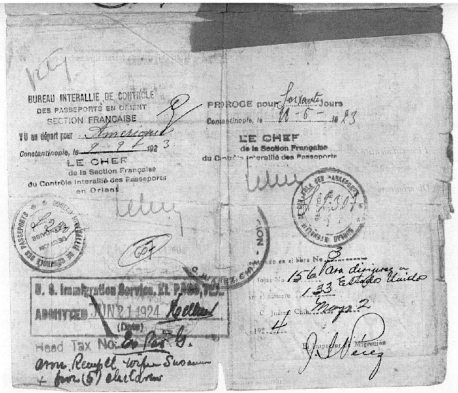

97 Top—Bulgarian Visa

98 Bottom—French Visa

257

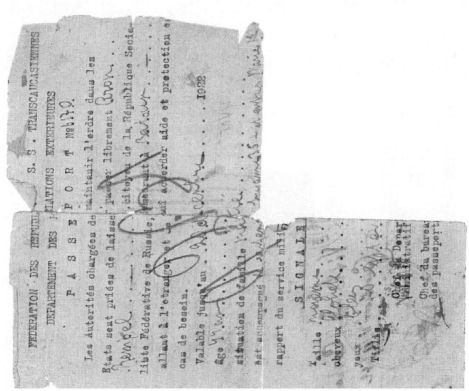

99, 100 Aaron and Susanna's passport from Russia

The Aaron Rempels, Carl and Agatha Rempel, and Jacob and Susanna Toews from Gnadenfeld received their papers and left for Constantinople before the rest of the Mennonites, including Oma Agatha Dirks and her family, who were still stuck in Batum.

What a relief to be leaving Russia, but when Carl and Agatha Rempel stepped on board the ship, Carl was immediately arrested. It was a case of mistaken identity. Carl was released within an hour's time, but for his poor bride Agatha, it seemed an eternity! [616]

On the boat, some of the travelers wanted some of Aaron's furs, so he was able to trade some of them for bread for his children. The furs had kept the family warm; they were slept on; and they also paid their way.

The skies were constantly grey and drizzled all the time. Each time they traveled, it drizzled, so their clothes became moldy. Aaron found his family a really nice, sheltered place on deck under a balcony for the children and baggage. A Syrian swung his great bundle around, ready to throw it right on top of the children, but Arron caught him and pulled him back. The Syrian had a knife in his pocket so he could have fought Aaron, but Aaron seized him in such a way, that if he tried, he would have been thrown overboard instead. So the Syrian left, stomping off.

Gonja wore a straw hat with a red band when a gust of wind came up and swept her hat off and into the sea. Aaron said, "That's it. No more hat." So when they arrived in Constantinople, and whenever the family was near the ocean, Gonja always went out to look for her hat.

At one port along their way, they anchored near a wharf, where men dressed in red sailor suits with white stripes and Turkish fezzes on their heads came on board to help load many cases of oranges being shipped to Constantinople.[617]

Much later, they learned their ship from Feodosia, Crimea to Batum, Georgia actually had landed in Turkey before they landed in Batum. Could they possibly have avoided all the horrors of Batum if they had known and gone ashore in Turkey? Would they have been able to get their passports in Constantinople without having exit papers obtained in Batum? They would never know.

---

[616] "Memoir of Agatha and Carl Rempel" as told to K. R. Lockwood, daughter, pg 13
[617] My Trip From Russia to Freedom in America, Herman G. Rempel, pg 31

Constantinople

When they arrived in Constantinople, a fellow Mennonite passenger on the ship was extremely ill. Their whole group squeezed into a fifth story room Aaron located their first night in Constantinople. Aaron was always the one who found places to stay. Soon he found two rooms for the same rent on the second story of another building. The Toews family of six took one room; they always seemed to get the better end of the deal. Toews had a room all to themselves and wouldn't let anyone else in their room. Everyone else: Aaron's family of six, Onkel Carl and Tante Gotcha, and the ill man and his wife squeezed into the other room. The wife of the sick man begged and begged Aron to take care of her husband, but Aaron made the difficult decision, "No, I have a family to take care of. I am not going to take care of him and get that disease too, yet."

In one place, they discovered a Red Cross kitchen right across the street from where they stayed, which provided one meal a day. However, this kitchen was unable to take care of additional people. They told the family of another Red Cross kitchen clear across the city of Constantinople which could serve more people. So Aaron took Marie, twelve, and Ronka, nine, and showed them the way seven miles across the city to the other Red Cross kitchen. They were given a pail, (an old ten pound Crisco shortening bucket) of thin soup, enough for one dish of soup for each one in the family, and a three inch square piece of bread for each person. Too much soda had been added to the soup, and it was soooooo thin—one bean chasing another.[618] That was the food ration for each day; it was all they had to eat.

Marie was the only one who stayed well. Because Ronka only felt sick one day, but much better the next day, he accompanied Marie across the city every other day.

As an adult, Marie often wondered how she made that long trip each way, usually by herself, unless a guardian angel watched over her. She left in the morning, arrived at the soup kitchen around noon, picked up the bucket of soup and bread for each one, and the family ate their one meal of the day around 4:00 pm or so when she returned. When a person is hungry, food is all they think about.[619]

Once they were given horse meat soup and the next day horse meat meatballs from that same horse. Gonja was extremely pleased to receive all the horse meat the others didn't want to eat. There was a lot of marble in Constantinople. The city was near the "marble sea." All the counters in

---

[618] Memoir of Agatha and Carl Rempel, as told to K. R. Lockwood, daughter, pg 14
[619] A Rempel Story, video of Susanna Krause Rempel and Marie Rempel Bergmann by William C. Rempel.

stores and columns outside buildings were made of marble. When Marie walked to get food, she passed by candy stores, with big chunks of Halvah, Turkish sesame candy about two feet square by ten inches high with a big knife stuck in them, lying on marble counters. Aaron brought some halvah home only twice. It wasn't just that they were so awfully hungry all the time; Halvah was a really desired, rare treat. Marie had to pass by it daily. She looked longingly at it through shop windows every day.

Marie and Ronka also passed by the St. Sophia or Hagia Sophia Mosque on each trip for food. A lot of lit candles marked the sites where important people were buried. When Ronka was with her, Marie dared to stop nearby, and look in from the sidewalk.[620]

When Aaron had a little more money, he bought himself yogurt that was sold in a small container, and really enjoyed it. It seemed to give him a bit more strength, which he really needed. The children looked on hungrily, but there simply wasn't enough money to buy any for them. Sometimes, Aaron had enough money to buy the whole family some fish. How delicious the fresh fish was, and what a welcome change in diet from horse meat and watered down borscht with a tiny bit of bread.

Shortly after arriving in Constantinople, it was time for the baby to arrive. Aaron took Susanna in a taxi to try and find a hospital where the baby could be born. Since the Crimean War, the Allies had built hospitals in and around the Galata Tower on the west side of the Bosphorus. The French hospital refused to take Susanna. The Italian hospital also refused to take her. Next, even the British Hospital refused to take her. It wasn't as if Aaron and Susanna were penniless. Aaron had enough money to pay. Those hospitals just didn't want to take money from such riffraff from Southern Russia. It seemed they just didn't want those low-lifes in their hospitals.

Susanna, in hard labor now, with the baby coming fast, left the hospital doors of the British Hospital, plopped down on the concrete steps outside and exclaimed in exasperation, "Here I stay. Here I have the baby, right here, right here on these steps! I go no farther!" Aaron rushed back into the hospital and cried out, "My wife is having the baby on the steps right outside the door. Do you want that? Do you want her to have the baby on the steps out there?"

The British Hospital finally took pity on them and relented. Aaron paid the hospital $25 so she could stay 10 days, but he forgot to mention that detail to Susanna. He just took her into the hospital, paid the $25 for her hospital stay, and left her there. Aaron, relieved to know that she was well cared for, did not visit her once after the baby was born.

[620] The young people traveling with the Aaron Rempel family, Heinz, Mieche, Katche Dirks and Carl and Agatha Rempel were able to do some sightseeing, visiting mosques, the subterranean reservoir (water supply for the city of Constantinople) and other interesting sites in and around the city.

Willie was born prematurely, perhaps five or six weeks early on 26 November, 1922. Because he was born in Turkey, he was designated a Turkish citizen. Susanna couldn't speak English or Turkish, and it seemed no one in the hospital could speak German or Russian. She had no communication with anyone, and didn't see her baby Willie, because, as a preemie, they kept him in the nursery or "intensive care." Understandably, she became frantic. Susanna wanted to leave right away, but they wouldn't let her leave. They had taken baby Willie from her, then only allowed her to see him once a day.

101 Hagia Sophia Mosque

Hagia Sophia, built 537 AD as St. Sophia, replaced two former Christian churches on that site which were destroyed by fire and rioting. The Emperor Justinian set out to make it magnificent, and it was the foremost church in Christendom until 1453, when Mehmet the Conqueror captured Constantinople. The floor exceeds three football fields in area, and the upper gallery is so large the fifth (AD 553) and sixth (AD 680-681) Ecumenical Councils were held there. Muslims added four minarets and large Arabic signs inside during its life as an Ottoman Mosque, 1453 until 1931, when it became a museum. Today's President Erdogan in Turkey would like to return its status to that of a mosque.[621]

---

[621] http://www.levantineheritage.com/hosp.htm   Courtesy of: http://levantineheritage.com/

102 British Hospital viewed from Galata Tower

Picture taken from the Galata Tower. The British Hospital red roofs and its own tower are in the center of picture, right across the cobblestone street from Galata Tower, looking across the Bosphorus toward the portion of Constantinople where Hagia Sophia (unseen) sits high upon a hill. Upper portion of picture is of the Docks, barely visible on the near shore, behind the hospital, where Rempels probably arrived from Batum, Georgia.[622] The Bosphorus is the strait connecting the Black Sea and the Mediterranean Sea, and which separates Asian Turkey from European Turkey.

---

[622] http://www.levantineheritage.com/hosp.htm   Courtesy of: http://levantineheritage.com/

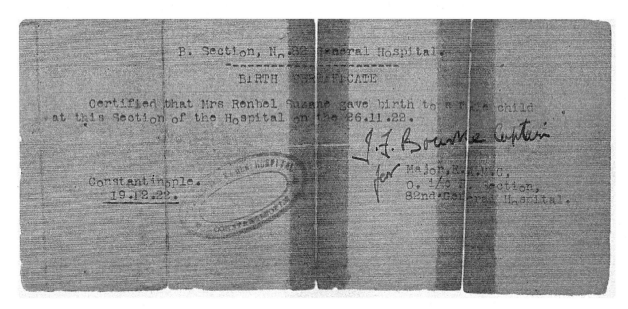

B. Section, N. ... General Hospital

BIRTH ... CATE

Certified that Mrs Renbel Susane gave birth to a r... child at this Section of the Hospital on the 26.11.22.

Constantinople. 19.12.22.

[signature] J.F. Bourke Captain

for Major, R.A.M.C, O. ... Section, 82nd General Hospital.

103 above Baby Willie's birth certificate

104 pebble mosaic

The pebble mosaic sidewalk leads to steps in front of the door where Baby Willie was almost born.[623]

Susanna remembered seeing Aaron's arms around those other two women back in Siberia. Yes, he had come back to her and the children. Yes, he had brought them safely, not without adventure and severe trials, but safely back to Gnadenfeld. And now he had brought them safely thus far to

---

[623] http://www.levantineheritage.com/hosp.htm   Courtesy of: http://levantineheritage.com/

Constantinople. But what if those important papers to immigrate to the United States came through while she was still here in the hospital with Baby Willie? She was terribly afraid she would be left behind all by herself, helpless and alone with a newborn, in a strange land.

Susanna recalled, "When Willie was born, I could not speak to nobody. I wanted to go to my family. They said, 'No, no. You stay here.' I thought they would keep us (Willie and me) forever, and I was afraid my family would go to America without me." Finally the hospital staff found a German girl who worked there, and brought her to translate. "I told her I wanted to go to my family. Then they understood I was so desperate to see my family. They knew I had come from a distance in a taxi. They gave me Willie. I almost never saw Willie. They had him all the time. They kept him away from me."

Susanna had no baby clothes, none whatsoever. The people at the hospital were able to gather a few baby clothes, a couple of diapers, and a blanket. The taxi driver wanted to know where Susanna wanted to go.

She did not know what to tell him, "Well, where all my others are."

"Are you immigrant?" he asked.

"Yes, I am immigrant. Go where the people from Russia are."

"Oh, then I know where you go," and he drove where Susanna could see the hill and the five story building where they were living perched upon the top. Susanna had to climb five stories, carrying baby Willie, to get to their quarters.

All the men were smoking. No one expected her to reappear for ten days, but here Susanna showed up unexpectedly after only five days. How had she found her way back? She never knew. Susanna showed up by surprise. The look on Aaron's face was one of disbelief when suddenly, without warning, she entered the room. "My girl! What do you want here? How did you get home? I paid for you to be there for ten days. You should have stayed there!" Initially Aaron thought that his money had been wasted. Poor Susanna was hurt that Aaron seemed displeased to see her so soon. Susanna thought he should have told her, or written her a note that he had paid for so long. She didn't even know. Why shouldn't she be afraid of being left behind, and want to come home so soon? After a while, Aaron mellowed. He really was happy they were all together again.

266

Salut de Constantinople. La tour de Galata.

105 British Hospital, Galata Tower—Old postcard Taken looking from the docks on the Bosporus, shows the tower of the British Hospital on the left and the Galata Tower on the hill to the right.[624]

Susanna used her nice big fur coat as an incubator for little baby Willie. The fur coat was valuable, made up of many tiny pieces of fur. So Baby Willie was always warm, wrapped up in one of their fur coats. He only had one blanket, but the fur coat kept him alive.[625] Unfortunately, Susanna was not able to breastfeed him like she could her other babies. Perhaps because he was so premature, and while in the hospital he had been kept from her, she did not develop the milk supply. Or perhaps it was because Susanna herself was starving. Susanna gave him sugar water in a bottle. His nails were not formed yet because he was premature, but in him was life. He wanted to live, and Susanna wanted that boy to go to America.

It was so very damp and humid, drops of condensation were always all over the ceiling. Marie had to wash diapers in ocean water. The only way Susanna could dry a diaper, was to put it on her own bare stomach, so by night time, Baby Willie would have a dry diaper to sleep in at night.

---

[624] http://www.levantineheritage.com/hosp.htm   Courtesy of: http://levantineheritage.com/

[625] The author visited Istanbul, Turkey in late December 2014, when it was sleeting, so snow and ice covered the ground. Many think because Istanbul is on the Mediterranean it must have a very temperate climate, but temperatures were in the low twenties that December. Baby Willie truly was kept alive and warm enough in that fur coat despite the cold.

Christmas in Constantinople

As Christmas 1922 drew nearer, Marie was on the lookout for anything that might resemble a Christmas tree or decorations as she trekked across the city for their daily ration of soup and bread. Now, even little Susie accompanied her occasionally. Marie was so happy when Susie found four or five colored bits of paper. Marie couldn't find a single green twig. Even in hard times in Gnadenfeld, they had a Christmas tree. It just wouldn't be Christmas without that tree. In the end, the best Marie could find was a small, bare branch, and she was glad even to find that. The poor little branch was brought home, stuck in a hole in the wall, and decorated with those tiny scraps of colored paper from gum or candy wrappers found on the ground. That was their Christmas tree.[626]

Susanna was preparing for Christmas too. She made some paste out of a little chocolate, flour, and sweetened condensed milk she had somehow managed to save. At least the children thought it was like candy. They thought they had something special.

One evening, Tante Gotche and Onkel Carl Rempel, Tante Susanna and Onkel Jacob Toews and their children crowded into the room, sat around and cried together as they sang old German Christmas carols, and thought about past Christmases in Gnadenfeld. They missed their Oma Agatha's family, still stuck in Batum, and remembered the good times in Russia: pfeffernüsse cookies and real Christmas trees with beautiful German handblown glass decorations, the big, grand church in Gnadenfeld all decorated with evergreens, the wonderful organ playing Stille Nacht, the three days of Christmas celebrations. They cried when they thought how hopeless their situation looked. Would they ever get to America?

The Red Cross kitchen said they all were invited for a Christmas party. They had a real, green Christmas tree, and each child received a Christmas present. Gonja received a china doll with yellow painted hair and Susie one with black painted hair. They were both the same size, about a foot tall, with cloth bodies and china heads, hands, and feet. The head was sewn on at the shoulders, with the sewing going right through the body. They even had clothes that could be taken off. Gonja and Susie decided they had to keep their precious dolls out of the rain. Marie received a set of dishes.

---

[626] My Trip From Russia to Freedom in America, Herman G. Rempel, pg 10 (Cousin of Aaron Rempel and son of Gustav and Elizabeth Electra Dirks Rempel) Herman wrote in his diary, *Batum, Monday, January 1, 1923: Today we went with Henry, Mary, and Katharine* (Dirks) *to the dacha (country house) where they had lived before. Roses and Alpen violets are in bloom. We cut some fir branches for a Christmas tree and made walking sticks from the bamboo.*

It was at the Red Cross Christmas Party they were taught the song "Vlasu Rodillas Elochka," and they sang that song as they danced around the Christmas tree. It was a Russian Christmas song about a little Christmas tree who was very sad until finally some children came and decorated him beautifully in the house, and the little tree was so happy. They didn't know that song when living in Russia. [627]

106 Vlasu Rodilas Elochka, public domain

---

[627] Even as an adult, Susanna cried as she again sang this song while the author was audio taping her story. *"We learned that there, just there in Turkey. We didn't know that Christmas song in Russia."* Gonja remembered that song as long as she lived. When she taught elementary grades at the Ballard one room school in Santa Ynez Valley, California in the 1960s, she taught her students to sing it.

After that Christmas, they were able to go to the Red Cross kitchen near where they lived. Marie no longer had to trek clear across the city and back every day.

The family moved into a big two-story house near the sea, on the Asian side of the Bosporus, their last house before leaving for America. Onkel Carl and Tante Gotcha lived on the second floor where they enjoyed an outside staircase. Even though they were only living there temporarily, Gotcha fixed their little room up pretty by putting in curtains.

Still stuck in Batum, Mennonite leader Peter Janzen was totally unflappable. The Soviet officials could taunt him, curse him, insult him, and he acted as if nothing touched him, like he was totally deaf. It all rolled off like water off a duck's back. Janzen was like a burr in their clothing. Finally, to be rid of him, they eventually granted the remaining German Mennonite refugees in Batum everything.[628] Moscow had completed a back-ground check on each remaining refugee, and sent their exit papers to Tiblisi, where Peter Janzen went to pick them up. At last the remaining Mennonites were granted visas. They didn't arrive in Constantinople until Saturday, April 7, 1923. Dick and Herman Rempel,[629] ended up rooming and boarding with Carl and Gotcha Rempel. Many were still sick with malaria. The quinine had been so watered down, it wasn't doing much good. Once they were able to procure good quinine through the Near East Relief Agency, German Mennonite deaths in Constantinople ceased.

By Monday this group rented an old but spacious two-story house with twenty rooms in Goetztepe. It was formerly owned by a merchant with a harem of twenty wives, and was now managed by a Turk with four wives. Each family's room had bright windows, and was carpeted with woven grass matting, inhabited with bedbugs that hid during the day and came out at night. To combat the bedbugs, they learned to spray the cracks with kerosene. This cut down on the number of bloodsucking critters, but did not eliminate them. They also learned to look out for scorpions.[630]

Oma Agatha's family and some Rempel cousins stayed in the old house Mennonites dubbed "that old harem," while Gonja's family lived in a nearby house with a swing. Gonja pestered her cousin Dietrich Rempel to push her in that swing. He ignored her, but she continued to pester and pester, until finally he gave her a memorable swing. He swung her, and swung her, and swung her higher, and higher, and higher; so high, it scared the life out of her. She yelled "Stop, stop, **stop**!" But the more she yelled, the more he pushed, and the higher she went. She went as high as the barn with Gonja hanging on for dear life. Gonja was so grateful when Dietrich finally quit and walked away.

---

[628] Mennonites in Ukraine Amid Civil War and Anarchy (1917-1920) Translated and Edited by John B. Toews, pg 189

[629] Dick (Dietrich) and Herman Rempel, children of Gustav and Elizabeth Electra Dirks Rempel, were cousins of Aaron, Jr.

[630] From Bolshevik Russia to America, A Mennonite Family Story, Henry D. Rempel, pp. 77, 79

Her swing gradually came lower and lower, until she stopped. She never asked him to swing her again. But that was probably what Dietrich wanted in the first place.[631]

Spring brought nicer weather. They were in the country, and seemed to have more hope of getting to America. Gonja again looked for her hat lost in the Black Sea. She looked for seashells and found oranges washed up on the beach. Ronka eagerly bit into an orange, then another, expecting a refreshing sweetness. He spit it out and never tried one again. Gonja was so hungry all the time, she ate the oranges even though they were soaked in brine. When the family lived near the ocean, they received United States relief help, including dried turnips. They all ate dried turnips for a long time. Marie thought they tasted pretty good when they were cooked, but Gonja preferred briny oranges.

Once, Tante Mieche Dirks boiled water in the middle of the yard preparing to do laundry. Gonja, walking backwards, stepped right into the pot of hot water, and scalded both legs. Another time when Gonja ran barefoot, she stepped into nettles.

Aaron had to cross the city frequently to try and get the necessary money and papers to go to America. The MCC (Mennonite Central Committee) had opened an office in Constantinople.[632] The MCC worked to secure sponsorships, matching American farmers with refugee German Mennonite workers, to obtain travel fare, exit visas, railway and steamship tickets so the refugees could immigrate to the United States or Canada.[633] Also, the refugees absolutely needed to be free of lice.

Aaron had to cross the Bosphorus, and disembark near Galata Tower on the bridge over the Golden Horn connecting Sambul and Constantinople. The place was busy with steamship horns blowing as ships arrived and departed, vehicle horns beeping on the bridge, and sea planes droning overhead. Warships held maneuvers daily, with canon and machine gun fire. Aaron in Gnadenfeld had never before seen Scotsmen wearing skirts (kilts), instead of trousers, let alone black skinned Negroes and very brown Arabs. A guard at each end of the bridge collected a toll from all traffic, both cars and pedestrians. Only at night when bridge traffic was greatly diminished, was a portion of the bridge raised to let ships pass through.

A short distance from the bridge, Aaron had to buy a ticket to go through an underground cable car tunnel, to travel to the Red Cross Office in Pera. Here too, Carl and Abram Rempel (both sons of The Old General), Jacob Toews, and Johann Pankratz went on Friday, April 13, 1923, to make a down payment on their trip to America. Because there were so many people, they had to take a

---

[631] Dietrich Rempel would one day own the Rempel Rubber Toy Manufacturing plant in Akron, Ohio
[632] Mennonites in Ukraine Amid Civil War and Anarchy (1917-1920), Translated and Edited by John B. Toews, pg 189
[633] Ibid, pg 192

number and wait their turn in line. It turned out far too many people were in line to be seen that day, and so their numbers would not come up until the next day. Carl did not have any malaria fever on the day they went, but he had so much fever that night, he was much too weak to go the next day.[634]

What was that noise? That continuing drumbeat? Looking out the window, Marie saw minarets illuminated throughout the night. At midnight, people gathered and walked through the streets carrying lanterns, as the drum kept beating. Who could sleep through all that racket? The Turks were celebrating "Bairam" (the feast at the end of Ramadan). It was one of their most important holidays, preceded by 30 days of fasting, when they could only eat at night. For a whole month, they had been marching through the streets around midnight always beating their drums. According to the Koran, "Bairam" must be preceded with a day of fasting, but since the Koran does not specify exactly which day, they had to fast for the whole month so they didn't miss fasting on that one, special day.

Mennonites in Constantinople had heard they could book passage to America for only 25 lyra. However, when they arrived at the Red Cross office May 7, they were told the passage was actually 50 lyra per person. Most did not have enough to book passage. On May 15, Miss Thringland of the Red Cross told them she would be able to obtain tickets for all the Mennonites in Constantinople at 90 lyra per person. Although this amount was considerably higher, visas could be granted without obtaining affidavits. Of course this would be a great advantage to those who could not obtain their affidavits, so the group's leader Peter Janzen prepared a list of all those who had not yet received their visas.[635]

Tuesday, May 8, the American Red Cross announced they would help four families go to the United States: Aaron Rempel, Jacob Toews, W. Rahn, and perhaps Carl Rempel. They paid for their ship tickets the following Thursday. The American consul started the paperwork to issue visas of entry to the United States.[636] Now Aaron had to get the required medical certificate signed by Doctor Hoover at the American Medical Clinic. They had to pass the health inspection.

Lice! The whole family appeared before the Medical clinic but were rejected because some were infested with head lice. So often they couldn't get the right papers because of lice! The Aaron Rempels didn't have actual lice, but eggs were still attached to their hair. It was impossible to comb out the eggs. They were stuck. Susanna had a very fine toothed comb, and by carefully combing each square inch of the head, would remove ALL the lice. Susanna also killed lice by

---

[634] My Trip From Russia to Freedom in America, Herman G. Rempel, pp. 36, 38
[635] Ibid, pp. 40-42
[636] Ibid, pp. 40, 41

dousing everyone's heads in kerosene mixed with lard. Marie remembered always walking around with her head reeking of kerosene. But kerosene did not remove or kill the eggs stuck to the hair. If it wasn't the lice, it was the eggs, and the government still refused approval. They would not be allowed to board that ship until they could thoroughly rid themselves of those persistent, pesky parasites, including their eggs.

German Mennonites from Russia needed to enter on America's Russian quota. After World War I, Congress established The First Quota Act, which took effect June 3, 1921. This system allowed 23,000 Russian born immigrants each year.[637] Baby Willy was born in Turkey, so he would have to enter under the Turkish quota, which had already been met for the United States fiscal year July 1, 1922 through June 30, 1923. The annual Turkish quota of only 100 immigrants conceivably could be filled entirely on the very first day of the **new** fiscal year, starting midnight, July 1, 1923. They would have to arrive then. A day later could be too late.

They needed to have the money, the papers, no lice, and come in under the quota all at the same time. But for immigrants from Greece and Turkey, and other eastern and southern Europeans, the newly opened quotas likely would last only days. Some could close by the Fourth of July, others within just hours. *First come, first counted, but then America's open doors slammed shut again . . . . Congress and President Harding in 1921 imposed severe quotas based solely, for the first time, on nationality. A popular song of the day was "O! Close the Gates." . . . By summer of 1923, quota controls had radically reduced the influx of "less desirables," immigrants from Greece, Turkey, Armenia, the Balkans, and Russia.*[638]

Passengers to be transported by the Red Cross were divided into two groups. Jacob Toews was fortunate to get into the first group, but Aaron and Carl Rempel were in the second group. Since few visas had been granted so far, only a few passengers were booking passage, so Aaron was able to get each ticket from the Buras line to board the SS Washington for the bargain price of only 60 Lyra.[639]

Now Aaron had already bought the ship tickets; their ship was present in the harbor, ready to sail soon. So Aaron decreed, "This is it. The hair must all come off!" They had tried and tried to get rid of all lice. Each time they wanted to get the mandatory papers, they wouldn't give Aaron the papers because of lice. The Mennonite Central Committee had found sponsors for these German Men-

---

[637] The Batum Story, God's Mercy and Man's Kindness, compiled by Mary Dirks Janzen, Third Edition, Edited by Mary E. Janzen 2011 pg 31
[638] Los Angeles Times, "Racing to America," William C. Rempel, July 4, 1998, pp. 1, 22
[639] My Trip From Russia to Freedom in America, Herman G. Rempel, pg 49

nonites who had been stranded in Turkey. Aaron had now been sent an $800 loan from his sponsor, Mr. C. C. Sommer in Iowa.

There would be room on the Turkish quota if they boarded the ship The Washington provided the ship made it to New York first, so all hair had to come off, and it had to come off **now.** There was no other way, and no time to lose.

The family marched over to Tante Gotcha and Onkel Carl's room upstairs, and she cut off everyone's hair. She had little clippers, and when she was done, all their hair was lying on the floor. No one had any hair left; all were bald. *Susanna's eyes overflowed. Silently she wept. Her hair had been so long she could sit on it. She really put up a fight, but in the end, it all came off.*[640] *Vanity was a sin in her tattered Mennonite Bible, so she prayed that God would forgive "my silly tears."*[641] Carl was gallant enough to tell his bride that he thought she looked cute.

So on Thursday, May 15, 1923, the Aaron and Carl Rempels all marched over to Dr. Hoover's office, and received a medical certificate from him, stating they had a clean bill of health, and could now enter the United States. But they would all be entering bald, very bald indeed.[642]

A letter arrived Tuesday, May 29 from Neufelds of Reedley, California, containing three affidavits, one each for Carl, Dick, and Herman Rempel, and stating their relative Wilhelm Neufeld would sponsor them. The letter also contained two checks: one each for Carl and Aaron, plus a letter from Aunt Margaret.[643] [644]

On Saturday, June 2, 1923, Captain Bacoyanis of The SS Washington brought his immigrant ship into Constantinople.[645]

Friday, June 8, Ronka was in bed with Susanna and Aaron, when suddenly blood came trickling out of his nose. The trickle became a little river which soon intensified. Susanna tried to stop it with cold water, but it still poured out of his nose. It would not stop. Much of it ran into his mouth and was swallowed, so he would vomit big blood clots as it continued to pour. Ronka became

---

[640] "Memoir of Agatha and Carl Rempel" as told to K. R. Lockwood, pg 14
[641] Los Angeles Times, "Racing to America," William C. Rempel, July 4, 1998, pp 22
[642] My Trip From Russia to Freedom in America, Herman G. Rempel, pg 42
[643] Ibid, pg 46
[644] California Mennonite Historical Society Bulletin, No 45, Fall 2006, "Russian Mennonite Choral Conductors," by Peter Letkemann, pg 4, "On the return journey from Russia to Germany, he (Wilhelm Neufeld) suffered from severe intestinal pain, which later was diagnosed as intestinal cancer. Neufeld died on 7 June 1923, at age sixty-eight, almost a month before the Rempels reached in NY harbor (See footnote #643, Wilhelm's son Herman said his father died of liver cancer.)
[645] Los Angeles Times, "Racing to America," William C. Rempel, July 4, 1998, pp 22A

weaker and weaker. They tried calling a doctor, but that was difficult because all the doctors were Turks, and Rempels could speak neither Turkish nor French. All Ronka could do was lie down, and all he wanted was to hold his mother's hand. Ronka thought he was dying. A Turkish lady heard about Ronka's nosebleed, so she went home, made a hot brew, and came back with a thick green soup for Ronka to drink. Because it was hot, thick, and a large amount, it took Ronka a long time to drink it all, but the bleeding finally slowed to a trickle, then stopped altogether. That evening Ronka was pale and weak, but still alive.[646]

By 2 o'clock Saturday, June 9, all papers were in order. So Henry (Heinz) Dirks Jr, Dick and Herman Rempel accompanied the Aaron Rempel family and helped carry their baggage to the harbor. They had to say their good-byes on the dock because the ship was anchored in the harbor, and the family had to take a tender to board the ship. Toward evening, Rempels started their long voyage to New York[647] aboard The SS Washington. Paradoxically, although Jacob and Susanna Rempel Toews were in the first group, they actually left later, on the following Monday, June 11 on The Canada.[648]

107 Passport photo L to R- Marie, Susanna holding little Susie, Aaron, Gonja, Ronka

---

[646] My Trip From Russia to Freedom in America, Herman G. Rempel, pg 48, Friday, June 1, 1923
[647] Ibid, pg 49
[648] My Trip From Russia to Freedom in America, Herman G. Rempel, pp. 49-52, 56, 57. The "Canada was the last steamer to leave Constantinople, until June 24th, when two large groups left on the "Marseille" and the "Madonna," docked in Marseille, France. Then Mennonites traveled by train to Paris and Cherbourg, France, to sail from there to Ellis Island. It was during this period that a sad letter arrived stating that Uncle Wilhelm Neufeld in Reedley California was deathly ill, and had to go through an operation for cancer of the liver. The Carl Rempels moved into the quarters vacated by Jacob and Susanna Toews, where the Rempels occupied the larger room, and Dick and Herman the smaller. Carl and Agatha Rempel left Tuesday, July 3, 1923, on the ship "Constantinople" of the Byron Line. Then a newspaper arrived giving notice that Wilhelm Neufeld had died on June 7 in Reedley, California. Oma Agatha Dirks family, along with Dick and Herman Rempel were not able to leave until Saturday, September 27, 1923, on the Saxonia. All the rest of the Mennonite refugees from Batum arrived in New York on the Saxonia. Susanna Rempel never saw her mother Agatha again.

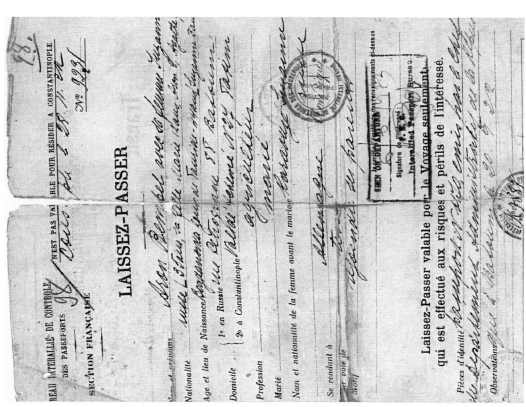

108, 109, Aron Rempel passport

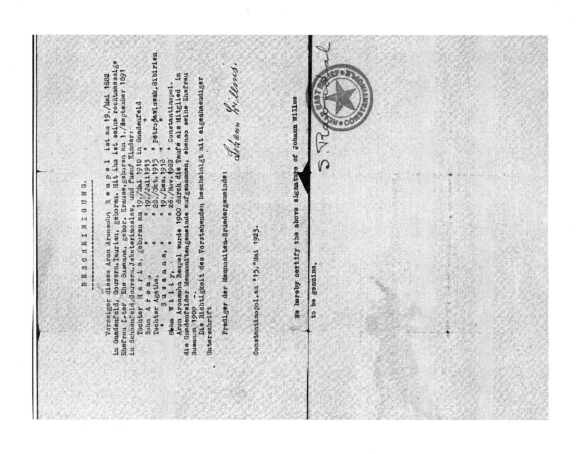

BESCHEINIGUNG.
————————

Vorzeiger dieses Aron Aronsohn R e m p e l ist am 19./Mai 1882 in Gnadenfeld, Gouvern.Taurien, geboren. Mit ihm ist seine rechtmaessige Ehefrau I.ter Ehe Susanna, gebor. Krauss,geboren am 1./September 1891 in Schoenfeld,Gouvern.Jekaterinoslaw, und fuenf Kinder:
Tochter Maria, geboren am 19./Mai 1910 in Gnadenfeld
Sohn Aron,   "   19./Juli1913   "
Tochter Agatha,   "   20./Okt.1915 : Petro,Pawlowsk,Sibirien
   "   Susanna, "   19./Dez.1918   "
Sohn Willy,   "   26./Nov.1922 : Constantinopel.
Aron Aronsohn Rempel wurde 1900 durch die Taufe als Mitglied in die Gnadenfelder Mennonitengemeinde aufgenommen, ebenso seine Ehefrau Susanna.1909 -
Die Richtigkeit des Vorstehenden bescheinigt mit eigenhaendiger Unterschrift

Prediger der Mennoniten-Bruedergemeinde: Johann Willms

Constantinopel,am "15./Mai 1923.

We hereby certify the above signature of Johann Willms
to be genuine.

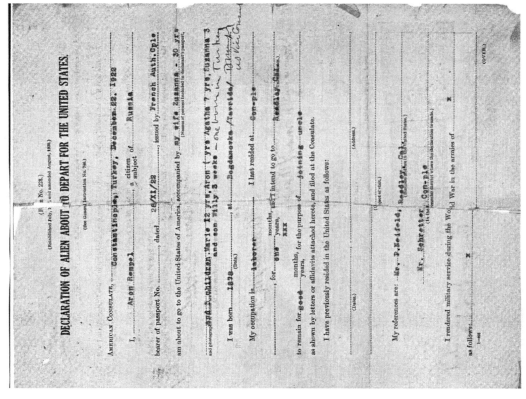

(Form No. 228.)
(Established Feby. ? and amended August, 1920.)

DECLARATION OF ALIEN ABOUT TO DEPART FOR THE UNITED STATES.

(See General Instruction No. 760.)

AMERICAN CONSULATE, Constantinople, Turkey, December 22, 1922

I, Aron Rempel, a citizen of / subject of Russia.

bearer of passport No. .... dated 25/XI/22 .... issued by French Auth.Cple

am about to go to the United States of America, accompanied by my wife Zusanna - 30 yrs children: Maria 12 yrs, Aron 9 yrs Agatha 7 yrs, Zusanna 3 and son Willy 3 weeks

I was born 1878. My occupation is laborer. I last resided at Con-ple. I do not intend to go to

to remain for good for the purpose of joining uncle as shown by letters or affidavits attached hereto, and filed at the Consulate.

I have previously resided in the United States as follows:

My references are: Mr. P.Reisfeld, Bradley, Cal.
                   Mr. Schretter, Con-ple

I rendered military service during the World War in the armies of
as follows:

(OVER.)

110, 111 US Consulate in Constantinople

I have informed myself of the provisions of section 3 of the Immigration Act of February 5, 1917, and am convinced that I am eligible for admission into the United States thereunder.

I realize that if I am one of a class prohibited by law from admission into the United States I will be deported or detained in the United States by immigration authorities, and I am prepared to assume the risk of deportation and of compulsory return in case of my rejection at an American port.

I solemnly swear that the foregoing statements are true to the best of my knowledge and belief, and that I fully intend while in the United States to obey the laws and constituted authorities thereof.

AMERICAN CONSULATE
CONSTANTINOPLE   No. 732   _Aron Rempel_
(City)   (Country)   (Signature of declarant.)

On journey to the United States

Subscribed and sworn to before me this _____

_____ day of _____, 192

$5 FEE STAMP

Thomas J Murphy
(American   Consul.)

CONSUL'S RECOMMENDATIONS

$2 FEE STAMP   CONSULAR SEAL.]   _Thomas J Murphy_

No. _____
($1.00.)

Visa granted _____
(Date.)

Visa refused _____
(Date.)

[Signed photograph of declarant.]

6 born in Russia
Turkey } not included in photo.

112 declaration — eligible to enter US

SS Washington

The gangway to America was open.

By the time they boarded the ship, Aaron had only $30 dollars in his pocket, but it was borrowed along with their fare for their steerage quarters.[649] He needed to show the inspectors when he arrived at Ellis Island that he had at least $25 for the trip to their destination.

Baby Willie was only seven months old, but extremely weak because he had been born prematurely,[650] poorly fed, and it had been a cold and very damp time of year. They didn't have any good clothes, and baby Willie had almost nothing to wear.

By the time they needed to board the ship, Gonja was sick with measles. That would have kept them from going, but Susanna hid her illness from all the officials and smuggled her on board. Of course, once safely on board, next little Susie, then the rest of the family came down with measles.

In those days, many steerage passengers didn't have separate cabins. By 1922, many ships were upgrading steerage compartments to family cabins, but the <u>Washington</u> was in financial straits so wasn't one of them. Everyone was crammed in together in big, old men's, women's, and family dorms with bunk beds. The noisy, clanking engine room constantly pounded directly beneath them. Sleeping compartments sometimes accommodated as many as 300. Lights stayed on all the time, even through the night. Aisles to walk between the bunks at the foot or the head were narrow, but the beds were all right next to each other with barely enough space to walk between them.[651] Each bunk might be six feet long, about two feet wide, and only 30 inches separated upper and lower berths. Perhaps the mattress was stuffed with straw. People usually slept in their clothes, since the only blanket that was supplied was so thin. If constant light and engine noise weren't enough, sleep was difficult because of additional noise of rats running just above their heads.

---

[649] <u>Los Angeles Times</u>, "Racing to America," William C Rempel, July 4, 1998, p 22
[650] If Susanna were pregnant as they left Gnadenfeld, baby Willie should have been born close to full term. However, because of poor nutrition from the Great Famine and Susanna's illness from malaria for months on end, he could have had a very low birth weight, and appeared like a preemie. It is unclear if the lack of finger nails and toe nails when he was born really indicated he was a 7 month preemie, or just reflected malnutrition. By the author's calculations, he may have been an 8th month preemie.
[651] <u>Ellis Island</u>, Wilton S. Tifft, pg 80; http://montalbine.com/steerage.html

Ship's profit lay in numbers, not in comfort. Overcrowding caused a lot of the children to come down with measles. Measles were the number one cause of death among the third class passengers both on the voyage, and later at the quarantine station on Hoffman Island in New York harbor. Because no facilities existed for storing the dead on the ship, if a child died at sea, the body was quickly and unceremoniously slipped into the ocean with the mother crying unconsolably.[652]

The Rempels were at sea 28 rough, stormy days. Most passengers were seasick throughout the voyage. They could see a lot of water through the portholes, but not see the sky. As far as the eye could see, waves, more waves, and higher waves, the whole ocean in an uproar. At first they feared a watery grave, but then they were so sea sick, they were afraid they might not die after all. Some people didn't know where the toilets were. No fresh air reached the cramped quarters; ventilation was almost non-existent and the smell was fierce. On many of the ships, in steerage, when someone was seasick, no one from the ship's crew would clean the floor, until shortly before inspection in New York harbor. Living conditions were almost unbearable. Because the air was so foul, most passengers would seek to be up on the open deck early in the morning during good weather, but the area was limited, crowded, and without chairs.

Even if they had not been sea sick, they could not have eaten, the food was so poor. They were only fed sardines [653], black salted olives, and orange jello made with oranges including the orange peels. That jello looked so pretty, so inviting, looked so soothing to eat, but it was extremely bitter with peels included. Once they actually received a whole orange to eat and another time an apple! What a treat!

Neither privacy, cleanliness, decency, nor comfort is possible . . . . sometimes two or three thousand persons are crowded into a space hardly sufficient to accommodate 1,200. Steerage passengers can not, with any degree of truth or justice, be said to be humanely or properly treated at any stage of their long and painful journey.[654]

As the ship neared its destination, the ship's crew finally scrubbed the floors and cleaned and readied everything else according to regulations. On arrival in port, customs officials came aboard

---

[652] Island of Hope, Island of Tears, David M. Brownstone, Irene M. Franck, and Douglass Brownstone, pg 129

[653] Ibid, pp. 126, 130, The "sardines" were probably actually pickled herring, the cheapest food available that might be relied upon to keep immigrants alive for a trip of up to three or four weeks. It was nourishing, and seemed to alleviate seasickness. Ships would have barrels and barrels of herring, and passengers often could help themselves any time. Furthermore, for strict religious Jews, herring was considered kosher. Many immigrants remembered their voyages in terms of herring; no matter how different their ships had been, the unifying experience was that pickled herring.

[654] Ellis Island, An Illustrated History of the Immigrant Experience, Ivan Chermayeff, Fred Wasserman, Mary J. Shapiro, pg 39, "Report of Conditions Existing in Europe and Mexico Affecting Emigration and Immigration, ca 1907"

to hold inspection. The ship only presented what the ship wanted inspectors to see, not what it was really like during the voyage. It was only by keeping their eyes on the prize of American freedom and citizenship that made the trip in steerage at all tolerable.

The entire passenger manifest was subject to the strictest quotas. If another ship arrived and was counted first, those quotas could be filled before a single SS Washington passenger finally reached the head of the immigration line.

The SS Washington, under new management, hired a crew of mostly Greek sailors, paying them only paltry wages. Just to break even, the ship needed to make their first trans-Atlantic crossing under new ownership with enough passengers who would not be rejected at Ellis Island. *Even a decrepit ship could find customers in that kind of market* [655] . . . and this ship was certainly decrepit. However, each ship was also responsible for returning those who were deported, and this possibility could ruin the new owners financially on their very first voyage.

The huge British King Alexander and French Canada dwarfed The Washington both in size and number of passengers, carrying about 10 times as many. Because the SS Washington was also much slower, Captain Bacoyanis decided not to pick up much needed revenue with additional passengers but made a dash for the Straits of Gibraltar and the Atlantic when those larger ships made scheduled stops in Italy. Only a few hours in their race across the Atlantic, passengers on the SS Washington spotted eight transatlantic steamers behind them, all bound for New York. Included was the French liner Canada, carrying the Jacob and Susanna Toews family.

At 4 p.m. on Saturday, June 30, The SS Washington steamed up the Ambrose Channel toward the Narrows. There, already anchored at a conveniently close distance from the entrance to New York Harbor, was the King Alexander. The winner would be the first to cross an imaginary line across the Narrows between Brooklyn's Ft. Hamilton and Ft. Wadsworth on Staten Island. But not until midnight, when the new quota went into effect. *Capt. Bacoyanis squeezed his smaller ship into Gravesend Bay between the British steamer and the Danish Polonia. He radioed Washington, D.C., for the official time, then set his bridge clocks precisely.*

---

[655] Los Angeles Times, "Racing to America," William C Rempel, July 4, 1998, p 22

113 <u>SS Washington</u>

Ten days of stormy weather in the final two weeks of the voyage, though hard on the passengers, had worked to the advantage of Capt. Bacoyanis and his crew. The slowest ship in the race had arrived in time to have its pick of excellent anchor sites.

But the other ships kept coming . . . . <u>The King Alexander</u> was reporting 1,328 passengers, mostly Greeks.

By nightfall, the outer bay resembled a parking lot for ocean liners. Port authorities diverted some late-arriving vessels to Boston. [656]

As if the twelve ships were not enough, small vessels of every kind, filled with friends and relatives of the aliens on board the competing ships, crowded the bay shouting greetings to their loved ones. Police boats had to clear them from the narrow channel where the last leg of the race would pass.

Because prohibition was in effect, ships departing or arriving in the United States were only allowed a very limited amount of alcohol or spirits for medicinal purposes only. <u>The Presidente Wilson</u> gave out free beer to all the passengers and crew, who were having a very good time on the eve of the Big Race, but even so, 20 barrels of beer had to be destroyed. Otherwise, some vessels left off their alcoholic supples in Bermuda, to be picked up again once they left American shores. Pas-

---

[656] <u>Los Angeles Times</u>, "Racing to America," William C. Rempel, July 4, 1998, pg 23

sengers disembarking from these lines seemed to be burdened with packages they kept with them at all times, never entrusting them to porters or stewards.[657]

The hopes of thousands of immigrants now rode on the outcome of one last nautical sprint . . . .[658]

Only a certain percentage of the yearly quota were allowed in each month, with all the excess immigrants for that quota automatically excluded and sent back. The First Quota Act had, in effect, created a new phenomenon in New York, a monthly steamship race with giant steamships competing to land their passengers before the quota was filled. On the night before the first of every month, sometimes as many as twenty ships waited outside the harbor until the stroke of midnight, the signal to race in. Immigration officers stationed at Fort Wadsworth, and Fort Hamilton on either side of the Narrows judged the winners, whose passengers would be counted in the new monthly quota.[659] However, the quota race July 1, 1923 was particularly unique, since that was also the start of the new quota fiscal year, which reset at the stroke of midnight.

On Manhattan, the Rev. Oliver Paul Barnhill was preparing for his Sunday sermon at the Marble Collegiate Church on Fifth Avenue. It had a patriotic theme in advance of the Fourth of July holiday: "How the immigrant influx was ruining the morals of America" . . . .[660]

The whole new quota legislation that would go into effect at the stroke of midnight threatened many passengers in two ways; the possibility of a horrendous accident from a melee in the impending harbor race, or of being deported. These strict quotas reflected strong anti-immigrant sentiment in America.

Out in the bay, Susanna Rempel read her Bible and prayed. She did so every night—in boxcars, sleeping with the pigs, at sea . . . .

As the ship's clocks counted down the last minutes of June, Capt. Bacoyanis plotted the distance and time required to weigh anchor and the lag time to full speed.

Then he waited, listening to the night sounds of the harbor, clanking buoy bells, waves lapping at the hull, the moan of taut anchor lines . . . music from a ship's band?

---

[657] http://www.theshipslist.com/ships/Arrivals/1923b.shtml,   accessed 6 April, 2018
[658] Los Angeles Times, "Racing to America," William C. Rempel, July 4, 1998, pg 23
[659] Ellis Island, An Illustrated History of the Immigrant Experience, Ivan Chermayeff, Fred Wasserman, Mary J. Shapiro, pg 251
[660] Los Angeles Times, "Racing to America," William C. Rempel, July 4, 1998, pg 23

It came across the water, from the Staten Island side of the bay, from the decks of the Italian liner Presidente Wilson. A rousing Fascist anthem, "Giovinezza!" (Youth!)

But "Giovinezza" was a ploy. Under cover of drums and trumpets of martial music, the Italian skipper had ordered his anchors up. Before any other captain knew what was happening, the Presidente Wilson was underway.

As the big ship steered into Ambrose Channel, the navigation waterway to the Narrows, passengers on her decks erupted in a great cheer heard on the Staten Island shore. The race was on.

In quick succession, anchor winches groaned into action from one ship to the next. The big ships jockeyed for position churning up the placid bay like so many giant yachts lining up for the start of a regatta.

The Italian liner set a zigzag course to discourage any other liner from trying to pass. The tactic was unfair. But there were no race stewards. There were no rules.

On The SS Washington, Capt. Bacoyanis watched his clocks and eased the steamer toward the fray. The smaller Washington was all but unnoticed among the giant hulls. . . .

For a few moments, it appeared The Canada and The Wilson were headed for the same spot in the channel. Then The Washington appeared . . . . Bacoyanis maneuvered between the zigzagging Presidente Wilson and the charging Canada. The French gave way . . . . The Washington cleared the Narrows running off the starboard quarter of The Presidente Wilson[661] at two and a half minutes past midnight. The first 8 ships all arrived within four minutes of each other.[662] It was a miracle there were no collisions!

The Italian liner won the race. But The Washington, 30 seconds behind in the official record, beat the rest—most notably the third-place Canada and fifth-place King Alexander, with their low-quota passengers. Last ship into the harbor was The Aquitania.[663]

Since there were around 10,000 aliens aboard the 12 ships, not all would go to Ellis Island at once, as Island personnel could only inspect about 2,000 a day. Passengers had to remain on their respective ships until their turn came according to how their ship placed in the Big Race. With 900

---

[661] Los Angeles Times, "Racing to America," William C. Rempel, July 4, 1998, p 23
[662] http://www.theshipslist.com/ships/Arrivals/1923b.shtml,   accessed 6 April, 2018
[663] Los Angeles Times, "Racing to America," William C. Rempel, July 4, 1998, p 23

already on Ellis Island for the weekend, and 420 waiting to be deported, there simply were not enough mattresses for more first and second class passengers. Additional mattresses of the best quality had been purchased, but not received yet. Third class or steerage passengers would simply have to sleep on the benches. However, by the next day, 232 more beds arrived, bringing the total to nearly 2,000. It was then announced that no one would have to sleep on a bench.[664]

The New York Times, July 1, 1923 headline blared, _Twelve Ships Make a Midnight Dash With 10,000 Aliens, RACE TO BEAT JULY QUOTA, MANY WILL BE DEPORTED, One Vessel Bringing more Greeks Than the Law will Allow to Enter . . . . and the next day are about 5,000 more immigrants, of a total of 15,000 racing to beat the quota . . . . Hundreds of the immigrants waiting on board the liners to know their fate were here last year and were sent back to their native lands because the quotas were full. After waiting for seven months, they are taking another chance of entering the United States._[665]

A new administrator of Ellis Island began his first day on the job that same momentous day, July 1, 1923. Curran recalled in his memoir:

Competing steamship companies would bring in immigrants from all over the world, trusting to win the race at the finish. It was dangerous to human life to have twenty great ships crowding through the Narrows at the stroke of midnight. It was tragedy to the immigrants who had pulled up stakes, left home behind, and come hopefully here only to be turned back at the gate, through no fault of their own, as "excess quota." They had no place to go—the old home gone, the new home forbidden—it was tragedy that tore the heartstrings of those of us who understood.

At 6 the first barge-load of immigrants came to be examined. There had been no collision at the Narrows. The ships were safely in, each with its moment of crossing the line recorded to the second. And, scattered among them at their piers, were 2,000 men, women, and children who were 'excess quota.' Here by our country's permission, the 2,000 would now be turned back, at the very gate, by our country's mandate.

In a week or two they all went back. I was powerless. I could only watch them go. Day by day the barges took them from Ellis Island back to the ships again, back to the ocean, back to what? As they trooped aboard the big barges under my window, carrying their heavy bundles, some in their quaint, colorful native costumes worn to celebrate their first glad day in free America, some carrying little American flags, most of them quietly weeping, they twisted something in my heart that hurts to this day.[666]

---

[664] http://www.theshipslist.com/ships/Arrivals/1923b.shtml   accessed 6 April, 2018
[665] New York Times, July 1, 1923 http://www.oocities.org/musetti.geo/race.html,   accessed 12 April, 2013
[666] Pillar to Post, Henry H. Curran, pg 87

Since there were 1,700 Greeks on the <u>King Alexander</u>, the Greek quota was the first to be filled. By July 2, the Turkish quota also had been filled by passengers who disembarked at Providence, Rhode Island. Greek "picture brides" arrived, but some of them remained unclaimed when they showed up. Eight quotas had been exhausted by the following month, August 1, 1923. [667]

Because it was so cruel to permit *immigrants to cross the Atlantic, and then to send them back for no other reason than that their boat was slow, or that they sailed a few days too late*, it was suggested that the United States establish a system of control whereby the American consuls in the country of origin examine the prospective immigrant and determine that admission or denial be made there, before departure to America, and so no passport visas would be granted in excess of the month's quotas. [668] The immigration law was changed for the following quota year starting July 1, 1924, putting into affect these much more humane recommendations.[669]

Also on July 2,1923, remnants of the Czar's White Army of Deniken and Wrangel, some still wearing the uniform, arrived in San Francisco. They had wandered the seas for two years, from port to port, no country giving men, women, children, or even orphans asylum until America finally relented.[670]

The rest of the other German Mennonite refugees stuck in Constantinople, left by ship for Marseilles, France at a later date. There they boarded a train to cross France via Paris to the port city of Cherbourg. Oma Agatha Dirks' family was among the last to arrive at Ellis Island in October, crossing the sea aboard the Cunard liner <u>Saxonia</u>.[671]

Another Mennonite family had a baby in Turkey after baby Willie Rempel was born. The United States didn't let them in because the Turkish quota had already been reached before they arrived at Ellis Island. They were not allowed to leave the ship but were sent back to Constantinople. Turkey wouldn't let them off the ship. So the ship went on to Greece. Greece wouldn't let them off either. They remained on the ship. Meanwhile, the Mennonite Central Committee appealed to President Calvin Coolidge, and finally they were allowed into America. They had been kept on that ship for fully three additional months.[672]

---

[667] http://www.theshipslist.com/ships/Arrivals/1923b.shtml,   accessed 6 April, 2018
[668] Ibid
[669] Later quota laws would also effect the ability of Susanna's brothers Jacob and Cornelius in efforts to immigrate to the USA.
[670] http://www.theshipslist.com/ships/Arrivals/1923b.shtml,   accessed 6 April, 2018
[671] <u>Mennonites in Ukraine Amid Civil War and Anarchy (1917-1920)</u>, Translated and Edited by John B. Toews, pg 192
[672] <u>Los Angeles Times</u>, "Racing to America," William C. Rempel, July 4, 1998. pg 24

Henry Wiens (pronounced Veens), another from their group in Batum and Constantinople, whose father had died in Batum while Henry was still very young, arrived and stayed on Ellis Island a week with his mother and two sisters. Their sponsor had died, so Ellis Island sent them back to Cherbourg, France. Cherbourg wouldn't let them off the ship, so they went to South Hampton, England. England wouldn't let them off the ship. A woman from the Mennonite Central Committee relief agency found another sponsor for them and finally got them back to America.

Even with their low wages, The SS Washington must not have paid their sailors, for by the time the family arrived in New York, the sailors had stolen all their goods in storage, including Susanna's and Aaron's fur coats and the down comforters the family hadn't kept right with them. The family was able to bring in a little box, Aaron's tobacco humidor, and Susanna's Bible, that same Bible Susanna had pretended was a cookbook. The Washington should never have made the trip, it was so decrepit; but it made even one additional round trip between Constantinople and New York, carrying two more German Mennonite refugee families, the Birkles and Kroekers.[673] Then it was junked and became scrap metal.

As dawn broke in New York harbor, and the fog lifted, the whole family was on deck and were amazed by the impressive skyline of downtown New York City. Seeing the Statue of Liberty, they knew for sure they were now in America, and everyone cried, clapped, or yelled, and waved to Lady Liberty as if she were an old friend, saying to each other in all sorts of languages, "Look at her. Look at her."[674] They had finally arrived, each tightly clutching a dream.

Ships from abroad stopped in Lower New York Harbor, where they were placed in quarantine pending clearance. They were boarded by teams of medical inspectors.

When The SS Washington arrived in New York harbor, one of her sailors had the pox, so everyone on the ship was vaccinated. Baby Willie was only a seven month old, undernourished, skin and bones, tiny baby; but he was vaccinated as well. They said Papa Aaron and Gonja's vaccinations "didn't take." [675]

---

[673] Herman G. Rempel, "My Trip From Russia to Freedom in America, pg 59 Tuesday, August 7, 1923. The ship "Washington" left for New York today with two families from our group: Birkle and Kroeker.
[674] Ellis Island, An Illustrated History of the Immigrant Experience, Chermayeff, Ivan; Wasserman, Fred; Shapiro, Mary J. pg 18
[675] The Anchor Light, Volume 25, Number 5, May 2007, page 4, "Sandy Hooks Pilot Service in World War II". Hoffman Island was man made during the 1870s as a quarantine station. When the functions of a quarantine station were moved to Ellis Island, Hoffman Island was abandoned. In both World War I and II the island was used by the military to protect the harbor from submarines. Today the island is part of the Gateway National Park, without access by the public, but valuable as a bird sanctuary.

114, 115 Aaron's humidor, one of the very few items, along with that blue plaid shawl and Susanna's Bible that made it to USA from Russia

Did Aaron and Susanna even know that Aaron's sister Susanna Toews and her family were on the competing ship The Canada; that the ship had left Constantinople just a few days later than they, yet had arrived in third place that same day, July 1, 1923?

The Toews on The Canada proceeded directly to Ellis Island July 1st, the same day their ship arrived. Once on the Island, little seven year old Jake Toews followed behind his parents as the family went in single file to be checked by doctors. All of a sudden, Jake was **gone**! He had become separated from them somehow. Susanna and Jakob were now frantic, and could hardly do anything the officials wanted them to do. They wanted to run around and search for their little Jake, but were not allowed. They had to remain in line, and go through all the prescribed requirements to check their ears, then their eyes, and open their mouths. "Wachten sie, wachten sie," was all the officials could say in German. "Wait and see, wait and see." But Jake did not show up. He did not show up that day, or the next, or the next! This really was an Island of Tears.[676]

July 4th, a little boat bearing a yellow quarantine flag came out to the SS Washington, and a doctor boarded. Captain Bacoyanis showed him a report and pointed quietly to the Rempel family standing among the immigrants. A few minutes later, the Rempels were on their way to Hoffman Island to be vaccinated again.[677]

From Hoffman Island Rempels saw the Fourth of July fireworks above the Statue of Liberty. It was especially beautiful over the ocean. "What is it?" asked Ronka. Aaron shrugged and shook his head. Ten year old Ronka could only think of one explanation: "Maybe it is to welcome the Rempels to America." "Oh, it was something!" remembered Susanna decades later. "We had found heaven."[678]

---

[676] The ship's manifest lists the Toews family as Tevs: Jacob head of family, age 40; Suzane, wife, age 35; Henry son age 11; Jacob, son age 7; Cornelius, son, age 3; and Helene, daughter, age 9, on their way to Uncle Wilhelm P. Neufeld in Reidley (sic) (Reedley), Fresno County, California. However, the Toews' settled with their actual sponsors in Lancaster County, Pennsylvania, where they remained.

[677] The New York Times, Magazine Section, November 27, 1910, pages 13 ff, "A Little Island Near New York Peopled with Babies: Taken from Incoming Steamers: Suffering from Measles, Scarlet Fever, and Other Ills, They are Cared for on Hoffman Island till They Get Well"

[678] Los Angeles Times, "A Search for Ancestral Soviet Home", William C. Rempel, Wednesday, August 4, 1982, pg 17

Ellis Island

Hoffman Island may have separated many families in the past because of quarantine, but the Rempel family stayed together. When they were first ushered into the dining room, Susanna suddenly stopped, as her children rushed past her to tables laden with good food. For the first time in a long time, an abundance of food was laid on the table. It was the Fourth of July and they had three really good meals that day. On following days the food was plentiful and good, but not as dramatically wonderful as on their first day there. They had all kinds of fancy fruit on the side, fruit they had never seen or tasted before, like bananas. Gonja picked up a pretty green banana and started biting, but it was hard and made her mouth pucker up. She needed to drink a big glass of milk, and didn't want any more banana. Marie watched someone sitting near her family take a pretty yellow one, peel it, and then take bites. Marie then picked up a yellow banana, peeled and bit it, before she gave bites to others in the family.

Susanna just started crying, tears flowing down her face because she was so happy. She saw all the food on the table, and the children could really eat."[679] She simply thanked God for America. [680]

The family slept in big, airy rooms. No mattresses were provided, but they were given blankets, disinfected between patients, some used as a mattress on the wire mesh bed, some for a covering, and one for a pillow. Even their packages, suitcases, and their contents were disinfected, before being returned to the owners as they left for Ellis Island.

Hoffman Island was huge, able to care for around 2,000 at once with lots of beds, but the Rempels were practically the only ones there. The family really enjoyed their stay, where they were well cared for.

Well, the health officials vaccinated. But instead of vaccinating Aaron and Gonja who apparently needed it, they vaccinated everyone else again, and poor baby Willie's didn't take. It actually had "taken" the first time when they were still on the ship, but didn't "take" the second, third, or fourth times. They kept scratching Baby Willie's thin little arm, and it simply wouldn't "take." Finally they gave up, and gave baby Willie some shots so he wouldn't get sick, and sent the family on to Ellis Island. They remained on Hoffman Island until July 7th.

---

[679] Even 60 years later, every time Susanna related this story to the author, she wept at the memory that her children could eat.
[680] California Mennonite Historical Society Bulletin, No, 54, Fall 2011, "The Rempel Family's Escape from Death by Famine", Corinna Siebert Ruth

116 Statue of Liberty & Ellis Island

117 Ellis Island ferry, public domain, New York Pubic Library digital collection

On Ellis Island, as they went in through the door, two doctors observed them closely. Each person was tagged with a number, showing where a person appeared in the registry book, the ship's manifest.

They had to go past more doctors who checked their eyes, ears, and inside their mouths. Everything was checked. Their biggest fear was of their family being separated from one another. One member could be sent back, and the others could stay, or go back with the rejected person. They were made to go here, and there, prodded and pushed by the Ellis Island staff. All the other immigrants were being handled, pushed, and prodded too, herded really, so a person just went with the flow. Occasionally, they glimpsed the promised land waiting for them across the water.

A very wide staircase, the Stairs of Separation, was divided into three sections: two sets of stairs lead to a bright future in America either going to Manhattan, or to New Jersey and the rest of the country. The other set of stairs lead to deportation. Being sent back was each immigrant's greatest fear. Sometimes officials would let the whole family except for one member in. If the rejected person were a small child, an adult had to return with him. Sometimes it was an aged parent, a grandmother or grandfather who was sent back, and they went back alone, completely destitute, and in worse condition than before they left the old country, their home either sold or destroyed by war, with no money, no resources, no job, and no income.

The prodded, pushed flow of humanity then went up the wide stairway into another large hall, where they were told to sit on benches and wait their turn.

The Susanna and Jakob Toews family were already there. When the Rempels and Toews finally met, the Toews told the story that this really was an Island of Tears, as they had only just found Jake again that same morning, July 7th, before the Rempels arrived. He had been missing for a whole week! They never did find out what had happened to him in the meantime; his disappearance always remained a mystery.

Men and women slept in different dormitory rooms. That first night, the other women had rushed into the dormitory and taken all the beds before Susanna arrived with her children. It was not that a person was actually lying on each bed. The beds were bunk beds hung from chains, three beds high. There were many Jews, escaping from the pogroms massacring Jews in southern Russia. These women were loud with much quarreling and shouting, quite demanding and pushy, most disagreeable.[681] They were just being selfish and ornery, trying to prevent anyone from sleeping in beds near them.

---

[681] Love and Remembrance, from the Journals of Dietrich and Katharina (born Matthies) Rempel, Volume 1, Origins to 1927, pg 46

No vacant beds were left at all. Susanna went in the women's dorm room with Marie, Gonja, Susie, and baby Willie. It was just too much for her. Where could she put herself and her children? Susanna plopped herself down on the floor with all their blankets, put her head in her hands, and cried.

119 ship manifest, left side

ALIEN STEERAGE

STATES IMMIGRATION OFFICER AT PORT OF ARRIVAL

States, or a port of another insular possession, in whatsoever class they travel, MUST be fully listed and the master or commanding officer of each vessel carrying such passengers must upon arrival deliver lists thereof to the immigration officer.

STEERAGE PASSENGERS ONLY

Arriving at Port of _____ NEW YORK., N.Y. _____ JUL 1 – 1923 _____, 19 23.

List 2

130

The entries on this sheet must be typewritten or printed.

No. on List.	By whom was passage paid?	Whether ever before in the United States; if so, when and where?			Whether going to join a relative or friend; and if so, what relative or friend, and his name and complete address.	Purpose of coming to United States			Whether a polygamist	Whether an anarchist		Whether alien...	Condition of health, mental and physical.	Deformed or crippled; Nature, length of time, and cause.	Height		Color of —			Marks of identification.	Place of birth.	
			If yes—												Feet	Inches	Comp-lexion.	Hair.	Eyes.		Country.	City or town.
			No., m. of pass., year	Where?																		
1	No. Self	No No			Uncle. P.Neifeld Reedley, Cal.	No Perm	Yes	No No	No	No	Good	None	5	7	Fr.	Fr.	Gr	Bone	Russia	Tavrida
2	do Husband	No			as above	do.	do.	do do	do	do	do	do	do	4 11	do	do	do	do	do	do
3	do Father	do			do	do	do	do do	do	do	do	do	do	4 6	do	do	do	do	do	do
4	do	do			do	do	do	do do	do	do	do	do	do	3 11	do	do	do	do	do	do
5	do	do			do	do	do	do do	do	do	do	do	do	3 2	do	do	do	do	do	do
6	do	do			do	do	do	do do	do	do	do	do	do	2 2	do	do	do	do	do	do
7	do	do			do	do	do	do do	do	do	do	do	Inft		do	do	do	do	Turkey	Const/ple
8	Yes Self	30 Yrs.12	Ely Home. 42 Ramanian St. New York City.			do	do	do do	do	do	do	do	5 5	Brn Brn	Brn	do	do	Balata
9	No do	do	Cal.	Brother. J.Arslanian 517 Recon St.Los Angelos, Cal.	do	do	do do	do	do	do	do	5 6	Fr	do	do	do	Russia	Kidashin
10	do Father	No			as above	do	do	do do	do	do	do	do	5 1	do	do	do	do	do	Alex-
11	do Self	No			Brother.Sapo Soghoyan. 456 S. Clarence St.Los Angeles, Cal.	do	do	do do	do	do	do	do	5 6	do	Gr	do	do	do	andropol
12	do Father	No			as above	do	do	do do	do	do	do	do	4 6	do	do	do	do	do	do
13	do Husband	No			Husband.Pedro Manankian 19 Virginia Ave.Hopewell,Va.	do	do	do do	do	do	do	do	4 10	do	do	do	do	do	Tiflis
14	Yes Self	25 No			Brother.Athanassos? Vetlic	do	do	do do	do	do	do	do	5 8	Fr	Gr	do	do	do	Savastopol
15	do Husband	No			133 Cambridge St.Brooklyn,N.Y.	do	do	do do	do	do	do	do	5 9	do	do	do	do	do	do
16	do Father	No			as above do	do	do	do do	do	do	do	do	5 6	do	do	do	do	do	do
17																				
18																				
19																				
20																				

118 ship manifest, right side

Tante Susanna Toews had been there for a week already, so she knew how to do it. "You just push aside, empty their stuff off the bed, and grab whatever you can. That is how you do it." She showed Susanna how to do it. She saw a few beds with stuff on them, and just pulled the stuff off, dumped it on the floor, and quickly put a child on each of the emptied beds. Oh there was fussing and grumbling in all sorts of different languages they didn't understand, but all the Rempel family members had beds for the night. It was aways the case. They had to do the same routine each night: to fight for a bed.

July 8, baby Willie developed a boil in his armpit from the repeated vaccinations and shots, so Susanna and Willie were whisked off to the hospital at Ellis Island. Susanna and little Willie would be separated from their family for 8 days.

While Susanna waited with baby Willie to be sent to the hospital, a Greek made all sorts of hand motions and gestures to Susanna, but she did not know what he wanted. Susanna had no hair since it had been cut off in Constantinople, so she always wore a kerchief. The Greek kept trying to say something, and gestured wildly with his hands, but Susanna still did not understand. So, she kept getting up and moving away, and the Greek became ever more agitated. Finally, Aaron came over and interrupted. The Greek just wanted her to sit still so he could paint Susanna and baby as a Madonna and child.

120 bunk beds— public domain

298

When Mama and baby Willie were finally taken to the hospital, the family was left alone.

Papa was with the children. Mama was taken away from them, and they didn't know what she was doing. Otherwise they stayed in the big hall during the day. The children had to amuse themselves as best they could. It was boring, just sitting all day, day after day, with nothing to do. Many families just sat looking dejected. The children stared in wonder at all the different people coming through in their various native dress. Jewish men wearing their yarmulke and prayer shawls stood, praying in the corners of the room. Sometimes their children would come and try to interrupt, but the father would cuff them, and go back to his prayers.

On Sunday, all the immigrants still at Ellis Island were hauled into an auditorium for a sermon. Even the Jews had to be in there on Sunday, and they were not happy about that. They didn't want to go to a Christian church service on Sunday! They grumbled; they complained, and fussed, but they were forced in anyway.

They were hauled off to the dining hall to eat three times a day. It was clean when they went in and smelled of disinfectant. They had different long, narrow tables with benches for the different nationalities, so they had food they were used to. The Jews had their own tables with Kosher food. It was not polite company. Each person had to grab his fair share quickly before it was all gone. Nevertheless, after all the starvation times in Russia, Batum, and Constantinople it seemed so wonderful to have such an abundance of good food.

Twice a day, afternoon and evening, people came by to give the children under 16 a delightful snack of a small paper cup of milk and 2 graham crackers. After the children's evening snack, everyone proceeded to a room where they each received two paper towels, a piece of soap, and went to a room where they could wash themselves. The men and women were separate, but there was no privacy in the room where they washed. Next they went to a room where a great big pile of green wool army blankets lay. Each person received 5 blankets, to put two underneath as a mattress on the bare springs, use two as blankets, and roll one up as a pillow. These blankets were not sterilized between use by different people as they had been on Hoffman Island, but were collected each morning and stacked in the blanket room, to be given out at night again, to whomever. So those who kept themselves relatively clean, in spite of their difficult living circumstances often received the blankets that had been used by those who had no concept of "clean." [682]

---

[682] "A Despatch from Sir Auckland Geddes, British Ambassador at Washington reporting on Conditions at Ellis Island Immigration Station". Presented to Parliament by command of His Majesty, 1923

121 Dining Hall, public domain, New York Pubic Library digital collection

122 Great Hall, public domain, New York Pubic Library digital collection

123 Hospital Wing

Papa Aaron took little Susie and Ronka with him to the men's side. Marie, age 13, had to take care of Gonja, age 8. There was a person standing at the door before they entered the dormitory with a counting gadget as they passed through. As usual, the women were all pushing and trying to get theirs. As Mennonites, they didn't want to be pushy, so they were often last. Now it was Marie's responsibility to push, empty, and grab the beds. Gonja was known to sleepwalk, so Marie made sure Gonja was on an upper bunk above her, so she would be sure to know if Gonja decided to sleepwalk some night. In the morning, they were awakened usually at 5:30 by someone pounding a large iron bar on an iron railing, making a horrible racket.[683] After they washed, they had a breakfast of oatmeal, bread, jam, coffee or milk before proceeding once again to the big hall.

Susanna and Baby Willie were in the hospital with many different nationalities, but no one who could speak German or Russian. Again she became frantic, thinking her family might leave without her.

Years later Susanna recalled of her stay in the hospital, "There were 8 women in the hospital. We had donder and blitzen (thunder and lightening) and we were all afraid. One Italian woman came and held me and said, 'I cannot breathe, I am so afraid.' My, she was afraid. She cried the whole

---

[683] From Bolshevik Russia to America, A Mennonite Story, Henry D. Rempel, pp. 103-104

time. It was just lightening, and it was a big hospital. The windows were all light. I said, 'I am not afraid. God will take care of us.' So they finally sat down too. I was a little bit afraid too, but I showed like I wasn't. Willie was in his little bed 8 hours every day, and I just sat there with nothing to do."

Susanna received a lot of good food, and even had some extra, special cookies. Finally, she understood she could write a letter to her family in the big hall, so she did and enclosed some of those extra cookies in the envelope.

When the people in Ellis Island's post office saw this unusual envelope, all bulging out suspiciously, instead of delivering the letter in the usual way, they called Aaron Rempel to present himself at the Post Office, to open the envelope right in front of them. The Ellis Island staff laughed when they saw the cookies and crumbs fall out of the envelope. Then Ellis Island officials gave Aaron a whole 2 pound box of graham crackers. From then on, Ellis Island staff saw to it that Marie, Ronka, Gonja, and little Susie had even more milk and crackers in the afternoon snack time. They took better care of them, and even let them have a bath for the first time since arriving. Before that they could only sponge bathe themselves with a little bit of water and used paper towels to dry off. Decades later, Ronka recalled, "One day we took a bath. I was kind of perturbed at that lady because she came right in the room with me to watch me take a bath, but that bath felt so good. It was just fantastic. It was the only time we had a bath on the whole trip."

Marie, Ronka, Gonja, and little Susie had nothing to do in that big hall, day after day. It was crowded, incredibly noisy, with crying babies, many different languages, all sorts of nationalities. One day Marie laid down on a bench in the Great Hall, and took a nap.

Gonja noticed their Toews cousins, now on the other side of a big iron grate, were yelling at them. They learned Aaron's sister Suse Toews' family was now leaving Ellis Island at last! Aaron, Ronka, Gonja and little Susie ran to the fence, to be able to say their last good-byes to Tante Suse, Onkel Jakob, and cousins Jake, Cornelius, Eric, and Henry. They were leaving for Pennsylvania, but Rempels were going to Iowa, so they might never see each other again.

Aaron shook Marie and said, "Well, Du hast alles gesloppen? (Do you always sleep)? It seemed kind of silly to Marie that now he was waking her up and telling her the Toews had just left the Island while it was too late for her to say, "Good-by."

Later that same day, Mama Susanna and baby Willie were reunited with the rest of the family, and the next day, July 16, their turn came to leave the Island forever.

This was when they would go before the inspector at the end of the great hall, and be asked to show $25 for the trip. Not always did immigrants actually have to show the money. For instance one Scandinavian couple was allowed in with only $1.50 between them. Later in the day, other immigration officials might have turned them back. Actually no government regulation required a minimum of $25 to exist, but an overzealous commissioner of Ellis Island in 1909 had made it a requirement anyway. Even though he was no longer commissioner, some of the inspectors continued to use the $25 as a yardstick for entry, so the whole world knew a person had to have $25 to enter. Sometimes immigrants who came together on the same ship, would surreptitiously slip $25 from person to person in line to help those who simply weren't able to raise the full amount before they left the old country.[684]

There were box lunches for sale for a dollar each for the long train ride to Iowa, with a loaf of bread, one orange, a piece of salami, just about enough for a meal or two.[685]

As they walked out of the building toward the ferry, they heard shouting from the top of the roof garden. There were their cousins. The Toews hadn't left after all. They actually left later than Rempels. In the end, it took a whole year and three months to emigrate, not the three months they had anticipated.[686]

An inspector led the family to the correct train. Each immigrant had a tag pinned on them with their name and the address of their destination. It was no problem that they did not know English and couldn't understand the names of the cities they passed; they stayed on the train until the conductor told them to get off.

These families left Ellis Island for their new lives in America, *an America that held mixed and even hostile feelings about newcomers. The American Legion, at its New York State convention that summer, called for immediate suspension of all foreign immigration. The Alabama State Democratic Party had earlier passed a resolution specifically opposed to Mennonite immigration because their pacifist views made them undesirable citizens. . . .*

---

[684] Island of Hope, Island of Tears, David M. Brownstone, Irene M. Fanck, and Douglass Brownstone, pp. 191-195
[685] Ibid, pp. 184-185
[686] Oma Agatha's family, along with Herman and Dietrich Rempel, arrived at Ellis Island aboard The Saxonia, October 7, 1923, fully a year and a half after leaving Gnadenfeld

But America's economy was booming. Jobs outnumbered workers. If they could get in, the immigrants could work. If they could work, in time, they would own homes, raise families, fill pews, pay taxes, contribute to charities and support their new homeland—whether they were welcomed or not.[687]

---

[687] <u>Los Angeles Times</u>, "Racing to America," William C. Rempel, July 4, 1998, pg 24

Iowa

The Mennonite Central Committee (MCC) was instrumental in finding sponsors for those German Mennonites trapped in Batum. Christian C. Sommer in Crawfordsville, Washington County, Iowa had sent the Rempel family $800 while they were in Turkey, understanding Aaron would work it off after arriving.

The train carried them from New York, as far as Kalona, Iowa, passing cities and farms, peaceful scenes with children playing, farmers working, no soldiers, no devastation caused by war. It was the end of July when they finally arrived. The Sommers married late in life. Christian aged 51 and Selma Clara 38, had a girl Dora 5, a boy Otto 3, and little Irvin Carl, less than a year old. Their children were about the same ages as some of the Rempel children, so it was kind of nice for the younger Rempel children to have some play mates. They had a farm with chickens and other farm animals, producing milk and eggs. The whole Rempel family of seven lived in one small room upstairs in the Sommer home. Susanna worked like a maid for Selma, and Aaron worked extremely hard out on the farm from sunup to sun down.

124 Kalona, Iowa train station, public domain

Although a Mennonite, Mrs. Sommer was very stingy with the amount of food, and did not cook enough food for people who had gone through severe drought and famine, starving times. Although plenty of food was available on this farm, there never was enough food on Sommer's table to fill those starved bellies. Because Aaron was doing such hard manual labor, he needed to help himself first, then the rest of his family could have what was left. The food tasted so good. Marie recalled, *In the morning we got corn flakes with milk and thought it was like something from heaven. Now when I eat corn flakes, I wonder why they don't taste as good to me.*

Gonja remembered being so hungry, that all she wanted was another helping of the potatoes. Gonja asked once, and Papa said, "No." He knew how many potatoes were on the table, and what he needed for energy to do his heavy work. Gonja asked again. Aaron then excused her from the table. She had to leave and couldn't have anything else to eat. She knew unripe apples were out in the orchard, so she went out there and filled her little aching belly with those green, unripe apples. Crying, even years later, Susanna recalled, *We were hungry there. We were so hungry. Our children were so hungry. That is what we filled up on, green apples. We lived for a while in a room in Sommer's house. I don't even want to talk about it. It's very pitiful. We were hungry there. Here we were living on a farm that had all this food, and yet we were so hungry.*

Eventually the Sommers finished a little house in the apple orchard with 4 rooms, each 12 X 12 feet, including the kitchen. The girls slept sideways, three in a bed, in one room; baby Willie with parents in another, and Ronka slept on a couch in the living room. They also had a kitchen, and an out house. The wood stove in the kitchen went all day long to barely keep the rooms slightly warm. In the winter the children undressed as quickly as possible and dove under the covers.

Mr. Sommer was a nice man, but Selma Clara Sommer was peculiar and she wore the pants in that family. She gave the Rempel's old, canned, rancid butter. She had canned butter in water, but it was stinky! They didn't eat it. They couldn't eat it. That canned, stinky butter was still there when Rempels left.

What saved the Rempels were some close neighbors, John, 67, and Rosa Richie, 63, who also went to their local Mennonite church. The oldest child was Beulah, 29. Gonja was friends with Edna, and Ronka with Stan and Dwayne Richie. The Richies knew the Sommers, and what they were like. Richies compassionately loaned Rempels a milk cow. Also, Mr. Richie went around to all the neighboring farmers and asked for a donation of chickens. He brought over 100 chickens to the Rempels. Ronka became good at milking the cow. The Rempel cow gave more milk than Sommer's cow. The Rempel chickens gave a lot more eggs than Sommer's chickens. Mrs. Sommer became suspicious and accused the Rempels of stealing eggs from them. "God gave us more than he gave the stingy," Susanna mused.

Aaron was paid $40 a month, and he saved $20 of that each month to help pay off the debt faster. He used some of the money for smoking tobacco. The Sommers had two big black walnut trees and raised vegetables, so Susanna made sauerkraut with the cabbage, enough for them and Sommers. The family ate what was produced on the farm. They needed to buy little from stores. Of course, Susanna bought flour to bake all her own bread. They had a lot of applesauce. They always had applesauce and fried potatoes. They had so much apple-sauce, the children liked to draw pictures in it before they ate it. They thought it was probably too hot and humid to dry apples in Iowa, so didn't try it. Susanna would never let them waste food, so they learned to be really thrifty. They had so many chickens, a lot of times they had chicken for dinner.

Aaron wanted to know how much the Sommers would pay him, and when he could work it off. They refused to tell him when he would pay his debt off, but tried to increase his hours and reduce his pay. It reminded them of Laban in the book of Genesis who kept changing Jacob's wages for his own benefit.[688]

When living in Kalona, Iowa, Ronka, already age ten, and Gonja went to school for the first time. They were both put into first grade. When they arrived, their hair was still growing in, but very, very short. At first, when children teased calling them, "Baldy, baldy," they didn't understand. The other kids liked to rub their knuckles into Ronka's head. Ronka did what was necessary to protect himself. The teachers on playground duty called Ronka over to be reprimanded. They knew he didn't know English, but they scolded, and Ronka just grinned at them. After a while, he realized that if he just kept acting dumb, and grinning, pretty soon they just sent him back to play again, and told the other children to leave him alone. As the year went along, Ronka and Gonja learned English, and they learned what the word "baldy" really meant. That word espe-cially stung Gonja. She never forgot.

---

[688] Obituary for CC Sommer in The Davenport Democrat, 25 Dec. 1924, listed his farm as the former William Moore Farm, one of the landmarks of the township, located 2 miles SW of Crawfordsville, Iowa close to the Eicher Mennonite Church in Wayland, Iowa. *He had been well to do financially but his long illness must have depleted his finances.*

125 Sleeping Sisters illustration by Margie Hildebrand

126 Eicher Mennonite Church, Wayland, Iowa

127 CC & Selma Sommer, Eicher Mennonite Church graveyard

Christmas seemed pretty lonesome. They had no three days of celebrating Christmas, for now Aaron's father was in Mexico, and Oma Agatha's family was in Connecticut. Carl and Agatha were in New York. Jasch and Cornelius and their families were still in Gnadenfeld. Christmas Eve they went to church at the Eicher Mennonite Church in Wayland, Iowa. The family was all dressed really warmly in coats, shawls, draped in blankets, with heated bricks under their feet. Aaron drove the horse drawn wagon, which had a canvas top. After singing Christmas carols at church, they went home frozen stiff.

On Christmas morning, Mrs. Sommer came and told Aaron, "Well, Mr Rempel. Get ready. We butcher pigs today." Christmas morning, and they wanted him to spend the whole day butchering pigs!

Aaron stood his ground, "Well, I won't do it."

"You are working for us now, and you will too do it."

"Nope. On Christmas morning I don't go." And he didn't go either.

Aaron did have the usual chores that each farmer must do every day of the year, to feed and water the animals, and milk the cows, but that was going to be it.

Oh, Selma Sommers was mad! She had buck teeth and a big goiter. Her anger made her goiter stick out that much more. There was nothing pretty about her, and her anger made it even more so.

Other Mennonite immigrants had sponsors who ended up becoming their best friends. J. P. Rogalsky started working for Eby . . . . *When I (Rogalsky) asked him when I could start working for him in order to repay the travel debt, he said, "I did not have you come in order to exploit you. You can work where you wish. I have given the money to MCC and I'll never accept it back. The sooner you pay the MCC, the sooner someone else can be helped over. God bless you."*[689] But the Rempels and the Sommers did not become close friends. They didn't even become friends.

The family was used to having a Christmas tree in Russia, and they were so happy that they could celebrate Christmas again. They had a tree with some decorations, which the children saw for the first time on Christmas morning. It was only about 3 or 4 feet high on the floor. No candles were on it. The gifts were given the same way as in Russia. Candy, cookies and fruit were put on each person's plate, and next to the plate was a gift. One gift was tinker toys, which the children played with all day.

One thing Aaron complained about was that they were invited to dinner each Sunday with different Mennonite families. He complained because when you are visiting, you can't relax. He was tired and wanted to take a nap. His work days were 10 to 14 hours long, and he suffered greatly from arthritis. Sunday was his only day to rest.

The whole community went to the Kalona Elementary School for a special program. The room was packed, with standing room only. Little kids, to see the program, were seated, cross legged, Indian style in front of the first row of seats, sitting almost on top of the feet of those in the front row. The room was hot and stuffy, with so many bodies squished together as tightly as possible, to get everyone inside.

---

[689] <u>Mennonites in Ukraine Amid Civil War and Anarchy (1917-1920),</u> Translated and Edited by John B. Toews, pg 192

After a hasty supper, their family had rushed in the horse drawn wagon to arrive on time. Papa had a Model T. Ford, but it couldn't be driven when it was rainy, as the wheels would get stuck in muddy roads. The children rushed inside the two story brick building with a bell tower on top, next door and to the left of the high school building, while Papa found a place to tie up the horses.

Gonja was dressed as a flower, draped in red crepe paper. But Gonja was hot and sweaty. The sweat on her face was melting the red crepe paper. Little red streams ran down her face, making her face even redder. Gonja's part in the program was finally over. She had learned a poem about a flower in English, and she had said her poem in English, with a Russian accent to be sure, but she had memorized her poem and said it in English! Since her part was done, and there was no way for her to join her family sitting somewhere in that crowded room, Gonja found a back door that was open to let in some cold air.

She stood in the open doorway, enjoying the wind rushing past her flushed face while she gazed over the plowed, bare cornfields in the moonlight. Somewhere in the distance a dog barked. More dogs barked, and Gonja froze in sheer terror. The cold, icy wind stabbed her heart. She was petrified, unable to move. Her stomach twisted into one huge knot. It was as if the air itself had been sucked out of the room. Dogs barking meant Makhno and his gang of bandits were coming! They were riding like the wind into the village to plunder, terrorize and kill. Oh no, what could she and her family do? People would be killed tonight. Where could they go and hide? They couldn't hide in this school. No, they would be found for sure. Could they get back to the farm in time, and hide there? She knew she needed to run and hide, but her feet seemed stuck to the floor; she couldn't move. Then it dawned on her. She realized this was Iowa. She was in the Kalona Elementary School in Kalona, Iowa. Makhno with his unspeakable, barbaric acts of cruelty couldn't get her or her family here, not here. Gonja was not in Russia any more. She was safe in America. Now she and her family were safe. Liesbet's words came back to her, "I hope you never come back!" Yes, she would never, ever come back!

128 Susanna Krause Rempel on her 100th birthday
Reedley, California, August 31, 1991

"If somebody would really write it all down, it is quite a busy life story for us in Siberia . . . in the beginning and all the time through, all the time through . . . till here I have a peaceful life."

Gnadenfeld Today

Today there are very few Mennonites left in the old Colony of Molotschna, or in any area of Ukraine, for that matter. *The area is agricultural, but does not seem to be prosperous.* [690]

In the village of Gnadenfeld, the original Zentralschule (high school), the post office, and the Doctor's clinic are still there. The church building is gone, its site now an empty field. [691] *Many homes and farm buildings have completely vanished. There are still only three dusty streets, but Susanna's home and Aaron's factory are gone . . . .*[692]

---

[690] <u>Molotschna Historical Atlas</u>, Helmut T. Huebert, pg 96
[691] <u>Ibid</u>, pg 128
[692] <u>Los Angeles Times</u>, Wednesday, August 4, 1982, "A Search for Ancestral Soviet Home," William C. Rempel, page 17   Cousin and journalist William C. Rempel visited Gnadenfeld in 1982. The author was scheduled to visit Gnadenfeld July 2014, until the Russians under Putin shot down a passenger plane over Ukraine, killing 298 civilians, July, 2014, by a surface to air missile, and the tour was canceled.

Appendix A

(3) Dear Katje   July 29 – 1989

This is a copy of the letter sister Susan wrote
to me in answer to some questions I had asked.
Sorry that she did not write more, but this helps
some.

Remember the funeral of grandfather Retzlaff
which was held in their "Scheune" when we were little
children? I do remember seing him all dressed up
lying in his casket. He was the one who married
of parents.

Since we come along later, we can only guess about
dates of birth or how old Kornelius was at this
wedding, we certainly need a love for arithmatic &
a calculator to compare birth & wedding dates. Surely
we are only guessing.

Now I understand why Kornelius & Jasch went off
to school to learn accounting & classical music on
guitar & mandolin, they must have disliked their young
stepfather because of his youth. Now at our old age
of 80 plus, we can quite clearly understand that situ –
ation coused by a marriage ordered by a guardian, as
was customary in those years for widdows.

        Later many tears were shed by husband & wife
because of heartach, and hostility from all directions.
I blame no one, let God in heaven be the judje. Only
the 3 sisters, Susan, you & I are allive to tell this story
all others are faded into dust, may they rest in peace.

                    ....' .   ... —

Appendix B

(translated)

To My Sister Mieche, (Maria),

My hand recently is getting very shaky, and my back and knee and sitting upright to write is barely possible, but I will attempt.

Here are a few answers that you ask of me:

The wedding of the parents was in our shed and our neighbor Heinrich Ratzlaff [693] married them. The wedding was in the summer. I was a 13 year old, Cornelius was 15 and Jasch (Jacob) was 11. According to my memory mother was 41 years old when our father so surprisingly died and she waited 3 years before she married Heinrich Dirks . . . so she had to be 44 years old when she married.

Everything is still very clear in my memory. This sad time, the cows and horses "by foot" on the way towards Gnadenfeld, a large wagon for the feed for the animals and the horses tied to the side of the wagon. Jakob Schlichting and 3 or 4 Russian men guarded everything.

Now one more error: Aaron and Heinrich Dirks were in the school together in the same grade. Aaron was 28 years old as I met him, he said that Heinrich was 29 years old.

Susanna Krause Rempel

---

[693] Heinrich Ratzlaff, lived in # 74, (born 1857, died 1922; Grandma Mennonite Genealogy database # 193814) was not only their neighbor, but was Heinrich David K. Dirks' brother-in-law, married to Heinrich Dirk's sister Helena, so he was Oma Agatha's brother-in-law by marriage, not by blood.

Dear Ant Mary!
Mother gave me
this letter to mail to
you. Mother is wrong
in the age of father
because he was 28 when
I was born.

Love Marie
Bergman.

An meine Schwester Mieke.
Meine Hand wird in letzter Zeit so unruhig
und mein Rücken und Knie das steilsitzen
zum schreiben nur so eben geht doch will
versuchen.

Hier einige Antworten die du von mir frägst.
Die Hochzeit der Eltern war in unser
Scheune und unser Nachbar Heinr. Ratzlaff
traute sie. Im Sommer war die Hochzeit.
Ich war 13 dreizen Jahre alt. Cornelius 15 und
Jash 11 elf. Nach meiner Erinnerung war
mutter 41 Jahre alt, als uner Vater so uner-
wartet starb und sie wartete drei Jahre
ehe sie Heinrich Dirks heiratete so muss
sie 44 alt gewesen sein als sie heiratete.
Habe noch alles sehr gut in Erinnerung.
Diese trauge Zeit, das Vieh Kühe + Pferde
"zu Fuss" auf dem Wege nach Gnadenfeld,
einem grosen Wagen fürs Futter fürs Vieh
und Pferde angbunden an seid am
Wagen. Jackob Schlichting + 3 or 4 Russen
Männer pasten nach all dem auf.

Nur noch ein Fehler: Aron + Heinrich Dirks
waren in der Schule zusamen, derselben Jahre
Aaron war 28 Jahre alt als ich ihn kennen
lernte, er sagte Heinrich war 29 Jahre alt.

317

Glossary

see pg 10,11 Mennonite Foods & Folkways from South Russia, Volume II, Norma Jost Voth

anwhoner—Mennonites who did not own land, called the landless

Barshtan—common area where the watermelons, pumpkins, and corn were planted (protected by a Russian watchman)

borscht—Mennonite cabbage soup flavored with dill

Brasol—also called Schönfeld, area in Ukraine north of the Molotschna Colony

Dachstube—attic above the house

Eckstube, Eckstov—the corner room, or winter room, used as the parents' bedroom

Faspa—afternoon snack, somewhat equivalent to the British tea time—Sunday afternoon Faspa was the social highlight of the week, with ironed tablecloth and the best china; always serving zwiebach

Fenstre—windows, all windows had shutters. Closed in summer, they kept out the heat and in winter the cold. They offered protection from burglary as well.

Grottestube or Grottestov—living room or parlor

Hinterhaus—Dining room

Hoff—the yard

kaputt—broken

Kirchensteg—church path

Kleinestube, kleinestov—little room, typically the girls' bedroom.

Kuche—the kitchen

ladde voge or leiterwagon,—ladder wagon, used for hauling in the hay harvest—the sides looked like ladders

MCC—Mennonite Central Committee, a relief agency

mooss—shortened form of plümemooss

Oma—grandmother

Onkel—uncle

Opa—grandfather

plautdeutsch—a low German dialect, the everyday language of German Mennonites

Plümemooss—a thick fruit soup made of dried fruit, somewhat like applesauce

Scheune—A shed attached to the barn, where hay, wagons, farm machinery were stored

Selbstschutz—self-defense league, manned by pacifist Mennonites

Sommastube, sommastov—the summer room, where the boys typically slept—so called the summer room because the stove (the brick wall oven) did not heat that room in the summer, so that room stayed cooler

Speisekammer—pantry

Stahl—barn

Zwiebach—two buns baked together, smaller one on top

Tante—aunt

verst—approximately two-thirds of a mile

Vorderhaus—front room, entry

wirtshaft—farm; wirtshaften—farms

Bibliography

Family History: Books, Memoirs, Diaries, Obituary

California Mennonite Historical Society Bulletin, No, 54, Fall 2011, "The Rempel Family's Escape from Death by Famine," Corinna Siebert Ruth , Feb. 10, 2013, http://www. calmenno.org/bulletin/fall11.pdf accessed Dec 3, 20014

Dick, Jacob P., The Dueck Family Genealogy, 1632-1978, (Holland-Germany-Russia-U.S.A.-Canada) ? ? ?

Janzen, Mary Dirks. The Baum Story, God's Mercy and Man's Kindness. 1974, edited by Mary E. Janzen, self-published, 2011

Janzen, Mary Dirks, My Memories. retyped and edited by Margie Friesen and Reuben Friesen. self-published, 1998

Klassen, Helene (Rempel), Editor and Translator, Love and Remembrance, Vol 1, Origins 1927, From the Journals of Dietrich & Katharina (Matthies) Rempel, Judson Lake House, Abbotsford, BC, Canada, 2012

Klassen, Paul. From the Steppes to the Prairies. Canada: City Press Limited, 1996

http://www.krausehouse,ca/krause/EasternFront.htm accessed Feb 8, 2013

http://www.krausehouse.ca/krause/EasternFront.htm California Mennonite, Historical Society Bulletin, No. 54, 2011 - http://www.calmenno.org/bulletin/fall11.pdf

Krause, Irvin D.. "Descendants of Jacob Krause", self published

Krause, Jacob C. "Gnadenfeld, Molotschna, South Russia" 1835-1943., translated by Carl Rempel, Yarrow, British Columbia: self-published, 1954

Jacob C. Krause, "Gnadenfeld, Molotschna, South Russia, Memories of Good Times and of Hard Times," translated by Carl Rempel, self published

Krause, Maria. Obituary of Jakob C. Krause, translated from the German by Soren Kern

Rudy Krause, "Memories", dated 13 July 1990 included in Rundbrief, (cousin round robin letter)

Loewen, Greta Rempel, "The Story of Greta", the letters of Greta 1923-1936 depicting the life of a young family under Communism and the reign of Stalin; self published by son Walter J. Loewen , and brother Arthur Rempel, Winnipeg, Canada 1995

Loewen, Walter Jakob. The Life Story of Walter Jakob Loewen, republished by Friede Thiessen, Winnipeg: 1999

Los Angeles Times, 4 August, 1982, "Quest: Search for Ancestral Roots in Ukraine," William C. Rempel

Los Angeles Times, "Racing to America," William C. Rempel, July 4, 1998

Neufeld, Bill, From My Memories, Riverside Community College, Riverside, C, 1992

"Pilgrims of the Promise." PDF. Mennonite Historical Society of British Columba, Anabaptist History

http://www.mennoniteeducation.org/MEAPortal/Portals/57ad7180-c5e7-49f5-b282-c6475cdb7ee7/Anabaptist%20History%20Lessons/AH11%20Traveling%20On.pdf accessed April 2013—taken from Mennonite Martyrs: People Who Suffered for Their Faith 1920-1940, pp. 31-35

Rempel, William C., "Quest: Search for Ancestral Roots in Ukraine." Los Angeles Times, 4 August, 1982

William C., "Racing to America." Los Angeles Times, 4 July 1998

Rempel, William C., "A Rempel Story" (video). Los Angeles: self-published

Rempel (Wolfenden), Susanna. "Kasha" self-published, 1943

Rempel, William. "Dinuba to Palmer." Diary of Bill Rempel, 1944

Rempel, William. "We Moved to Alaska in the Dead of Winter, Lock, Stock and Barrel!". self-published 2001

Rempel, Agatha (Krause), "Memoirs of Agatha (born Krause) and Carl Rempel, as told to Katherine Ruth Lockwood", unpublished manuscript

Rempel, Arthur G. "A Letter To My Children: The Memoirs of Arthur G. Rempel". self-published 1993

Rempel, Evangeline G., "My Trip to America, The Diary of Evangeline G. Rempel 1922-1923", AHSGR (American Historical Society of Germans from Russia Journal) Fall 2000

Rempel, Herman G, My Trip from Russia to Freedom in America, diary 1922-1923 self-published,

Remarks by Walter Bergmann, son of Marie Rempel and Henry (Heinrich) P. Bergmann on the occasion of his parents' 50th Wedding Anniversary Sunday, September 13, 1981

Rempel, Dietrich and Katharina (Matthies), Love and Remembrance: Stories and Recollections from the lives of Dietrich and Katharina (Matthies Rempel, edited and translated by Helene (Rempel) Klassen, Abbotsford, B.C. Canada: Judson Lake House Publishers, 2012

Schroeder, Gerhard P., Miracles of Grace and Judgment, Kingsport Press, Kingsport, Tennessee, 1974

Toews, Henry, Letter to the Editor, The Mennonite Historian, pg 8, East Petersburg, PA www.mennonitehistorian.ca/29.1MHMar03pdf accessed Feb 10, 2013,

Voth, Norma Jost, Mennonite Foods & Folkways from South Russia, Volumes I and II, Good Books, Intercourse, PA, 1990, with numerous contributions from Mary Dirks Janzen

Wiens, Elisabeth L. (born Braun), <u>Wir die Braunskinder</u>, Filadelfia, Chaco, Paraguay: Imprenta Off y Graph; Ascuncion, Paraguay: Imprenta MODELO S.A., 2000 translation from the German by David Föhles

German Mennonites from Russia General History

Birdsell, Sandra, <u>The Russlander</u>, Fresno, CA, Center for Mennonite Brethren Studies, 2013

<u>California Mennonite Historical Society Bulletin</u>, No 45, Fall 2006

<u>California Mennonite Historical Society Bulletin</u>, No, 54, 2011, <u>http://www.calmenno.org/bulletin/fall11.pdf</u> and Mennonites in Ukraine Amid Civil War and Anarchy (1917-1920) Translated and Edited by John B. Toews

<u>California Mennonite Historical Society Bulletin</u>, No, 54, Fall 2011, "The Rempel Family's Escape from Death by Famine", Corinna Siebert Ruth

Chipman, Josephine, Master's Thesis, <u>Selbschutz</u>, Canadian Mennonite University, Winnipeg, Manitoba, 1988

Dyck, Harvey L., Staples, John R., and Toews, John B. <u>Nestor Makhno and the Eichenfeld Massacre, A Civil War Tragedy in a Ukrainian Mennonite Village.</u> Kitchener, Ontario: Pandora Press, 2004

Dyck, Peter and Elfieda. <u>Up From the Rubble, The epic rescue of thousands of war-ravaged Mennonite refugees</u>. Scottdale, Pennsylvania and Waterloo, Ontario: Herald Press, 1991

Dueck, David. <u>And When They Shall Ask, a Docudrama of the Russian Mennonite Experience</u>. Winnipeg, Manitoba: Mennonite Media Society, 1984

Epp, Irmgard (editor). <u>Constantinoplers, Escape from Bolshevism</u>. Victoria, B.C.: Trafford Publishing, 2006

Christian Family Calendar, published in Halbstadt, Molotschna, years 1905-1913, http://chort. square7.ch/FB/D0663p.html pictures #28, 29, 30, 33, 34, 40, accessed May 24, 2018

Friesen, Abram and Loewen, Abram J., Escape Across the Amur River. Winnipeg, Manitoba: CMBC Publications Manitoba Mennonite Historical Society, 2001

Friesen, Katie. Into the Unknown. Steinbach, Manitoba: Derksen Printers Ltd., 1986

Funk, Cornelius, Escape to Freedom, translated and edited by Peter J. Klaassen, Hillsboro, Kansas, Mennonite Brethren Publishing House, 1982

Gislason, Leona Wiebe, RÜCKENAU, The History of a Village in the Molotschna Mennonite Settlement of South Russia, From It's Founding n 1811 to the Present, Windflower Communications, Winnipeg, Canada, 1999

Harder, John A., Editor, translator, From Kleefeld with Love, Pandora Press, Kitchener, Ontario, Canada, 2003

Horsch, John, The Principle of Nonresistance As Held by the Mennonite Church, Scottdale, PA: Mennonite Publishing House, 1940

Huebert, Helmut, Events and People: Events in Russian Mennonite History, And the People That Made Them Happen, Springfield Publisher, Winnipeg, Canada, 1999

Huebert, Helmut, Hierschau: An Example of Russian Mennonite Life, Winnipeg, Canada: Springfield Publishers, 1986

Huebert, Helmut T., Mennonite Estates in Imperial Russia, Winnipeg, Canada, Springfield Publishers, 2008

Huebert, Helmut T.; Schroeder, William, Mennonite Historical Atlas, Winnipeg, Canada, Springfield Publishers, 1996

Huebert, Helmut T, Mennonite Medicine in Russia 1800 to 1930, Winnipeg, Canada, Springfield Publishers, 2011

Huebert, Helmut T. Molotschna Historical Atlas. Winnipeg, Canada: Springfield Publishers, 2003

Kennedy, Tim. Where Roads Diverge, Eighth Grade Reader, Harrisonburg, Virginia: Christian Light Education, 2005

Klassen, Robert L., Life and Times of a Renaissance Mennonite Teacher: Cornelius A. Klaassen, (1883-1919 and Beyond), https://sites.google.com/site/mennonitehistory/cornelius-a-klassen, accessed November 16, 2016

Kroeker, N.J., First Mennonite Villages in Russia, 1789-1943, Khortitsa-Rosenthal, D.W. Friesen & Sons, Cloverdale, BC, Canada, 1981

Kroeker, Wally, An Introduction to the Russian Mennonites, Intercourse, PA: Good Books, 2005

Lapp, John A. and Snyder, C. Arnold, editors, Testing Faith and Tradition, Intercourse, PA: Good Books, 2006

Lohrenz, Gerhard. Stories From Mennonite Life. Steinbach, Manitoba: Derksen Printers, 1980

Martens, Cornelius. Beneath the Cross. Altona, MB, Canada: English translation from the German "Unter dem Kreuz by Helene S. Fast, 2010

Martens, Katherine, They Came From Wiesenfeld, Ukraine to Canada, translated and edited by Katherine Martens, Winnipeg, Canada, Art Bookbindery, 2005

1996 Mennonite Heritage Cruise, Part Four http://home.ica.net/~walterunger/Rudy-4.htm accessed Feb 10, 2013

Mennonite Historian, a publication of the Mennonite Heritage Centre for Mennonite Brethren Studies in Canada, file:///Users/karen/Desktop/MAKHNO%20&%20EICHENFELD.pdf accessed 16 March, 2018

Nickel, John P., Editor and Translator, <u>Hope Springs Eternal, A Legacy of Service and Love in Russia During Difficult Times</u>, Sermons and Papers of Johann J. Nickel (11859-1920), Nickel Publishers, Nanaimo, BC, Canada, 1988

Neufeld, Justina D., <u>A Family Torn Apart</u>, Kitchener, Ontario, Canada: Pandora Press, 2003

Nickel, <u>Hope Springs Eternal</u>

Quiring, Dr. Walter and Bartel, Helen. <u>In The Fullness of Time, 150 Years of Mennonite Sojourn in Russia.</u> Waterloo, Ontario: Reeve Bean Limited, 1974

Reedley First Mennonite Church, <u>The First Seventy-Five Years 196-1981</u>, No. Newton, Kansas: Mennonite Press Inc. 1981

Reimer, Al, <u>My Harp is Turned to Mourrning</u>, Windflower Communications, Winnipeg, Manitoba, Canada, 1990

Rempel, Henry D., <u>From Bolshevik Russia to America</u>, Boston, MA, Pearson Custom Publishing 2001

Rempel, Jacob J., <u>Consider the Threshing Stone</u>, Writings of Jacob J. Rempel, A Mennonite In Russia, translated and edited by David J. Rempel, Smucker, Kitchener, Ontario, Pandora Press, 2008,

Schmidt, A. Lowen. <u>1835-1943 Gnadenfeld, Molotschna.</u>, self published after the Gnadenfelder Reunion in Winnipeg, 1988

Smucker, Barbara Claassen, <u>Days of Terror</u>, Clark, Irwin & Company Limited, Toronto/Vancouver, 1979

Smucker, Barbara Claassen. <u>Henry's Red Sea</u>. Scottdale, Pennsylvania and Waterloo, Ontario: Herald Press, 1955

<u>The Mennonite Treasury of Recipes</u>. Steinbach, Manitoba: Derksen Printers Ltd., 1960

The Davenport Democrat, 25 Dec. 1924, obituary

Tiessen, Henry Bernard. The Molotschna Colony, A Heritage Remembered, Kitchener, Ontario:

Toews, Arthur, (compiled by) The Eichenfeld Collection, Winnipeg, Manitoba, 2004

Toews, Aron A., "Pilgrims of the Promise", page 182 taken from Mennonite Martyrs, People Who Suffered for Their Faith, 1920-1940, Hillsboro, KS, Kindred Productions, 1990 pp. 31-35

Eichenfeld, Dubowka, Heinrich Toews, translated from the German by Arthur Toews Krahn, Cornelius.

Toews, John B., Czars, Soviets, & Mennonites, Newton, Kansas: Faith and Life Press, 1982

Toews, John B., Lost Fatherland, Scottdale, Pennsylvania, Herald Press, 1967

Toews, John B., Mennonites in Ukraine Amid Civil War and Anarchy (1917-1920), Center for Mennonite Brethren Studies, Fresno, California, 2013

Toews, Ron, 'Notes on the history of the Schoenfeld Colony,' Heritage Cruise 1999

Turner, Selma Willms, From Oma's Kitchen, Abbotsford: Judson Lake House Publishers, 2006

Unger, Walter, 1996 Mennonite Heritage Cruise, Part Four http://home.ica.net/~walterunger/Rudy-4.htm accessed Feb 10, 2013

Willms, H. J., At the Gates of Moscow, translated by George G. Thielman, Ph.D, Abbotsford: Judson Lake House Publishers, 2010

http://www.krausehouse.ca/krause/EasternFront.htm Feb 8, 2013 accessed Dec 3, 2014 (http://www.blackseagr.org) accessed Aug 2017

"Molotschna, Mennonite Settlement (Zaporizhia Oblast, Ukraine)", Global Anabaptist Mennonite Encyclopedia Online. 1957, accessed 2012 http://www.gameo.org/encyclopedia/contents/M6521.html   source Mennonite Encyclopedia accessed Dec 3, 2014

http://www.gameo.org/encyclopedia/contents/O567.html accessed March 14, 2018

http://www.mhsbc.com/news/pdf/RB07-3_2001_Summer.pdf, Mennonite Historical Society of British Columbia, pg 5

Other Related History

A Despatch from H. M. Ambassador at Washington reporting on Conditions at Ellis Island Immigration Station Presented to Parliament by command of His Majesty, 1923

Annie's Ghosts, A Journey into a Family Secret, Steve Luxenberg, Hyperion: New York, 2009

Bell, Friedl E. Semans, She Cried for Mother Russia, San Luis Obispo, Graphic Communication Institute at Cal Poly, 2009

Brownstone, David M; Irene M. Fanck; and Douglass Brownstone; Island of Hope, Island of Tears, New York, Barnes & Noble, 197:

Charques, Richard, The Twilight of Imperial Russia, Oxford University Press, London, Oxford, New York, 1958 paperback 1974 USA

Chermayeff, Ivan; Wasserman, Fred; Shapiro, Mary J.; Ellis Island, An Illustrated History of the Immigrant Experience, New York: Macmillan Publishing Co., 1991

Curran, Henry H., Pillar to Post, New York: Charles Scribner's Sons, 1941

Duffy, Francis James. "Sandy Hooks Pilot Service in World War II." San Pedro, CA: The Anchor Light, a publication of U.S. Merchant Marine Veterans, P.O. Box 629, San Pedro, CA 90733, Volume 25, Number 5, May 2007

Engel, Beverly, The Right of Innocence, New York, Random House, 1989

Gillette, Ned. and Rowell, Galen. "Adventure in Western China."(Kirghiz), National Geographic, February 1981

Island of Hope—Island of Tears. the Ellis Island Immigration Museum Film

Jonas, Susan, edited by, Ellis Island, Echoes From a Nation's Past, Hong Kong; Aperture in association with the National Park Service, U.S. Department of the Interior and Montclair State College

MacArthur, Dr. John, The Master's Current, Vol. 21, No 2, "Our Sacred Duty', The Master's College, Santa Clarita, CA

MacArthur, Dr. John, sermon "How God Restrains Evil in Society," February 22, 2015

Mossolov, A. A., 'At the Court of the Last Czar,' http://www.alexanderpalace. org/mossolov/one3.html accessed 4 Nov 2016

Reeves, Pamela, Ellis Island, Gateway to the American Dream, New York: Crescent Books, 1991

Richards, John F., "The World Hunt: An Environmental History of the Commodification of Animals, Chapter 2 the Hunt for Furs in Siberia", University of California Press, 2014

Russian History Atlas, Martin Gilbert, Macmillan 1972,

Savalas, Telly. "Remembering Ellis Island, Everyman's Monument." Beverly Hills, CA: Panorama International Productions

Smele, Jonathn D., "Civil War in Siberia, The Anti-Bolshevik Government of Admiral Kolchak. 1918-1920," from a review by Eva M. Stolberg http://www.h-net.org./reviews/showrev.php?id=1925, accessed 10 Feb, 2017

The Anchor Light, Volume 25, Number 5, May 2007

The New York Times, Magazine Section, November 27, 1910

Tifft, Wilton S., Ellis Island, Chicago: Contemporary Books, Inc., 1990

Ellis Island, Wilton S. Tifft, pg 80; http://montalbine.com/steerage.html accessed 15 Feb., 2017

http://en.wikipedia.org/wiki/Hoffman_Island accessed
Dec 3, 2014

https://en.wikipedia.org/wiki/Katorga accessed 11 Feb 2017

Wikipedia https://en.wikipedia.org/wiki/Kumis, accessed October 24, 2016

http://en.wikipedia.org/wiki/Meningitis accessed Dec 3, 2014

Civil War in Siberia, The Anti-Bolshevik Government of Admiral Kolchak. 1918-1920, Jonathan D. Smele, ed., from a review by Eva M. Stolberg http://www.h-net.org./reviews/showrev.php?id=1925, accessed 10 Feb, 2017

http://en.wikipedia.org/wiki/Revolt_of_Czechoslovak_Legion, accessed 14 March, 2018

http://www.levantineheritage.com/hosp.htm Courtesy of: http://levantineheritage.com/

http://en.wikipedia.org/wiki/Typhus accessed Dec 3, 2014

https://en.wikipedia.org/wiki/Petropavl accessed 4 Nov, 2016 average weather

http://econfaculty.gmu.edu/bcaplan/museum/czar.htm accessed 11 Feb 2017

New York Times, July 1, 1923 http://www.oocities.org/musetti.geo/race.html, accessed 12 April, 2013

New York Times, http://www.theshipslist.com/ships/Arrivals/1923b.shtml, accessed 6 April, 2018

"Russian Revolution, 1917". Wikipedia .http://en.wikipedia.org/wiki/Russian_Revolution accessed Dec 3, 2014

http://encyclopedia2.thefreedictionary.com/Petropavlovsk+Operation+of+1919 the free Dictionary by Farlex This source is written from the viewpoint of the Bolsheviks, the Red Army. accessed Dec 3, 2014

The free Dictionary by Farlex http://encyclopedia2.thefreedictionary.com accessed 14 March 2018

http://www.petropavl.kz/module/mg106_1.shml
Petropavlovsk history accessed April 2013

http://www.rushunting.com/siberian_brown_bear.html hunting brown bear, wolf in Russia, accessed 2016

https://en.wikipedia.org/wiki/Siberian_fur_trade, accessed 10 Feb 2017

https://isedphistory.wordpress.com/russian-revolution/diary-entry-of-tsar-nicholas-ii/ accessed 27 March, 2016

http://www.mhsbc.comfamhistories.html accessed prior to 2016

Romanov DNA https://www.livescience.com/7693-case-closed-murders-russian-czars-family.html accessed 13 April, 2018

https://isedphistory.wordpress.com/russian-revolution/diary-entry-of-tsar-nicholas-ii/ accessed March 27, 2016

http://alphahistory.com/russianrevolution/cheka/
Cheka, accessed 2 February, 2018

https://www.systemaspetsnaz.com/history-of-the-cheka-ogpu-nkvd-mgb-kgb-fsb Cheka accessed 2 February, 2018

GRACE, Godly Response to Abuse in the Christian Environment https://www.facebook.com/Godly-Response-to-Abuse-in-the-Christian-Environment-GRACE-102403896480483/

Myron Horst, on ATI Parents Recovery site, 2014 (private access) used by permission